THE AMERICAN POET LAUREATE

# The American Poet Laureate

## A HISTORY OF U.S. POETRY AND THE STATE

Amy Paeth

Columbia University Press
*New York*

Columbia University Press
*Publishers Since 1893*
New York   Chichester, West Sussex
cup.columbia.edu
Copyright © 2023 Amy Paeth
All rights reserved
Library of Congress Cataloging-in-Publication Data
Names: Paeth, Amy, author.
Title: The American poet laureate : a history of U.S. poetry and the state / Amy Paeth.
Description: New York : Columbia University Press, [2023] | Includes bibliographical references and index.
Identifiers: LCCN 2022039191 (print) | LCCN 2022039192 (ebook) | ISBN 9780231194389 (hardback) | ISBN 9780231194396 (trade paperback) | ISBN 9780231550796 (ebook)
Subjects: LCSH: American poetry—20th century—History and criticism. | American poetry—21st century—History and criticism. | Poets laureate—United States—Biography | Poetry consultants—United States—Biography. | Literature and state—United States—History. | Poetry—Appreciation—United States—History. | Library of Congress. Poetry and Literature Center—History.
Classification: LCC PS153.L38 P34 2023 (print) | LCC PS153.L38 (ebook) | DDC 811/.5409—dc23/eng/20230111
LC record available at https://lccn.loc.gov/2022039191
LC ebook record available at https://lccn.loc.gov/2022039192

Cover design: Milenda Nan Ok Lee
Cover image: Elizabeth Bishop writing at her desk in the Library's Poetry Office, with the U.S. Capitol in the background, circa 1949-1950. Image courtesy of the Library of Congress.

*To Dr. Alan William Paeth, in memory of his
generous spirit and omnivorous intellect*

# Contents

Acknowledgments  ix

INTRODUCTION  1

I  State Verse Scandals: The Bollingen Affair and Postwar Poets at the Library of Congress, 1945–1956  27

II  Inaugurating National Poetry: Robert Frost and Cold War Arts, 1956–1965  63

III  The Politics of Voice: The Poet-Critic, the Creative Writer, and the Poet Laureate, 1965–1990  100

IV  Civil Versus Civic Verse: National Projects of U.S. Poets Laureate, 1990–2022  150

EPILOGUE: "AN INVISIBLE BERLIN WALL," THE U.S. INAUGURAL POEM, AND THE FUTURE OF STATE VERSE  192

Appendix I: Occupants of the U.S. National Poetry Office  209
Appendix II: Fellows in American Letters at the Library of Congress  212

Appendix III: U.S. Inaugural Poets  213
Notes  215
Bibliography  275
Index  295

# Acknowledgments

*The American Poet Laureate* shows how the relationship between institutions and individuals shaped the landscape of postwar American poetry after World War II, and the book itself is no less a product of both institutional and individual support.

I am grateful to the Library of Congress, the University of Pennsylvania, the Northeast Modern Language Association, and my editor and team at Columbia University Press. I am indebted to the resources of the Manuscript Division at the Library of Congress, where I conducted archival research beginning in the summer of 2011. My research over the last decade was supported by many knowledgeable helpers, including Peter Armenti, literature specialist for the Digital Reference Section, and Cheryl Fox, Barbara Bair, Michelle Krowl, and Bruce Kirby at the Manuscript Division.

Equally, this project owes to the Poetry and Literature Center at the Library of Congress, now under the auspices of the Literature Initiatives Office. The head of PLC, Rob Casper, and his colleagues were invaluable to this book. His warmth, patience, and expertise helped improved the book immeasurably. I am also grateful to Shawn Miller, the Library of Congress photographer, who welcomed me on a visit and has shared his work with me and now my readers. As this book hopes to show, administrative labor gives life to and sustains access to magical things, including poetry.

An earlier version of this manuscript was awarded the Northeast Modern Language Association's Annual Book Prize in 2018. I am grateful to NeMLA for their support, and especially for the counsel and support of Ben Railton.

The earliest version of this project was based in my dissertation research conducted at the University of Pennsylvania, and it owes to the resources I accessed as a doctoral student there. My dissertation chair, Bob Perelman, and my committee of readers, Jim English, Max Cavitch, and Charles Bernstein, have supported the project in various ways. Jim and Charles offered invaluable help with the publication process. Many others at the University of Pennsylvania have supported this project as well: thanks to Joseph Squillaro at the Philomathean Society, Chris Mustazza at PennSound, Al Filreis at the Center for Programs in Contemporary Writing, Valerie Ross, Matthew Osborn, and Stacy Kastner at the Marks Family Center for Excellence in Writing, and Deborah Burnham, Chi-Ming Yang, and Jed Esty in the Department of English. I also received important guidance from Mayelin Perez, a specialist in Literatures in English, Theatre Arts, and Comparative Literature at the University of Pennsylvania Libraries, and Christine Weller, assistant general counsel and copyright advisor, also at Penn Libraries.

Finally, I owe tremendous thanks to my editor, Philip Leventhal at Columbia University Press. After my first conversation with Philip, I knew immediately that my project was in excellent hands. The book is better because of Philip's criticism and counsel. And it would have not been possible without Monique Laban, Susan Pensak, and other members of the CUP team.

In addition to the support of Library of Congress, NeMLA, the University of Pennsylvania, and Columbia University Press, I received extrainstitutional support from individuals who provided publishing advice, editorial help, critical feedback, and lodging during archival research trips. Special thanks to Cal Biruk, who believed in this project from the very beginning, and to Michelle Taransky, SaraEllen Strongman, Nazia Hasan Kazi, Greta LaFleur, Fayyaz Vellani, Kate Kramer, Julie McWilliams, Beth Dalmut, Betsy Siddon, Neesha Shah, Raquel Salas Rivera, Monika Bhagat-Kennedy, Jenny Xie, Marissa Nicosia, Janet Paeth, and the late Steve Reeder.

Jonathan Fedors has been my most reliable interlocutor, providing valuable feedback at every stage of the project. In 2019, I was doing a deep dive back into the manuscript, and I wrote an email thanking him for his sharp editorial eye when we were both graduate students at the University of the Pennsylvania. By chance he was moving back to Philadelphia, where I live, that summer. Now he is my husband, and he has remained an incredible source of support for this book since.

Lastly, thanks to the many participants in this book's story who took time to speak with me, including Poet Laureate Joy Harjo and Librarian of Congress Carla Hayden; Stephen Young at the Poetry Foundation, Poet Laureate Tracy K. Smith, and Poet Laureate of Philadelphia Raquel Salas Rivera, who were generous with their time in interviews; and again Rob Casper, head of the Poetry Office at the Library of Congress, for his consistent support. Their perspectives have ensured that this literary history accounts for the literary present.

The following textual permissions are gratefully acknowledged: excerpts from "View of the Capitol from the Library of Congress" from *Poems* by Elizabeth Bishop. Copyright © 2011 by the Alice H. Methfessel Trust. Publisher's note and compilation copyright © 2011 by Farrar, Straus and Giroux. Reprinted by permission of Farrar, Straus and Giroux. All rights reserved. Excerpts from "The Gift Outright" by Robert Frost from *The Poetry of Robert Frost* edited by Edward Connery Lathem. Copyright © 1923, 1969 by Henry Holt and Company. Copyright © 1951 by Robert Frost. Reprinted by permission of Henry Holt and Company. All rights reserved. Excerpts from Dream Song #354 "The only happy people in the world" and Dream Song #373 "My Eyes" from *The Dream Songs* by John Berryman. Copyright © 1969 by John Berryman, renewed 1997 by Kate Donahue Berryman. Reprinted by permission of Farrar, Straus and Giroux. All rights reserved. Ron Padgett's "Voice" is reprinted by permission from *Collected Poems* (Coffee House Press). © Ron Padgett. Excerpt from Reed Whittemore, "The Lines of an American Poet" is reprinted by permission from *The Feel of Rock: Poems of Three Decades* (Takoma Park: Dryad, 1982), and originally appeared in *An American Takes a Walk* (Minneapolis: University of Minnesota Press, 1956). Excerpt from "Notes on a Certain Terribly Critical Piece," is reprinted by permission from *Past, the Future, the Present* by Reed Whittemore, University of Arkansas Press, 1990. Excerpt from "For All of Us, One Today" by Richard Blanco. Copyright © 2013 by Richard Blanco. Reprinted by permission of Beacon Press, Boston.

# THE AMERICAN POET LAUREATE

# Introduction

> No art is more stubbornly national than poetry.
> —T. S. ELIOT, "THE SOCIAL FUNCTION OF POETRY"

> "'What does the Consultant in Poetry do?'"
> —GWENDOLYN BROOKS, "ANNUAL REPORT TO THE LIBRARIAN
> OF CONGRESS FROM THE CHAIR OF POETRY"

In her last days in office as the national poet of the United States, Gwendolyn Brooks opened the 1986 Annual Report of the Consultant in Poetry to the Library of Congress with this question. Brooks, the first Black American woman to hold the post of the "Consultant in Poetry," would also be the last to hold it in name. Earlier in her term, Congress passed legislation retitling her position the office of the poet laureate: formally, the "Poet Laureate Consultant in Poetry of the United States" and, conversationally, PLOTUS among library administrators today.[1] What Brooks would return to in her report, twenty-one-pages long and written by hand, as *"that delicious question,"* again emphatically—"What does the Consultant in Poetry do?"[2]—is an even more active one in the twenty-first century. Is the national poet a symbolic post, an activist position, or a bureaucratic title for a state official? What does it mean for a poet to represent American literary culture, the federal government, or national interests? Is the post "political?" The history of the national poetry office—first established as the Consultantship in Poetry in the English Language at the Library of Congress in 1937 by a private gift[3]—provides competing answers to these questions. It observes poets acting as librarians, archivists, and sound recording administrators; later as cold warriors and cultural diplomats abroad; and most recently as domestic ambassadors of the seemingly apolitical cause of poetry itself. Today, the official mission of the poet laureate is "to raise the national consciousness to a greater appreciation of the

[ 1 ]

reading and writing of poetry."[4] What it means to promote the "appreciation of poetry" as a representative of the state, however, is a complicated question.

The figure of the poet is often pictured as a lone artist—scribbling the stuff of the soul from an attic garret or romantic odes from a Keatsian flowerbed. But the history of the U.S. national poetry office reveals the poet as a sometimes calculating, and sometimes ambivalent, institutional and political actor. It is also a history that reveals the central role of the state in American poetic production since World War II.

Consider Elizabeth Bishop, who served as the national poet from 1949–1950. During her post—which she held in the tumultuous aftermath of *New York Times*-headlining controversies at the Library of Congress—Bishop sat down at her desk on the top floor of the Jefferson Building, which faced a broad window overlooking the Capitol, and wrote a poem rather pointedly titled "View of the Capitol from the Library of Congress." On the day she described, the Air Force Band was performing. "Moving from left to left, the light / is heavy on the Dome, and coarse," she wrote, observing in the opening lines, "the Air Force Band / in uniforms of brilliant blue," who played "hard and loud, but—queer— / the music doesn't quite come through." First published in the Fourth of July issue of the *New Yorker* in 1951, the poem offers a suggestive, but restrained, critique of state power: "The gathered brasses want to go / *boom-boom*," the final lines conclude. The "*boom-boom*" symbolizes the bombs and guns of U.S. military might. But it is also an imitation of the stolid rhymes and uniform meter of the poem itself, which Bishop—working as a state official, seated at her official desk—uses to sympathetically mimic the bass line of the military band:

> It comes in snatched, dim, then keen
> then mute, and yet there is no breeze.
> The giant trees stand in between.
> I think the trees must intervene,
>
> catching the music in their leaves
> like gold dust, till each big leaf sags.
> Unceasingly the little flags
> feed their limp stripes into the air,
> and the band's efforts vanish there.[5]

Was she, as a state-appointed poet, performing the same work as the military band—turning "leaves" into "flags?" Bishop wrestles with this question, conscious of the unique situation of her "View." On the one hand, she takes pains to present herself as a dispassionate observer of the nationalistic display. She dispenses with the personal pronoun *I,* for example—which she used in other, more famous poems—in an attempt to differentiate her own art from the crude pomp of the Air Force Band. But, on the other, she makes no effort to disguise her physical position at the Jefferson Building or institutional position in turn: a poet, at least functionally, in service of the state. And the latter stanza does strain to gild some lyric flight onto the band's song, entertaining a departure from strict meter into the flexible type of form Bishop tended to prefer. In "View of the Capitol," Bishop wants to distance herself from—while uncomfortably acknowledging that she finds herself complicit in and not merely a "viewer" of—the state performance.

Indeed, Bishop and other national poets were not just self-aware observers: they were participants in an evolving state project, which included the expansion of U.S. global power through cultural programming during the Cold War. Some national poets, like Robert Frost, actively embraced this project. Frost believed that "a great nation makes great poetry, and great poetry makes a great nation."[6] He delivered the first-ever inaugural poem at President John F. Kennedy's 1961 inauguration and the following year shared a bedside chat with Premier Nikita Khrushchev on a state-sponsored Mission to Moscow in the former USSR. In the years following the formal end of the Cold War, too, U.S. national poets beginning with Russian émigré Joseph Brodsky would champion a populist vision of poetry at home. Brodsky praised the English language as "the best,"[7] promising to distribute volumes of poetry in public places such as airports and hotel rooms à la Gideon Bibles. Like Frost, Brodsky believed that poetry—or, at least, certain kinds of poetry—could be the bastion of an "enlightened democracy."[8]

But other national poets would interpret their responsibilities differently. When Gwendolyn Brooks submitted the requisite Annual Report to the Library of Congress at the end of her term, it was no accident that she answered with a question—"What does the Consultant in Poetry do?"[9]—or, indeed, what *should* the consultant do? Her question echoed the Annual Report of Robert Hayden, the first Black writer to hold the position in

1976–78—"What does the Consultant in Poetry _do_?," his report had similarly opened.¹⁰ For Brooks, the relationship between the poet and the state was a loaded proposition. Several years before her appointment, she had participated in the Sixth Soviet-American Writers Conference, a cultural diplomacy mission to the Soviet Union, but found herself "angry" and then "sorrowful" in response to the reception of her reading of "The Life of Lincoln West," a poem that described the "traumas of a little black boy who, in a roundabout way, begins to recognize and value his identity" growing up on the Chicago South Side.¹¹ What infuriated Brooks was that both sides of the table—Soviets and Americans—were "*pleased* with me [Brooks]," as though she had, by reading this poem, palatably fulfilled her token role as the only Black writer at the conference. In response, Brooks gathered the conference's attention two meetings later not to read her poetry but to deliver a strident speech addressing the lamentable state of race relations in both countries. She acknowledged the formal purposes of the conference—yes, "a nuclear blast would abolish everything"—but "nevertheless," she said, "I am going to call attention to *blackness*, a matter no one else feels any reason to cite."¹² Although she was called to attend the conference to project American values of democratic pluralism to her Russian counterparts, Brooks instead leveraged her role as a cultural diplomat to call attention to domestic social inequities. And, as we will learn, she would also challenge official directives when she assumed her role as the national poet several years later. At the Library of Congress, Brooks began a lunchtime and an evening reading series held on-site and open to D.C. community members, for example, and paid the poets who read out of her own government stipend—to the apparent distress, my archival research shows, of some administrators.¹³ Today, however, the Poetry Office at the Library of Congress remembers her as a poet who "did what the position does best" and "connected the office to the community in ways that still resonate."¹⁴

Bishop, Frost, Brooks, Brodsky, and other national poets self-consciously negotiated their relationship to the state. Their individual negotiations reflect the changing relationship of the United States government to poetry. Through the careers of national poets, we can observe the evolving role of the state in poetic production—including the interested role of the state in the cultural uses of poetry at home and abroad during the Cold War. National poets offer us, as Bishop put it, a "View of the Capitol." This is why the office of the poet laureate is a crucial lens through which we can understand the increasingly influential—and confoundingly underexamined—role of the state in American poetry since World War II.

The national poet was not always "national." State poets became crucial arbiters of national values at home and abroad after World War II, but the position now known as PLOTUS began as a custodial role—effectively a librarianship. When Allen Tate assumed the national poetry office in 1943, the reference librarian issued a memorandum defining the duties of the post:

1. To survey the existing collections in order to determine their strengths and weaknesses.
2. To initiate recommendations for the purchase of additions to the collection.
3. To engage in correspondence with authors and collections with a view to securing important gifts of books and manuscripts.
4. To respond to reference questions submitted by mail, and to compile occasional bibliographies.
5. To confer with scholars using the Library's collections and facilities.
6. To make suggestions for the improvement of the service.[15]

This was not a public-facing position; certainly, state bodies outside of the Library of Congress were not yet interested in how a "Consultant in Poetry," endowed by a private benefactor, could be instead understood as a "national poet"—one that could be used as a symbolic figurehead representing American values—or in how the position could productively yoke state, private, and patron interests in the arts. Nor, in the early years of the office, was that how the poets saw their role. The prewar consultant was not "limited in his work to the single field of poetry" but free "to take all English and American literature for his province, including such forms as the essay, the drama, the novel, indeed creative writing of any and every sort," as well as literary scholarship, "studies in literature, and the biography and bibliography of literary personages." He should be warned, however, that "some of the questions referred to his attention will be trifling." These would be the queries of "poetry 'groups'" and "program makers": "school girls, women's clubs, catch-penny anthologists and talent testers . . . novices too ponderous to be raised by Pegasus." "Such work is part of the job; but it can be rather instructive and amusing."[16]

Today, the then "trifling" business of "poetry 'groups'" and "programs" is the job itself. Since the 1980s, national poets have increasingly led groups and programs at the library, and since the early 1990s, poets laureate have undertaken more ambitious cultural initiatives—poetry projects with public-facing, national reach. The library now keeps to a "modest minimum the specific official duties" of the office "in order to afford each incumbent maximum freedom" to pursue these projects,[17] all of which limit national poets' province to the genre of poetry. These national poetry projects are funded by a network of state and private players, which typically include the National Endowment for the Arts; literary-professional organizations, most importantly, since the early 2000s, the Poetry Foundation; individual and corporate patrons; and educational institutions. The Library of Congress provides institutional centralization for these projects through the administrative resources of the Poetry and Literature Center and symbolic centralization through the figurehead of the poet laureate.

The transformation of the U.S. national poet from a library custodian to a public servant represents a broader shift in the cultural function of poetry and the role of institutions in literary production after World War II. The history of the national poetry office is not only a history of national poets, therefore, but a history of the institutions that shaped the field of postwar verse. It is also the story of how the state effectively facilitated and consolidated various institutional interests: American poets relied on state support, and thus served its interests, in new ways during the Cold War. Since the 1960s, the state has adopted an increasingly important role as the central pivot between the institutional infrastructure of literary professionalism, on the one hand, and of higher education, on the other. To understand the function of the national poetry office, then, we must understand how its station at the Library of Congress operates among four sets of players: first, 1. cooperatively with other federal bodies, including the Department of State, the Central Intelligence Agency, the Office of the President, and the National Endowment for the Arts, which invest in the projects of 2. literary-professional organizations, chiefly *Poetry* magazine, administered by the Modern Poetry Association and later by the Poetry Foundation, the Poetry Society of America, and the Academy of American Poets. As we will learn, the collaboration between federal bodies and private cultural organizations has been typically initiated or facilitated through 3. private patrons, such as the philanthropist Paul Mellon, in later generations Mellon Endowment trustees, and the pharmaceutical heiress Ruth Lilly. Finally, public-private-patron initiatives are carried out in 4. institutions of higher education and, increasingly since the 1990s, K-12 public schools and other civic spaces.

This cooperation of public and private interests is crucial to the development of what I call *state verse culture*—recognizable at the first National Poetry Festival in 1962, and dominant following the formal end of the Cold War in the 1990s through the 2010s. By that time, the state, through its nexus of private partnerships, became the dominant organizing force in American poetry, even for poets with wide-ranging ideas about national poetic voice and citizenship.

In other words, by learning about national poets and the history of the U.S. national poetry office, we can better understand the increasingly active relationship of the state to poetry—and more broadly to the arts—in the United States since World War II. The national poetry office sits at the nexus of institutional actors in the field of postwar poetry. It is a lens through which to observe cultural transformations in the American literary field on a systemic level. Through the careers of national poets, we can better understand the development of state interests in poetry arbitrated through universities, literary organizations, and patrons. But individuals are also important to our story. National poets—this study highlights the state careers of Robert Lowell, Elizabeth Bishop, Robert Frost, Gwendolyn Brooks, Robert Pinsky, Billy Collins, Juan Felipe Herrera, Tracy K. Smith, and Joy Harjo, among others—were strategic agents. They sometimes subtly, and in the case of Robert Frost, sometimes momentously, affected institutional courses. Their various paper trails implicate other individual actors—arts administrators, government officials, lawyers, IRS employees, an heir and an heiress of a pharmaceutical fortune, journalists, businessmen-cum-poets, senators, and secretaries—and their interested participation in wider cultural agendas in turn. The story that this book tells therefore plays out on both an institutional and granular level.

The institutional story explains how initiatives of the State Department and other federal agencies during the Cold War have evolved into the cultural programming of poets laureate today. Since World War II, the state project has prioritized a model of poetic voice that emphasizes the expressive agency of the individual citizen, an ideology instrumental to the coherence of midcentury American nationalism and to the longer project of neoliberal identity formation. But the state did not always have an active role in verse culture—as we know, the national poetry office began as more of a functional librarianship and custodial position at the prewar Library of Congress. When the office began to evolve—and met considerable controversies—in the years immediately following World War II, the federal government was wary of supporting the arts, especially after the Library of Congress's awarding of the first government-sponsored prize in the arts, the Bollingen Prize, to the politically scandalous figure of Ezra Pound in 1949. In response to the scandal surrounding the award, the government, by an act of Congress, abolished all state-sponsored prizes in the arts.

Despite *Poetry*'s bid to take over the administration of the now infamous Bollingen Prize, it was relocated to Yale University after the controversy— and fittingly so, as poetic production was meanwhile relocating to the rapidly expanding university system. The particularly expandable disciplines of English and creative writing accommodated a disproportionate influx of veterans, and later baby boomers, following the passage of the G.I. Bill and the Higher Education Act, respectively, and provided poets and writers with newly created degree-granting programs and teaching positions. Meanwhile, during the early years of the Cold War, the state continued to question what appropriate *explicit* relationship it should maintain with artists and the arts. The appointment of William Carlos Williams to the national poetry office in 1952 prompted another political scandal at the Library of Congress—Williams was accused of, and then investigated by federal agencies for, alleged communist sympathies. The appointment was rescinded, and the national poetry office sat vacant for four years.

A member of the House of Representatives proposed reviving the office with legislation authorizing the president to designate a poet laureate in 1956, but the Library of Congress rebuffed the attempt, which never made it out of congressional committee. In a "democratic civilization," Librarian of Congress L. Quincy Mumford wrote, it would be inappropriate to "pu[t] the Government's imprimatur on one [poet's artistic] style as opposed to another."[18]

Despite this false start at creating a figurehead position for national poetry, during the later Eisenhower years and under the Kennedy administration the state invested in poetry, and other creative arts, with gusto both at home and through cultural missions abroad. These initiatives were undertaken by federal agencies, but often in cooperation with formally private philanthropic or cultural organizations with shared staff members and political priorities. "In this Eisenhower splurge I might possibly get enough from Ford or Rockefeller to take a trip to Europe," Bishop (1949–1950) wrote to Robert Lowell, who had also held the post in 1947–1948, in 1960.[19] The national poetry office proper reflected the government's new interest in poetry and in the arts, which Robert Frost, the national poet in 1958–1959, called a "golden age of poetry and power" in a poem for President Kennedy.[20] Not only did Frost's delivery of the first inaugural poem exemplify the symbolically vested domestic role of the American poet, but his bedside chat with Khrushchev was also publicized as ideological weaponry in the global Cold War. One month later, Paul Engle, director of the nation's flagship creative writing program, the Iowa Writers' Workshop, approached a State Department official about an international venture. He was met generously—the federal government supplied him with both overt and covert material support, including through CIA fronts, for the creation of Iowa's International Writing Program.

An emergent state verse culture became visible at the first National Poetry Festival in 1962, which demonstrated that poetry had special use both at home and abroad, symbolizing values of individuality and freedom contra the totalitarian groupthink of the Soviet Union. In the creative writing workshop, phonocentric voice was emphasized over restrictions of metrical form; the dominant model was individual, expressive, and narrative, and, as the material investments of industry leaders and the CIA suggest, a convincing proxy for the American citizen. The National Endowment for the Arts, established in 1965 under President Lyndon Baines Johnson, modeled this conviction in its language: the artist sustains "a climate encouraging freedom of thought," and moreover "the world leadership of the United States" depended not only on military strength but creative expression in "the realm of ideas and of the spirit."[21]

The professionalization of creative writing was marked by the formation of the Association of Writers and Writing Programs two years later, and Master of Fine Arts degree-granting programs boomed alongside university enrollments and the arms race. By the mid-1980s, "the workshop poem" had calcified as a dominant model in the field of American poetry, although one often polemically opposed by avant-garde practitioners. Community-based, experimental, and avant-garde poetry groups, including the Black Arts movement and the Language poets, advanced various critiques of the Cold War–era expressive voice. In these years, poetry took on a more conflicted role in the domestic sphere: did the creative writing workshop's "I" reflect the identities, or political realities, of a multicultural society? The state tried to answer this question affirmatively—not through increasing funding for minority voices, as the NEA budget was scaled back during the Reagan administration, but by recasting the Poetry Office at the Library of Congress as nationally representative. After appointing Gwendolyn Brooks, celebrated by the library in a press release as a "portrayer of black urban life," as the consultant in poetry in 1985–86, the library next appointed Robert Penn Warren, who had publicly recanted the racist views he held as a consultant in poetry in 1944–1945, as the nation's first poet laureate.[22]

The national poetry office, while still privately endowed, during its 1985 rebranding from the national poet as the "Consultant in Poetry" to the "Poet Laureate," began receiving annual funds from the NEA to undertake public programming. True to the Kennedy-Frost vision of state arts with a capitalist spirit, the office draws not only from patron trust funds and NEA money but since the 2000s increasingly collaborates with other organizations to undertake national poetry projects. National poetry projects are the best examples of contemporary state verse culture, in which institutions share common cultural priorities through their Cold War legacy and state interests are advanced through collaboration with formally private actors.

Poet Laureate Joseph Brodsky (1991–92) would provide the catalyzing "spark" for these projects,[23] vocally campaigning for the civic responsibilities of the office in ways that had not been seen since the state career of Robert Frost during the Eisenhower and Kennedy years. Brodsky, who had been expelled from the Soviet Union in 1972 after being charged with "social parasitism" and serving a sentence of five years of hard labor, was appointed U.S. poet laureate in 1991. In his opening press conference as the poet laureate, held a month before the dissolution of the USSR, Brodsky recited the poetry of Robert Frost before delivering a passionate mission statement advocating for more popular access to poetry in America.[24] Large-scale national projects by subsequent poets laureate in the late 1990s and 2000s followed this civic charge and, like Frost and Brodsky, typically emphasized as primary values standard American English, populist accessibility of poetry, individualism, and the individual spoken voice.

These poets laureate–led projects continue into the present, although their values and institutional affiliations have varied, especially in recent years. But the coherence of institutional support for civic-minded poetry initiatives has never been more robust or centralized. In 2002, the Modern

Poetry Association, publisher of *Poetry*, the nation's oldest magazine of verse, received a $100 million gift from pharmaceutical heiress Ruth Lilly—the largest single donation ever awarded to a literary group or journal in the United States.[25] The Modern Poetry Association was reconstituted as the Poetry Foundation the next year, and its mission statement was also recast to prioritize large-scale, civic programming, which includes collaborations with poets laureate. When the Poetry Foundation opened its massive new headquarters in Chicago in 2011, its president, John Barr, even designated one of its rooms as an office for the poet laureate—a kind of corporate Camp David for PLOTUS.[26]

The Poetry Foundation and the Library of Congress are also now members of the Poetry Coalition, a national alliance of twenty-five-plus government, private, and nonprofit poetry organizations created in 2016 and administrated by the Academy of American Poets.[27] The coalition marks the culmination of a series of important transformations in the field of American poetry, literalizing the consolidation of state verse culture. As we will learn in chapter 1, organizations like *Poetry* magazine and the Poetry Society of America were fierce antagonists in the postwar period. Today they, along with other national and local poetry organizations, share a common mission statement and common funding. The coalition received a $200,000 grant from the Ford Foundation in 2017 and shared with the AAP proper the second part of a $2.2 million grant from the Andrew W. Mellon Foundation in 2019.[28] The consolidation of public and private interests—and, with this, *the blurring of previously diverse aesthetic and political values*—defines state verse culture today. On the one hand, the consolidation of institutional interests provides historically unmatched support for poetry projects across the country. It also means that quasi-private organizations like the Poetry Foundation are now firmly allied to the state project, advancing apparently wide-ranging cultural missions that are often united, and bound, by a vocabulary of neoliberal multiculturalism and ambivalent nationalism.

This is a précis of the institutional story. However, many key events that shaped it were affected, and sometimes crucially determined, by the individual interests and by interpersonal interactions. For example, at the end of World War II, the Paul Mellon–funded Bollingen Foundation supported both the Library of Congress and *Poetry*, but after the library's scandalous awarding of the Bollingen Prize to Ezra Pound, the foundation decided to relocate the administration of the prize to Yale University. That decision spoke to the expanding role of universities in the literary field—increasingly influential as cultural tastemakers and canonical gatekeepers—but, as we will see, personal connections were important: James Babb, Yale's chief librarian, and Ernest Brooks, secretary of the Bollingen Foundation, belonged to the same country club. Days after *Poetry* editor Hayden Carruth wrote to Brooks offering "the facilities of the magazine to the Foundation for the administering of the prize"—it would "be appropriate for such an important prize for poetry to be awarded by the country's most prominent magazine of poetry,"[29] after all—Babb at Yale wrote in turn, smoothing his own bid with social niceties: "Peg and I very much enjoyed meeting your wife at Biddeford Pool."[30] Whatever the role such niceties played, Brooks moved the prize not to the foundering magazine, whose interwar glory days seemed long past, but to the university.

When *Poetry* was transformed into the Poetry Foundation fifty years later, becoming the most important private institutional player in the field of postwar verse, it was by way of a reclusive philanthropist. Had *Poetry* editor Daryl Hine not taken the time to craft a gentle, handwritten note of rejection to one slush pile hopeful in 1972, who submitted her poems under her former married name of Mrs. Guernsey van Riper Jr.,[31] it is unlikely the magazine would ever have received the $100+ million beneficence of so-called Prozac heiress Ruth Lilly—she had by then reclaimed her maiden name—in 2002. And, as my archival research at the Library of Congress reveals, *Poetry* editor Hayden Carruth had also exchanged letters with Ruth Lilly's brother, J. K. Lilly III, a half-century earlier. Carruth anxiously sought Lilly Endowment funding for the then-faltering magazine from the Lillies in 1949, a month before he was fired.

Such contingent personal details, then, can sometimes function as the gearshifts driving larger structural movements. For that reason, throughout this book we will at times observe the letters and the lives of poets and, just as important, the labor of arts administrators, secretaries, and mid-level government officials in the work of cultural production. Robert Frost is a symbol of national culture in part thanks to Academy of American Poets founder Marie Bullock using her connections at the U.S. Post Office for the issuing of his commemorative Frost stamp; Phyllis Armstrong, longtime poetry office secretary, contributed far more to the nation's first poetry recording archive than any one of its official stewards; and as the Annual Reports of national poets including Maxine Kumin and

Gwendolyn Brooks document, many workers arrived hours before and stayed hours after Library of Congress and other state events.

Appointing a poet laureate, moreover, is in practice a different administrative process each year. While the national poet has always been formally appointed by the librarian of Congress, historically the librarian's decision has involved the advice of former national poets, attendees of recent library events, and on occasion the behests of proximate federal officials, leaving behind a paper trail witness to the complex negotiations of individual interests within bureaucratic systems. Had Robert Lowell and Elizabeth Bishop not met at a New York dinner party in the winter of 1947—he was then the national poet—Bishop would never have been a contender for the office in 1949. (Indeed, had William Carlos Williams's health not been in decline, had Marianne Moore not been working on a translation project, or had Léonie Adams not hoped to "reach a compromise" with her husband,[32] Bishop would still never have been offered the position.) In later decades, librarians of Congress would continue to seek the advice of former national poets to make their appointments. "I wouldn't mind seeing Allen Ginsberg in the office," Richard Eberhardt wrote to Librarian of Congress Daniel J. Boorstin in 1978, "[and] I think highly of the work of Anthony Hecht, 55, an opposite kind of a poet [from Ginsberg], lapidary, perfectionist."[33] Eberhardt, who had served from 1959–1961, also recommended Maxine Kumin, Donald Hall, Gwendolyn Brooks, W. S. Merwin, and Philip Levine, all of whom, with the exception of Allen Ginsberg, would later serve as national poets.

Today, the Library of Congress is attuned to a broader swath of individual and institutional interests. Robert Casper, who runs the office of the poet laureate as the head of the Poetry and Literature Center, has recently sought to "institutionalize" the process of poet laureate selection.[34] For the twenty-third poet laureate selection process, which resulted in the appointment of Joy Harjo in 2019, the library asked 118 experts in the field in 15 different categories (including former national poets, i.e., poets laureate, but also academics; bookstore owners; festival, conference, and center directors; publication editors; and others).[35] A tiered voting procedure was used to tally the nominations,[36] which were then discussed by an internal recommending committee chaired by Casper and composed of leadership in the Library of Congress's service unit (the Center for Learning, Literacy, and Engagement), the Poetry and Literature Center staff, and a literature specialist in the Library's Humanities and Social Sciences Section.

The internal recommending committee reviewed the nominations, read and discussed poems, watched video performances, and then extended recommendations to the librarian.

This is a process that has evolved over the last decade. When Casper assumed his role at the Library of Congress in 2011—the first MFA holder and first noninternal government hire to run the office of the poet laureate—the process was still less formal; Casper would then meet with Librarian of Congress James Billington (1987–2015) to discuss the appointment, "often multiple times," and meanwhile reach out to experts in the field as well as previous poets laureate for nominations, although to a much smaller group. During several nomination processes—including with the last laureate he appointed, Juan Felipe Herrera—the librarian asked Casper to vet finalists with experts to make the selection. Casper has gradually increased the number of institutions and individuals involved in the search for the poet laureate, emphasizing the role of transparency in the nomination process with participant nominators and other stakeholders. "The [PLC] staff and I have tried to develop an ever more comprehensive and robust process—connecting to both the field and to other key library staff—to assist the [current] Librarian [Carla Hayden] in her appointment," Casper explained in a personal interview in 2019. In 2017, when the library appointed Tracy K. Smith as poet laureate, seventy-two nominators from twenty-six states nominated ninety-one poets discussed by the internal recommending committee; whereas in the 2019 appointment, ninety-two nominators from twenty-nine different states participated, and the Library of Congress received ninety-three nominations of poets for the position.[37] In the case of Harjo's appointment, which reflected an even wider swath of nominations, the internal recommending committee sent their recommendations to the librarian after reviewing the nominations, and members of the committee then met with the librarian and her team to discuss them. After the appointment decision, Casper arranged a call with Joy Harjo during which the librarian of Congress, Dr. Carla Hayden, offered Harjo the position.[38]

This book, *The American Poet Laureate*, is the first modern history of the national poetry office—and the only history of U.S. poets laureate. William McGuire's *Poetry's Catbird Seat* provides a history of the office from 1937–1986.[39] Commissioned by the Library of Congress to occasion its fiftieth anniversary, the existence of McGuire's study itself testifies to the transformation of the office, retitled the poet laureateship by an act of

Congress the same year. McGuire's history thus anticipates, but does not document, the expanded cultural role of U.S. poets laureate in the three decades to follow. This history, and especially McGuire's research notes and materials, has been an important resource for this book, alongside other previously unexplored Library of Congress archives. Drawing from archival research at the Manuscript Division at the Library of Congress as well as materials at the John F. Kennedy Presidential Library; from interviews with the administrators of the Poetry and Literature Center at the Library of Congress; and from conversations with Poetry Foundation administrators, local poets laureate, and former U.S. poets laureate, *The American Poet Laureate* traces the longer history of the national poetry office from 1945 to the present.

While McGuire wrote *Poetry's Catbird Seat* as a celebratory literary history of the office, this book has different methodological priorities and theoretical convictions. It is impossible, my research suggests, to understand the office of the national poet without asking broader questions about the role of the state in poetic production, or of the arts more broadly, during the Cold War and in the present. It is also impossible to understand the office without involving the sometimes overwhelmingly large—and today often only superficially distinct—cast of private institutional players that participate in its functions.

In other words, this book contributes to a growing body of institutional and sociological approaches to U.S. literary production in the postwar era. Most important, it takes heed of more recent work in this field that attends to the role of the state in literary production, in particular the work of Juliana Spahr and Eric Bennett, about which I will say more shortly. First and more broadly, the book responds to a growing body of research that attends to the institutional production of literary values, canons, and readerships in the postwar era. Most recently, Kamran Javadizadeh's work on the institutionalization of the postwar poet and the "institutionalized lyric" positions midcentury poets and poetry in the institutional contexts of universities, state offices, and the psychiatric hospital;[40] Evan Kindley's study of the "administrative" functions of the poet-critic, *Poet-Critics and the Administration of Culture*, which describes the role of modernist poet-critics in the shift from aristocratic patronage to technocratic bureaucracy in the field of literary cultural production; Merve Emre's *Paraliterary: The Making of Bad Readers in Postwar America*, on the institutional formation of contemporary "paraliterary" readers; and Joe North's *Literary Criticism: A Concise Political*

*History*, which treats the political role of poet-critics in historical perspective, have all been informative to this project. Earlier, critics like Alan Golding, Jed Rasula, most importantly in *The American Poetry Wax Museum: Reality Effects, 1940–1990*, and Christopher Beach have also treated poetic production from an institutional perspective. Others have included poetry in fiction-centered postwar literary histories—most important here, James English's history of the cultural economy of literary and cultural prizes, *The Economy of Prestige*; and Mark McGurl's groundbreaking history of the rise of American creative writing programs, *The Program Era*.[41] Scholars who have built on the work of McGurl include Christopher Kempf, whose *Craft Class: The Writing Workshop in American Culture* points to creative writing as a form of alienated labor with institutional values that are linked to neoliberal economic values resonating well beyond academia and the cultural economy.[42]

All the aforementioned studies variously describe or rely on the premise of the disassembly of the traditional literary professional establishment and the absorption of literary production by the academy after World War II. This scholarship points to both the new centralizing force of the higher education industry and to its proliferative effects—the social and formal diversification of poetic production in the U.S. writ large. This narrative is useful, but by looking only at the pre-1950 literary establishment of nationally circulated magazines, large trade presses and publishing houses, institutions of higher education, or small press–based and coterie writing communities, these studies also often rewrite the reductive opposition between establishment and avant-garde poetic production. While the dawn of what McGurl calls the creative writing "program era" is historically concurrent with Michael Davidson's sociologically inflected analysis of 1970s Bay Area poetries, for example, these two histories fail to intersect, with no players, individual or institutional, in common.[43] This disjuncture is due in part to the divide between poetics criticism and literary sociologies—the former privileging one or several writing constituencies, the latter working from market-driven definitions of the center. Moreover, both narrate writers' bids for patronage or independence—typically sought through academic or literary market institutions—in ways that often occlude the roles of private sponsorship and, especially, of state interest.

This book bridges the divide between poetry criticism and literary sociologies—the former privileging particular writing constituencies, the latter working from market-driven definitions of the center—by looking through the lens of the *state*. As the history of the national poetry office shows, state interest and cooperation with grant foundations and individual patrons are crucial to understanding postwar poetic production.

*The American Poet Laureate* thus more fully contextualizes the role of institutions of higher education in the U.S. literary project after World War II. Booming university enrollments, the expansion of English Departments, and burgeoning creative writing degree programs dominated mainstream postwar poetic production: while this book does not contest that the university became a primary site of literary production in this era,[44] it illuminates the role of other, arguably more critical institutional stakeholders. Not only have literary histories and critics forgotten poets laureate, but the Library of Congress—the nation's oldest federal institution, which hosts the largest library in the world—has been typically disregarded. By introducing players operating outside the university system itself, I extend existing accounts of *how* the university laid claim to postwar literary production.

This book also hopes to contribute to poetry and poetics scholarship of the postwar era, particularly from the 1980s to the present. By placing the national poet at the center of institutional cultural production, I highlight competing aesthetic and material interests of the stakeholders in the poetic field and dispense with the two-camp model of poetic affiliations that dominates many literary histories of the era.[45] I aim not to show that the "poetry wars"—i.e., the divide between what Robert Lowell in 1960 called "the raw" versus "the cooked," and what critics in later decades broadly understood as the divide between avant-garde poetics and establishment verse—have been fictionalized. Rather, I suggest, these debates are more accurately narrated by the institutions and the institutional contexts that produced them. For example, when the commercially popular poet Billy Collins was named poet laureate in 2001, one group protested with the election of an "anti-laureate." The coherence of this group and its rhetorically civic gesture, however, was itself made possible through the POETICS listserv and institutional support of the University of Buffalo. One methodological insistence, then, and the argument of the book, is that *all* verse is establishment verse, even while complex position-taking occurs within and between multiply interested establishments.

Moreover, I argue that there is an important distinction to be made between establishment, mainstream, or what Charles Bernstein of the Language poets called "official verse" or "official verse culture,"[46] and *state* verse culture, *precisely because* they so often overlap. This distinction is not only an intervention into histories of American poetry but also the broader body of institutionally focused or attentive histories of postwar American literature that have so consistently undervalued the role of the state.

Among these studies, then, I am especially indebted to the work of Juliana Spahr and Eric Bennett. Spahr and Bennett have both pointed to the role of the state in postwar American poetic production in important new ways, developing a historical record this book will expand. Bennett's *Workshops of Empire*, and his earlier archival research, explore the role of federal agencies in the rise of the MFA-granting creative writing workshop industry during the Cold War. The operations of federal bodies, Bennett shows, were often intertwined with the work of only formally private philanthropists or organizations such as the Rockefeller Foundation. *Workshops of Empire* extends the findings of a broader growing body of work that emphasizes the importance of the state-private network in Cold War cultural diplomacy, which has also been informative to my research in *The American Poet Laureate*.[47]

Whereas cultural histories of Cold War arts have focused on the visual arts, music, dance, and publishing,[48] and while most institutional histories of postwar literary production have focused on fiction, Juliana Spahr has provided influential accounts of the role of the state in the field of American poetry, most recently in *Du Bois's Telegram: Literary Resistance and State Containment*.[49] To what extent *can* poetry escape state containment? Spahr asks this question of literature more broadly in *Du Bois's Telegram*, but its history of state interest in literature is told primarily through its activities in the field of poetry. This is no accident. If poetry is both the most potentially resistant or even "radical" form of art, as Spahr implies, it is also the most "national," as T. S. Eliot warned us,[50] or the most susceptible to nationalization. Spahr suggests that even the most avant-garde or socially revolutionary aesthetic projects are often co-opted by state interests, at least in the history of twentieth-century U.S. literature and poetry. *The American Poet Laureate* expands the historical account of how nationalism shapes literature in the United States through a unique "synergy between private foundations and the U.S. government,"[51] describing the bureaucratic centralization of players in the field of American poetry through the lens of the national poetry office.

While Spahr's *Du Bois's Telegram* considers politically resistant writers and movements, I examine poets that have typically represented the dominant cultural norms of their time. Foregrounding American poets who operate from the national center, I attend to what Robert von Hallberg calls "centrist poetry," or what Karl Shapiro, who took over the editorship of *Poetry* after Hayden Carruth in 1950, called "culture poetry."[52] While I borrow sociologist Pierre Bourdieu's language of a cultural "field" and its "players," this book rejects the now more historically distant model of the artist as necessarily an adversary to culture at large. Understanding the national poet at the intersection of multiple social fields and modes of cultural capital is also to insist that these intersections determine the whole of the poetic field as well: the poet in postwar American culture, far from belonging to an isolated domain where capital operates by the inverted or unique "rules of art," is a multiply invested figure produced by and acting on competing interests. This is a recognition shared by more recent work on the institutional production of American literature and American poets, including Kindley's study of the modernist poet-administrator and the broader body of work surveyed previously.

Rather than writing in a distinct cultural sphere as one type of professional work, the institutional commitments of poets laureate—and indeed of the postwar American poet—have, moreover, typically required a politics of assimilation. Unfortunately, most critical treatments of poets at the center also advocate, as does von Hallberg, an Arnoldian position where it is the best poets who occupy "themselves with the center of ideas in their time."

This book, however, is not an advocacy project, examining instead how postwar poets laureate performed strategically, and sometimes ambivalently, to gain "access to the cultural authority of a centralized culture."[53] Likewise, I am not principally concerned with finger-pointing where recent projects of U.S. poets laureate channel institutional agendas, e.g., that the Lilly-funded Poetry Foundation signals "the consumerization of poetry," as poet-critic Carol Muske-Dukes has suggested, or, like Stephen Yenser, that the projects are "funded by drug money—literally—Lilly pharmaceutical!"[54]

Instead, I describe how the poetic field itself has articulated the problem, namely as one of representative voice. "Voice" has different entailments in different contexts. For instance, the poet laureate who elevates individualism to a heroic and transcendent status, much like what Language poets called "the dominant 'self' (or workshop 'I')" of the MFA or creative writing workshop poem, serves as the "vehicle for an aesthetic project in which the specifics of experience dissolve into the pseudo-intimacy of an overarching authorial 'voice' "[55]—but here as the voice of the model citizen. Building upon von Hallberg's account of poetry in the context of American empire, Piotr Gwiazda argues that U.S. poets have since 1979 "take[n] it upon themselves to perform the role of public intellectuals," driven by a "civic ambition."[56] In an era that witnessed "the *simultaneous* acceleration of globalization and nationalism,"[57] American poets increasingly "adopt[ed] centrist positions and often address[ed] public events from the standpoint of personal experience."[58]

My history of the national poetry office, and of the broader poetic field that it represents, shares Gwiazda's estimation: since around 1980, poets have increasingly occupied civic or public-facing positions as stewards of national values, voicing "what it means to identify oneself as American" or indeed modeling "the idea of America," as in Robert Pinsky's *An Explanation of America*.[59] However, I understand this important shift in the cultural functions of the American poet in the context of the institutions that motivated it and in relation to the state explicitly. Pinsky did not only "explain America" through his poetry, but through his national representative position as poet laureate (1997–2000), and through institutionally formalized civic initiatives. Pinsky's "Favorite Poem Project," for instance, instructs reader-citizens to recite a favorite poem for the national archive. It also inherits the national poetics with the longest shadow: Robert Frost's phonocentric "ethics of personal and political sovereignty."[60] Where "civil verse" poets like Frost, and, as von Hallberg suggests, Poets Laureate Pinsky, Robert Hass, and Louise Glück, demonstrate the "flexibility, exactness, and vitality of standard American English as an artistic medium," it follows for citizens that "if gorgeous or acute art can be made in this medium, one may have faith that just legislation, judicious litigation, and progressive social policy can also be crafted from this general social position."[61] These civil verse poets naturalize dominant national narratives and demonstrate that political agency is available to citizens who articulate themselves through legible identity positions. In this way, national poetry projects of the late 1990s and early 2000s participated convincingly in the neoliberal state project.[62]

Chapter 1 examines the postwar origins of key institutional players in state verse culture today: the Library of Congress, *Poetry* magazine and its administration, and patrons Paul Mellon and J. K. Lilly III of the Lilly Endowment. "State Verse Scandals: The Bollingen Affair and Postwar Poets at the Library of Congress, 1945–1956" highlights the state careers of national poets Robert Lowell and Elizabeth Bishop, who among other national poets navigated major controversies at the Library of Congress: first, and most seismically, the awarding of the Bollingen Prize to known fascist Ezra Pound in 1949. In response to the decision, a congressional act abolished all government awards in the arts later that year, forcing the Mellon-funded Bollingen Foundation to move its prize to the private sphere. Yale and *Poetry* both bid for the prize, as well as for the prestige it represented. Archival documents reveal how the debate around the politics of the prize resulted in the overhaul of the editorial regime at *Poetry* and helped to catalyze the movement of poetic culture into the university system—predicting the increasingly influential role of universities in American poetic production that we see in later chapters. The Bollingen affair also foreshadowed the way private money interests, here the Lilly family, would continue to calibrate the relationship between universities, private literary organizations, and the state in the decades to follow. Several years later, the Library of Congress underwent another scandal: the red-baiting of William Carlos Williams out of the national poetry office during the McCarthy years. ("We don't want any communists or cock-suckers in this Library," Librarian of Congress Luther Evans had told Karl Shapiro, who held the office from 1946–47, in their first meeting.)[63] Both scandals defined modernist experimenters as fascist and communists, in turn, as "enemies of good, old-fashioned poetry."[64] While the university emerged the institutional victor in the wake of these state verse scandals, I argue that the moment the government *lost* the Bollingen Prize in fact marks a historical turn to a new centrality of the state in the administration of literary culture. The broader arc of this book traces how state patronage restructured its investments through public arts initiatives and corporate interests.

Chapter 2, "Inaugurating National Poetry: Robert Frost and Cold War Arts, 1956–1965," examines the U.S. federal government's investment in the creative arts during the pivotal years 1956–1965. I tell this story through national poet Robert Frost, focusing on two periods of his career—the early development of his poetic theory (1912–1916) and his politically active late years (1956–1962). Frost's poetics were rooted in notions of natural speech and expressive individuality, and, after his repatriation from London to the United States in 1915, they increasingly politicized questions of voice and form. His politicized poetics became important on the national stage later in his life: the chapter describes Frost's largely unexplored relationship with President Kennedy. Through correspondence and policy measures, the poet and the president expressed a common vision of an American "golden age of poetry and power" in cultural competition with the Soviet Union.[65] The role of poetry in the cultural front of the Cold War would become especially visible at events such as Frost's controversial Mission to Moscow in 1962, when the poet, in addition to meeting with Khrushchev under the auspices of the State Department, gave readings in Moscow, Peredelkino, and Leningrad in the weeks preceding the Cuban Missile Crisis. The Kennedy administration placed a new and special value in the symbolic power of the American artist, expanding cultural missions abroad and setting forth the founding of a federal arts agency at home—what would become the National Endowment for the Arts under President Johnson in 1965. The Frost-Kennedy years, we will observe, transformed the function of poetry in national culture. Poetry, and particularly the phonocentric narrative poem—exemplified in Frost's recitation of "The Gift Outright" at Kennedy's 1961 inauguration—modeled the expressive agency of the artist-citizen to provide ideological weaponry in the global Cold War and a blueprint for later national poets in the longer project of neoliberal identity formation.

Chapter 3, "The Politics of Voice: The Poet-Critic, the Creative Writer, and the Poet Laureate, 1965–1990" describes how the rise of MFA programs was central to the development of state verse culture. The recentralization of poetic production in the academy after World War II is a phenomenon that must be understood in relationship to federal bodies, which not only funded the public education system responsible for the postwar expansion and disciplinary solidification of English Departments, but treated the country's flagship creative writing program, the Iowa Writers' Workshop, as a training cell in the cultural front of the Cold War. This chapter argues that the academicization of poetry is a twofold legacy: the poet-critic of the English Department and the MFA workshop poet constitute two distinct cultural roles for the poet in postwar America. In response to the mainstreaming of accessible, voice-centered verse by the MFA industry and poets laureate, experimental successors to first- and second-generation modernists, such as most members of the previously anti-institutional Language poetry group, moved into English Departments and other non-MFA university teaching positions by the early 1990s.

Chapter 4, "Civil Versus Civic Verse: National Projects of U.S. Poets Laureate, 1990–2019," describes the solidification of state verse culture. Federal bodies, market presses, private patrons, and educational institutions now more typically cooperate their initiatives—cultural programming typically informed by nationalistic ideals—in the aftermath of MFA culture. In 2002, pharmaceutical heiress Ruth Lilly donated $100 million to *Poetry*, reconstituting the Modern Poetry Association as the Poetry Foundation and crystallizing long-standing relationships of the institutional triumvirate this book shows are key to postwar poetic production: corporate patron families, *Poetry*, and the Library of Congress in partnership with other federal agencies. The Poetry Foundation—in a far cry from its antipopulist origins during the interwar period—is now, like the National Endowment for the Arts, "committed to a vigorous presence for poetry in our culture," seeking to "place it before the largest possible audience."[66] I examine poets laureate initiatives funded through this state-private nexus in the late 1990s and 2000s, including Robert Pinsky's "Favorite Poem Project," Ted Kooser's "American Life in Poetry," and Billy Collins's "Poetry 180." I argue that these civic verse projects are in fact more accurately understood as *civil verse* projects, modeling the voice of the citizen in the speech-based narrative tradition of Robert Frost. Prizing vocality, expressivity, and accessibility for poetry that is written in standard American English, these projects make implicit claims about the model of voice, and of citizen, that is valued in American culture and about what kind of language is or should be appropriately considered "accessible" to reader-citizens.

This chapter also considers more recent poets laureate projects and how their missions, content, and administration have adapted—and in some instances challenged—predecessor programming. It highlights the work of the Poetry and Literature Center at the Library of Congress with Poets Laureate Juan Felipe Herrera (2015–2017) and Tracy K. Smith (2017–2019). Juan Felipe Herrera's three formalized projects included multilingual, multiauthored, and multiparticipant initiatives, and Tracy K. Smith's "American Conversations: Celebrating Poems in Rural Communities" engaged in geographical spaces previously outside the scope of poets laureate programming, including Puerto Rico and communities in Alaska, South Dakota, and Louisiana. Smith told me in 2019 that she viewed her project as a departure from the initiatives of some of her predecessors.[67] Smith was appointed under a new librarian of Congress, Dr. Carla Hayden, the first Black woman to lead the nation's oldest federal cultural institution. The most recent appointment to the office of the poet laureate under Hayden was Joy Harjo in 2019. Like Herrera, Harjo—a member of the Mvskoke Nation and the first Native American poet laureate—is a poet laureate who works across genres, including theater, film, and musical performance. She was appointed to a second term in 2020 and later to a rare third term, serving through April 2022.

By understanding the history of state verse culture through the lens of the national poetry office, we can better evaluate the uses of poetry in classrooms, civic spaces, and public life. The poet laureate is, finally, not a merely symbolic position, but rather an institutional hub that represents the investments of taxpayer dollars, wealthy corporations, individual philanthropists, and public schools. That since 2011 the poet laureate has not only an office overlooking the Capitol and the Washington Monument—but also a "between unofficial and official" office at the Lilly Pharmaceutical–funded Poetry Foundation—literalizes the fuller and fuller imbrication of state and private interests in the American poetic field.[68] As national poetry projects are increasingly undertaken in civic spaces such as K-12 schools, the Cold War origins of such projects—and of the dominant national values of state verse culture—should remind us of the important role that poetry has in structuring conceptions of self, citizenship, and national belonging.

It is also a history that helps us to better understand our political present. The poetic values of individual voice and cultural pluralism remained dominant in the transition from a Cold War liberalism, which opposed them to totalitarian communism, to neoliberalism, which associates these values with privatization and economic growth. Examining literary politics in the context of state interests, and especially against the backdrop of U.S.-Russia relations, *The American Poet Laureate* is an especially relevant history today, when the Cold War is increasingly understood as ongoing. The epilogue, "'An Invisible Berlin Wall,' the U.S. Inaugural Poem, and the Future of State Verse," therefore considers the role of poetry in national culture and international politics since 2013. It considers the functions of state, city, and locality-based poets laureate across the country and their relationship to the national poetry office. It also examines other symbolic uses of poetry by the state, namely poetry read at U.S. presidential inaugurations. Comparing Robert Frost, the nation's first inaugural poet, and Richard Blanco, the nation's inaugural poet in 2013, I highlight the use of poetry by the state to convincingly advance notions of national identity and citizenship at key moments in the global Cold War. Frost read at the inauguration of John F. Kennedy in January 1961, less than three weeks after the United States severed diplomatic relations with Cuba. And Cuban American Richard Blanco, who was selected to read at the second inauguration of President Barack Obama, restaged the ethos of its first precedent. While Blanco's inaugural poem, "One Today," ostensibly expressed values of multiculturalist inclusion, I argue that it also guarded the agential voice of the anglophone speaker as a stubborn analogue for the American citizen. Blanco, who would pay direct homage to Frost in a book about his inaugural reading, was subsequently commissioned by the State Department to read at the reopening of the U.S. Embassy in Cuba in August 2015. The history of the inaugural poem is also a story of the Cold War still ending.

Like those of so many national poets examined in this book, the state careers of Frost and Blanco spotlight the role of American poets on the geopolitical stage—and more broadly of state interest in poetic production, popularity, and canonization. Moreover, Blanco, who performed what he described as an "invisible Berlin Wall" at the U.S. Embassy in Cuba, enacted a ceremonial role that is distinct from the projects of poets laureate. Inaugural poets are products of executive branch, rather than legislative branch, decisions. As even more direct mouthpieces of the state than the networked projects of poets laureate, then, Frost and Blanco call our attention to those less visible ways that politicized interests operate in the field of American poetry today.

The role of the poet, and indeed of the artist, in contemporary American political culture is markedly different than during the middle Cold War years when American musicians, writers, and poets held active and more visible partnerships with the federal government. There was no inaugural poet present at the presidential inauguration of Donald Trump in 2017, for example, and the Trump administration's first federal budget called for the elimination of the National Endowment for the Arts and the National Endowment for the Humanities. More recently in 2021, twenty-two-year-old Amanda Gorman's performance of "The Hill We Climb" at the inauguration of President Joe Biden was met with wide public acclaim—provoking a response to poetry on the national stage not seen since the eighty-six-year-old Frost delivered "The Gift Outright" at the inauguration of President Kennedy in 1961. In a fractious political environment that bears little apparent resemblance to the Kennedy-era national arts "golden age," it may seem cynical, or even nostalgic, to recall prior and ongoing uses of federal arts programming for nationalist and imperialist ends. Yet precisely because of the increasingly limited—albeit, as we will see, only formally limited—role of the American artist in statecraft, the work of the poets who are tasked to represent the nation is increasingly important to understand.

CHAPTER I

## State Verse Scandals

*The Bollingen Affair and Postwar Poets at the Library of Congress, 1945–1956*

### The Capitol and the Colony

On the Inauguration Day of President Harry S. Truman in 1949, Elizabeth Bishop wrote to Robert Lowell about an employment opportunity. "Dearest Cal," she scrawled from her remote hatch cabin in Key West, "If I get the Washington job—I don't *have* necessarily to give a lot of 'readings' do I? . . . I've always felt that I've written poetry more by *not* writing it than writing it, and now this Library business makes me really feel like the 'poet by default.'"[1] Lowell had first written to Bishop about "this Library business" a month earlier, encouraging her to take up his former post as consultant in poetry, today the office of the poet laureate, at the Library of Congress in Washington, D.C. As a former consultant, Lowell sat on the Fellows in American Letters, the library's committee of nomination for the post, and had maneuvered on Bishop's behalf.[2] "You will be the next consultant unless you decline. You'd better keep this to yourself. The details of the selection are intriguing, but you've got to come here to hear them," he wrote on December 18. "You see what pressure I'm putting on you."[3] Lowell then preempted the official offer to Bishop—"on its way through the Library machinery to you"—with a personal appeal:

> I don't want to force advice on you—one's dear friends can be so obtuse that way; but I think you would enjoy it. The salary is $5700.

You work five days a week and *more or less* have to be there; but what you actually have to do for the Library takes no more than 2 days.... The duties are simple and untechnical—nothing you couldn't do better than I, except the meeting (you couldn't be more nervous than Léonie [Adams, the current consultant]).[4]

"Library machinery" moved slowly to Key West—Bishop was, as it would later turn out, fourth in line for the job—and she worried during the time lag between private and institutional correspondence. By Inauguration Day, she had considered and reconsidered Lowell's offer: "first I felt a little overcome and inclined to write you a frantic 'no,' but after having thought about it for a day or two I've concluded that it is something I *could* do (there isn't much, heaven knows)"—but having not heard from Washington, "of course I suspect that everyone has changed his mind & I am not breathing any of this to anyone and if they have changed their minds I hope you're not going to be embarrassed, etc."[5] Lowell had meanwhile sought to "lure you [Bishop] to Yaddo,"[6] the artists' colony where he then resided. Until "the [Library of Congress] thing is certain one way or another," Bishop decided she would look into this alternative residency.[7]

Since they had met a year and a half earlier, the younger but more institutionally savvy Lowell had variously coached Bishop's career moves. He had convinced her to visit Washington to record for the new Archive of Recorded Poetry and Literature at the Library of Congress, which he shepherded as consultant in poetry in his 1947–48 term; he then arranged for her to assume the consultant post herself and, throughout, to apply for a residency at the Yaddo artists' colony in Saratoga Springs, New York. (Or at least to visit—"Now my refrain & ending from now on: / Do come to Yaddo next summer, / I miss you, / Cal.")[8] "I still haven't heard from Washington," Bishop wrote Lowell on January 31, "but I did hear from Mrs. Ames [the director of Yaddo] and am hastening to fill out the forms. She says graciously that she thinks I need not send any manuscripts."[9]

Before Bishop could secure either residency, scandals erupted at both the Capitol and the colony. She would not hear from Lowell, the Library of Congress, or Yaddo for months. The "details" of library meetings were, as Lowell had put it, indeed "intriguing." At the same library fellows meeting during which Lowell had nominated Bishop for the consultant position, he had also cast his vote for the winner of a new book award. The Bollingen

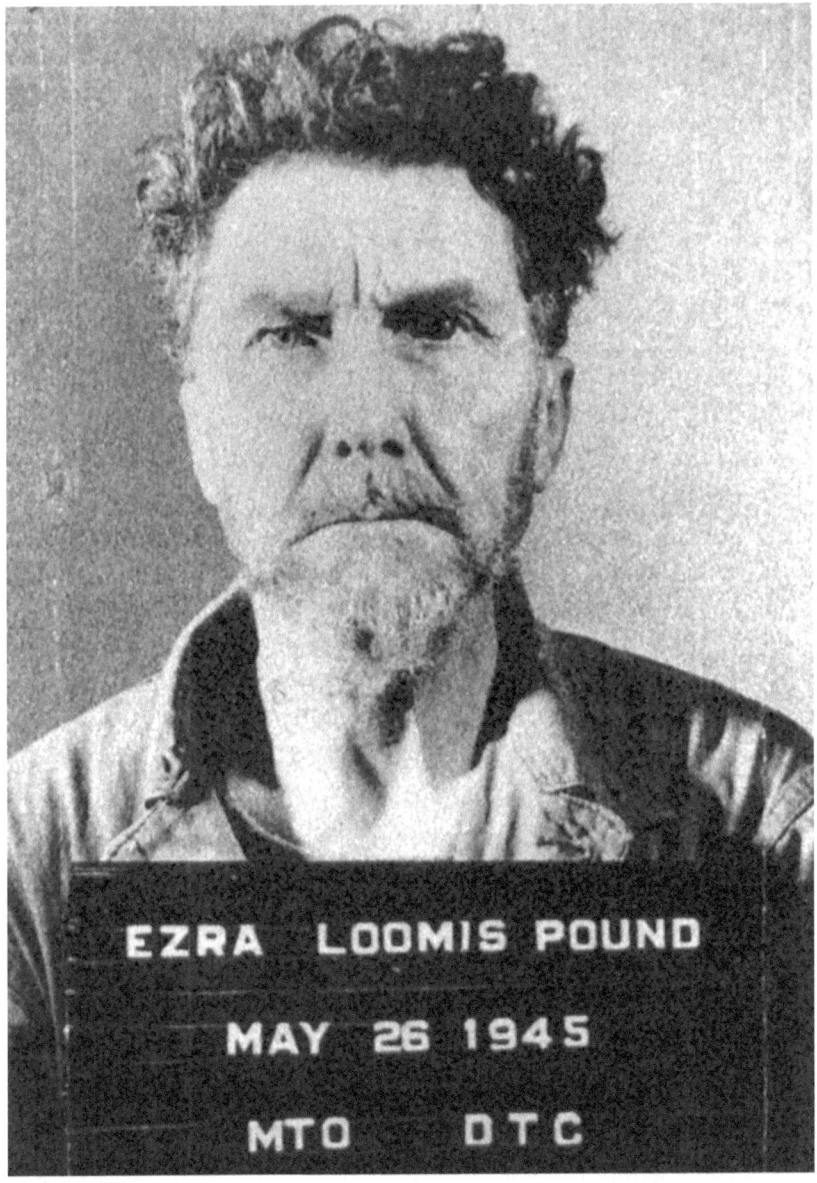

*Figure 1.1* Mugshot of Ezra Pound, taken by Morris J. Lucree of the U.S. armed forces in Italy. While in a U.S. Army Detention Camp, Pound worked on drafts of *The Pisan Cantos*. The collection received the first Bollingen Prize from the Fellows in American Letters at the Library of Congress in 1948, touching off a scandal that reverberated beyond the literary world.

Prize for the Best American Poetry of 1948, sponsored by the Paul Mellon Endowment and selected by the library fellows, was to become the first federal government–issued prize in literature. On February 20, the Library of Congress announced that the prizewinner was Ezra Pound—a poet infamously arrested for profascist and anti-Semitic radio broadcasting in Italy during the war, tried for high treason three years earlier, and incarcerated a few miles away from the library at St. Elizabeths Hospital. The $1,000 purse honored *The Pisan Cantos*, partially composed in a detention camp north of Pisa where Pound had been held in 1945: "Pound, in Mental Clinic, Wins Prize for Poetry Penned in Treason Cell," ran the *New York Times* headline.[10]

Since casting votes for Bishop and Pound in Washington, Lowell had retreated to Yaddo, working on *The Mills of the Kavanaughs* in his room above the driveway. He had also been writing back and forth with the fellows, crafting a press release addendum defending the fellows' Bollingen Prize decision as proof that "poetry doesn't have to pass a political test," thus an affirmation of "the validity of that objective perception of value on which any civilized society must rest."[11] The same week the press release was published, Lowell repeated this liberal defense of aesthetic autonomy—but now to accuse the Yaddo artists' colony director Elizabeth Ames of sheltering communists. He testified to the Yaddo board that Ames was "deeply and mysteriously involved in the political activities" of journalist Agnes Smedley, a recent colony resident and an accused Soviet spy.[12] While poetry need not pass a political test, the same was not true of journalism. Lowell had read Smedley's work, and, judging that it lacked "literary merit," thought it deserved no ideological immunity. Yaddo was an artists-only political safe house: "Would any of you object to the presence of a Communist here per se if he were *a genuine artist*?" Lowell asked the board. For Lowell, his sanctuary in upstate New York literalized the ideal of aesthetic inviolability—it was a quarantine against the politics of the outside world. In a letter to Pound, he would call Yaddo "St Elizabeth's [sic] without the bars."[13] And Lowell's testimony at Yaddo would foreshadow the broader ideological debates unfolding in the wake of the Bollingen Prize—was the poet, the "genuine artist," uniquely exempt from politics?[14] What was the proper relationship of poetry, or indeed the arts, to the American state after World War II? The prize decision—which would become known as the "Bollingen Affair"—launched a trial that unfolded not in a residential artists' colony but on the national stage. Its verdict would prove more seismic, reconfiguring the relationship of the government to arts patrons, literary institutions, and the university system. And it would help to transform the relationship of poets, and poetry, to the state during the Cold War.

Lowell left Yaddo after the trial in the midst of a manic break and wrote his next letter to Bishop from Baldpate Hospital. Bishop meanwhile received an official invitation to serve as consultant in poetry from Librarian of Congress Luther Evans in mid-April.[15] She would also hear back from Elizabeth Ames at Yaddo—the charges against Ames had been dismissed—and spend the summer of 1949 at the colony before moving to Washington in September.

As middle-generation poets who served as consultants in poetry to the Library of Congress in the years following World War II, Robert Lowell (1947–48) and Elizabeth Bishop (1949–50) offer a revealing window into the institutional life of the postwar poet. The consultant's view is that of a poet within the establishment—that is, within the central cultural institutions that supported, and shaped, postwar American poetry.[16] The national poet's office in the Jefferson Building not only intersected with federal bodies—Congress, the State Department—but also with the university system, literary trade institutions, private patrons and their trustees, and even seemingly remote sites of literary production like the artists' colony and the psychiatric hospital.

More important, the national poet's "view of the Capitol from the Library of Congress," to take the title of the poem Bishop wrote from her desk while consultant, is a historical view of postwar poetic production that recognizes the central role of the state. Lowell and Bishop held the national poetry office in a moment of federal government solidification and expansion in spheres of cultural production.[17] The Central Intelligence Agency, for example, was created the same month that Lowell moved to Washington, and he would later benefit from its investments in poetry.[18] The postwar poet's "view of the Capitol" pans out to depict a rapidly widening field of state interest, both domestic and international. In 1950, the State Department asked Bishop to survey the "current national interest in poetry; the number of poetry magazines, poetry clubs, fellowships and awards" for the State Department–run magazine *Amerika*, "intended to project the various phases of American life to foreign readers."[19] This was among the first of many collaborations to follow between the State Department and the office of the national poet.

The lives of postwar state poets were gripped both by political scandal and by bureaucratic routine. Bishop's predecessor Léonie Adams (1948–49), who occupied the poetry office during what she called the "siege" in the most heated months of the Bollingen affair,[20] nonetheless spent most of her time administering the library's Archive of Recorded Poetry and Literature: settling copyright questions with publishers, preparing leaflets to accompany recordings, and managing routine correspondence. Bishop's "Annual Report to the Librarian of Congress from the Chair of Poetry 1949–1950," too, painstakingly itemized the administrative labor of "earning a living by poetry" for the government:

1946 general telephone calls
1071 administrative calls
88 reference replies by letter
684 routine letters
445 visitors seen and talked to
120 readers given assistance . . .[21]

At the time, the consultant in poetry was less a public-facing national poet than a bibliographer, administrator, and occasional tour guide for the nation's poetic canon. Moreover, the growing cultural authority of this canon was institutionally entangled—and institutionally fraught. It was the same organization, the Paul Mellon–endowed Bollingen Foundation, that funded both the bureaucratic burdens of the recording archive and the scandalous administration of the Bollingen Prize. In this sense, organizations like the Bollingen Foundation, no less than the state poets they supported, are the true narrators of postwar American poetry. The national poetry office, as the archives of the Library of Congress reveal, is a site where we can not only view the relationships between the state, literary institutions, universities, and private patrons, but how the politicized relationships between these institutional players were reconfigured during the postwar years.

The awarding of the Bollingen Prize to Pound in 1949 was a crucial catalyst of this reconfiguration. During the Bollingen affair, *Poetry* and Yale University would both bid to take over the administration of the Bollingen Prize from the Library of Congress. The Bollingen Foundation and other patrons—including J. K. Lilly III of Lilly Pharmaceutical—were arbiters of the fight, acting as influential intermediaries between the state, the literary establishment, and the university system.

To understand the national poetry office, then, we must attend to seemingly dry memoranda, letters, and financial documents exchanged within the private state network taking shape in American letters during these years, much as we already attend to the individual poets and poems—now canonical—that these institutional relationships produced. The negotiations of these institutions would not only dynamically shape the postwar poetic canon but also American poetry in the present. Archival records of J. K. Lilly III's exchanges with cash-strapped *Poetry* in 1949 might appear superficially less interesting than a close reading of a poem. But they reveal a deeply influential institutional legacy. In 2002, J. K. Lilly III's sister, Ruth Lilly, would make a massive donation to the magazine that would shake the contemporary poetry world, illuminating the institutional relationships within it that, as we will see, were structured fifty years before.

In the aftermath of the Bollingen affair, the state would suffer a series of apparent losses: the loss of the right to give prizes and of the Fellows in American Letters as a body. And *Poetry*, which shared the Bollingen Foundation as a common patron, would suffer the loss of funding and of its entire editorial staff. After the appointment of William Carlos Williams to the national poetry office in 1952 resulted in another political controversy—Williams was accused of communist sympathies, underwent a federal loyalty check, and was investigated by the FBI—the library would also lose a representative consultant in poetry from 1952–56. This chapter is a history of the poetry scandals at the postwar Library of Congress, which is the first important chapter in the history of the national poet. It narrates, through these losses at the Library of Congress and at *Poetry*, the relocation of poetic culture to the university system in the years after World War II. However, as we will see, the state learned to adapt. Although the Bollingen affair brought mostly unwelcome attention to the Library of Congress, the political functions of poetry, and the nationally representative functions of the poet, would become increasingly important to federal bodies in the years to follow.

## The Bollingen Affair

The Bollingen Foundation was a reliable patron of the Library of Congress in the immediate postwar years. Its first donation created the Archive of Recorded Poetry and Literature, the first national poetry sound archive.

Paul and Mary Conover Mellon had established the foundation in 1945 principally to circulate the work of Carl Jung in the United States, subsidizing the Bollingen Series of translations published by Pantheon Books in New York.[22] But Huntington Cairns, a Washington lawyer, secretary-treasurer of the National Gallery of Art, and a trustee of the new foundation, rapidly led Mellon to issue two additional outside grants: one to the Modern Poetry Association of Chicago to support the publication of *Poetry* magazine and the other to the Library of Congress to support a national sound archive. Former consultant Allen Tate (1943–44) had met Cairns as a colleague on a radio program, "Invitation to Learning," and then put Cairns in touch with Librarian of Congress Luther Evans.

"Mary and I have decided that the Library of Congress record project will be excellent for the Bollingen Foundation," Paul Mellon wrote to Cairns in January 1946. "We wonder if we may add two names to their proposed list."[23] Only a month after the foundation was officially established, the trustees granted $10,500 for the current consultant, Louise Bogan, to prepare "five albums of twenty-five 78 r.p.m. records of twentieth-century poetry in English."[24] The correspondence between Mellon and Cairns testifies to the powerful function of the patron as a cultural gatekeeper, directing the flow of contemporary ("twentieth-century") poetic production and preserving its canonical record in the national library. Mellon was proactive in his approach to the project, monitoring and appending names to the library's recording catalogue as in his letter to Cairns. As significantly as the patron's power to include or exclude specific poets, determining the content of the canon, however, was the power to determine the form of the canon. Mellon funded the preservation of voice: the first audio canon in U.S. poetry.[25] The Archive of Recorded Poetry and Literature aestheticized the individual speech act while the heightened internationalism of the postwar period animated spoken American English as a tortured object of national identity.

The Mellon-Cairns correspondence testifies to the powerful function not only of the patron but also of the administrator as a cultural gatekeeper. The Bollingen Foundation renewed the $10,500 recording grant in 1947, and the next year Tate approached Cairns with another proposition. Tate had discussed establishing a national poetry prize at a meeting with the Fellows in American Letters of the Library of Congress, a body he formed during his tenure as consultant, constituted by former consultants and consultant-nominated literary advisers.[26] Poetry office secretary Phyllis

Armstrong's meeting notes indicate that Willard Thorp proposed the idea of the prize, and the fellows appointed Allen Tate and W. H. Auden to sound out the Bollingen Foundation.[27] As Tate ultimately approached the grantor, however, literary histories have recalled the prize as exclusively his enterprise. Jed Rasula writes that "the decision to award a prize in poetry was made possible by the Bollingen Foundation, but the initiative was Tate's."[28] Armstrong's dutiful minutes complicate this individualizing narrative. Reading the notes of administrators, and not only the letters of literary figures, serves importantly, if not to illuminate Willard Thorp in the stead of Tate as a key mover, as a record of the fundamentally collaborative nature of the venture. To call the prize "Tate's initiative" obscures the precipitating conversation between Thorp, Tate, and other fellows; and to say the prize was "made possible by the Bollingen Foundation" obscures the intermediary role of cultural administrators like Huntington Cairns, through whom Tate accessed the Mellon Endowment. Cairns proved an instrumental site of capital convergence in the poetry world in the postwar years. Not only did he facilitate the Bollingen Foundation's support of the library's poetry recording and prize programs and of *Poetry*, but, several months before pitching the library's prize proposal to the Bollingen Foundation's board of trustees, he also mobilized the foundation to help subsidize an international literary criticism symposium at Johns Hopkins University, where Allen Tate, John Crowe Ransom, and R. P. Blackmur lectured in the spring. Indeed, throughout the postwar period, Cairns acted as a middleman between Paul Mellon and the Bollingen Foundation, the Library of Congress, *Poetry*, the Internal Revenue Service, Johns Hopkins, and Yale—magnetizing diverse interests to support New Critical programming, which treated the poem as an ahistorical and autonomous artifact.

The Bollingen trustees approved Cairns's proposal to subsidize a prize at the library and endowed $1,000 to honor "the best book of verse published during the previous calendar year by an American author and citizen" for the next ten years. The fellows would act as the jury of selection. In 1948, the first award year, the fellows were composed of fourteen members: current consultant in poetry Léonie Adams; previous consultants Allen Tate (1943–1944), Robert Penn Warren (1944–1945), Louise Bogan (1945–1946), Karl Shapiro (1946–1947), and Robert Lowell; and Conrad Aiken, W. H. Auden, Katherine Garrison Chapin, T. S. Eliot, Theodore Spencer, Willard Thorp, Paul Green, and Katherine Anne Porter. The fellows set nominations for the Bollingen Prize during meetings on November 19 and 20, 1948.

Verner Clapp, acting librarian of Congress for Luther Evans, instructed the fellows on November 19 not "to be deflected by political considerations or other questions of expediency from a decision rendered strictly in terms of literary merit."[29] When the fellows met again the next day, they settled around four contenders: Ezra Pound's *The Pisan Cantos*, William Carlos Williams's *Paterson II*, Randall Jarrell's *Losses*, and Muriel Rukeyser's *The Green Wave*. In a preliminary ballot, eight votes were cast for Pound and two for Williams; two members abstained and two were absent.[30] As the fellows would not meet again until February, when the prize would be announced, and more eligible poetry collections would be released that year, Lowell, Karl Shapiro, and Consultant in Poetry Léonie Adams formed a committee for the procedure of the official vote by mail.

In the next months, the fellows grappled with the stakes of awarding the prize to Pound. Lowell, Shapiro, and Adams exchanged a flurry of letters with Tate and with Librarian of Congress Luther Evans. Karl Shapiro, whose *Trial of a Poet* (1947) had taken Pound to court the year before with an ambivalent verdict, voted for *The Pisan Cantos* at the meeting in November, but "wrestl[ed] with his soul" through the next months. He wrote to Evans suggesting that the first Bollingen should be delayed a year, and the "highly compromising business of Pound be forgotten." His plea ignored, Shapiro changed his vote in favor of Williams's *Paterson* in late January. Tate tried to convince Shapiro to change his vote another time: "I simply don't think that your point of view is sufficiently searching," he argued. The objective critic, Tate argued, necessarily divorces literary merit from person and politics: "I am not pro-Pound . . . I voted for the *Pisan Cantos* because it was the best book available."[31] When Shapiro did not relent, Tate held him to his ambivalence: "these public statements of yours are inconsistent with the views expressed [earlier and in letters]. . . . Shall I accuse you of dishonesty?"

Save Katherine Garrison Chapin—a poet who, interestingly, was also the wife of Francis Biddle, the attorney general who had indicted Pound for high treason in 1943—Shapiro was the lone dissenter among the fellows in the vote for Pound's Bollingen Prize. Shapiro would later declare that his "dissent from dissent" caused "the literary and cultural 'Establishment' [to] tur[n] its back on him."[32] In *Reports of My Death*, the second volume of his autobiography, Shapiro would maintain that his vote against

Pound "cost him his standing among fellow poets, marking him forever as 'just another refuser' and a Jew."[33] In fact, Shapiro had not been alone in "great distress" and "confusion" prior to the award announcement.[34] In its wake, the fellows unilaterally banded behind Tate as a spokesperson in the press, but an untitled memorandum in the archives records a late ballot of seven votes for Pound (Adams, Lowell, Bogan, Tate, Eliot, Spencer, and Auden), four for Williams (Shapiro, Aiken, Chapin, and Thorp), with three fellows not voting or absent (Warren, Green, Porter). Warren and Thorp, when interviewed decades later, could only recall voting for Pound.[35] These instances of faulty memory are telling: during the controversy that followed, Pound would represent an aesthetic position for which Thorp and Warren stood. If they had not voted for *The Pisan Cantos*, the book, by private ballot, they voted for *The Pisan Cantos*, the symbol, after its public hearing.

The final ballot was cast by mail in February: ten for Pound, two for Williams, one abstention (Paul Green).[36] "The Fellows [were] aware that objections may be made to awarding a prize to a man situated as is Mr. Pound," and Tate, consulting with special committee members Lowell, Shapiro, and Adams, drafted the statement attached to the library's February 20 press release:[37]

> To make a choice for the award among the eligible books, provided any one merited such recognition, according to the stated terms of the Bollingen Prize. To permit other considerations than that of poetic achievement to sway the decision would destroy the significance of the award and would in principle deny the validity of that objective perception of value on which any civilized society must rest.[38]

Some press responses echoed the sentiments of the fellows' statement.[39] "This emphasis on an objective criterion of beauty and excellence, akin to belief in an objective truth, is fundamental to a free and rational society," accorded one editorial in the *New York Herald Tribune*. *Politics* called the Bollingen Prize decision "the brightest political act in a dark period." Meanwhile, a columnist in the *Daily Worker* declared a cabal in the United States government: "the anti-Semites Eliot and Pound . . . [are supported by] giant Mellon industrial and financial interests."[40] Robert Frost privately called the prize "an unendurable outrage," and the press release its "wild manifesto":

In the list of names I saw at once the Chapin lady at the head . . . as Mrs. Francis Biddle, the wife of the former Attorney General the explanation of why Ezra had been protected by the New Deal from being tried for treason like poor friendless Axis Sally. . . . I suppose Louise Bogan wrote the manifesto of the wild party. Well if her logic carries through it will say that we should admire Ezra for being a great poet in spite of being a great traitor, so we must condemn him for [being] a great traitor in spite of his being a great poet.[41]

Protests flooded the library mail: "Why do we have such people as . . . the present Librarian of Congress in tax-paid Government positions?" demanded the Georgia superintendent of schools; the Contemporary Writers League wrote urging the library to rescind "the most serious disgrace to American poetry."[42] The president of the Poetry Society of America, Robert Hillyer, reanimated headlines in an inflammatory double-issue segment for the *Saturday Review of Literature* in June. Hillyer printed excerpts from *The Pisan Cantos* and T. S. Eliot's *The Waste Land*, conducting exposé close readings that revealed an institutional conspiracy: the Library of the Congress was linked to the Bollingen Foundation, which "through the generosity of Paul Mellon . . . supports the Pantheon Press, a publishing house which issues many outpourings of the new estheticism, the literary cult to whom T. S. Eliot and Ezra Pound are gods," and moreover to Mellon's favored Jung—and Jung's "services to the Nazi cause."[43] On the one hand, Hillyer's claims were patently sensationalist, intended to attract mass audiences and sell papers. On the other, the library took him seriously: Librarian of Congress Evans submitted an official reply printed in the next issue,[44] and the library issued a press release on August 11. Copies were sent by special delivery to the *Saturday Review*, and when the editors declined to reprint the statement the fellows revised it to a seventy-two-page "counterattack." The Modern Poetry Association, the publisher of *Poetry*, would print this as *The Case Against "The Saturday Review of Literature,"* aligning itself against Hillyer's Poetry Society of America, which had positioned itself as the steadfast commons of "honest American" literary populism. "It is by my authority as a citizen that I protest!," Hillyer wrote: "A terrible thing has been done in the name of my Library of Congress!"[45]

In the wake of the Bollingen Prize, New Criticism as an identifiable program acquired national prominence. Hillyer had previously attacked

Eliot and Pound, but in the *Saturday Review* pieces they became exemplars of "new aestheticism" as an institutionally located dogma. The "new aesthetes" achieved, "where Oscar Wilde had failed," institutionalizing the ideology of art-for-art's-sake, or aesthetic autonomy, within the Library of Congress as well as in "the Ivory Tower." For the *Saturday Review*'s editorial board and readership, the fact that the fellows issued the prize decision under the auspices of the federal government—and not within the private sphere of "the Ivory Tower"—was at the heart of the scandal. "Even if all political aspects, pro and con, are brushed aside, the fact remains that 'The Pisan Cantos,' for the most part, seem to us to be less poetry than a series of word games and hidden allusions," wrote Norman Cousins and Harrison Smith for the editorial board, "hardly deserving of an award bearing the name of the United States Library of Congress."[46] But the most "fundamental question" was the role of the government in the arts: "Government prizes do not fit in too well with democratic ideology, and the early laws of this county specifically discouraged donations to Government agencies by private individuals or organizations. Totalitarian states specialize in prizes. . . . For a democracy, however, the danger, made explicit in this case, is that a single school might use the prestige of the Government for advancing its own idiom."[47]

It was the first and last time the Bollingen Prize would be awarded by the U.S. government. Congressman James Patterson entered the *Saturday Review* articles and the library's responses into the Congressional Record on July 19, fulminating before the House: "Should we encourage the activities in literature of moral lepers?" Congressman Jacob K. Javits ordered an investigation of the award decision. Two months after the press storm cloud, the Congressional Joint Committee on the Library of Congress resolved that it was "bad policy for the government to give prizes and awards, especially in matters of taste."[48] In keeping with the resolution, passed August 19, 1949, the library also discontinued the Elizabeth Sprague Coolidge Medal for eminent services to chamber music as well as three prizes endowing national exhibitions of prints. The joint committee would not approve the library's awarding of literary or artistic prizes for another forty years.[49]

After the congressional ruling, the library wanted to cleanse itself of the negative publicity of the Bollingen affair, but also to maintain rapport with the Bollingen Foundation as a patron. To trace the subsequent negotiations around the temporarily homeless purse—the path of material capital linked warily to its symbolic capital as a prize—is to trace the institutional relocation of poetic prestige in the years following World War II.

## *Poetry* Versus Yale

If "government prizes do not fit in too well with democratic ideology," who would administer the Bollingen—an already powerful, albeit infamous, marker of poetic celebrity? The first contender was *Poetry*, which had been in dire straits since the end of the war and owed its survival in no small part to Paul Mellon's funding through the Bollingen Foundation.[50] Like the library, *Poetry* owed Mellon's support in turn to the crafty facilitation of Huntington Cairns. When leading Paul Mellon to support *Poetry* alongside the Library of Congress in 1946,[51] for example, Cairns first helped the magazine acquire federal government tax exemption to secure the Mellon trustees' support. Correspondence among Cairns, Paul Mellon, *Poetry*, and the IRS shows how *Poetry* relied on Cairns's internal help in Washington. *Poetry* administrator Thomas Lea wrote to Cairns on November 27, 1946, thanking him for his "many kindnesses in this matter:" "Today we received the new ruling from the Bureau of Internal Revenue confirming our tax-exempt status. . . . If, as we assume, this remarkable speed on the part of the bureau is the result of your prompt intercession—you are a genius."[52] The same day, Cairns wrote to Paul Mellon: "The Bureau of Internal Revenue ruling Poetry has been pried loose and mailed to Chicago. It was favorable, which means that we will be able to make our grant at once."[53]

The Bollingen Foundation continued supporting the magazine until January 1949. A month before the Library of Congress announced the Bollingen Prize decision, the Bollingen trustees issued *Poetry* a $15,000 check—but warned it may be their last.[54] The possibility of renewed support would remain up for discussion, but the trustees hoped that *Poetry* would in the meantime find additional backers. When the editor of the magazine, Hayden Carruth, read the Library of Congress's press release announcing the termination of the Bollingen Prize, he immediately and strategically wrote to the Bollingen Foundation. "I should like to express to you . . . my extreme misgiving for this unfortunate action," he wrote to the foundation's secretary, Ernest Brooks, on August 26, 1949. "I believe that the Joint Congressional Committee on the Library has committed an exceedingly unwise act in depriving American poets and other artists of their only official recognition," he sympathized, moreover offering "the facilities of this magazine to the Foundation for the administering of the prize": "I believe it would be appropriate for such an important prize for poetry to be awarded through the country's most prominent magazine of poetry. I contemplate an award made upon the basis of judgment of a committee of writers very much like that comprised in the Fellows to the Library."[55]

Carruth viewed the Bollingen Prize as an opportunity to help replenish at least the symbolic capital of *Poetry*, suggesting that "the announcement of the award would be made in the magazine." Carruth pitched the potential acquisition to Brooks, however, as a basically equitable exchange: as "the country's most prominent magazine of poetry," *Poetry* could brand the Bollingen Prize with "the mark of high literary distinction, which this country, unlike many others, has lacked for so long." More practically, he offered administrative support: *Poetry*'s staff "would handle administrative matters—nominating books, collecting votes, conducting correspondence, etc." Most important, Carruth made the bid for the prize based on an argument for the relocation of the prize to the *private* sphere: "A continuance of the prize would give very real moral support to serious American writers and editors, and it would demonstrate as well to the discriminating and reasonable members of the general public that hysterical political action can be counteracted by *private stability and private judgment*."[56] This was a good bid, assuring that *Poetry* magazine would not be involved in the controversies of a government-sponsored award. But if the Bollingen Foundation's support of the Library of Congress and of *Poetry* were not always publicly correlated aesthetic missions, they had become one when *Poetry* published the fellows' "counterattack" to the Poetry Society of America as *The Case Against "The Saturday Review of Literature."* Having stood behind the fellows' prize decision would cost the magazine.

Four days after Carruth's appeal, on August 30, Chief Librarian James Babb of Yale University wrote to Brooks at the Bollingen Foundation in turn: "The Yale Library, through the Yale Collection of American Literature, could issue the prize." Babb, who was friends with Librarian of Congress Luther Evans, made the proposition in a markedly casual tone: Babb had happened to read about the controversy in the paper and judged simply that Evans had been "forced" to give up prizes "because of pressure from Congress." Unlike Carruth's heavy-handed assessment of the congressional decision's broader ideological stakes, Babb addressed the decision's effect not on society or even on the institutional entity of "the Library," but on the individual "Luther Evans"—against whom the "pressure from Congress" flattens into a political abstraction. As Babb demonstrates, the future of the prize was a question most comfortably posed within an interpersonal domain—he offers Brooks a close-quartered business proposal, disassociated from fist-thumping senators and squeamish *Saturday Review* editorialists. As if to avoid association with such journalistic argumentation, Babb writes without rhetorical excess. He performs only perfunctory flattery—the Bollingen [Prize] "would be a distinguished thing for us here at Yale"—but, unlike Carruth, Babb makes no attempt to guise the potential symbolic capital gain for the university: "it undoubtedly would indirectly help the Yale Collection of American Literature." Donning the persona of the curmudgeonly scholar, Babb assumes a posture of indifference: "Of course, as a cold-blooded librarian, I would rather have the $1,000 a year to buy books of poetry. This would enable us to buy all the important current books and have a few hundred dollars a year to buy a good old book." To the Bollingen trustees, Babb's disinterest surely seemed a welcome palate cleanser. The "cold-blooded librarian" or dispassionate archivist would have seemed a far preferable cultural administrator to the headily desperate poets and journalists dueling it out in the news rags. "If my suggestions above are out of order, just throw this letter away," Babb insists. His relative indifference was at least mostly genuine; unlike *Poetry*, Yale Library was not, after all, on the brink of collapse. "Peg and I very much enjoyed meeting your wife at Biddeford Pool. We also had a nice chat with her parents. They are an attractive, lively couple. Sorry you weren't around."[57] A postscript redoubles Babb's effect of country club intimacy: "P.S. I should have to clear this poetry prize business with higher authorities here, but I cannot see that they would object in any way." In the formally tidy addendum, Babb relieves himself of explicit identification with institutional power while simultaneously providing its assurances against any potential bureaucratic headache—thus ensuring the epistolary sanctity of the letter as a "chat around Biddeford Pool."

On December 21, Brooks reported in a memorandum after a phone call with James Babb that the librarian had cleared Yale's sponsoring of the prize with the university's president, Charles Seymour. The university promised to reconstitute the Bollingen award name: "As to the name of the prize,

Babb said that continuation of the name 'Bollingen' would be agreeable," though "some have suggested the name 'Yale-Bollingen Prize in Poetry'":

> Babb said that he was conscious of the fact that some friends of the Yale Library might criticize Yale for carrying on the prize. However, he seemed to be thinking less of the Jung controversy and of Pound's politics than of the acrimony caused by the sharp division in the world of poetry between the traditionalists and the modernists. Among the good friends of Yale who he thought might be bothered were William Rose Benet, an editor of the Saturday Review of Literature, and Leonard Bacon. He said, however, that he understood that Benet had not sympathized with SRL's attack on the Pound award. I assured him that Leonard Bacon felt the same way.[58]

Babb wrote to Brooks the next day making their phone call official. "Dear Ernie, / I am very happy to say that the Yale University Library will be pleased and honored to have the opportunity to award annually the Bollingen Poetry Prize of $1,000 to that volume of poetry published in the preceding year which was selected as the best poetical effort of the year by a Committee of Award which, in the future, will be appointed by the President of Yale University." Babb echoed the two politicized considerations—"I think that it should be called the Bollingen Prize" and "I feel fairly certain that we should wish to ask all of the previous Committee to act again."[59]

The literary authority of the fellows was thus reassembled at Yale—all agreed to serve on the prize committee again[60]—and a new relationship established between the arts patron and the university: "Please tell Paul [Mellon] that I am delighted at the outcome of all this," Babb concluded to Brooks.[61] Babb and President Seymour would collaborate with Brooks to carefully construct a proposal for the establishment of the prize and a press release smoothing over politicized concerns.[62] Chiefly, Babb "want[ed] to be sure that no impression is created in the minds of the public that Yale is taking the prize away from The Library of Congress, as Luther Evans is a good friend of his. There should be no difficulty on this score. Any announcement by Yale can make it clear that The Library of Congress discontinued the prize; and I have every reason to believe that Luther Evans will be glad to have the prize continued by Yale."[63] While Babb drafted the primary material for the press release, Brooks would add a final paragraph: "The Library of Congress established a similar poetry prize in 1948, but subsequently all prize awards by the Library of Congress were discontinued. Yale University is very glad to have the opportunity of re-establishing this prize, the purpose of which is to encourage and afford recognition to outstanding achievement in the field of American poetry." Brooks recorded in a memorandum for his personal files that he phoned Huntington Cairns to read "my draft suggesting material to be included in publicity release by Yale." The addendum reflected genuine goodwill between the institutions: Yale University had reclaimed the notoriety of the prize as an honor and, by extension, increased the symbolic prestige of the Bollingen Foundation. The university had, in effect, siphoned off the symbolic value of the scandal. By reestablishing the prize, Yale granted its apolitical fresh start, but the prize now came with value added—the cultural attention the Bollingen affair had magnetized. Save the Pulitzer, the Bollingen Prize remains arguably the most prestigious national prize in American poetry today.

Throughout the fall, *Poetry* editor Hayden Carruth had meanwhile sought new sources of funding for the magazine. In the first weeks of September, Carruth traveled to the East Coast to meet personally with potential benefactors. He had taken a similar trip earlier that summer. After this second trip proved a failure, Carruth, increasingly frenetic, frequently implicated the Bollingen Foundation in communications with other potential funders—despite the foundation's tenuous status as a continuing donor and meantime silence in response to his August inquiry about the magazine taking over the Bollingen Prize. In November, Carruth wrote to Brooks excitedly with a new lead: the Lilly Endowment of Indianapolis, an organization he "had never heard of . . . until about two weeks ago." In an unusual, and to Carruth's mind promising, reply to a routine solicitation letter, the Lilly Endowment secretary, Mr. J. K. Lilly III, requested a more detailed picture of *Poetry*'s circulation and cultural affiliations. He inquired especially about the individuals or foundations interested in supporting the magazine: "In an enterprise of this sort it is the policy of the Endowment not to support the entire project, since it is felt that a broader base of support is healthier for the project itself."[64]

In the wake of the Bollingen affair, Carruth might have worried that the institutional and cultural alliances of the magazine might alienate the

Lilly Endowment. *Poetry*'s sole source of support and Lilly's only potential funding partner had just become famous for honoring a fascist, anti-Semitic, mentally ill poet. But, under Carruth, *Poetry* remained an uncompromising ideological ally to the fellows. "It may very well turn out that they [the trustees of the Lilly Endowment] are the Saturday Review sort of people who will lose interest when they learn more about the magazine," he had written to Brooks, "but I hope not. We can only wait and see what happens." Carruth naturally viewed Brooks and the Bollingen Foundation trustees as being of like minds with the fellows against the "Saturday Review people." In the same letter to Brooks, Carruth mentioned "the pamphlet"—it would, he promised, "be out on Monday. The first shipments of copies went today to the distributing agents in New York."[65] This pamphlet was *The Case Against "The Saturday Review of Literature."* The library fellows' soon to be notorious "counterattack" hitting "virtually all of the literary establishment" was presented as a collaboration by *Poetry* and the library fellows. In fact, the Bollingen Foundation would seek to distance itself from this publication, later making clear that it was not directly involved in its funding. As the Bollingen Foundation sought a clean break from the stink that its first prize decision had caused in the press, Carruth's readiness to hold court on the controversy would prove one compelling reason for the Bollingen Foundation to disassociate its name from *Poetry*. Already, it had encouraged the publication to seek new funding; now, this became a more urgent priority.

Carruth, meanwhile, did not hesitate to advertise "the Bollingen Foundation's interest in the magazine" to Mr. Lilly. When enclosing "a copy of the letter we sent today to Mr. J. K. Lilly of Lilly Endowment, Inc." to Brooks, in fact, he sounded penitent for this reason: "I realize that perhaps my letter sounds as if the Trustees of the Bollingen Foundation had already made their decision to renew the grant [to *Poetry*]." Carruth acknowledged that he had perhaps exaggerated the Bollingen Foundation's commitments to *Poetry*:

> I hope you will not think I have stated the case too strongly; it was certainly not my intention to obligate the Bollingen Foundation in any way to the Lilly Endowment.... Every effort should be made to keep the Lilly Endowment interested. It will be easier to explain to them later, I think, exactly what the situation at Bollingen is when there are negotiations between Bollingen and Lilly.[66]

But Carruth's hopes that the Bollingen Foundation and Lilly Endowment would "come to an arrangement for the joint subsidy of the magazine" were soon dashed.[67] "It is my duty to tell you that the decision was not to offer a grant for this purpose (support of POETRY)," Lilly wrote on December 10, 1949, to Carruth, who in turn quoted Lilly's refusal in a letter he wrote to Brooks the same day he received it. "The feeling was that this project is slightly outside the scope of activities of the Endowment since support of literary efforts in the past has been more for research and bibliography rathern [sic] than for publication of current material."[68]

Whether the Bollingen affair per se proved decisive in the Lilly Endowment's decision not to fund *Poetry* is not clear. What is clear is that the Lilly Endowment's expressed agenda for its involvement in literary culture—a commitment to "research and bibliography" over "current material"—parallels the Bollingen Foundation's realignment toward the academy. In a last appeal to Brooks for support, Carruth diagnosed the magazine's struggle as a symptom of the new era of the university stronghold: "Everyone is interested in scholarship, nobody in creative writing of the good kind."[69] The universities were increasingly linked in with patronage in a way *Poetry* was not: "We have found that today charity—if literature can be called that—is an organized, big business, and we can't crack it." Despite having "written literally thousands of letters, hav[ing] applied to many foundations, and hav[ing] spok[en] with as many people as we could," *Poetry* could not "compete with the universities in getting money, even though we are doing more for the state of American culture as it is right now than any university. The universities are safe and respectable, and there is a certain amount of truth in the observation that creative writing, in order to be good, cannot be entirely safe and respectable."[70] Carruth, denied the support of the Lilly Endowment and the Bollingen Foundation, was fired at the magazine's next board meeting.[71]

What the fired editor never could have predicted is that the Lilly family—the very patron that helped guarantee his ousting—would reemerge to grant *Poetry* a windfall fifty years later. We will learn more about J. K. Lilly III's sister, Ruth Lilly, in chapter 4. The so-called Prozac heiress would transform *Poetry* from a literary magazine into a massive cultural institution with a $100 million grant in 2002. But Carruth certainly predicted the fifty years ahead. As the Bollingen Prize moved to Yale, so too poetry moved to the academy. Like the Lilly Endowment and the many foundations that refused Carruth's appeal, the Bollingen trustees felt safer stashing its symbolic capital with "cold-blooded librarians."[72] Patronage, in this sense, was helping birth the age of criticism and the solidification of literary prestige in the university.

The Bollingen Foundation; presciently, the Lilly Endowment; the Library of Congress; and the faltering *Poetry* magazine thus all emerge as key institutional players in the relocation of the poetry establishment—most immediately, the Bollingen award committee, a coup of big-hitter poets who were also literary critics[73]—to the academy. On the one hand, the discontinuation of government prizes "in matters of taste" had offered a swift historical corrective to the Fellows' decision, apparently settling "the values involved in th[e] cultural and political fight" in favor of the *Saturday Review*'s affronted patriots.[74] Yet by admitting the Bollingen Prize to the "private sphere," the federal government redoubled the fellows' liberal state apology for the "objective perception of value": the university became a safe house for politically inconvenient art like *The Pisan Cantos*, and meanwhile the library could assume ideological neutrality: state-supported poetry would be reconstituted as a de facto public good during the Cold War, and in the educational and civic initiatives of the state arts and neoliberal-era poets laureate. The ascendant New Critical program at Yale quarantined the literary object to yet a narrower sphere of perceptual autonomy, adopting the regulative values of "objective perception" the fellows defended in the context of national culture. For Jed Rasula, the Bollingen affair is straightforwardly "integral to the hegemony of New Criticism": desperate to contain and cure history, the Library of Congress absorbed a politically punishable act of treason "into the carceral apparatus of pedagogy at a time when heuristic protocol meant that Pound's poetry, not his life, would serve the curriculum."[75] Yet to say the Bollingen affair catalyzed the academic institutionalization of New Criticism eclipses the broader stakes of the fellows' relocation to the university.[76] Inasmuch as Pound and the high modernist project served academic and culturally elite curricula for the second half of the twentieth-century, poetry was news that stayed news on the syllabus. But the relocation of the fellows to Yale was not the only result of the Bollingen affair. The move would subsequently impact the administration of poetry programming at the Library of Congress and the ways in which the state related to poetic production. It also impacted the administration of *Poetry*. The fellows' dissenter, Karl Shapiro, had moved with the library's body to Yale, but maintained his outlier view. Shapiro's dissent echoed throughout the literary trade establishment, and it was loud enough in the Modern Poetry Association boardroom to topple *Poetry*'s editorial regime.

## *Poetry*'s Regime Change: Dissent from Dissent

The day after he was fired, Carruth wrote to Brooks at the Bollingen Foundation, "feel[ing] obliged to tell you that, at a general meeting of the Board of the Modern Poetry Association yesterday, I was fired from the editorship of Poetry. This action was brought about largely through the influence of Marion Strobel." "There is not very much I can add to that flat statement," Carruth wrote. He had not been told the name of his successor. The purpose of the letter was less to inform Brooks about the termination of his editorship—he rightly "suppose[d] [Brooks would] be informed of such matters by the officials of the Modern Poetry Association or by somebody on the Poetry staff"—than to make one last bid for Bollingen Foundation support, this time on behalf of himself.

> I wonder if you could tell me whether or not the Bollingen Foundation ever considers grants to individual[s] engaged in literary projects. And if there is the possibility of such a grant, what one must do to apply for it. Now that I am unemployed, I can begin again to turn my attention to my own work. . . . But I won't be able to do much about [my projects] unless I can find some means of support.[77]

The foundation did not; patron support to individuals still tended to work on an informal and interpersonal basis. Institutionally formalized "grants to individuals engaged in literary projects" were still uncommon. Individuals found institutional support through university sabbaticals or occasionally as residents at artists' colonies like Yaddo.[78]

Brooks received the forewarned letter from "the officials" the next day, which recast Carruth's firing at the hands of Marion Strobel as the nonrenewal of his appointment by consideration of the board.[79] Karl Shapiro, who became editor in February, would meanwhile refer to Carruth's "resignation."[80] Brooks thus heard three different versions of *Poetry*'s regime change.[81]

Shapiro, whom the MPA board apparently selected "unanimously," is a notable choice in light of the Bollingen Prize scandal. His anti-Pound stance may have caused most of "the literary and cultural 'Establishment'"—represented by the fellows, now at Yale—to "tur[n] their back on him," but to the MPA board it made him an antidote to Carruth.[82] The MPA—which less than a year before had defended the fellows against the *Saturday Review*—now preferred the fellows' dissenter. The appointment of Shapiro as editor marked a decisive shift in the cultural politics of the magazine.

Indeed, it necessitated an editorial overhaul. Upon assuming "active control" on February 1, Shapiro fired everyone at the magazine. "Except for Miss Udell, the Business Manager, there is no staff at present," Shapiro wrote to Brooks. "The Trustees voluntarily granted me full editorial powers, including the prerogative of choosing a new staff and introducing whatever editorial policies I saw fit . . . I hope to develop a strong small staff and myself to formulate the policy of POETRY."[83] Shapiro also changed the name of the magazine that year, dropping the subtitle from *Poetry: A Magazine of Verse*.

By firing Carruth, the board may have enabled the magazine's survival. The Bollingen Foundation now felt comfortable reassigning an annual endowment to *Poetry*, which they had threatened to terminate, under Shapiro's more moderate stead.[84] Shapiro wrote to Brooks on February 22, 1950—a year since the Library of Congress had announced the Bollingen Prize—thanking him for the trustees' continued "generous assistance" for the upcoming year: "All of us connected with the Association are deeply cognizant of the fact that POETRY would be defunct today were it not for the Bollingen Foundation. We are also aware that your assistance cannot continue indefinitely, and that it is part of our responsibility to make the magazine financially independent."[85]

## Aftershocks of the Bollingen Affair: Losses at the Library of Congress

Despite Lowell's encouraging letters to Bishop in early 1949, she had not been the obvious choice for the 1949–1950 consultant post. Lowell had explained to Bishop that she would be offered the post if her mentor, Marianne Moore, refused. Bishop was likely never told that after Moore could not "in conscience digress" from a translation project,[86] Librarian of

Congress Luther Evans had also asked the current consultant, Léonie Adams, to stay on another year. Adams declined.[87]

The first choice, meanwhile, had been Williams Carlos Williams. Williams in fact initially accepted the formal offer to serve as consultant in early 1948. "Aware of the honor that has been bestowed upon me," Williams wrote to Luther Evans on March 3, "I will do my best to live up to it."[88] He had already suffered the first of a series of heart attacks, however, and by October withdrew his acceptance—leaving the fellows to vote on the Bollingen Prize and on Williams' replacement—in their last meetings of 1948. The fellows hoped that Williams would take the post in 1950–51 instead, which he declined, though in the meantime he joined the fellows as a member;[89] and in January 1950 Williams again refused the 1951–52 term, in poor health and wrapping up his medical practice. When Conrad Aiken, who held the office during those two terms instead, wrote to Williams in 1952—noting that the librarian had now raised the position's stipend—Williams agreed. "At $7500, I could do it . . . perhaps I'd get used to it and even like it in the end," he wrote, and arranged to rent Aiken's apartment on Capitol Hill.[90]

Appointing Williams as consultant in poetry, however, proved to be the fellows' second major, and ultimately last, scandalous decision. Not only was Williams associated with Pound, whom he had publicly supported during the Bollingen affair—his review of *The Pisan Cantos* in *Imagi* had even prompted letters of protest to the librarian of Congress[91]—but Williams's own political record would prove suspect in the climate of early Cold War America. Senator Joseph McCarthy had made his infamous Wheeling, West Virginia, declaration that the State Department had been infiltrated with communists two years before; the House Un-American Activities Committee's investigation of communist propaganda in the film industry—resulting in the blacklisting of the "Hollywood Ten"—had unfolded three years before that, several months before Lowell accused Elizabeth Ames of sheltering communists in the trial at Yaddo.[92] When the library issued a press release announcing Williams's appointment on August 8, it was met with a series of loyalty accusations, beginning with a list of charges in the weekly newspaper *Counterattack: Facts to Combat Communism*. Williams, the article pronounced, had signed seven petitions and letters between 1937 and 1941 advocating for cooperation with Russia, clemency for Earl Browder, and the elimination of HUAC; he had published in the *Partisan Review* before it became anticommunist; and he had been billed to speak at a rally in April 1951 in defense of three members of the Hollywood Ten.[93]

Within days of the *Counterattack* story, letters protesting Williams's alleged communist sympathies began arriving in the library office. In literary circles, too, the Poetry Society of America's witch-hunting rhetoric during the Bollingen affair—asserting that the fellows had "defied the decencies of the American tradition[;] Let us find out more about these people"[94]—would be echoed. The charge now was not against the library's support of Pound as a disloyal fascist, but of Williams as a disloyal communist. The Lyric Foundation, for example, published a nationwide circular that called Williams's appointment "an insult to American citizenship," and his poetry "the very voice of Communism": "O Russia, O Russia, come with me into my dream and let us be lovers. . . . I lay my spirit at your feet" (a 1946 poem published in the *New Republic*).[95]

Acting Librarian of Congress Verner Clapp, who in 1948 had exhorted the fellows not "to be deflected by political considerations or other questions of expediency from a decision rendered strictly in terms of literary merit" on the question of the Bollingen Prize, now fast relented to "political considerations." Issuing the request for Williams's federal loyalty check—President Harry Truman's Executive Order 9835, the first general loyalty program designed to guard against communist influences among federal executive agency employees, had been issued in March 1947—Clapp also had HUAC records checked, revealing one reference to Williams: in mid-1939, he had cosigned an open petition calling for greater cooperation with antifascist forces and the Soviet Union.[96] Denunciations from legislators on behalf of angered constituencies followed, including Senators George Smathers and Spessard Holland (Florida), Alexander Wiley (Wisconsin), Lyndon B. Johnson (Texas), and Congressman Franklin D. Roosevelt Jr. "One of the Truman administration patronage job-holders who probably will be given a careful going-over by the Republicans is the Librarian of Congress, Luther H. Evans," wrote one Hearst columnist: "he seems to be running a sort of employment service for indigent Left-wingers."[97]

Before Williams, who had already delayed his trip to Washington because of his health, arrived at the library, his wife, Flossie, received a letter from Clapp. "I very much regret to have to tell you that we have received from the Federal Bureau of Investigation a preliminary report resulting from our request for a loyalty investigation, on the basis of which we have felt it necessary to ask for a full and fuller investigation." Due to the allegations in the preliminary report, and in light of the pending investigation, Clapp announced that it would "not be possible for Dr. Williams to enter upon the duties of his appointment." He had sent the letter to her, Clapp explained, rather than to Williams directly, "out of regard for his [health] condition."[98]

The fellows, whose relationship with the library had been tense since the Bollingen affair,[99] would further deteriorate during the Williams imbroglio. After 1952, they would never again meet on Capitol Hill, holding only occasional satellite meetings in New York. On January 11, 1953, under the auspices of Yale, the fellows honored Williams as the winner of that year's Bollingen Prize.

Two days later, as if in response, the library officially withdrew Williams' invitation to serve as the national poet. Having already endured the Bollingen affair, Librarian of Congress Evans was tired of finding his name in the news, as well as of the apparently political business of poetry. "I have determined that the conditions no longer exist which at an earlier date made your appointment . . . appear desirable and profitable to the Library," he wrote tersely to Williams. "I accordingly hereby revoke the offer of appointment." He also halted the loyalty inquest.[100] When Williams's attorney sent an incredulous response, Evans rebuffed it: "I propose not to reply," Evans noted on the attorney's letter. "I agree," wrote Clapp. Four administrators then marked their initials. In March, Williams, hospitalized for depression, wrote to Evans that he did not plan to "sue anyone"—and in April Evans conditionally reinstated his appointment, reinitiating the loyalty investigation. But the appointment expired in September, and Williams would not hear from the library for another year.[101]

While Williams and Pound, tried on the national stage, sat in mental hospitals, the national poetry office sat vacant. In October 1954, L. Quincy Mumford replaced Evans as the librarian of Congress. He received a forewarning brief from Chief of the General Reference and Bibliography Division Roy Basler and Clapp on the politically animated situations of the fellows and the role of the consultant in poetry and soon wrote to Williams that matters with the fellows would need to be settled before any new consultant could be appointed. The poetry office would remain unoccupied until the appointment of Randall Jarrell in 1956.

By that time, the fellows had wholly disbanded. Standing behind Pound, and now Williams, had strained their relationship with the library to the breaking point. By 1955, eight members' seven-year terms had expired or the members had resigned. "The failure of the relationship between Fellow and Library to work out is a disaster," Lowell pleaded with the new Librarian of Congress. "I think the position of Consultant in Poetry will have little meaning or prestige unless he is chosen by other writers."[102] The library was allowing its tastemaking authority "to die on the vine," as Conrad Aiken lamented, but, after all, the library was to now abstain in deciding "matters of taste."[103] When Mumford eventually called for a fellows meeting to nominate a consultant for 1956, only two members accepted, and the meeting was canceled.[104]

In five years' time, the Library of Congress had lost the prize; the fellows, or as Aiken joked, the "poor castrated Felons," who had been deprived of the prize;[105] and finally a nationally representative poet.

## Reading for Red Tape: "Mumbling contentedly" for the Canon

Most of the day-to-day work has been connected with the leaflets that will occupy the [Archive of Recorded Poetry] records. Short biographies of each of the poets had to be written, as well as bibliographies, lists of references examined, and first publications checked. The results of this, when printed, appear rather slight; however, a great deal of time goes into them and since most of the poets send incomplete or incorrect information, or none at all, it means a good deal of checking and re-checking to be done.
—ELIZABETH BISHOP, "ANNUAL REPORT TO THE LIBRARIAN OF CONGRESS FROM THE CHAIR OF POETRY, 1949–1950"

Even as the Bollingen affair and its aftershocks rocked the Library of Congress, national poets meanwhile had to mind day-to-day business. There was paperwork to do, a recording archive to create, and visitors to greet. Meanwhile, the consultant and fellows were navigating their increasingly tense relationship with Library of Congress administrators. In one office mishap in the spring of 1950, both Conrad Aiken and Randall Jarrell were offered the 1950–1951 consultantship. Aiken had formally accepted the post in March, but "the letter was seen by only one girl in the reference department who filed it away safely, while everyone else just wondered what had happened to Mr. Aiken for five weeks," Bishop—then the consultant—explained to Lowell. In the meantime, "someone had told Randall [Jarrell] (not me) & he had started to make plans."[106] Jarrell would be invited again, however, the next time formally. But it would not be until the fellows had dissolved. He would serve from 1956–1958.

After losing the Bollingen Prize and the cultural authority of the Fellows in American Letters to disperse its capital, the library still had one remaining endowment of Paul Mellon's Bollingen Foundation: the Archive of Recorded Poetry and Literature. During their terms in office, Lowell, Adams, Bishop, and Aiken variously cited—and often complained—about the administration of the archive, having earned their keep at the library not by standing behind Pound and Williams, which had created scandals, but by managing the archive's recordings. Bishop characterized her "work for the year 1949–1950 [as] chiefly centered around the preparation of the second series of albums of recordings of <u>Twentieth Century Poetry in English</u>"—more specifically, "most of the day-to-day work has been connected with the leaflets that will occupy the records." Bishop was careful to defend the value of these leaflets: "when printed, [the material may] appear rather slight"; "however, a great deal of time goes into them." She refers to the written record that accompanies, explains, and understands itself in proximity to the recorded archive: this is Bishop's "day-to-day work"—the work of the poet-administrator—that she worried will be misrecognized or forgotten.

Unlike the Bollingen Prize, the archive would grow up unsullied by publicly political "matters of taste." While in these middle decades of the twentieth century the American university would systematically treat the poem as a textual object, especially in the tradition of New Critical close reading techniques, the Archive of Recorded Poetry and Literature represented an alternate tradition of the speech-based, and phonocentric, narrative poem—one that would prove important for future state poets. In later years, it was activated as an ideologically unblemished tradition of the American poetic voice.[107] In chapter 2, for example, we will witness Robert Frost project an ideology of national voice in the spontaneous recitation of sixteen lines of blank verse from memory at President Kennedy's inauguration and, even more directly in later chapters, observe how more recent poets laureate have extended this phonocentric tradition of "saying" poems into civic space. As discussed in chapter 4, Robert Pinsky's

Favorite Poem Project's audio and video recordings of "Americans saying their favorite poems out loud" (1998 to the present) constitute a more recent substantial addition to the Archive of Recorded Poetry and Literature. Following Frost, this archival tradition has been typically instrumentalized to model the expressive voice of the individual citizen and to project evolving ideologies of national identity. But earlier state poets often voiced measures of resistance as they constructed the national audio canon: in private jests about its bureaucratic business, in decisions about to who to include or exclude, and especially in wariness about its representative capacity. The archive was not only an administrative burden, but an outlet through which national poets understood their relationship to a canonical tradition—and to state power. Lowell and Bishop, for example, frequently voiced critiques of the national tradition by performing failed speech acts in a written archive that placed itself self-consciously adjacent to the Archive of Recorded Poetry.[108] Lowell complained of his *boredom*, Bishop would *mumble*—acts not, exactly, of defiance, but that mark a kind of complicity and ambivalence about working for the nation in the years it asserted itself as a new global and imperial power.

Bishop despised reading for live audiences or for tape. As the national poet, she would embody the sometimes incapacity, and more typically the passive refusal, of the poet to act as a "voice" for the state. Lowell was keenly aware of her aversion—and he would frequently cater to it in letters. In his first epistolary reportage to Bishop when he was the consultant, Lowell claims that, written on library stationary, "this is a dull letter"—"but I've just been on a tour to the library annex, had my teeth x-rayed, and when [I] look up I see the dome of our capitol." The matter of bureaucratic necessity is announced immediately—"I'd like to have you record when you come here"—and undermined in turn. "You'll be amused when you see the list of poets that the 'fellows' have provided me for the first album"; "So much for that . . . I hope you'll really come here this fall & we can go to the galleries & see the otters"; "P.S. Of course you don't have to be recorded, but I'd like to oust some of the monstrosities on my list, if you want to let me know a few days before your arrival, so I can . . . can [sic] get the red tape rolling."[109] Lowell's pun on audio recording tape and "red" tape is jest at the expense of bureaucratic duty, but it is also designed to purchase confidence with Bishop, still a new friend, as his interlocutor.[110] The plotted ineptitude of the postscript's ellipses—"I can . . . can"—refuses two forms of competence. It is first a refusal to ably get "the red tape rolling," or Lowell's reluctant capacity as a poet-administrator, and more specifically a performative haplessness as a government employee. It also imitates the verbal stutter or failed oral delivery of the poem to be recorded on "red tape."

"I'd like to see you, recordings or no," Bishop replied. "Maybe you will send me a card about this so I'll know whether to practice my vowels and consonants or just keep on mumbling contentedly until next year."[111] Both Lowell and Bishop, in poems and letters that represent proximity to the Capitol, i.e., through what Jerome McGann calls "bibliographic codes"—such as writing on Library of Congress stationary or through indicating a "view of the dome" or "view of the Capitol from the Library of Congress"—also represent the disrupted or difficult act of producing recorded poetry, music, or expressive sound. Lowell's critique of the recording archive in letters to Bishop is neither subtle nor perhaps ultimately serious: "Today I record myself—the hangman with no one left to hang but himself."[112] Bishop's critique, meanwhile, is systematically presented in her written record that accompanies the archive, such as administrative reports, correspondence, as well as her poetry proper written as the national poet.

Bishop composed the poem "View of the Capitol from the Library of Congress" in late 1950, at the same office desk where she prepared her Annual Report. "View of the Capitol" describes the Navy Band as "hard and loud, but—queer— / the music doesn't quite come through." First published in the *New Yorker*'s Fourth of July issue in 1951, Bishop qualifies—or indeed questions—the performance of sound for a national audience.[113] "View of the Capitol," like Bishop's famous poem "One Art," is a metered poem that stages a syntactic disruption in its penultimate and final lines. In "One Art," this disruption occurs in the typographically demarcated, visual imperative to "(*Write* it!)." In "View of the Capitol," the Navy Band sounds "queer" and strained: the brasses "want" to pound out a bass line rhythm. Rather than render music through fluent language, Bishop renders noise through base onomatopoeia:

Great shades, edge over,
give the music room.
The gathered brasses want to go
*boom—boom.*

The *"boom—boom"* is the sound of the state, yet the imperative to the trees that produce paper—the "shades" that stand as written pages—to "give the music room" is issued by Bishop. The observer-poet is on the side of the Army band music, ventriloquizing the state command: "edge over." Bishop's willingness to ventriloquize this command provides a historical record of her "view," that is, her institutional position at the Library of Congress, doing poetry work for the state. While Lowell would confess his privileges and sins—and moreover catalogue his antiestablishment triumphs—throughout his poetic corpus, Bishop refuses confession to record her complicity within the national establishment. The poem's geographical and institutional location decisively links speaker to author but is evacuated of personal subjectivity. Bishop registers her resistance not by speaking out but by "mumbling" along, unwilling to perform voice where she had only a view—sounding a quiet discontent, but also measured complicity, with state projects of empire.

Lowell was meanwhile eager to obscure through wit or undermine the actuality of bureaucratic "day-to-day work." The "boredom" he felt at an

*Figure 1.2* Elizabeth Bishop writing at her desk in the library's poetry office, with the U.S. Capitol in the background, circa 1949–1950. Image courtesy of the Library of Congress.

office job was, after all, one way to claim a fundamentally artistic persona as well as to register his disinterest in work for the state. A conscientious objector during World War II—he described himself a decade later as once a "fire-breathing Catholic C.O. [conscientious objector]" who "made my manic statement, / telling off the state and president"[114]—Lowell would also decline his invitation to a 1965 White House Arts Festival in protest of the Johnson administration's policies in the Dominican Republic and in Vietnam, writing a public letter in refusal of attendance.[115] But while in the national poetry office Lowell did not "tel[l] off the state"—he more often complained about administrivia and boredom. It was, after all, a job. Conrad Aiken would treat the position similarly and cheekily boasted to his daughter that he "disregard[ed] office hours, drifting in . . . out or nigh two hours for lunch, then vamoose[ing] at 5 to the awaiting orange blossoms." He echoed Lowell's estimation that "Washington is dull"—"This Lib Cong job is . . . largely a matter of receiving visitors and answering peculiar questions and turning down invitations to speak or read. . . . The best thing is my office, generally reputed to be the handsomest in the city, top floor, overlooking Capitol on one side and Supreme Court on the tother [sic], with view out to river an country too."

From the same office, Bishop did not perform such self-avowed "haplessness" in administrative labor, but competence. Administrative competence enabled, for the archival record, the recognition of other workers, in particular Phyllis Armstrong—"a nice [E]nglish gal . . . who is of course really the Chair of Poetry and does the real drudgery,"[116] as Aiken described the poetry office secretary in a letter to his daughter. Armstrong meanwhile appeared on the first page of Bishop's Annual Report to the Library: "With Miss Armstrong's help I edited these recordings and made the selections to be used for the albums." Bishop further explicitly acknowledged Armstrong, with whom she worked on a daily basis, throughout her Annual Report—frequently recounting office labor using plural pronouns, e.g., "we were busy," "our work"—and throughout the written record of her year in office.[117] No other consultant's report exhibits a similar attention to administrators as collaborators (in the cases, that is, where poetry consultants submitted reports that offered more than "incomplete or incorrect information" for posterity). Moreover, Bishop renders transparent and identifies with the administrative capacity of her position, signing a response to a State Department inquiry as "Elizabeth Bishop / Chair of Poetry / General Reference and Bibliography Division."[118]

If "mumbling" her poems for the archive was a refusal to ventriloquize state power, Bishop meanwhile did not mumble where it would obscure extraliterary labor. In other words, where Bishop performed incompetence—a quiet ambivalence—about her work as a state poet, it is never in the written record of her administrative work with Armstrong, only in the phonetic record of her individual expression as a poet. The archive itself would otherwise conceal the work of those who "edit and select" the sound material, as with the Robert Frost recordings that occupied much correspondence time that year—as well Adams's schedule the year before.[119] The recording archive itself preserves voice, which leaves no written trace of this labor, for national posterity. And while Aiken boasted of his idleness, he—who, like Bishop, despised reading—oversaw the publication of the archive's second series and recorded a number of new poets, including Williams's physician, Merrill Moore. When Robert Hillyer of the Poetry Society of America, however, wrote to belatedly accepted an invitation to record for the archive—the initial invitation, from Warren in 1945, had preceded his attacks on the library during the Bollingen affair—Aiken demurred. "After the Saturday Review ruckus, I don't really feel that any useful purpose would be served by our meeting."[120] He arranged for Hillyer to record in his absence that summer. It was Phyllis Armstrong who handled the recording.

The Archive of Recorded Poetry is not only an example of the bureaucratic work of postwar state poets, nor only of the work of government administrators and office workers in the formation of a national canon. The written archive that accompanies it, the "day-to-day" labor of the office, is also a registry of the national poets' muted frustration and complicity with the national project. (In contrast to the publicity of the postwar scandals, this apparently politically neutralized work is a better model for the projects of contemporary state poets who no longer administer the recording archive but rather civic-minded initiatives.) Postwar state poets departed from state interests most loudly during the Bollingen affair and by dissolving as a body after the red-baiting of Williams out of his post. But their meanwhile office work would represent the voices of a nation that had newly assumed enormous global power—"*boom—boom.*" State poets may have been uncomfortable with this power, as we hear in the "queerness" of Bishop's "View of the Capitol" from her desk or as Robert Lowell would later express in "July in Washington."[121] But they also accommodated and represented state interests, and, in the years to follow, not only at the Library of Congress.

In the postwar period, the national poetry office was less a public platform for its occupants—Lowell, Adams, Bishop, Aiken, and their predecessors—than for its antilaureates. The scandals at the Library of Congress catalyzed political debates and institutional negotiations that meant that Ezra Pound and William Carlos Williams would not be honored as national poets. Instead, the scandals made them Bollingen Prize winners and would help to solidify their canonical status as modernist giants in the university[122]—the new center of poetic production in the decades to follow.

The Bollingen affair would prove the most important event of the early years of the national poetry office. Revealing the national poetry office as a position that was articulated by complex institutional relationships, it also assembles the core cast of characters we will see reappear throughout this book. The Bollingen affair transformed the relationship of the library, *Poetry* magazine, and their then common patron, resulting in administrative and aesthetic regime changes at both institutions. The Bollingen affair made *Poetry* an enemy to the Poetry Society of America and a friend to what we now see as the modernist canon, but nearly lost its patron in the fight. The negotiations surrounding who would take over the funding of the Bollingen Prize, moreover, presciently demonstrate the role of patrons, from the Mellon Endowment to pharmaceutical families, that structure the magazine's commitments in the present. And the losses of prestige at the library—of the prize, the fellows, and, after the librarian of Congress could not handle a second scandal, the failed appointment of William Carlos Williams and the loss of a national poet—would recalibrate the relationships between the state, private literary organizations, and the patron families that continue to shape American poetry today.

It may be accurate to call the university the institutional victor post-1949—the newly codified locus of literary authority—but it is shortsighted to imagine that other institutional investments in cultural production simultaneously vanished. Indeed, the moment the government *lost* the Bollingen Prize marks a historical turn toward its effective centrality in the administration of culture. The state had to abdicate its explicit and public interests in poetry but also learn to reinvest them. By formally disclaiming guardianship of taste or literary value proper, the state accomplished a kind of ideological sanitization project via New Critical methodology, instrumentalizing the university as a vessel of potent if messy political judgments and cultural values. Of course, federal support, most importantly the G.I. Bill and later the Higher Education Act, supported the university's growth. And the State Department and other bodies would fund writers and poets in cultural missions abroad, as it would later support the growth of the creative writing industry. The state could then later use poetry as a value in and of itself to deploy as cultural weaponry in the global Cold War and a commodity instrumental to the literary-cultural production of neoliberal discourses of identity.

The broader arc of this book, and the history of national poetry programming, traces how the state—alongside, and often in concert with private patrons—remobilized its agendas, and restructured its investments, within the apparatus of higher education and semiprivate, semipublic arts initiatives. Bishop and Lowell served as consultants in poetry for only one-year terms at the postwar Library of Congress, but in fact they would remain state poets in the decades to follow. When Lowell wrote to Bishop about the consultantship in 1949, such a post was rare. By the early 1960s, the means of state support for the American poet had dramatically expanded. What Bishop described as the "Eisenhower splurge" enabled her, and many other poets, to travel and write on Ford or Rockefeller grants.[123] Then, under the Kennedy administration, poets and artists were increasingly honored on the national stage. "The White House!" Lowell remarked excitedly after a White House arts dinner in 1962,[124] "200 guests, a third maybe I think actually known to us . . . New York types like Mark Rothko . . . nothing objectionable though there were many florid compliments to the U.S."[125] In the global Cold War, poets would also prove increasingly useful as cultural missionaries abroad. "I talked to a guy at the Rockefeller Foundation who advised us to stop at Trinidad and come home by way of Lima," Lowell wrote to Bishop the same year, "[and] Jack Thompson thinks the Congress for Cultural Freedom might partially finance us. Do you know someone in Rio named Keith Botsford? I knew him at Iowa. He's the agent for the Congress."[126] There were now Rockefeller grants, the generosity of the CIA-funded Farfield Foundation, and the support of the Congress for Cultural Freedom. "WHO pays for the Congress for Cultural Freedom, anyway?" Bishop wondered to Lowell a few months later.[127] The Congress for Cultural Freedom was funded by the CIA. By 1965, there were more formal, federally funded NEA grants. And in the years that followed, the growth of the creative writing industry—whose flagship program, the Iowa Writers' Workshop, would receive State Department and Farfield Foundation support—dramatically expanded teaching and publishing opportunities.

In the postwar period, the state had learned the lessons from the Library of Congress not to involve itself outwardly in "questions of taste," to avoid the undemocratic business of awarding prizes, and to make politically safe appointments to the national poetry office. But it had also learned the power of poetry in shaping political ideologies and that poetry could be a useful symbol and exporter of democratic values if channeled through state-private networks. By the end of the 1950s, the national poetry office would be reenergized, after sitting vacant for years, with an occupant who shared this conviction.

CHAPTER II

## Inaugurating National Poetry

*Robert Frost and Cold War Arts, 1956–1965*

> Knowing the pride of the Russian people in things Russian, R.F. [Robert Frost] was quick to explain that he, too, had a "nationalist" approach to art: "The first reason for a strong nation is to protect the language, to protect the poetry in it" he said, [sic] "it works both ways. A great nation makes great poetry, and great poetry makes a great nation."
> —STEWART L. UDALL, SECRETARY OF THE INTERIOR,
> ON FROST'S MISSION TO MOSCOW, APRIL 1963

> I don't want to run for office, but I want to be a politician.
> —ROBERT FROST, CONSULTANT IN POETRY,
> LIBRARY OF CONGRESS (1958–59)

In December 1958, three months into his term as consultant in poetry at the Library of Congress, Robert Frost called a press conference to announce he had "come down here [to Washington, D.C.] on a misunderstanding." Since taking office, he had been approached only three times by the White House, once by the Supreme Court, and not at all by Congress: "I thought I was to be poetry consultant . . . in everything—poetry, politics, religion, science. I'll tackle anything." He offered national educational policy advice, a field in which he considered himself the world's "greatest living expert": "A lot of people are being scared by the Russian Sputnik into wanting to harden up our education or speed it up. I am interested in toning it up, at the high school level . . . I have long thought that our high schools should be improved. Nobody should come into our high schools without examinations—not aptitude tests, but on reading, 'riting, and 'rithmetic. And that goes for black or white."[1]

Set in the context of domestic race relations and Cold War cultural competition with the Soviet Union, Frost emphasizes *tone* as a singularly powerful indicator of the health of the American education system and by extension the American state. The difference between "hardening" or "speeding up" and "toning up" curricula is no less the difference between Frost's terms of "Spartanizing" or "democraticizing," or the difference between Sparta and Athens, the Greek nation-states Frost frequently contrasted to analogize the Soviet Union and the United States. Rejecting Sparta as a social model of militaristic conformity—the hard, fast Spartan Sputnik—Frost championed Athenian conflicts of "opinion and personality," democracy with "all risks taken." America ought "rather perish as Athens than prevail as Sparta." "The tone," he said, "is Athens. The tone is freedom to the point of destruction."[2]

Poetry had an important part to play in the Athenian fight: "One reason I'm here is my ambition to get out of the small potatoes class," he said of assuming the national poetry office. "Poetry can become too special, isolated and separate a thing."[3] This conviction echoed his earliest articulations of a poetic theory—Frost first declared in 1913, then an unknown expatriate in London, that poetry was "a language absolutely unliterary." "The great fight of any poet is against the people who want him to write in a special language," Frost wrote, "that has gradually separated from spoken language." He determined his verse "would never use a word or combination of words that I hadn't heard used in running speech."[4] The poet's faculty was not command of a "special language," but of everyday speech: to capture the political pulse, here the Athenian tone, of American life.

Frost understood his role in relation to federal power, as evident in his rhetorical self-positioning vis-à-vis the three branches of government (enumerating solicitation by "the President, Supreme Court, Congress"). At the time he assumed the consultancy, this understanding had considerable premise. His appointment followed a formally unrealized invitation earlier that year to act as a White House cultural adviser: "what we really need is a person who thinks about the arts," Sherman Adams, the assistant to President Eisenhower, wrote to Frost, addressing him "Dear Mr. Poet Laureate": "Perhaps we need you on the White House staff. What think you?"[5] In the middle years of the Eisenhower administration, Adams requested Frost's membership on a reelection lobby, the Committee of Artists and Scientists for Eisenhower,[6] and assisted in State Department and Information Agency overtures to Frost as a cultural emissary, in one instance sending an official to his home in Ripton, Vermont, to request he showcase "American life" in short essays for foreign circulation.[7] The same year, 1957, Frost traveled to England on a goodwill mission as the "distinguished representative of the American cultural scene" for the Department of State.[8] Frost first determined "the behest [was] on a high enough level"—he wrote to the secretary of state that he "wouldn't want to be shot off like an unguided missile"[9]—and was assured the importance of "the task of emphasizing the common Anglo-American heritage."[10] Upon his return, Frost dined with President Eisenhower;[11] when Librarian of Congress L. Quincy Mumford wrote to Frost about the post, he understood Adams had already directly promised it to Frost.[12]

In the context of his own ambitions during this period,[13] Frost's assertion that the purpose of the consultant in poetry was to make "politicians and statesmen more aware of their responsibility to the arts" is unremarkable. But, in the history of the office, it was unprecedented.[14] Consultants previously acted as writers-in-residence and custodial stewards of the Library of Congress's recording archive. The vision of the office as a public-facing national platform is particularly startling following its four-term vacancy from 1952–56. After the Bollingen affair and the failed appointment of William Carlos Williams, the library was wary of the politically sensitive labor of appointing another consultant—and struggling to solicit funds to support one. Indeed, the library's relations with its donors had been tenuous since the Bollingen affair. In 1954, the library (Roy Basler and Phyllis Armstrong) prepared an appeal to the Bollingen Foundation for renewed funding; the foundation sat on the proposal. The recording archive project had also come to a standstill. During these years, the library's modest poetry programming was supported by Gertrude Clarke Whittall,[15] known for her stubbornly traditional literary tastes and eccentric hatbox-style donations: in one instance casually removing $100,000 in bonds, "which she handled carelessly," from her hatbox and handing them to Librarian of Congress Luther Evans after a cafeteria lunch.[16]

In 1956, Congressman W. Sterling Cole of New York proposed legislation that would authorize the president to designate a "poet laureate." The library would finally fill the consultant position that year—Randall Jarrell served from 1956–1958—but idea of designating a "laureate" was rejected. The library hastened to avoid the politicized business of promoting the arts, and the proposal never got out of committee. "I am thoroughly in accord with your objective of providing an incentive for creative effort in the field of poetry. I must confess, however, that I have doubts as to whether the arts, in a country such as ours, can successfully or indeed should be promoted by the Government through the creation of prizes and other similar distinctions," Librarian of Congress L. Quincy Mumford wrote to Cole. Mumford makes clear in this letter that the library had not forgotten the lesson of Pound's *Pisan Cantos* and the Bollingen affair—"here at the

Library of Congress we have had an unfortunate experience in the making of awards"—nor the congressional resolution that followed. Mumford's letter elaborated the 1949 decision that it was "bad policy" for a democratic government to exercise judgment in "matters of taste":

> In our cosmopolitan and democratic civilization the arts survive by their ability to establish themselves with relatively large groups[,] and few artistic styles or movements fail to secure adherents. For the Government to make a choice from among the practitioners of one or another school would, I believe, tend to discourage rather than encourage experimentation and artistic development by putting the Government's imprimatur on one style as opposed to another.[17]

Two years later, however, the library's "doubts" were scattered by Frost's conviction that "the connection should be closer between Government and the arts."[18] Pound may have been the antilaureate of Washington over the last few decades, casting a long shadow from his nearby cell at St. Elizabeths—but in 1958 Frost arrived on the scene to secure his release. He met with Justice Department officials in February, following his dinner with Eisenhower. When the federal district court dropped charges against Pound in April, the *New York Times* reported that "the person most responsible for today's announcement . . . is Robert Frost, the poet, who has waged a persistent public and private campaign during the last two years for Mr. Pound's release."[19] Frost received the official invitation to serve as consultant in poetry just a few days later.[20] Cast in the light of his "first raise on the Capital City,"[21] Frost read the invitation as a summons to more political action.[22]

The congressional mandate that it was "bad policy" for the library or federal government to play gatekeeper in the arts issued in the wake of the Bollingen affair thus expired in the wake of Pound's release. Randall Jarrell had pursued his preceding two terms in office with gusto, giving a number of talks on the poet's role in society and the nation. Unlike Frost, however, he did not express a strong desire to influence federal policymakers. "I would if I knew what they were," Frost replied when a reporter asked if he would, as Randall Jarrell's successor, "continue Mr. Jarrell's politics"—a comment met with laughter.[23] Frost's dismissive jest was also the assurance that creative artists were nonpartisan civic representatives. He and his predecessor were artists representing the "the clean and wholesome life of the ordinary man."[24] During his consultancy, and in his politically active late years, Frost sought to reactivate policy makers' commitment to the creative arts. But rather than defining national arts support as the ethical imperative to protect aesthetic freedom, per the dominant rhetoric observed in the defense of Pound during the Bollingen affair, Frost saw a role for the artist as a model citizen, taking what he called the "middle" or "measured way."[25] By the "measured" way, Frost referred to the assimilative discipline of his poetic practice—for example, where speech rhythm is contained by metrical law, a dialectical moderation he analogized with the checks and balances of democratic government—and by extension a social ideal of "chartered freedom."[26]

The creative artist—relocated from St. Elizabeths to "the middle way," but still representing the freedom of the "road less traveled"[27]—held symbolic promise in the Cold War climate. The federal government and the American artist forged a new alliance during the Cold War, and the avant-garde visual artist, and the minor voice of the poet, were particularly well positioned to portray the values of individuality and freedom. Unlike New Deal domestic arts programming, the government now invested in the artist on the global stage. Serge Guilbaut's *How New York Stole the Idea of Modern Art*, which describes how the CIA invested in Abstract Expressionist painting, is one compelling example of how U.S. national arts funding worked in cultural competition with the Soviet Union, promulgating the creative, individual voice of the American artist-as-citizen contra the collective groupthink of the communist threat.[28] This cultural competition also played out in the field of American poetry. Recent scholarship has begun to account for this importantly, including Eric Bennett's *Workshops of Empire*, which examines how the Cold War state worked in concert with private interests to support the rise of the creative writing industry, and Juliana Spahr's *Du Bois's Telegram: Literary Resistance and State Containment*, which considers the Cold War within a longer history of state interest in literature.[29]

In this chapter, we will examine the U.S. federal government's investment in the creative arts in the pivotal years of 1956–1965 through the lens of the national poetry office at the Library of Congress. The state career of Robert Frost, perhaps the most influential occupant of the national poetry office to date, is exemplary not only of how the Cold War state invested in poetry as ideological weaponry abroad but of how it changed its relationship to arts funding at home. We will focus on two periods of Frost's career (1913–15 and 1956–62), beginning with his articulation of a speech-based and phonocentric theory of poetic composition in the early 1910s in London. By tracing the development of Frost's poetics, which increasingly politicized notions of voice and form after his repatriation to the United States in 1915—natural speech and national identity becoming core preoccupations of his poetics—we can better understand Frost's goals and legacy as a national poet in his politically active late years.

After his official post as consultant in poetry in 1958–9, Frost remained active as the national poet, proposing to President Kennedy an alliance between "statesmen and poets" to advance a national arts "golden age."[30] As we will see, the proposal was taken quite seriously, and with lasting consequences. Though well documented, the relationship of Frost and Kennedy typically receives only anecdotal notice. Our study directs explicit attention to Frost and Kennedy's political partnership, invested in a vision of American "poetry and power" in cultural competition with the Soviet Union.[31] Under Kennedy, poetry achieved a particularly important status among the cultural, or nonmilitary tactics, used to compete with the Soviets for global prestige. The State Department sent Frost on goodwill trips to Israel and Greece two months after Kennedy's inauguration and a month before the Bay of Pigs, and to the Soviet Union in September 1962, where he would meet with Khrushchev at the premier's private dacha in the weeks preceding the Cuban Missile Crisis.

At home, the Frost-Kennedy years also transformed the function of poetry in national culture. They did so through both symbolic actions and policy changes. At Kennedy's inauguration, Frost's recitation from memory of "The Gift Outright"—the country's first inaugural poem—symbolized, before tens of millions of viewers, the expressive agency of the individual citizen in relation to state power. Poetry provided a blueprint of citizenship—the individual convinced of his continuity with national history and agency in a national future—for the Kennedy and Johnson administrations, which supported this model of expressive agency through federal arts initiatives in cooperation with private interests. Under Kennedy, the creation of the position of special consultant on the arts to the president, and later an Advisory Council on the Arts, would lay the groundwork for the creation of the National Endowment for the Arts under the Johnson administration in 1965.

In the Frost-Kennedy national arts "golden age," the state acted as an increasingly central pivot between the infrastructure of literary-professional organizations, private patrons, and the rapidly expanding higher education

*Figure 2.1* President John F. Kennedy presenting a Congressional Gold Medal to Robert Frost in the White House's Fish Conference Room, March 26, 1962. Left to right, pictured are Representative Edward P. Boland of Massachusetts, Representative James A. Burke of Massachusetts, Erma Lee Udall (wife of Secretary of the Interior Stewart Udall), President Kennedy, Senator Leverett Saltonstall of Massachusetts, Robert Frost, Secretary Udall (mostly hidden behind Frost), Senator A. Willis Robertson of Virginia, Senator George Aiken of Vermont, Vice President Lyndon B. Johnson (partially hidden behind Senator Aiken), and Representative Carl Albert of Oklahoma. Abbie Rowe, White House Photographs, John F. Kennedy Presidential Library.

industry. This was most visibly marked in the institutional collation of the first National Poetry Festival, celebrated in Washington in October 1962 as the Cuban Missile Crisis simultaneously unfolded. Held at the Library of Congress and funded by the Bollingen Foundation and the Poetry Society of America, the event occasioned *Poetry* magazine's fiftieth anniversary and Frost's last public reading. Savvy networker Paul Engle, head of the Iowa Writers Workshop, the nation's flagship creative writing program, was also making the rounds. The Frost-Kennedy model of state-private institutional collusion articulated a national poetry project for the middle Cold War period and transformed the structure of federal arts funding in the second half of the twentieth century.

*Figure 2.2* An envelope addressed by Robert Frost from his Cambridge, Massachusetts, residence to President Kennedy. Image courtesy of the John F. Kennedy Presidential Library (Special Correspondence, Papers of John F. Kennedy). Used with permission of the Robert Frost Copyright Trust.

### Frost's Early Years (1913–1915): Literary Repatriation and an American Poetics

> Another such review as the one in Poetry [Ezra Pound's "Modern Georgics"] and I shan't be admitted at Ellis Island. This is no joke. . . . You can imagine the hot patriot I will have become by the time I get home. And then to be shut out!
> —FROST TO SIDNEY COX, JANUARY 2, 1915[32]

> Another experience I cant [sic] seem to get over is Ellis Island. I dreamed last night that I had to pass a written examination in order to pass the inspection there. There were two questions set me.
> 1. Who in Hell do you think you are?
> 2. How much do one and one make?
> —FROST TO NATHAN HASKELL DOLE, MARCH 26, 1915[33]

In December 1915, Robert Frost wrote to Louis Untermeyer that he was so "discouraged it would do my enemies (see roster of the Poetry Society of America) good to see me."[34] "You needn't tell anyone I am so down or I shall have everybody on top of me," Frost confided. "Sometime I will do as you tell me—write a little more poetry and a little prose too. Not now." Meanwhile Frost was writing letters. Since repatriating to the United States from England in February, the forty-year-old newcomer to the New York literary establishment had launched an epistolary campaign disseminating "the story of how I see my own development and some of my theories of art" to American poetry editors and critics.[35] Frost had published his first two collections of poetry in London, where the second, *North of Boston*, found considerable acclaim. The British reviewer Edward Garnett called Frost a "New American Poet" who was "destined to take a permanent place in American literature."[36]

But the critical approval Frost won in England translated uneasily at home. "When an American poet comes to us with an English reputation and prints upon his volume the English dictum that 'his achievement is much finer, much more near to the ground, and much more national than anything that Whitman gave to the world,' one is likely to be prejudiced, not to say antagonized, at the outset," Jessie Rittenhouse wrote for the *New York Times*. Her review of *North of Boston* reacted to what she understood as English critics' implicitly patronizing terms of praise: "Just why a made-in-England reputation is so coveted by the poets of this country is difficult to fathom, particularly as English poets look so anxiously to America for acceptance of their own work."[37]

Rittenhouse was the recording secretary and an influential cofounder of the Poetry Society of America. While Frost was developing his poetic theory in London, seeking approval from "the critical few who are supposed to know," Rittenhouse had been meanwhile fighting for the PSA's secession from its parent organization, the London society, determined to build the first "authentically American" poetry organization. "She had no right to imply of course that I desired or sought a British-made reputation," Frost wrote to a friend after reading Rittenhouse's review. "You know that it simply came to me after I had nearly given up any reputation at all."[38]

The day after Frost repatriated to the United States, via Ellis Island, he attended a Poetry Society of America banquet. It was an inauspicious literary homecoming. Rittenhouse would prove the ringleader of what Frost called his "roster of enemies," taunting his "made-in-England reputation" not only in reviews but also, as he would later learn, at PSA meetings when he was not in attendance. "Someone writes to tell me that the Poetry Society had one of my poems to abuse in manuscript the other night.

Absolutely without my knowledge and consent," Frost fumed to Untermeyer. "Protest for me, will you? I wonder how in the world they got the manuscript."[39] This particular humiliation prompted Frost to write to Amy Lowell, chief promoter of American Imagism, and a tenuous confidante at best, with a begrudged concession: "I shall hope to see you sometime a good deal sooner than I can promise to be at the Poetry Society to be reduced to the ranks."[40]

Not only, however, would Frost eventually join his "roster of enemies," but he would eventually serve as the honorary president of the PSA for over two decades,[41] a reliable "honored guest at dinners given to celebrate [other] medals or award[s]."[42] He was among the first sponsors of the "College Poetry Society of America,"[43] and the PSA established its major prize, the Frost Medal, in his name. When Frost accepted a Gold Medal for Distinguished Service from the society in 1958, President Eisenhower interrupted the banquet with a congratulatory telegram.[44] Indeed, Frost's initially fraught relationship with the PSA would outlast all other literary affiliations of his early career.

But in the fledgling years of the Poetry Society of America, founded in 1910, and the fledging years of Frost's career—his first publication was in 1912—Frost's initially "made-in-England" reputation conflicted with Rittenhouse's vision for a poetry society built along "national lines."[45] The Poetry Society of America's mission formed in stark contradistinction to transatlantic modernist literary experimentation. That it would be the most strenuously vocal critic of the Bollingen Prize decision in 1949, by which time Frost served as the organization's honorary president, the PSA's disgust with "alien expatriate" Eliot and "alienated citizen" Pound is unsurprising given the organization's ideological origins.[46] Rittenhouse, the recording secretary during its first decade, shepherded what began as a high society couple's salon into a public-minded institution with an explicitly national project. The first meeting, at the home of Mr. and Mrs. Isaac L. Rice in the Ansonia Hotel, was a mid-winter New York social event: "a colorful painting" assembling poets, painters, musicians, novelists, and actors "to consider the possibility of an organization for the appreciation of poetry," as Rittenhouse describes in her autobiography.[47] The Rice event imagined the PSA as a group of poetry writers "united largely through the hospitality of [its] hosts" at individual members' apartments, "founded upon the salon idea." However "pleasant" a monthly meeting with "associations of wealth and hospitality," Rittenhouse rejected the salon model for its clubbish tendency to "degenerate into a social affair," preferring the "stable basis" of "an organization in the formal sense of the word":

> When, after much enthusiastic speech-making, a committee was appointed to retire and discuss the details, I had no hesitancy in saying—though at the risk of seeming ungrateful to our hosts—that it was much too big an idea to be narrowed down to a social function, into which it would inevitably deteriorate, and if the Society were developed at all, it ought to be along national lines, and should meet in a public rather than a private place.[48]

Rittenhouse understood the governing values of artistic assembly through a series of oppositions—hospitality versus bureaucracy, private versus public, and society versus nation. Her preference for a bureaucratically formalized, public organization was motivated less by a populist vision—the PSA would remain itself clubbish at least through the 1960s, with a highly exclusive membership list—than a nascent literary nationalism. When the Poetry Society of England sought to incorporate the group, she stood firmly against affiliating as a degraded subset: "In vain we explained to Mr. Browne [of the Poetry Society of England] that we had banded together on wholly different lines, that our objective was entirely the appreciation and encouragement of living poets, *whereas the English Society operated almost as a university extension*, having centres throughout the country where the classic as well as contemporary poets were studied."[49] On the one hand, Rittenhouse did not want the PSA to resemble the salon-style enclaves of American literary experimenters in London. On the other, she sought to resist the bureaucratic hierarchies of academia. While the "English Society" operated as an extension of the university, as a static limb, the Poetry Society of America would be a living body that refused parental affiliation: "Here was a chance to found in a few months a powerful body functioning from a parent centre throughout the whole of America, and we were content to remain a handful of ineffectual dreamers taking years to do what could so soon have been accomplished by an expert."[50] "Never was there a more disgusted man than Mr. Browne nor one more disillusioned," Rittenhouse wrote, "as to American enterprise." For Rittenhouse, refusing the parental expertise of British affiliation modeled American willful self-determination as a national value.

An influential player in a nascent New York poetry establishment, Frost would rapidly adapt his poetic persona to align with the institutional values of the Poetry Society of America. Yet cultivating a reputation as an "American" poet was only in part a reactionary answer to the PSA and reviews in publications like the *New York Times*. His poetic theory had already developed a concern with national identity, animated by a rivalry with Pound in London. Abroad, he had come to understand himself as an "American poet" that stood in contrast to Pound and his cosmopolitan internationalism, and this identity would be threatened, and then anxiously reclaimed, during a traumatic event of repatriation. Frost's nationalist strain was thus primed—by modernist contemporary Pound, gatekeepers like Rittenhouse, and officials at Ellis Island—before it cohered as a commercially strategic posture within the U.S. literary marketplace.

### Declaring American Independence in London: Frost's Early Poetic Theory

Frost had first sought to establish himself as an "English writer" during his England residence (1912–15), seeking "success with the critical few who are supposed to know."[51] Impressing himself upon the London literary-critical elite was instrumental to his careerist vision. Frost imagined success in London as a requisite step to securing a broad audience in America, and a defined theory of versification as a rite of passage before entering the marketplace: "really to arrive where I can stand on my legs as a poet and nothing I must be outside that circle to the general reader who buys books in their thousands."[52]

"The critical few" were a complex set. Frost was the beneficiary of literary personages with diverse aesthetic commitments; both the London literary avant-garde and rural Georgian poets shaped his early poetic theory during his England residence. When he met his most important contact, F. S. Flint, at a bookstore opening, he found himself stationed at the nexus of a poetic battleground: Harold Monro, who was opening the store, had just taken over the *Poetry Review* of the London Poetry Society with his incipient school of Georgians; Flint and T. E. Hulme were advocates of French symbolism and contemporary French poetry. Flint would facilitate Frost's meeting with fellow American Ezra Pound, who was influenced by Hulme in turn, albeit temporarily, commandeering the London avant-garde through successive doctrines of Imagism and Vorticism. Viewing the literary scene as a playing field, or, as he often called it, a "game," Frost initially accepted favor wherever it was offered; he was not shy to recommend himself ("You *know* I want you to use my poem in your catalogue").[53] At the same time, Frost resented feeling indebted to his advocates—particularly Pound.

Frost found in Pound a "bullying" advocate and came to view himself the victim of a dictatorial mentorship. After Flint spoke to Pound on behalf of Frost, Pound sent a calling card to Frost's residence at 10 Church Walk, Kensington: "At home—sometimes."[54] The terse quasi invitation anticipated what Frost would call a "quasi-friendship."[55] At their first meeting, coincidentally the day Frost's very first published work, *A Boy's Will*, came off the printers, Pound insisted they walk to the publishing house. To Frost's horror, Pound held the first bound copy before he did.[56] Pound also lost no time reviewing it for *Poetry*: "I think we should print this notice at once as we ought to be first," he wrote to the editor, Harriet Monroe; his "booming" of *A Boy's Will* was "sure to make fuss enough to get quoted in N.Y."[57] In Frost's correspondence, Pound physically laying claim to his first volume dramatically enacted a psychic power struggle. The more he considered it, Frost found Pound's review an insulting depiction of him as "the untutored child."[58] Moreover, he had incurred a debt, which Pound demanded he pay, pedagogical interest due, in aesthetic allegiance:

> You will be amused to hear that Pound has taken to bullying me on the strength of what he did for me by his review in Poetry. The fact that he discovered me gives him the right to see that I live up to his good opinion of me. He says I must write something much more like vers libre or he will let me perish of neglect. He really threatens. I suppose I am under obligations to him and I try to be grateful. But as for the review in Poetry (Chicago, May), if any but a great man had written it, I should have called it vulgar. . . . The more I think of it the less I like the connection he sees between me and the Irishman who could sit on a kitchen-midden and dream stars. It is so stupidly wide of the mark. And then his inaccuracies about my family affairs! Still I think he meant to be generous.[59]

Frost casts Pound as an oppressive pedagogue: the "great man" is the provider, a parent who "threatens" "neglect"; Frost must "live up" to his expectations and "try to be grateful." Frost would like to keep Pound's "good opinion" while simultaneously rejecting it as "inaccura[te]." Rather than a gift outright, Pound's "generosity" required an immediate and unequal return: not the abstract condition of gratitude, but the performed compliance of a student.

Frost would not be deemed "an untutored child" taught to write in vers libre (free verse). He sought to distance himself from Pound and the poetic principles of the London avant-garde—Frost described Pound as leading a band of "American literary refugees"—in a series of "declarations of independence" that month. He cast his own theory of versification as an American invention, first pronouncing it by letter on Independence Day, July 4, 1913. "To be perfectly frank with you I am one of the most notable craftsmen of my time," he wrote to longtime family friend John Bartlett. "I am possibly the only person going who works on any but a worn out theory (principle I had better say) of versification. . . . I alone of English writers have consciously set myself to make music out of what I may call the sound of sense."[60]

Two weeks after announcing his theory of versification by letter to Bartlett, Frost drafted a free-verse satirical poem in a letter to Pound that he would never send. Despite its parodic use of open form, the poem is a remarkably self-disclosing narrative, equal parts confession and accusation: "I clung to you / As one clings to a group of insincere friends / For fear they shall turn their thoughts against him / The moment he is out of hearing."[61] The proximity of these two compositions—Frost's poetic theory written on Independence Day and his declaration of independence from Pound—is telling. Frost's rivalry with Pound helped motivate, and moreover usefully highlights, the nationalist gesture of his July 4 date-stamped poetic theory. To refuse his domineering "expatriate" mentor, Frost became an American "patriot"—indeed a "hot patriot," as he asserted in a letter to his friend and literary critic Sidney Cox.

In between his declarations of American independence, Frost petitioned American publisher Thomas Mosher to help connect him to different, decidedly non–vers libre literary ilk: "I wish sometime if you know [Edwin Arlington] Robinson you could put me in the way of knowing him too."[62] Notably, Frost pursues affiliation with the populist poetic sensibility of Robinson in the same letter in which he refuses to be taken as an "untutored child." Frost's aesthetic identification with Robinson, an American "people's poet," was forged in reaction to Pound. Moreover, impugning

Pound's "merit for caviar" made Frost in the next breath a "poet for all sorts and kinds" and a "People's Poet" in letters to Bartlett and Monro.[63]

Frost's declarations of American independence were not wholly successful. When he sent his parody of Pound to Flint, the savvy moderator pacified Frost, casting Pound in the role of the misbehaving child: "We mustn't be too hard on E.P. . . . Your 'poem' is very amusing! . . . You know I think his bark is much worse than his bite. . . . All the same he irritates; and we mustn't allow ourselves to be irritated, don't you think? Don't you feel it as a weakness?"[64] Frost did not send the poem to Pound, nor would he express his irritation to Flint directly again—even when Pound's review of his second book enraged him.

After the publication of *North of Boston*, Frost had sent Garnett's and other favorable British reviews, in self-made press kit style, as clippings in letters to editors and reviewers in America. But when the first long review of *North of Boston* appeared in the States, two months before his planned departure, Frost realized this might have been a tactical mistake. This first, stand-out review was written by Pound: "It is a sinister thing that so American, I might even say so parochial, a talent as that of Robert Frost should have to be exported before it can find due encouragement and recognition."[65] For Pound, *North of Boston* was instrumental in a wider polemic attacking American literary culture. Frost, like any talent (although his is "parochial"), had been forced to publish abroad:

> It is natural and proper that I should have to come abroad to get printed, or that "H. D."—with her clear-cut derivations and her revivifications of Greece—should have to come abroad; or that Fletcher—with his tic and his discords and his contrariety and extended knowledge of everything—should have to come abroad. One need not censure the country; it is easier for us to emigrate than for America to change her civilization fast enough to please us. But why, IF there are serious people in America, desiring literature of America, literature accepting present conditions, rendering American life with sober fidelity, why, in heaven's name, is this book of New England eclogues given us under a foreign imprint?[66]

Frost understood the implications of being labeled an American "export." "I fear I am going to suffer a good deal at home by the support of Pound,"[67] he wrote to Cox. "Another such review as the one in Poetry [Pound's

"Modern Georgics" in December 1914] and I shan't be admitted at Ellis Island. This is no joke."⁶⁸ Their personal relationship had also soured—"we quarreled in six weeks," and Pound was "doing his best to put me in the wrong light. . . . Nothing could be more unfair, nothing better calculated to make me an exile for life." Frost determined to now publicly define himself against Pound's London-based "party of American literary refugees." To Cox, he issued a breathless request:

> I dont [sic] see that it is possible to do anything publicly to disassociate myself from Pound but do you think it would be a discreet thing for you to say a word to [Stuart P.] Sherman or perhaps (what do you think?) even write a short letter to the Sun or The Times or both saying that you have reason to know that I would have no pleasure in that part of Pound's article in Poetry that represented me as an American literary refugee in London with a grievance against Amer[ican] editors.

A few paragraphs later, Frost reconsidered: "P.S. We won't stir the Pound matter up I think . . . but what I have written in the body of the letter you could use should I be attacked when Holt sends out copies for review. Of course it is quite possible that I exaggerate the importance of Pound's article. Let's hope so."⁶⁹ Frost's composure then waned, and he subsequently wrote Harcourt, his publisher in America, with a similar request.⁷⁰

Frost's fear of being perceived as insufficiently loyal to the American poetry establishment leaves a striking, even compulsive, paper trail, but it was not unfounded. As PSA secretary Rittenhouse's *New York Times* review had warned, Frost would experience backlash at home for his success abroad, though less thanks to the review by Pound than that by Garnett. Moreover, Frost's seemingly hyperbolic paranoia that he would not be "admitted at Ellis Island" in fact turned out to be "no joke."

### *Literary Customs: Enemies at Ellis Island and the Poetry Society of America*

The day after his repatriation to the United States, Frost met two ordeals he would later refer to as a singular trauma—Ellis Island. After three years abroad, Frost made his homecoming accompanied by a friend's son and an underage British citizen, thirteen-year-old Mervyn Thomas. Immigration officers stopped Frost at customs. No alien under sixteen could enter the United States without a suitable sponsor able to prove his financial means prevented the alien from becoming a public charge. The next morning, the poet stood trial. He held no teaching position; how, then, "would he be able to support himself, his family, and this boy on the earnings from his poetry?"[71] A panel of three immigration officers questioned an "infuriated" Frost, who yelled to Thomas: "Tell them you wouldn't stay in a country where they treat people like this!"[72] Frost found his status as a professional poet on trial at U.S. customs.

Meanwhile Frost had to smuggle "a British-made reputation" through the customs of the New York poetry establishment. The evening of his customs trial, Frost made his first homeland literary appearance: Harcourt, his publisher, hoped the PSA banquet would provide a warm welcome to the American poetry scene.[73] Instead, Frost found himself surrounded by a "roster of enemies" led by the aggressive national vision of recording secretary Jessie Rittenhouse. Frost expected to return home to some degree of repute: he hoped to farm and find a respectable teaching position, the latter "on account of his successes with prosody in England."[74] Instead, during his first days back in America, he was questioned by gatekeepers of the nation and gatekeepers of the New York poetry establishment. The overlap of these ordeals cohered Ellis Island as a site of trauma—the troubled threshold to literary-national acceptance. It was a symbol producing nightmarish anxiety, as he records in letters, in the months to follow.[75] The conflation of national and poetic gatekeepers during repatriation heightened Frost's sensitivity to questions of national belonging, bearing crucially on the development of his poetic theory and the self-styling of his literary persona.

After all, Frost had won rapport and respect in London's literary circles, and he wanted to carry his hard-won international cultural capital back to the U.S.—and now, it turned out, to do so without being read as international. Yet cultivating his patriotic persona was not merely strategic at PSA meetings and to a commercial readership[76]—his relationship with Pound had already made national identity a source of Frost's professional self-definition. Pronouncing his first poetic theory on Independence Day had not been a pitch to an American audience but a private gesture of liberation.

Most finally, the traumatic coherence of literary and national gatekeepers in New York during repatriation had animated Frost's eagerness to claim an American reputation.

Frost's campaign to be seen as an American poet, in contrast to an expatriate modernist, would prove successful. In contrast to what Rittenhouse at the PSA rejected as the bannered chaos of the "modern phase in literature"—the American poetry scene was in danger, in her view, of becoming "an army with banners, and each insurgent poet has a different brand of revolution . . . you will find imagism, on another vers libre or free verse, cubism, futurism, and a dozen other things"[77]—Robert Frost finally appeared, by the summer of 1916, refreshingly *"American to the core."* In her address to the annual meeting of the American Library Association, "The New Poetry and Democracy," Rittenhouse urged librarians to the task of "bringing [democracy] to the public" through literature; two "new American" masters, Edgar Lee Masters and Robert Frost, prevailed:

> Robert Frost is democratic to the core; he is American to the core, and the types Robert Frost writes of are strictly out of America. . . . You know Robert Frost is a farmer . . . he had a little farm up in the New England hills, and had a very difficult time to keep the farm going. . . . He sold it and went to England. He coined his soul and his last dollar to bring out his book, and with this book he is buying back another farm! . . . He is a beautiful character with the face of Christ.[78]

Rittenhouse, the ringleader of his "roster of enemies" only a year earlier, now found in Frost an exemplary national mythos. Although he had "coined his soul" by moving to England, this Faustian deal had been undone by buying another stony hill lot in New England; he had redeemed himself through his renewed commitment to the admirably "barren" but "ground up" American way, choosing life on a New England farm rather than in London literary salons. Frost had become palatable, even praiseworthy to Rittenhouse, against the growing influence of "eccentric" Amy Lowell and "ragbag" Ezra Pound; along with Masters, he promised "an assimilation." The democratic American type did not write "absolutely free verse," after all, and represented a compromise where poetry's new forms would "modify the old forms" for "a certain freedom within the law"[79]—or what Frost called the "middle way."[80]

## Saying "Iamb" to the Listening Public: Phonocentric Populism

> In "North of Boston" you are to see me performing in a language absolutely unliterary. What I would like is to get so I would never use a word or combination of words that I hadn't heard used in running speech. I bar words and expressions I have merely seen. You do it on your ear. Of course I allow expressions I make myself.
> —FROST TO JOHN T. BARTLETT, DECEMBER 8, 1913[81]

> I must be outside that circle to the general reader who buys books in their thousands. . . . I want to be a poet for all sorts and kinds. I would never make a merit of being caviare [sic] to the crowd the way my quasi-friend Pound does.
> —FROST TO JOHN BARTLETT, C. NOVEMBER 5, 1913[82]

Frost's major poetic theory, what he called the "sound of sense," advances a way of composing poetry according to the "ear," following the "natural" rhythms of American speech. Frost's discovery was poetry as "a language absolutely unliterary," a nonspecialized discourse that reached "the crowd." Preferring the sense of the ear over the eye, and enchanted by the "aural imagination," Frost's theory privileged aural experience over semantic content: "It is the abstract vitality of our speech. It is pure sound—pure form. One who concerns himself with it more than the subject is an artist."[83] Frost rejected the process of making or constructing the poem on the visual field of the page: "Of course the great fight of any poet is against the people who want him to write in a special language that has gradually separated from spoken language by this 'making' process.'"[84] This fight was against Pound's "special language" that privileged the eye—enough, he wrote to Bartlett in his Fourth of July letter, has been said about the eye already. "Time we said something about the hearing ear—the ear that calls up vivid sentence forms." Once confined to a separate and specialized domain of paper, a word or sentence lost its vital, "natural" capacity: "I bar words and expressions I have merely seen. You do it on your ear." Frost's poetic principle valued sound over sight, speech over the written, and blank verse over vers libre.

If the phonocentric principle of Frost's poetic theory was polarized in contradistinction to Pound, his belief that "sound-sense" could communicate the natural or essential quality of the individual spirit was influenced by other thinkers in London. William James and Henri Bergson's discussions of "the stream of consciousness" contributed to Frost's notion of a "natural" experience and "natural sound-sense" in language.[85] But while James and Bergson understood "the stream of consciousness" as experience prior to analytic discrimination, Frost rejected the mediation of stream-of-consciousness experience through technologies of writing, that is, automatic writing. The *sound* of words, deprived of semantic content, was a more unmediated expression of the "rhythms of life and the centre of our minds."[86] "The best place to get the abstract sound of sense is from voices behind a door that cuts off the words. Ask yourself how these sentences would sound without the words in which they are embodied," he explained in his Fourth of July letter.[87] The exercise of listening to voices behind a door activates what Frost would later call the "audile [aural] imagination."

"Sound-sense" and "aural imagination" are importantly connected to the notion of individual spirit. Tyler Hoffman argues that Frost promotes an "ethics of personal and political sovereignty" and "political belief in the dignity and value of the individual"; James and Bergson's vocabulary secures the "scientific backing [in the language of this aesthetic theory] that will help him achieve literary success."[88] Extending Hoffman's observation, an appreciation of the rhythms of the mind, or spiritual center of the self, affirms the sovereignty of the individual through the form of the spoken sentence. "Unless we are in an imaginative mood it is no use trying to make them [sentences]. We can only write the dreary kind of grammatical prose known as professorial,"[89] Frost wrote on the eve of his departure back to the United States, a period of prolific and urgent theorizing. Linking the notion of aural imagination to the sentence unit, Frost developed a distinction between the "grammatical sentence" and the "vital sentence." The grammatical sentence is read by the eye, uninspired and academic; the vital is heard by the ear, summoned naturally from a spiritual wellspring of creative energy:

> The grammatical sentence is merely accessory to the other and chiefly valuable as a furnishing clue to the other. . . . Just so many sentence sounds belong to man as just so many vocal runs belong to one kind of bird. We come into the world with them and create none of them. What we feel as creation is only selection and grouping. We summon

them from Heaven knows where under excitement with the audile [aural] imagination.[90]

Unlike the sentence that is written or read, the sentence that is said and heard is both a more natural and divinely sourced language.

In the initial development of his poetic theory, Frost cleaves to an "aural" language of the ear more than he emphasizes the voice or orality, yet I refer to Frost's poetic theory as "phonocentric." Frost cast his poetic theory in letters to other poets as a *compositional* guide or practicum. The poet takes inspiration from what is heard and writes to record this inspiration to subsequently "speak" or "say" it. Poetry on the page is only a record of what is more primarily, in its natural form, speech. A phonocentric poetics appeals to the listener over the reader.

*North of Boston*, the collection most closely contemporaneous with Frost's articulation of his poetic theory, was by his account its test case—an attempt to "perfor[m] a language absolutely unliterary."[91] Frost claimed to have used only words and word combinations he had himself overheard, "bar[ring] words and expressions I have merely seen."[92] Nearly every poem contains a quoted speech act, usually between two interlocutors. Pound compared *North of Boston* with recent experiments in short fiction: "He is quite consciously and definitely putting New England rural life into verse."[93] *North of Boston* strives to be as "absolutely unliterary" as a phonograph, where Frost acts as the omnipresent narrator recording a regionally spoken American English. At the Kennedy inauguration in 1961, when Frost put aside the page he brought to the podium and recited a poem from memory, he would project the contents of this archive as the voice of the individual citizen.

On the one hand, then, Frost's poetic theory connects natural "speech rhythm" to the individual spirit, understanding spoken voice as the most natural expressive vehicle of the willful subject. On the other, speech rhythm is necessarily ordered by metrical form: "Tell them Iamb, Jehovah said, and meant it."[94] While the iambic rhythm of blank verse was "honest"—the rhythm at the center of the mind and north of Boston— free verse poets displayed an unnatural "desire . . . to play always on the insane fringe of things. Their interest is only in the abnormal. . . . When a man sets out consciously to tear up forms and rhythms and measures, then he is not interested in giving you poetry," Frost said. "He just wants to perform; he wants to show you his tricks." The inspiration for blank verse, however, "lies in the clean and wholesome life of the ordinary man": Frost persistently associated the laws of meter with the laws of social propriety and the state.⁹⁵ The containment of speech rhythm by meter worked as Frost's personal mythology for the healthy checks and balances of democratic government—or "'chartered' freedom."⁹⁶ Iambic poetry, such as the blank verse of "The Gift Outright," which Frost recited at Kennedy's inauguration, emblematizes this dialectical relation between individual expression (speech rhythm) and state order (metrical form). Frost viewed the "measured way" and the "middle way" as overlapping prosodic and social ideals: the responsibility of the poet is to maintain the middle path in poetic and, by extension, social expression,⁹⁷ thus modeling self-regulatory creative practice in parallel function to the state.

In a "fiction of form,"⁹⁸ fictionalization is the analogizing leap between the figural and social. In this case, Frost's speech rhythms symbolize "rational control" for Katherine Kearns;⁹⁹ "blank verse stands for self-reliance and democracy, and free verse for self-surrender and socialism" for Hoffman.¹⁰⁰ Here, I want to emphatically redirect attention to Frost, rather than to later critics, as author of his own "fiction" whereby rhythm and meter stand for self and state. This is a worthwhile distinction, as this chapter will subsequently demonstrate how Frost's politicization of poetic form was also, critically, *non*fictional: Frost's blank verse was not just imaginatively imbued with democratic ideology, but broadcast as a live event at Kennedy's inauguration; Frost expressed the synchronicity of his poetic and political vision not only in letters regarding prosody but also in conversations with Eisenhower, Kennedy, and Khrushchev; and thousands of American youth would recite Frost's poems in classrooms under the curricula of citizenship training.

Frost in Washington and Abroad (1956–1962):
The Years of "Poetry and Power"¹⁰¹

I CAN ACCEPT IT FOR MY CAUSE—THE ARTS, POETRY, NOW FOR THE FIRST TIME TAKEN INTO THE AFFAIRS OF STATESMEN.
—FROST TO KENNEDY, ACCEPTING HIS INVITATION TO READ AT THE 1961 INAUGURAL CEREMONY¹⁰²

As his politics of poetic form suggests, Frost viewed poetry and the creative arts as deeply relevant to the health of U.S. democratic ideology. Especially after 1949, Frost considered himself a political and social commentator: "My specialty is talking ideas and reading my own poetry,"[103] Frost wrote to the secretary of state on the eve of a trip to England, his second "goodwill" mission abroad. Frost traveled as a cultural emissary to South America and delegate to the World Congress of Writers in São Paulo, Brazil, in 1954, where he acted as a poet-diplomat: in extemporaneous remarks to the conference assembly, for instance, he sought to correct any image of the United States as a "monster": "I won't say anything about Russia, which perhaps does want to dominate the world, but I do want to make it very clear that my country does not in any way want to rule the world."[104] The State Department also underwrote trips to Israel, Athens, Greece, and London (March 1961) and to the Soviet Union (August-September 1962), where he would meet with Khrushchev in the weeks preceding the Cuban Missile Crisis. Frost "began playfully but half-seriously to boast that he might become one of the 'unacknowledged legislators of the world.'"[105]

In other words, Frost was an active player in the international "cultural" missions undertaken by the Truman and Eisenhower administrations, through which many American artists acted as cultural emissaries through the Department of State, United States Information Agency (known overseas as the United States Information Service), Central Intelligence Agency, and semiprivate bodies, operating with both overt and covert federal support. Sending artists on "goodwill missions" or "cultural missions" was intended to legitimize American leadership on the world stage, disseminating the discourse of artistic freedom against totalitarian cultural economies of the Soviet bloc—a worldwide Marshall Plan in the field of ideas.[106] Frost would also play an important role in the extension of this international cultural programming—and moreover the development of new national arts initiatives—undertaken by the Kennedy and Johnson administrations.

Although Frost's role would become most publicly visible, especially after later state performances—namely of the nation's first poem read at a presidential inauguration, at President Kennedy's televised ceremony in 1961, and his later Mission to Moscow—he represents many other state poets who were employed to represent notions of the individuality and creativity of American voice at home and abroad during the Cold War.[107] During the Eisenhower administration, Sherman Adams, assistant to the president, was a key figure in recognizing the potential uses of the creative artist in the Cold War state project. While he was still the governor of New Hampshire (1949–1953), Adams had met Frost at the St. Botolph Club, and quoted to him from his poem "New Hampshire": the two would become close, and Adams facilitated many of Frost's connections in Washington. Adams managed Conger Reynolds at the U.S. Information Agency, for example, who solicited artists' work for international circulation, and had him visit Frost in Ripton. When he visited Frost, Reynolds "described various areas around the world where American prestige was threatened and various ways . . . to defend the nation's image abroad." One of the most effective of these was to have public figures write pieces about American life for international audiences.[108] Adams also connected Frost to Eisenhower, pitching that Frost serve as a goodwill ambassador to England.[109]

Adams prompted Eisenhower to send a telegram—one he likely also drafted—to Frost at the annual PSA banquet in January 1958, where the poet was being presented with a Gold Medal for Distinguished Service.[110] Frost "of course [sic] saw your hand in it [the "splendid telegram" from Eisenhower]"—that is, the hand of Adams, whom he flattered:

> You have a great influence up there. Few in your position have ever thought of the arts at all. Some day it seems as if you might want to have me meet the President to thank him in person at a meal or something, so that it needn't go down in history that the great statesman and soldier never dined socially with any but big shots, and these preferably statesmen, warriors, and Holly woodsmen [sic]. I read in today's paper that you are sending Bob Hope and Bing Crosby to represent us in the arts at the World's Fair in Brussels. And when I say this half seriously it is not just for myself that I am speaking.[111]

In these few lines, Frost appeals to Adams's interest in Eisenhower's standing in posterity ("it needn't go down in history" that Eisenhower was a snob, refusing contact with anyone but "big shots"); in the eyes of the domestic populace (strategically crouched among the general populace, Frost is able to speak "not just for [him]self"); and on the international stage (questioning the administration's ability to choose artists equipped to "represent us" at the World's Fair). Perhaps this was not a subtle ploy to get a dinner invitation, but it worked. Adams secured the meeting with Eisenhower.[112] He also suggested that Frost act as cultural adviser to the administration, meanwhile asking that Mumford appoint Frost as consultant in poetry.[113]

From the term of his consultancy until his death, Frost remained active in Washington and as a cultural missionary abroad. As library aide and observer Roy Basler summarizes, in these years Frost

> lent considerable impetus to the movement culminating in the establishment of the Kennedy Center and the National Foundation on the Arts and the Humanities; helped bring about the continuing series of Cabinet and White House sponsored literary and performing arts presentations in the State Department Auditorium; and the White House receptions, dinners, awards presentations, and festivals honoring prominent figures in the arts and humanities which became . . . something of an established pattern in the national capital.[114]

After his term as consultant in poetry, a position was created for Frost to serve as honorary consultant in the humanities.[115] In May 1960, he visited Washington to lecture as consultant in the humanities in Washington and to testify for a bill to establish a National Academy of Culture before a Senate subcommittee. Frost told the senators that poetry should be considered an equal to business, science, and scholarship by the state:

> Last night I had a real consultation with some Members of Congress. . . . We talked about poetry in relation to other things. I was not defending or even talking particularly about poetry. . . . We discussed politics and the affairs of the nation. Poetry can become too special, isolated and separate a thing. The connection should be closer between Government and the arts. Wouldn't it be wonderful if there could be something for the arts like the Morrill Act was for education in establishing the Land Grant colleges? . . . Congressmen should personally be interested in this Consultantship. The Consultant must have a broad vision for Congressmen and take an interest in what they think. The Consultant should be something the Government consults as part of the Government.[116]

The Eisenhower administration honored Frost in turn for his contribution to the national arts agenda. In March 1959, a Senate resolution observed Frost's eighty-fifth birthday; Eisenhower signed a "Robert Frost Medal" bill "in recognition of his poetry, which has enriched the culture of the United States and the philosophy of the world" on September 13, 1960.[117] The occasion also initiated his relationship with Kennedy. While celebrating the event at the Waldorf Astoria, hosted by the publisher Henry Holt, Frost gave an "endorsement" of the young senator tinged with regionalist pride. "Somebody said to me that New England's in decay," he said to a reporter. "But I said the next President is going to be from Boston.... Can't you figure it out? It's a Puritan named Kennedy." This prompted their first correspondence.[118]

The Kennedy administration would place unprecedented stock in the symbolic power of the American artist, expanding cultural missions abroad and setting forth the mission of founding a federal arts agency at home.[119] In September 1961, Kennedy appointed Roger L. Stevens as chairman of the board of trustees of the National Cultural Center; and in March 1962 Kennedy appointed August Heckscher as his special consultant on the arts, asking him to prepare a report on the relationship between the arts and the federal government. Heckscher completed the report, "The Arts and the National Government" in May 1963, and submitted it to Congress and the president six months before his death. That report would lead to the creation of the President's Advisory Council on the Arts, or what is today the National Council on the Arts.[120] While little domestic legislation passed under Kennedy's New Frontier—much of the work of cultural and arts initiatives would come to fruition under Johnson—Kennedy created precedents for later policy changes and relied on the representative function of exemplary figures in culture and the arts to champion American values, frequently entertaining artists, writers, and musicians at the White House. For example, cellist Pablo Casals, who refused to return to his native Catalonia under the dictatorship of Francisco Franco, performed at the White House in 1961. "An artist must be a free man," Kennedy trumpeted as the message of the event.[121]

The most significant legacy of the Frost-Kennedy national arts "golden age" was the creation of the National Endowment for the Arts in 1965 under Johnson. State Department cultural missions or acts of nonmilitary defense, and not New Deal programming, were the policy scaffolding for the NEA. Unlike job-creating initiatives like the Federal Writers Project, the NEA responded not to a domestic economic imperative but rather followed the precedent of nation-building through demonstrations of artistic leadership and cultural diplomacy on the global stage. In the Frost-Kennedy national arts "golden age," the artist was viewed as vital to expressing the nation's strength and global authority. The act establishing the NEA and NEH records this view; the nation's global political leadership and cultural leadership are effectively intertwined in its language: "The world leadership which has come to the United States . . . must be solidly founded upon worldwide respect and admiration for the Nation's high qualities as a leader in the realm of ideas and of the spirit," reads section 2 of the Public Law. The nation-state could gain 'worldwide respect' through military power but also through cultural and artistic output.[122]

The new "golden age" of "poetry and power" was unveiled at Kennedy's inauguration, which featured notable attendees in the arts—including Carl Sandburg, John Steinbeck, and Ernest Hemingway, Abstract Expressionist painter Mark Rothko, and playwright Arthur Miller—and the first inaugural poet in United States history.

*Broadcasting American Voice: The Kennedy Inaugural Recitation, or Poetry at the "Hour of Maximum Danger"*

On January 20, 1961, Frost delivered the first inaugural poem in United States history. Frost had planned to read the seventy-two-line "Dedication," written the day before the ceremony during a Georgetown snowstorm. The strictly occasional poem would have followed the British model of the poet laureate's inaugural contribution, praising the president-elect for "summoning artists to participate / In the august occasions of the state."[123] In the glare of the sun and snow, however, Frost struggled to read from the pages he had brought to the podium. After stuttering out the first lines, he abandoned the written script and recited a different poem from memory.

That poem, "The Gift Outright,"[124] sixteen lines of what Frost called the "measured way" of blank verse, proved a more effective service to the U.S. nation-state than the poem he intended to deliver. Broadcast live in living rooms across America, Frost's spontaneous recitation was almost instantly mythologized as a triumph of human memory and of individual voice. Secretary of the Interior Stewart Udall would recall that Frost's "faltering . . . added a special note of human warmth to the occasion."[125] The rejection of the failed technologies of writing and eyesight in favor of oral authenticity "ca[ught] the hearts" of the American public. Rather than honorifics "editorial in tone," Frost provided a national history that could be extemporaneously recalled—the "sound-sense" of speech more natural and authentic than its written record.[126] Frost's recitation of "The Gift Outright" can be understood as an extension of the work of the Archive of Recorded Poetry and Literature into mass culture, hailing a listening public.

The poem, recited from memory, presents the colonial possession of American land as always already embodied knowledge:

> The land was ours before we were the land's.
> She was our land more than a hundred years
> Before we were her people. She was ours
> In Massachusetts, in Virginia,
> But we were England's, still colonials,
> Possessing what we still were unpossessed by,
> Possessed by what we now no more possessed.[127]

The ahistorical temporality that the poem proposes—"the land was ours before we were the land's"—further naturalizes the description of colonial possession while moving chronologically forward to look "to the land vaguely realizing westward / But still unstoried" in the last lines. "The Gift Outright" is assured of the "historic inevitability" of American manifest destiny and westward expansion;[128] simultaneously, listeners are assured that the national story is *un*storied—without history; "no slavery, no colonization of Native Americans, a process of dispossession and then possession, but nothing about the dispossession of others that this destiny demanded," as Derek Walcott, among many others, have noted.[129]

In the context of the inaugural performance, moreover, the territorial and imperial expansion of the United States became not only a historic inevitability but prophetic. Since its publication in *A Witness Tree* (1942), the last lines of the poem had referred to the expansion of the land "westward, / But still unstoried, artless, unenhanced, / Such as she was, such as she *would* become."[130] When Udall had suggested the poem to Kennedy for the inauguration, however, the president had requested that "would" be changed to "will." From the podium, Frost issued a halting and emphatic revision: "Such as she was, such as she *would* become, *has* become, and I—for this occasion let me change that to—what she *will* become."[131] By reciting the poem from memory—and going a bit off script—the territorial expansion of the U.S. state is presented as so natural that the representative citizen can tell it in his own words. It is a story he knows "by heart." The poem's national history and projected future (what America "*will* become") acquired, in effect, the authenticity of its extemporaneous utterance.

More basically than naturalize an ideology of nation, however, Frost's spoken performance provided individual agency as a convincing description of modern American citizenship. The performance conveyed features of modern liberal identity: voice, the capacity for authenticity, and capable self-expression of that which is ostensibly "true to oneself."[132] Overcoming conditional limitations—the weather, the failed technologies of eyesight and writing, age—Frost as a representative citizen voiced the "will" of the individual as nation in visible proximity to state power. The voice of the poet, in other words, became proxy for individual agency and for the self-determination and capacity of the citizen.

Earlier poets laureate, i.e., in the United Kingdom, historically functioned at inaugural occasions to tender public faith in state authority, but did not provide a representative model of citizenship.[133] Due to the ceremonially quarantined role of the laureate as one who honors a head of state, the poet laureate represented the state itself rather than contact *with* the state. In other words, state poetry did not present the speaker as an individual in contact with the nation-state so as to instrumentally document or model an instance or expression of citizenship. By contrast, Frost acted as a "distinguished guest in the arts" and representative citizen.

The majority of Americans watching the ceremony would hear this description of citizenship echoed by Kennedy a few minutes later. Kennedy's inaugural address was itself historically exceptional, focusing almost entirely on international affairs.[134] Rather than emphasize the moment as an extension of peacetime after World War II, with Eisenhower having ended the conflict in Korea, the president emphasized the United States as a new world leader charged to protect democratic values abroad. Declaring "freedom at the hour of maximum danger," Kennedy famously impelled citizens to assume the "price, burden and hardship" of state interests in an antithetical reversal of terms in the burden of care: "And so, my fellow Americans: ask not what your country can do for you—ask what you can do for your country." This new neoliberal ethic followed persuasively upon Frost's performance of the citizen's expressive capacity in explicit relation to state power. As the nationally representative voice, Frost assisted not only in the transfer of power to the new president but in the transfer of agency to the individual citizen.

### Frost's "Mission to Moscow"

> Khrushchev saw him [Frost], and under very fascinating circumstances because Khrushchev was moving the cuban [sic] missiles in and was making a lot of other moves at that time. No one knew that. This was the first week in September.
> —STEWART L. UDALL, SECRETARY OF THE INTERIOR, 1961–1969, ORAL HISTORY INTERVIEW, MARCH 12, 1970[135]

Not only did Frost exemplify the symbolically vested domestic role of the poet at Kennedy's inauguration, but the uses of poetry as ideological weaponry in the global Cold War were publicized dramatically by Frost's trip to the USSR the next year. During the trip, a cultural exchange through which Alexander Tvardovsky, viewed as a "leader of the movement for freedom of expression in Soviet art,"[136] meanwhile visited the States, Frost would accompany the secretary of the interior, Stewart Udall, under the auspices of the State Department on a two-week Russian tour.[137] "I shall be reading poems chiefly over there [the Soviet Union] but you may be sure I won't be talking just literature," Frost wrote to Kennedy in late July 1962, accepting the president's formal invitation with a digressive rumination on his purpose in the broader American mission. "How like you to take the chance of sending anyone like me over there affinitizing with the Russians," Frost opened the letter: "You must know a lot about me besides my rank from my poems but think how the professors interpret the poems! I am almost as full of politics and history as you are."[138] With this rather remarkable assertion, Frost sketched out a chauvinistic understanding of the geopolitical stakes of the Cold War: "I see us [the US and USSR] becoming the two great powers of the modern world in noble rivalry while a third power of United Germany, France, and Italy, the common market, looks on as an expanded polyglot Switzerland," he explained. "Forgive the long letter. I don't write letters but you have stirred my imagination and I have been interested in Russia as a power ever since Rurik came to Novgood":

> These are my credentials. I could go on with them like this to make the picture complete: about the English-speaking world of England, Ireland, Canada, and Australia, New Zealand and Us versus the Russian-speaking world for the next century or so, mostly a stand-off but now and then a showdown to test our mettle. The rest of the world would be Asia and Africa more or less negligible for the time being though it needn't be too openly declared. Much of this would be the better for not being declared openly but kept always in the back of our minds in all our diplomatic and other relations. I am describing not so much what ought to be but what is and will be—reporting and prophesying. This is the way we are one world, as you put it, of independent nations interdependent.—The separateness of the parts as important as the connection of the parts.
> Great times to be alive, aren't they?[139]

Frost departed Washington on August 28. Accompanied by Secretary of the Interior Stewart Udall, longtime friend Frederick Adams of the Pierpont Morgan Library in New York, and Franklin Reeve of Wesleyan University, who served as his translator, Frost spent a week and a half giving readings, interviews, and dining with writers across the USSR.[140] "Poetry's the most national of the arts, not so much painting or music. A great nation makes poetry, and great poetry makes a great nation," Frost told reporters when he arrived in Moscow on August 29.[141] At readings there and in Leningrad, the poem "Mending Wall"—in which the narrator questions the need for a division "where it is we do not need the wall," but his neighbor concludes "good fences good make neighbors"[142]—became a ready-made allegory for the escalating tensions of the Cold War. "Some of the gentlest mockery the Soviet Union has endured came recently from the 88-year-old poet, Robert Frost, a cultural-exchange visitor," reported the *Times*.[143] In Moscow, too, a reporter "unfortunately interpreted" the poem as commentary on Berlin.[144]

Throughout the trip, Frost expressed his desire to meet Soviet premier Nikita Khrushchev, whom he considered a "great leader" because he was a "man who wasn't afraid of power."[145] As he had written to Kennedy, he hoped to convey to the premier his view of the Soviet and U.S. systems as "rivals in magnanimity."[146] And, in the final days of the trip, Frost was invited to meet Khrushchev in Gagra. The night before the meeting, however, Frost fell ill, and after the flight from Moscow was driven to the guest house of the Georgian SSR Ministry of Health to rest before continuing to the premier's dacha. When Frost appeared unable to travel further, Khrushchev met the poet at his bedside. According to Udall, the "kernel" of his "big message" to Khrushchev resembled a model of Hegelian dialectics: a dualist battle romanticized against the possibility of synthesis where "coexistence is negative and sterile." Frost expressed to Khrushchev that "over the long haul . . . the mettle of the two systems would be tested by the nobility of the thinkers and leaders each produced."[147] Franklin Reeve, who was present and interpreting during the hour-and-a-half exchange, likewise records that Frost expressed his theme of a "noble rivalry" between "two nations laid out for rivalry in sports, science, art and democracy." After a discussion of a Berlin solution, NATO, and the Warsaw Pact, Khrushchev asked Frost to tell Kennedy about their conversation. Frost finally presented Khrushchev with *In the Clearing*, inscribing it "from his rival in friendship."[148] Frost was by all accounts elated after

*Figure 2.3* Robert Frost sharing a bedside conversation with Nikita Khrushchev, Gagra, Abkhazia, September 7, 1962. Courtesy of the Dartmouth College Library. Used with permission of the Robert Frost Copyright Trust.

the meeting: "he knew it had been a big inning for poetry and power."[149] Indeed, the diplomatic stakes were high: Khrushchev was meanwhile installing nuclear missiles in Cuba, ninety miles from American soil, resulting in a two-week standoff between Kennedy and Khrushchev the following month.

When greeted by the press at home, however, and asked by reporters to share Khrushchev's message for Kennedy, Frost provided an inflammatory soundbite, saying that the premier "feared for us because of our lot of liberals. He said we're too liberal to fight." This comment, widely reported—"Frost Says Khrushchev Sees U.S. As 'Too Liberal' to Defend Itself" ran a headline in the *Washington Post*—was in Reeve's account inaccurate and "stung" the president,[150] sensitive to charges from congressional conservatives that he was soft on communism, especially in the wake of the military buildup in Cuba.[151] Kennedy would not personally communicate with Frost again. During the height of the Cuban Missile Crisis, Frost attempted to correct his statement, conceding that he may have misrepresented the premier's comments.[152] Although it would be inaccurate to say that the meeting between Frost and Khrushchev materially shaped the policies between the U.S. and Soviet Union, it stands as a powerful demonstration of the symbolic importance of the role of the poet, and moreover of the artist, in the cultural front of the Cold War.

"'Art,' as President Kennedy said recently, 'is political in the most profound sense,'" Udall reflected.[153] Playing on the language of Frost's poem "The Road Less Traveled" in his state report of the trip, Udall allied the poet with American values of choice, privacy, and individualism: "The roads [Khrushchev and Frost] had taken to the year 1962 could scarcely had [sic] been more divergent. The younger man had walked the harsh road of social revolution; the older had, by choice, taken a 'less traveled' private path. The Premier was a shrewd master of a totalitarian political system; the only 'government' familiar to the poet was the kingdom of the individual."[154] The symbolic power of the poet on the world stage, for Udall, was to model the agency and individuality of the American citizen. And while the president would decline to communicate with Frost after his gaffe with reporters, his special consultant on the arts, August Heckscher, who would lay the groundwork for the National Endowment for the Arts, wrote to the poet with congratulations: "You did wonderfully. I am sure that on both sides of the Iron Curtain your visit will be long remembered."[155]

Frost's Mission to Moscow is only one, and uniquely public, example of how state poets participated in transnational ambassadorships and cultural missions abroad during the Cold War. Bishop and Lowell were, the same year, globetrotting on the dime of the Congress for Cultural Freedom: "The Congress people are rather breathless; they now plan for us to end up in Mexico City after Argentina, Uruguay, Chile and Peru," Lowell reported to Bishop,[156] who meanwhile wondered about its operations: "I really know nothing about it."[157] What Bishop sometimes shorthanded as "C for CF," and other times the "Congress for Cult F,"[158] was an anticommunist advocacy group, active in thirty-five countries and covertly funded by the CIA, as we saw in the last chapter.[159] The congress was one among many arms of the state that supported American poets in representing the individual creative voice as liberal values abroad. But much of this "the whole Culture-Government business" was, as in the case of the Congress for Cultural Freedom,[160] less visibly state-supported, or, more precisely, supported through a complex of state and private interests. In contrast, Frost's Mission to Moscow, an explicit state mission, received ample media coverage—and placed his performance of individual, expressive voice at Kennedy's inauguration within the geopolitical framework of the Cold War for everyday citizens. The sixty-plus million American viewers who tuned into Kennedy's inauguration witnessed Frost model the triumph of individual narrative voice in his spontaneous recitation of "The Gift Outright."[161] Now, there could be no doubt that the voice of the poet, representing "the kingdom of the individual" across from Khrushchev, "the master of a totalitarian system," in turn represented democracy abroad.

### The National Poetry Festival: "America's outstanding poets" in Cold Wartime

No one could have foreseen that this gathering [the National Poetry Festival, October 22–24, 1962] would have fallen in the same weeks as the Cuban crisis, and no one would have planned it that way. But now that it is over, we can all feel that these readings and discussions by America's outstanding poets reminded us of the real meaning of the struggle being carried on at other levels.
—AUGUST HECKSCHER TO L. QUINCY MUMFORD[162]

A month after Frost returned from Moscow, he would travel to Washington for a poetry festival. The event was not only remarkable as the occasion of the national poet's last public reading before his death. The first National Poetry Festival, held October 22–24, 1962, displayed a new institutional coherence in the field of American poetry. The event marks the emergence of a new *state verse culture*. The National Poetry Festival collated key institutional and individual players in the production of postwar verse: the event was sponsored by the Bollingen Foundation, held at the Library of Congress, and celebrated the fiftieth anniversary of *Poetry*.[163] The Poetry Society of America—which aligned against *Poetry* and lambasted the library a decade earlier during the Bollingen affair—cosponsored the event with the Bollingen Foundation. Bollingen Foundation representatives, including Huntington Cairns and Paul Mellon, attended; and well over one hundred copies of the fiftieth-anniversary double-issue of *Poetry* were distributed to all participants and guests. Two thousand more copies were purchased by the U.S. Information Agency for distribution abroad. Frost, among the eighty-some poets who attended, read "The Gift Outright"—which he had read not only at Kennedy's inauguration, but a month earlier in the USSR, calling it his "most patriotic poem."[164] Paul Engle, the ambitious director of the young Writers Workshop at Iowa, was also in attendance. He would use the trip as an opportunity to meet with State Department officials about his international vision for the American creative writing workshop. His weekend at the festival would lay the groundwork for the creation of the International Writing Program at Iowa five years later. Indeed, in the next chapter of our story, the domestic and international investments of the Cold War state would be funded in a new way: not only through diplomatic arts exchanges but also in the rise of a new industry: MFA-granting creative writing programs.

Gertrude Clark Whittall, the patron who dictated Library of Congress poetry programming during the early 1950s, attended as an invited guest; she reportedly grumbled throughout the lectures and readings, fiddling with her hearing aid in the front row.[165] With the increasingly robust cooperation between private organizations and the state, individual philanthropists had much less power as gatekeepers. Whittall, like Paul Mellon through the Bollingen Foundation, could support organizations whose taste she sought to promote, but she could no longer singlehandedly ordain the library's program of readers by pulling $100,000 in bonds out of her hatbox.[166] The expanded scope of interested players bureaucratized the support for decision-making in matters of literary taste. Cosponsorships for poetry programming between the Library of Congress and private literary organizations, notably the Modern Poetry Association and *Poetry* magazine, the Poetry Society of America, and public and private universities and primary schools—as in the exemplary case of the two-day program of the National Poetry Festival—rendered "hatbox patronage" increasingly obsolete.[167] Apparent political divisions among these institutions, which had excited scandal at the library in the immediate postwar years, had also diminished. Aesthetically opposed organizations, as in the case of PSA and *Poetry* previously, were now centralized by the state.

Collating institutional players in the postwar verse, the festival also drew together the poets they supported: "a living anthology" of American poets. A complex of cultural institutions now articulated the canon: "As a veteran anthologist, I had brought many of these poets together between the covers of a book. I had never seen many of them in flesh at one time—a living anthology, an extraordinary collection," then national poet Louis Untermeyer (1961–1963) reflected. "[The National Poetry Festival] was a refutation of the oft-repeated charge that the modern poet was only writing for himself and a few other poets," signaling a new "rapport between the poets and the public."[168] In fact, this symbolic and literal coming together of players in American poetry had been his initiative as the current national poet. Untermeyer solicited funds for the festival from the Bollingen Foundation through Huntington Cairns, who succeeded in winning the trustees' support in December 1961—uniting institutions and individuals under the banner of a new "national poetry."[169]

The National Poetry Festival assembled the canonical figures in postwar verse, moreover, at a crucial historical moment—the very days the Cuban Missile Crisis came to a head. The first day concluded with Kennedy's televised national broadcast announcing the discovery of Soviet missile bases in Cuba, the order of a naval quarantine against Cuba, and the preparation of U.S. armed forces for any necessary action.[170]

The next morning, the festival program was devoted to "The Poet and the Public." While it might seem that "the speech from the White House last night would seem to obliterate every other matter for consideration," contended Babette Deutsch, the program's first speaker, the opposite was true.[171] Karl Shapiro considered the event "prophetic": "What we are honoring here is . . . the dawn of a great American poetry, such as Anglo-Saxon bears to modern English literature. We are in our Beowulf years"[172]—what Frost described to Kennedy as the "golden age" of "poetry and power." "Looking back upon the past week with all its great and fearful events in the public scene, I remember the National Poetry Festival as a bright and . . . fitting interlude," Heckscher, who had been appointed earlier that year to the newly created position of the president's special consultant on the arts and who delivered greetings to the festival convocation, later wrote to the librarian of Congress.[173] As a geopolitically charged event, the National Poetry Festival drew on the recently established role of poetry in national discourse. "America's outstanding poets," as Heckscher observed, proved useful as ideological reinforcements during the Cuban Missile Crisis, "remind[ing] us of the real meaning of the struggle being carried on at other levels." The "real meaning" of an anticommunist world order was exemplified in the expressive voice of the individual citizen-poet. Robert Frost's reading provided the reigning example. "If anyone present [at the National Poetry Festival] held doubts that Frost was *the national poet*," Basler wrote, "his talk and reading on the night of October 24, in the midst of the Cuban Crisis, dispelled those doubts in a moment."[174]

Only six years earlier, "doubtful" that the government of a "free society" could ethically intervene in the private domain of the arts, the Library of Congress had rejected the proposal to institute a poet laureateship. Now, poets were "America's" and "reminders" of the ideological values of a free society. They spoke at presidential inaugurations; they shared bedside chats with world leaders. Presenting a Congressional Gold Medal to Robert Frost the same year, in March of 1962, Kennedy called the poet "distinctively American," whose "wholeness as a man and artist somehow symbolize the inner strength of our people—and summarize our heritage."[175] In turn, "The Library of Congress no longer held its unwanted distinction of being a very modest literary and musical oasis in the federal cultural desert," as Basler put it.[176] The National Poetry Festival marked a new era of government interest in poetic production and made visible an emergent state verse culture.

CHAPTER III

## The Politics of Voice

*The Poet-Critic, the Creative Writer, and the Poet Laureate, 1965–1990*

> So now his thought's gone, buried his body dead...
> will they set up a tumult in his praise
> will assistant professors become associates
> by working on his works?
>
> —JOHN BERRYMAN, *SONG* 373

> I do not know when Creative Writing became a full-fledged program, respectably housed in the Department of English. The first step towards this must have been the Poet in Residence, alias Mr. Robert Frost. In addition to the false position in which the M.A., or the M.F.A, or the Ph.D. in Creative Writing finds himself, we may observe still another abuse resulting from the confusion of literary with academic discipline: the academically certified Creative Writer goes out to teach Creative Writing, and produces other Creative Writers who are not writers, but who produce still other Creative Writers who are not writers.
>
> —ALLEN TATE, "WHAT IS CREATIVE WRITING?"

Will assistant professors become associates / by working on his works?" asks Henry House, the narrator of John Berryman's *Dream Songs* (1969). Here the poet's age-old anxiety over literary posterity finds its quintessentially postwar American expression. In the years Berryman composed the spasmodic tunes of his American epic, between 1960 and 1969, U.S. postsecondary school enrollments more than doubled. More professors were hired than had been in the entire 325 years before. Since the war, 2 million veterans had taken up the 48 months of free tuition provided by the G.I. Bill; the Higher Education Act of 1965 offered millions more secure federal grants and loans for college. This influx resulted in the expansion and disciplinary solidification of the English Department, and by 1967—the year the first professional association of academic creative writers, the Associated Writing Programs, formed—a surge in creative writing degree programs.

It is difficult to understate the transformations in American poetic culture during the 1960s–1980s. These decades saw the nearly full-scale movement of poetry into universities—most seismically with the rise of the creative writing program industry. In turn, these decades saw the experimental reactions of coteries and community-based poetry groups and the evolution of the role of the poet-critic. When Berryman accepted a National Book Award for *The Dream Songs*, the creative writing "workshop poem" was not quite yet a fixture in literary culture, but his occupation as a poet-critic was enough of a fixture in the English Department for him to stage literary posterity as a question of departmental status. Already in 1953, "the poet as the sentimental professional rebel ha[d] vanished; in his place was the young instructor of English in privately endowed colleges wearing a Brooks Brothers uniform."[1] As the relocation of the Bollingen Prize to Yale University in late 1949 had augured, the university system was now the primary arbiter of poetic culture and authority in the United States. And this new means to relative institutional security meant that postwar poets were stuck in the decidedly nontranscendental "muck, administration [and] toil" of careerist jockeying.[2]

The concentration of U.S. poetic production in the academy in the second half of the twentieth century is by now an accepted story. But what remains strikingly underacknowledged is that it is a story we cannot understand without reference to federal bodies. The state underwrote the transformation of the university system and, during the 1960s, made possible an institutional role for the creative writer as the expressive voice of national values—at home and, even more actively, abroad. Indeed, the creative writing workshop would become the most important outlet of a new state verse culture observed at the inauguration of John F. Kennedy in 1961 and the inaugural National Poetry Festival of 1962. In the first U.S. inaugural poem, Robert Frost successfully conflated poetic voice, the speaker of the phonocentric narrative, with political voice, the agential will of the individual, on the national stage. And at the National Poetry Festival individuals and institutions converged in a new way under the auspices of the Library of Congress while the Cuban Missile Crisis loomed over Washington. The expressive, individual voice of the American poet, a powerful symbol in the context of a heightened Cold War, was in the decades that followed often disseminated through the creative writing industry. Working with influential industry leaders like Paul Engle, the director of the Iowa Writers' Workshop, various arms of the state supported the growth of creative writing—the State Department; the United States Information Agency (known overseas as the United States Information Service); and the Central Intelligence Agency through the Farfield Foundation and the Congress for Cultural Freedom as well as through cooperation with formally private organizations, such as the Rockefeller Foundation. The second generation of creative writing programs of the 1960s—which professionalized creative writing into a full-fledged industry that still dominates the field of American poetry today—were, from the perspective of the state, privileged training grounds in national ideologies of sovereign individuality and expressive freedom. In the prototypical workshop poem, a coherent, expressive "I" acted as the democratic assertion of the individual voice against communist groupthink. Creative writing workshop pedagogy emphasizing the personal experience of the individual evolved to embrace the unique details of personal experience as markers of cultural identity, reflecting the values of a pluralistic society during the 1970s–1980s.

While many have described, or decried, the postwar "academicization" of poetry,[3] it is crucial to understand the movement of poetry into universities as a *twofold legacy*: the academic poet of the creative writing industry (housed in MFA programs) is a distinct historical phenomenon from the academic poet-critic (housed in the English Department). While the creative writing industry allied more closely with the cultural missions of the Cold War state—a legacy borne out in present-day national poetry programming—poet-critics often adopted a more politically restive and formally experimental poetics.

At the time that MFA programs were first burgeoning, this distinction was murkier. Berryman, for example, lectured in English Departments, and his late work in many respects troubled the model of individual voice that was becoming a staple of the creative writing workshop. On the other hand, Berryman taught at the Iowa Writers' Workshop, the nation's flagship creative writing program, received one of the first grants administered by the National Endowment for the Arts, and was invited to dine with President Lyndon Johnson. Yet in the still-consolidating state verse culture of the late 1960s, the agenda of the poet-critic already appeared distinct from the national agenda for poetry as "creative writing." "A Kennedy-sponsored bill for the protection of poets from long poems will benefit the culture / and do no harm to that kind Lady, Mrs Johnson," Berryman jests in *Dream Song* 354 (10–12). After all, "The only happy people in the world / are those who do not have to write long poems" (1–2). Berryman's speaker, Henry, still resigns himself to work on his long poem—*The Dream Songs*—alongside "'The Care and Feeding of Long Poems' . . . his next essay." In Berryman's account, the long poem is allied with the essay, or criticism and distinct from the creative writing workshop poem supported by the Kennedy and Johnson administrations. "He would have gone to the White House & consulted the President / during his 10 seconds in the receiving line / on the problems of long poems." But "Mr Johnson has never written one."[4]

John Berryman refused the invitation to dine with President Johnson and never served as consultant or poet laureate at the Library of Congress. His career marks an uneasy shift in the institutional tradition of the poet-critic—in close proximity to but increasingly distinct from the new breed of the "creative writer." Alongside Berryman, the careers of national poets Robert Lowell, Elizabeth Bishop, and Randall Jarrell, who represent the "Middle Generation" and the "age of criticism" in most accounts of twentieth-century American poetry, also reflect this institutional transition—teaching in both English Departments and creative writing workshops, critiquing some aspects of state power, but more often supporting their careers with its resources. Lowell, as we know, would, like Berryman, take a stand against the Johnson administration, refusing to attend a White House Arts Festival in 1965 in protest of American foreign policy, but meanwhile enjoyed foreign travel on the CIA's dime through the Congress for Cultural Freedom. Later poet-critics would challenge the increasingly nationalized model of the MFA creative writing workshop poem more directly. These experimental successors to first- and second-generation modernists, including Lyn Hejinian, Charles Bernstein, and Bob Perelman among the Language poets, moved into university teaching positions not in creative writing workshops but in English Departments as poet-critics in the 1990s.

Certainly, the relationship between the academically institutionalized creative writer and the poet-critic remains complicated in the present. Just as Berryman was both a poet-critic and a teacher of creative writing at the Iowa Writers' Workshop, there are many individuals today who move between these roles. Viewed through the lens of the *state*, however, they are historically distinct institutional traditions.

This is often obfuscated by literary histories and critical debates that narrate postwar American poetry as a battle between two dominant strands:

between the "raw and cooked," as Lowell described the two camps when he accepted a National Book Award in 1960, contrasting politically engaged and formally innovative Beat poets like Allen Ginsberg with the traditional verse of poets like Donald Hall (poet laureate 2006–7) or later between the "establishment" verse that Language poets attacked in a 1988 manifesto and the Language poets' own "experimental" poetics. But, as this era of our story shows, the institutional history of traditional literary study, on the one hand, and of creative writing, on the other, is today perhaps the starkest, if least often explicitly acknowledged, dividing line of the so-called poetry wars.[5] Indeed, the cultural sensitivity animating this divide—particularly given the institutional intimacy of the professional practices—is a significant reason scholarship has not accounted for the historical development of the creative writing industry (the MFA poet or creative writer) vis-à-vis the English Department (the poet-critic). Instead, critics have frequently adopted a more shrilly polemical pro- or anti-MFA rhetoric, such as Anis Shivani in *Against the Workshop: Provocations, Polemics, Controversies*;[6] or, meanwhile, an anti-"academic poetry" stance, as seen in the populist rhetoric of poets laureate of the 1990s and 2000s like Joseph Brodsky and Billy Collins, whose state projects prized poetry written in accessible standard American English.

In fact, both creative writers and poet-critics participate in what Charles Bernstein calls "official verse culture"—both publish in publications including *Poetry* and the *New Yorker*; both partner variously with organizations like the Modern Poetry Foundation (now the Poetry Foundation), the Poetry Society of America, and the Academy of American Poets; and both typically earn livings through the university system.

But the creative writing industry has a closer historical relationship to Cold War nationalism and is more squarely rooted in *state* verse culture. We can see the proximity of the creative writing industry to the national poetry office as early as 1947. As David Dowling describes in his history of the Iowa Writers' Workshop, Robert Lowell backed out of Paul Engle's offer of a teaching position with the workshop so that he could receive the $5,700 stipend—the same one he would recommend to Bishop—in return for the more "nominal" demands of the consultancy at the Library of Congress. This withdrawal did not prevent Lowell from assuming a teaching position at Iowa a mere three years later—a position vacated by Karl Shapiro, also a former consultant.[7] In the decades that followed, the state began supporting the growth of the creative writing program industry, understanding that the representative and symbolic capacity of the American poet, both domestically and internationally, had new and special value in the cultural Cold War. The creative writing industry welcomed this support.

The national poetry office at the Library of Congress reflected the state's new conviction about the capacities of American poets, expanding its international programming in the 1960s and 1970s. Meanwhile, the state also supported the program era's model of individual voice in civic projects proper undertaken by the National Endowment for the Arts after 1965—and especially after 1985, when the missions of the NEA and the national poetry office became formally linked. That year, congressional legislation renamed the consultant in poetry the "U.S. Poet Laureate" and designated NEA funds for the Library of Congress to undertake a new annual poetry program cooperatively with the agency.[8] No longer a custodial position or librarianship, the national poet, now under a more ceremonial and symbolic title, assumed an explicitly public-facing civic charge. The mid-1980s, like the immediate postwar years, saw poetry "pressed into the service of national identity formation" during a cultural climate of American political and economic expansion.[9]

By the mid-1980s, the office of national poet assumed new domestic significance. Gwendolyn Brooks, the last national poet to hold the title of "Consultant in Poetry to the Library of Congress" in the transitional 1985-1986 term, and also the first Black woman to hold the title, would be remembered as "one of the best examples of what [a national poet] does" by the Library of Congress decades later.[10] She was succeeded by Robert Penn Warren (1986–87), who had previously served as a consultant in 1944–1945 and had since publicly recanted his expressed racist views. In conjunction with Robert Penn Warren's inaugural poet laureateship, and with the fiftieth anniversary of the post in 1987, the library commissioned an official history of the office by William McGuire, who was meanwhile also at work on a history of one of the library's first patrons, the Bollingen Foundation.[11] In the wake of the U.S.'s booming new creative writing industry, the rebranding of the national poetry office marks the consolidation of state verse culture, accomplished through the cooperation of the NEA and other national federal bodies with supportive private patrons, literary professional organizations, and, most important, educational institutions.

We can therefore see the development of state verse culture during this period not only in the rebranding of the national poetry office as the "poet laureate" but also in the creation of the American creative writer: the individual voice that represented democracy and freedom and who received their training thanks to the funding of American cold warriors—at first businessmen and philanthropists and then thanks to the various and often covert arms of federal bodies and agencies. In the wake of the industry's success, the creation of a U.S. poet laureate literalizes the central role of the state in shaping an expanded, popularized, and professionalized poetic field in America.

## Pedagogy as Patron: The Rise of Creative Writing

In Cold War America, creative writing programs grew at pace with the arms race. When Frost delivered his last public reading at the National Poetry Festival in 1962, there were five creative writing programs in the United States.[12] By 1970, 44 programs in the U.S. offered master's degrees in creative writing or in English with a creative thesis;[13] by 1980, there were over 100.[14] Programs multiplied to meet the demand of growing enrollments: between 1971 and 1989 the number of creative writing degrees awarded tripled from 345 to 1,107.[15] When the Associated Writers Program was founded in 1967, it consisted of twelve member colleges and universities. In 1986, as Robert Penn Warren assumed the inaugural poet laureateship, the Associated Writing Programs claimed 150 member institutions.[16] The expanded Association of Writers and Writing Programs boasts over 500 today.

The rise of creative writing programs is central to the history of postwar literary production in the United States. Mark McGurl calls it "the most important event" of twentieth-century American literary history, the second half of which is now often considered "the program era" in keeping with the terms of his pioneering study.[17] While much of the important work that has followed McGurl has undervalued the role of the state, Eric Bennett's *Workshops of Empire* demonstrates how state interest and cooperation with grant foundations and individual patrons are crucial to understanding the rise of the creative writing industry. As the first chapters of our study have shown, the postwar state operated as a central pivot between the infrastructure of literary professionalism, on the one hand, and of higher education. on the other. In this capacity, the state would support the second wave (mid-1960s) growth of creative writing as a Cold War cultural mission.

This history helps us to understand the commitments of the creative writing industry in the present and to what extent it is distinct from other forms of contemporary poetic practice in the United States. The discourse of the "poetry wars," most active in the 1990s, highlighted the difference between program-era voice and the priorities of community-centered, often experimentally formal, and more often politically engaged—sometimes antistate and at other times potentially antistate—poetry writing practices, typically more aligned with the cultural imperatives of the poet-critic. The Association of Writers and Writing Programs reflects this two-camp discourse. Today, the AWP asserts a division between academic (specialized) poetry versus public (populist) poetry, not unlike the division between modernist and populist verse in the discourse that surrounded the Bollingen Prize. When the AWP points to the weaknesses of "academe"—such as the "tendency to reward those with the most academic connections, and this sometimes tends to make intellectual endeavors more specialized, in a domain remote from the public," as the AWP director David Fenza assessed in his 2013 Annual Report—"academe" implicitly refers to the poet-critics, but not the creative writers, who work at academic institutions. Despite the rhetoric of the creative writing industry's governing body, the AWP, historically the divide is not properly "between work in academe and work in the real world."[18] In the balkanized sides of the so-called poetry wars, *both* the creative writer of MFA-granting creative writing programs and the poet-critic of the English Department claim the university as base camp. The AWP understands full well that many MFA poets are, in fact, professors, which Fenza refers to as "teachers": "One of AWP's achievements is its promotion of those teachers who connect with the public—writers who teach and publish works that attract large general audiences."[19] By equating civic relevance ("teachers who connect with the public") with commercial relevance ("works that attract large general audiences"), the AWP defines MFA poets contra the poet-critics of a specialized "academe." Richard Blanco, who delivered the inaugural poem for President Barack Obama the same year as Fenza's report, and is discussed in our epilogue, has similarly criticized the "academization of poetry."[20]

The Association of Writers and Writing Programs discourse that pits academic against "real world" poetry thus obfuscates the position of the

MFA poet, although distinct from the poet-critic, as a career position *within* the academy. More broadly, the rhetoric is misleading about the historical relationship of the university to poetic production. In the second half of the twentieth century, the so-called academicization of poetry did not mean that poetry became less accessible to the general public: it meant that it became *more* accessible, with more people writing, publishing, and reading poetry. "The relationship between poetry and academia has increased rather than diminished poetry's public presence," Gwiazda affirms in a study of American poetry in the *Age of Empire*.[21] Moreover, public-facing, commercially successful state poets in this era could not have survived without universities, nor do they in the present.

But to understand the origins of the AWP's populist rhetoric, so insistent on the cultural function of the "nonacademic" poet, we will first have to understand the origins of the creative writing industry itself. Our next section traces the early history of the discipline through its flagship program.

### *Professionalizing Poetry: Iowa Writers' Workshop, 1939–1967*

"It is conceivable that by the end of the twentieth century the American university will have proved a more understanding and helpful aid to literature than ever the old families of Europe," Paul Engle said in 1961 from his position as director of the Iowa Writers' Workshop.[22] Whereas "the old families of Europe" offered literary patronage, in Cold War America the university offered literary professions.

The first creative writing programs in the United States were established in the years following World War II.[23] Iowa, the early exception, introduced courses in creative writing in its 1939–40 course catalog, and with the appointment of Engle as writers' workshop director in 1942 assumed a prototypical stature in the industry. Elliott Coleman founded the Johns Hopkins Writing Seminars in 1946. In 1947, Stanford began a fellowship program in writing. The University of Denver opened a writing program the same year; Cornell established one in 1948. The early postwar years saw the consolidation of creative writing as a discipline that reflected the ideals of universal high culture. Progenitors of the discipline, specifically Coleman, Wallace Stegner, Alan Swallow, and Baxter Hathaway, sought "to bring the teaching of literature more closely in line with the ways in which (they believed) literature is genuinely created," as D. G. Myers has summarized; "to impart the *understanding* of literature through the *use* of it."[24] The *use* value of creative writing, however, meant something different to the poets of the age of criticism in the literary climate of the 1940s and 1950s than it would to the second generation of creative writing program founders during the 1960s and 1970s,[25] and different than what it means to the AWP today. The originating disciplinary conception of creative writing sought to bridge the gap between literary knowledge and literary practice: between philology, literary history, and critical theory, on the one hand, and cultural studies, rhetoric, business English, and composition, on the other. Creative writing forged a "third way"[26]—it provided an alternative to producing literary criticism "as a branch of science" à la New Criticism, but it did *not* seek to provide professional training for a career as a creative writer. Norman Foerster, mentor to Stegner and Engle and director of Iowa's School of Letters from 1930–1944, was instrumental in the vision of creative writing as a methodological "third way," establishing "Imaginative Writing" as a field of graduate study in literature in 1931.[27] Ph.D. candidates were expected to have familiarity in language, literary history, literary criticism, and imaginative writing as subfields of literary study; a specialist in the latter submitted a poem, play, or other work of art instead of the typical dissertation. Foerster emphasized that his project was "to give all types of literary students a rigorous and appropriate discipline," rather than to "establish a vocational school for authors and critics."[28] "Imaginative critical" writing, a pursuit within literary study, was not intended to be a source of professional livelihood.[29] Creative writing was not born of a populist impulse toward socially engaged art, but quite the opposite—as "an effort to systemize and transmit the knowledge required to enjoy the vertical compensations of art rather than satisfying the horizontal demands of a great public."[30]

However, this disciplinary ideal sought to articulate itself at the very moment that the American university—in size, shape, and social role—was wholly transfigured. After the war, a newly centralized and powerful federal government assumed increased control of academic institutions. While federal aid had been distributed during the Depression, this was no precedent for the postwar growth of state funding for higher education.[31] The G.I. Bill, or the Servicemen's Readjustment Act, of 1944, allotted veterans 48 months of free education at the college or university of their choice. The Veterans Affairs administrator predicted only 700,000 would take advantage of the program; in fact, 2,232,000 veterans entered colleges and universities. More than a million enrolled during AY 1947–48 alone.³² In the new multiversity, Clark Kerr's term for the cultural flowering of the university that plays on Karl Polanyi's 1944 description of the emergence of a market economy,³³ creative writing held a special role. It was an expandable discipline. As the postwar university grew, so did the need for teachers, and writers met this demand more readily than professionals in hard-skill fields. Moreover, creative writing programs could exist within already established English Departments. They did not require new facilities or equipment, but could still function as independent programs, bringing in federal dollars via tuition for each student who enrolled. By 1964, poet-critics like Allen Tate—Tate, who ran a first-generation creative writing program at Princeton, would have preferred to call it an "Imaginative Writing" program—vocally critiqued the direction of what he believed should not be a professionally "certifying" or degree-granting discipline. "Creative Writing is a risk for the university and a risk for the student, and it is an academic anomaly," he warned. "I do not know when Creative Writing became a full-fledged program respectably housed in the Department of English. The first step towards this must have been the Poet in Residence, alias Mr. Robert Frost."³⁴

In Myers's account, the originating disciplinary ideal of creative writing was more or less lost in the noise of the rapid expansion of higher education. He argues that the "three-way split in English departments" collapsed, if messily, when creative writing split off from English Departments proper; the idea of creative writing put forward by its progenitors failed when it became a fully autonomous branch of curricula. But Eric Bennett identifies several influential founders, namely Stegner and Engle, as key agents in the ideological evolution of the project. Engle, in particular, successfully adapted values of his new humanist training to fit the cultural priorities of the Cold War.³⁵ In the 1940s and 1950s, Engle began promoting the Iowa Writers' Workshop to conservative Midwestern businessmen, publishing moguls, and philanthropic organizations such as the Ford, Guggenheim, and Rockefeller Foundations. The latter shared personnel with the Department of State and the Central Intelligence Agency, and by the mid-1960s, as Engle's international ambitions for Iowa grew, he received support from the State Department, CIA-funded channels, and other federal bodies directly. A savvy fundraiser, Engle gradually guided creative writing's flagship program toward a more socially ambitious mission, marketing the creative writer as the beacon of individual self-expression against the threat of totalitarianism. First tapping into state contacts at the emergent state culture at the National Poetry Festival in 1962, Engle, with the support of the Cold War state, was instrumental in establishing the reputation of the nation's first creative writing program and exerted incalculable influence on the institutional values and aesthetic norms of the creative writing programs that followed in its wake. Iowa became an important participant in the national arts agenda, and it was the blueprint for the programs that followed—more than half of the approximately fifty second-wave programs were founded by its graduates, in what Donald Justice called "a kind of pyramid scheme, it seems now [in 1984], looking back."[36]

While poet-critics like Tate regarded this second wave with disdain—"nobody can be academically certified in an art which, in its very essence, is not subject to the objective discipline that the scholar passes on from one generation to another,"[37] Engle also emphasized the division between the poet-critic and the creative writer in appeals to funders. The creative writer had civic utility that scholarship and criticism did not. In his first appeals to the Rockefeller Foundation, Engle pitted the productive capacity of the creative writer against the futile close readings of the critic: "How much longer can the body of English and American literature go on supporting thousands of presumed scholars without their production descending to the merely trivial? . . . In another 75 years what can this lead to but a glossing of every stanza of poetry and chapter of novel and act of play?"[38] Creative writing workshops, at least to their funders, became spaces not where students went to "enjoy the vertical compensations of art," but where citizens expressed widely held national values.

McGurl, and others, have written the rise of creative writing as a triumph of New Criticism. Bennett's archival study of Engle-Rockefeller correspondence helps to "correct the lingering overestimation of the role that the New Criticism played in the rise of creative writing programs"[39]—not to mention Tate's active disdain for the field's professionalization. While an organization like the Bollingen Foundation sought to support New Critical ventures proper—pulling its prize money from the Library of Congress when it became contaminated with postwar American state politics and relocating it to Yale, a veritable bastion of New Criticism—the Rockefeller Foundation did not shy away from the civic uses of literature. Engle's letters to the Rockefellers and other potential funders reflect the influence of his mentor Foerster, whose new humanist conceptions of "integrated individuality" and personal responsibility helped form Engle's "visionary conviction that literature mattered not only to the academy but to the nation and the world."[40] David H. Stevens, a director of the Humanities Division at the Rockefeller Foundation, praised Engle's Foerster for "work[ing] against old methods of graduate teaching in English" in *The Changing Humanities: An Appraisal of Old Values and New Uses*, a volume that details the philosophy behind the foundation's postwar funding decisions. Allied and often sharing personnel with the CIA and the State Department, the Rockefeller Foundation "put its money behind ideas larger than both the waning New Humanism and the waxing New Criticism . . . its munificence subsumed them more and more."[41] The foundation supported a broader vision of American liberalism, holding sacred the values of "secular humanism, democratic individuality, and the living voice of the artist as social glue" in a world torn between democratic and communist rule.[42] The Rockefeller Foundation did not support the limited ends of New Criticism at Yale, then, but the broader vision of creative writing at Iowa—granting Engle $40,000 between 1953 and 1956.[43]

Engle appealed to the Rockefeller Foundation and other corporate and individual donors as generals in a cultural battlefield of the Cold War, promising Iowa's creative writing students as their soldiers. Engle regularly highlighted the role of university students in the fight against communism. "I trust you have seen the recent announcement that the Soviet Union is founding a University at Moscow for students coming from outside the country," Engle wrote the foundation in 1960. "Thousands of young people of intelligence, many of whom could never get University training in their own countries, will receive education [and] the expected ideological indoctrination."[44] Creative writing programs, meanwhile, stood against communist and totalitarian ideas. The creative writer was a beacon of individual expression. The creative writer, like the Abstract Expressionist painter, stood for the values of an open society and provided an image of American cultural leadership abroad.

A more regionalist strain of this ethos helped sell the value of the creative writer to Midwestern investors. Much like Frost cultivated his brand as a national poet by emphasizing his regional, New England roots in *North of Boston*, Engle pitched articles to generalist readerships throughout the 1950s that helped cohere his persona—and the face of institutionalized

*Figure 3.1* Paul Engle with Iowa Writers' Workshop students, University of Iowa, 1950s. Image courtesy of the Frederick W. Kent Collection of Photographs, University of Iowa Libraries.

creative writing—as a regional and thereby all-American brand. He composed a handful of holiday specials for *Better Homes and Gardens* and pieces such as "Poetry, People, Pigs" for *The Iowan*.[45] Media relationships assisted Iowa in turn. Publishing mogul Henry Luce of *Time* and *Life* and Gardner Cowles Jr., who published *Look* and several newspapers in the Midwest, "loved to feature Iowa: its embodiment of literary individualism, its celebration of self-expression, its cornfields."[46]

Rejecting the experimental modernist abroad, or the writer "alienated from his country," Engle admired Frost's model of the writer as citizen.[47] "One of the powerful themes of literature in the twentieth century has been the alienation of the writer from his times and his country because he felt that he had no home there," Engle wrote in the opening of his 1964 collection *On Creative Writing*, dedicating it to the "heartening variety of individuals, foundations, and corporations who have refused to believe that this must be true."[48] Also like Frost, Engle understood the role of the writer as a unique but representative citizen: "The young writer is not merely a student. Far more than any other person of talent, he creates an image by which a country sees itself, and the image by which other countries also see it," Engle stated in the 1959 publicity materials accompanying "Proposal for Founding the Iowa Industries Fellowships in Writing at the State University of Iowa."[49] The student writer as the image of the nation: this was the persuasive ethos of the creative writing workshop. Previous and ongoing funders were convinced. Howard Hall of the Iowa Manufacturing Company in Cedar Rapids, for instance, explained why funders should consider Iowa's international students a national priority: "Their presence here means that they will later act as cultural missionaries, taking the name of Iowa around the Free World." The Iowa ethos was also endorsed by Henry Rago, then the editor of *Poetry*: "Paul Engle's plan is valuable not only for this region, and for the country as a whole, but to all that part of the world which still believes in the free individual and the free artist."[50]

To expand the imperial vision of the Iowa Workshop across the "Free World," Engle would need more than the support of Midwestern businessmen. Iowa had "attained national eminence by capitalizing on the fears and hopes of the Cold War" with private funders.[51] For the first two decades after the war, Iowa had been supported by private gifts. Now, it would pursue international ventures, culminating in the founding of an International Writing Program in 1967 with the overt and covert aid of the state. The formation of the Associated Writing Programs established creative writing as a professional industry at home the same year. We should therefore understand the second generation of creative writing programs, which bloomed during the 1960s, not only as the transition from the disciplinary consolidation of creative writing to the professionalization of creative writing. We should understand it as the industry's transition from private to state support.

In June 1962, a USIS contact encouraged Engle to "write the White House, since the welcome mat is supposed to be out for new ideas these days."[52] This "welcome mat" had in part been laid out by Frost, the national poet who, as shown in chapter 2, worked instrumentally with President Kennedy and his administration to secure a privileged role for the individual artist in projects of Cold War cultural imperialism. While Engle argued for the geopolitical stakes of the creative writer to Iowa shareholders, Frost had been making the same case to the White House, although here a more difficult one. State-sponsored arts sounded suspiciously like the propaganda of the USSR. By conceiving of national arts as a cooperative venture with private industry, as well as a "volunteer effort" of the free-willed citizen (in line with the "ask not" exhortation of Kennedy's inaugural address), the Kennedy and subsequent Cold War administrations effectively distinguished national arts programs from those of a socialist state. If a government-supported arts initiative was also supported by an industry giant like Rockefeller, after all, it could hardly seem anticapitalist. State investment in creative writing during the mid-1960s was not provided through any one single fund, then, but followed Kennedy's model of state arts with a capitalist spirit.

Engle's appointment to the Advisory Committee on the Arts was instrumental in securing the eventual state support for creative writing. Congressional legislation had formally created the board of trustees for a National Cultural Center in 1958, but the center was not effectively mobilized until Kennedy took office, and an Advisory Committee on the Arts was assembled to plan and fundraise for the center in January 1962. (A June 1963 executive order formally established the President's Advisory Council on the Arts, which exists today as the National Council on the Arts.) Engle was appointed.[53] Encouraged by the national arts "welcome mat," Engle contacted the assistant secretary of state for educational and cultural affairs, Lucius D. Battle, regarding his work in Asia. This was the first of many fruitful exchanges that would lead to the state funding of Iowa's International Writing Program.

In his capacity as an advisory committee member, Engle communicated with the cultural center's chairman, Roger L. Stevens. He also had cause to follow up with State Department officials during visits to Washington. In October 1962, Engle made a key trip to attend the National Poetry Festival. In Bennett's telling, Engle attended "a poetry conference at the Library of Congress, an event overshadowed by the Cuban Missile Crisis"; although he was not mentioned in news coverage of the attendees, he "was both at the conference and making the rounds."[54] Library of Congress records also document Engle having attended the reception.[55] At the festival, Engle found a longtime network of state and private endowments convening to celebrate the national poetry office at the Library of Congress and *Poetry*'s fiftieth anniversary—a fortuitous atmosphere in which Engle could make a case for the state support of Iowa. Though indeed "overshadowed" by the missile scare, the resulting political tension in Washington animated the festival's nationalist strands. During this visit, Engle met with Stevens, invited Mrs. Jacqueline Kennedy to serve on the University of Iowa's Arts Council, and followed up in person with Battle at the State Department to solicit support for Iowa's Asia venture. Here, he was referred to specialized State Department staff "much interested in exploring with you the possibilities for collaboration" on the project Arthur Schlesinger Jr., special assistant to President Kennedy, meanwhile, deemed "promising."[56]

Engle spent half of 1963 on a "world recruiting tour" supported by the Rockefeller Foundation and the State Department. He made stops in London, Karachi, Lahore, New Delhi, Bombay, Calcutta, Bangkok, Taipei, Manila, Tokyo, and elsewhere. Bennett describes Engle's letters from his six months abroad as effusive political appraisals; sometimes they "verged on treatises, letters having little to do with literature."[57] He felt himself "an important emissary." Engle's trip abroad solidified his international vision for Iowa's future. The success of the Program in Creative Writing at the University of Iowa "suggested that, in an open society such as ours, writer, businessman, and university can join to make an environment which is useful to the writer, friendly for the businessman, and healthy for the university"—and an international Iowa would model the values of an open society to the world, where "young writers from all regions of the USA and many areas of the earth could come here and make an international community of the imagination."[58] When they returned home, moreover, "international creative writers were presumed to be unmediated agents of change in their native countries."[59] The state agreed that creative writing was a potent tool to spread values of individualism and democracy both at home and abroad. The State Department, rather than the Rockefeller Foundation, would directly fund Engle's next international mission.

Engle's activities in 1965, when Iowa's enrollment reached a new peak of 250 students, show the Kennedy-Frost national arts agenda coming to fruition. President Johnson appointed Engle to the National Council on the Arts in February.[60] Over the summer, the council worked to help draft the National Foundation on the Arts and the Humanities Act, which established the National Endowment for the Arts as an independent agency of the federal government: "The world leadership which has come to the United States . . . must be solidly founded upon worldwide respect and admiration for the Nation's high qualities as a leader in the realm of ideas and of the spirit," the act declared. Hence "national progress and scholarship in the humanities and the arts, while primarily a matter for private and local initiative, are also appropriate matters of concern to the Federal Government. . . . While no government can call a great artist or scholar into existence," it could avoid breeding "unthinking servants" by "help[ing] create and sustain not only a climate encouraging freedom of thought, imagination, and inquiry but also the material conditions facilitating the release of this creative talent."[61] Engle's first useful state contact, the former chairman of the National Culture Center Roger L. Stevens, was appointed the first chairman of the NEA. While in Washington for Johnson's ceremonial signing of the bill on September 29,[62] Engle planned the details of his next trip abroad. He would deliver lectures on American poetry in Norway, Denmark, Ireland, Sweden, and Germany later that fall.[63]

Two years later, Engle's work on scouting trips abroad was realized in the founding of an International Writing Program at Iowa. The International Writing Program was subsidized by the State Department, the Asia Foundation,[64] and the Farfield Foundation,[65] which operated as a CIA front, funding cultural operations through the Congress for Cultural Freedom. A product of the combination of covert state support through the Farfield Foundation, explicit state support through the State Department, and Rockefeller Foundation grants, Iowa's International Writing Program provides an instructive example of how the participation of formally private enterprises secured the national arts agenda as distinct from Soviet propaganda.

The NEA also made its first complete series of grants the in fiscal year of 1967. None of the awardees had applied for NEA support; the new agency had not yet developed a system for applications. The first series of grants in literature, totaling $737,010, were awarded to twenty-three creative writers, including Maxine Kumin, who would serve as the national poet in 1981–82; Iowa graduate Mona Van Duyn, who later became the first female poet laureate in 1992; former *Poetry* editor Hayden Carruth, Robert Duncan, and Kenneth Patchen. It also provided grants to nine literary organizations. These organizations, such as the Coordinating Council of Literary Magazines, were instrumental to the shaping of state verse culture, providing publication and career advice to aspiring creative writers, many of whom were Iowa graduates as well as providing funds to the publications, including *Poetry*, the *Hudson Review*, the *Kenyon Review*, the *Southern*

*Review,* and the *Virginia Quarterly Review,* that would publish these Iowa graduates in turn.[66] The same year, the Associated Writing Programs was founded, formalizing creative writing as a national industry.[67] Two years later, the Apollo 11 made the first crewed moon landing, a conquest in the space race symbolizing geopolitical dominance over the USSR. The front page of the *New York Times* featured three images of the two Americans on the lunar surface; the headline story, "Voice From Moon: 'Eagle Has Landed'; and "Voyage to the Moon"—a poem by former Librarian of Congress Archibald MacLeish.[68] President Richard M. Nixon had asked MacLeish to write for the occasion,[69] which, appearing on the front page of the *Times,* was perhaps the most important national occasional poem since Frost's spontaneous recitation at Kennedy's inauguration. "Presence among us / wanderer in our skies, / . . . and we have touched you! // From the first of time, before the first of time, before the / first men tasted time, we thought of you." Like "the land that was ours before we were the land's," the moon was cast as territory that men "thought of before the first of time," "Now / our hands have touched you" and made destiny manifest. The Kennedy-Frost era vision for cultural dominance—to send a man to the moon by the end of the decade, and of "poetry and power," had come to fruition.

The institutional biography of the Iowa Writers' Workshop reflects the consolidation of the national arts agenda in the mid-1960s. Initially underwritten by anticommunist businessmen, the creative writing industry's flagship program increasingly developed relationships with official and unofficial organs of state support. State support of Iowa occurred alongside wide-ranging legislative changes, the creation of the NEA and the passage of the Higher Education Act in 1965, so as to appropriate and programmatically reproduce the creative writing project of expressive voice within the mainstream ideology of the nation-state.

### *Stating the Self: The Creative Writing Industry's Project of Poetic Voice*

I have always laughed
when someone spoke of
"finding his voice." I took it

> literally: had he lost his voice?
> Had he thrown it and had it
> not returned? Or perhaps they
> were referring to his newspaper
> the *Village Voice*? He's trying
> to find his *Voice*.
>     What isn't
> funny is that so many young writers
> seem to have found this notion
> credible: they set off in search
> of their voice, as if it were
> a single thing, a treasure
> difficult to find but worth
> the effort. I never thought
> such a thing existed. Until
> recently. Now I know it does.
> I hope I never find mine. I
> wish to remain a phony the rest of my life.
>     —RON PADGETT, "VOICE"

*Write what you know. Show, don't tell. Find your voice.* Describing what he calls "the subjective turn in postwar American aesthetics," Fredric Jameson recalls these three injunctions—the tripartite doctrine of the postwar creative writing workshop—as a "precious clue for exploration both of the new postwar society and economy, and of the evolution of that subjectivity so often loosely identified as individualism."[70] Like the poems and short stories they shaped, the pedagogical dicta of the creative writing workshop are symptomatic reflections of a wider cultural ethos. Significantly, workshop directors and pedagogues themselves understood this. We must read Engle's command to students to "find your voice" alongside his assertion that a "young writer" is "not merely a student, but the image of the nation"—that is, a representative citizen. As his correspondence and prose show, Engle was mindful that crafting the psychology of the "I" was not only the crafting of the "I" of the student, but the "I" of the citizen-subject.

The national value of individualism, in the context of creative writing programs, was articulated through what Bennett calls a "kind of ethic of raw particularity."[71] Bennett points to Engle and Warren Carrier's didactic interpretation of Archibald MacLeish's "Ars Poetica," which argues that "expressing significance in poetry demands sharp, specific *detail*. The concrete symbols, the things in this world as we know it—these are the invariable stuff of poetry. . . . Poetry must operate through such concrete symbols."[72] As Bennett describes, "this was the vision of a poetry of concrete symbols—of symbols so particular that they issue from and return to a single mind—and no longer of doves and roses and serpents, no longer the old public symbolism, but instead William Carlos Williams's red wheelbarrow glazed with rainwater beside the white chickens."[73] While it is true that Engle "concentrated on particulars in his poetry, his teaching, and his occasional work as a critic and educator," these were *not* the concrete details of imagism, but the concrete details of personal experience.[74] In creative writing pedagogy, the particular legitimized the authenticity of the speaker. That is, the ethic of raw particularity reflects the imperative to "show, don't tell," but perhaps equally to "write what you know"—where concrete details provide the evidence of difference, or the unique value, of the individual voice.

On his world recruiting tour that led to the creation of Iowa's International Program, Engle recorded observational travelogues that provide an instructive view of the workshop director's conception of voice as "American" voice. "I have been places no American had been before," he wrote the Rockefeller Foundation from India, "in the chawls of Bombay where the smell of urine was the same color as the cup of tea I looked at grimly, in open drain paths of Calcutta where I saw on a pad cross-legged on the floor and discussed the social novel with a man who looked like Buddha."[75] In Engle's travelogues, representations of cultural difference serve as the chief claim to narrative authority or indeed the speaker's exemplary status: "*I* have been places *no American* had been before, in the chawls."

"I became very close to the Bengali poets, went out with them at night across the bazaars of that dreadful city, down to the burning ghats along the Hooghly [River] at midnight, the crisp stench of flesh and wood burning, the Untouchables pushing heads and legs back into the fire, the filthy water next day splashed over the faces of old women from lovely brass jugs at one of the Khali temples."[76] In this single breathless sentence, Engle includes four proper nouns and adjectives (Bengali, Hooghly, Untouchables, and Khali) as well as culturally specific or "untranslatable" terminology, the "bazaars," or enclosed marketplaces, and "ghats," a series of steps leading down to a body of water, particularly a holy river, here the Hooghly. The proper or culturally specific noun marks difference and specialized cultural knowledge. We see this again in Engle's description of his time in Pakistan: "In the first row to the right there were women writers in 'purdah,' sitting with black hoods over their faces ('burkha'), an embroidered opening giving them a view but keeping them invisible. Spooky, man!"[77] Here, "purdah" and "burkha" provide the narrative authority of the speaker, who assumes a pedagogical role in providing the reader with access to cultural difference through these terms. The exclamation of "spooky, man!" assures the reader that the speaker does not identify with, nor expect the reader to identify with, the cultural experiences related to these terms, only that he has access to them as tokenized markers.

In addition to the culturally specific proper noun, Engle represents difference through the sensory detail and stark, dualistic contrasts: the *"filthy"* fills the *"lovely"*; and, in an elemental opposition of fire and water, the ritually impure work of the Untouchable caste "pushing heads and legs into the fire" is held against another body part, "faces," being "splash[ed] with water." Cultural difference is reduced to sensory details of smell, for example, "crisp stench of flesh and wood burning," or image, "Untouchables pushing heads and legs back into the fire," which also contrast with the cultural position of the speaker. Such techniques thus endow the speaker with the value of difference, or unique personal experience, and at the same time stabilize his own position as American.

The strategies we see in Engle's travelogues used to represent cultural difference—stark, dualistic contrasts; the use of proper nouns and non-English words and sensory details—mark the seeds of what McGurl calls "high cultural pluralist" aesthetics in program-era writing.[78] Consequentially, as Engle's travelogues show, the origin of this aesthetic was rooted in an imperialist literary nationalism "approaching smugness": "I am simply more convinced, with a fervor approaching smugness, that the sort of hard critical approach, along with a study of the development of poetry and fiction in Europe and the USA over the past 100 years, *is precisely what these people, in their cloudy minds, need most. The self-critical, questioning mind on which we were raised is rare out here*, and yet it is the basis of any real enhancement of natural talent."[79]

The unique detail as a marker of difference would also hold an important role in creative writing ethos in the age of identity politics. The individualism of the 1950s would evolve to accommodate a new national priority to embrace demographic pluralism in the late 1960s and multiculturalism in the 1970s–1980s. As creative writing workshop voice evolved to advance identity over individuality, the details authenticating narratives of personal experience increasingly functioned as markers of identity. The high-cultural pluralist writer, McGurl explains, is "called upon to speak from the point of view of one or another hyphenated population, synthesizing the particularity of the ethnic—or analogously marked—voice with the elevated idiom of literary modernism."[80] In the workshop poem, too, markers of cultural difference authenticate the voice of the speaker. The particular detail, especially when framed through semantic, and by extension cultural, contrast, marks *difference* that is incorporated into an "elevated idiom of literary modernism"—the name or sensory description of "ethnic" food, for example, a non-European proper name, an untranslated adjective, or otherwise simulation of local color provide evidence of otherness—but do not threaten to challenge the intelligibility of the speaker in narrative standard American English. The unique detail also serves to authenticate the speaker as author. A fundamental operation of high-cultural pluralism is to "associat[e] the individual writer with a group from which she draws a claim to personal literary distinction,"[81] but again, also to synthesize this distinction back into an "American" canon. Richard Blanco's 2013 inaugural poem provides an exemplary instance of this operation and is discussed in this volume's epilogue.

While the individual represented the antitotalitarian values of a democratic society, then, the *unique identity* of the individual represented the values of a pluralistic society. Creative writing programs "help[ed] to affirm the messy peopleness of people, their difference from each other, and the value of respecting such differences."[82] Increasingly, the creative writer's voice was not a megaphone of the multiversity, but—where creative writing programs understood themselves as anti-academic, connected to public and not university life—of a multicultural society. Indeed, today "creative writing depends on and affirms difference in content. Everybody has a story to share, and the value of a story is its uniqueness." In his 2013 Annual Report of the Association of Writers and Writing Programs, the executive director, David Fenza, affirms this vision: "Walter Lippmann wrote, 'The great social adventure of America is no longer the conquest of the wilderness but the absorption of fifty different peoples.' It's the job of writers, of course, to help with that adventure of embracing so many others—narrating their lives, making sympathies among like and unlike characters, illuminating our world."[83] But while MFA program writers display multiple and contradictory formulations of voice as writerly identity, that is, multicultural identity, these identities often provided a fairly uniform formulations of the voice as an American citizen. There are certainly exceptions, enough to warrant treatment beyond the scope of this study. Meanwhile, poet-critics asserted projects outside of, and in visible opposition to, program-era voice. But before we turn to the protests of the poet-critic, who offered alternate formulations to the dominant models of voice and citizenship: how did the national poetry office evolve under the priorities of state verse culture during the program era?

## The Poet Laureate as the Expressive Subject

Lines off his line became smoother
And smoother and more and more
Know-how came in the window
And verses rolled out the door.
Now everyone in the market
Knows his new works are sure
To be just as the country wants them:
Uniform, safe, and pure.
—REED WHITTEMORE, "THE LINES OF AN AMERICAN POET"[84]

I went into Russia armed with mental pictures of marching men, wide peasant women in shapeless skirts. . . . I expected to see dark babushkas galore . . . Russia. Land of the cold heart, the regimented mien. . . . Among the poems I offer is my longish "The Life of Lincoln West," detailing the traumas of a little black boy who, in a roundabout way, begins to recognize and value his identity. Fedorenko is enthralled. Missing my point entirely, he rhapsodizes over little Lincoln. . . . I ponder on this, and I begin to get very angry.
—GWENDOLYN BROOKS, "BLACK WOMAN IN RUSSIA," 1997[85]

In "The Lines of an American Poet," Reed Whittemore compares the "creative" labor of writing poetry to mechanized assembly-line production:

"His very first verses were cleverly / Built, and the market boomed / Some of the world's most critical / Consumers looked, and consumed." His critique is self-suspicious: "the smooth lines" describe the "lines off *his* line." Satirizing the creative writing industry's production of uniform commodities, Whittemore was wary of writing for readers as consumers. He meanwhile worries that the potentially slower production of the poet-critic refuses his responsibility to "the country." In "Notes on a Certain Terribly Critical Piece," Whittemore positions himself not as the assembly-line poet but as the poet-critic:

> I have been busy writing a terribly critical
> Piece on the nature of poetry.
> Poets should never do this. They should look out,
> Not in. They should be terribly
> Vital, as I understand it, not as my piece
> Is, lethal. God forbid. All the same
> I have been writing my piece and when I have finished
> I shall rest a few days, then revise and revise it.[86]

Here again, we see the divided pursuits of the poet-critic retard the process of "rolling verse the door." Critical labor demands "rest" and "revision." However, this rest is likened to death—more "lethal" than "vital" and less connected to its public audience. The poet-critic turns "in" rather than "looking out." Whittemore's several layers of self-conscious irony digest the fraught new implications for the role of the poet-critic vis-à-vis the new role of the American creative writer. He describes the division between poets who "look in . . . [to] writ[e] terribly critical / [p]iece[s]" and those who "look out . . . just as the country wants them." Whittemore hoped to poke fun at both.

When Whittemore assumed the national poetry office in 1964, the role was still described as a librarianship:

> The Library's consultant in Poetry gives advice on improving the literary collections; recommends new material for purchase; assists in acquiring manuscripts and books through authors and collectors; and advises on bibliographic and reference work in his field. He also meets with scholars and poets using the Library's facilities, and he gives

editorial supervision to the Library's program to tape-record contemporary poets in readings of their works.[87]

At least on paper, the job description had not changed much since the library defined the duties in 1943. The perception of the office, however, had evolved since Frost's occupancy and the National Poetry Festival. Whittemore assumed the motto of "The Useful Arts" and "set out to stir up a cultural storm . . . and became convinced that all poetry consultants hereafter should do the same." Like Frost, who saw a natural collaboration between the poet and politician, Whittemore understood the office as one in service of the state—if from a more critical perspective: "the language of Washington . . . could use poets." As consultant, he arranged two informal meetings with "officials in various governmental agencies" to address the role of artists and writers in government.[88] And, in a practical simulation of the "useful arts," Whittemore also wrote the text of the Thomas Jefferson Memorial pamphlet for the National Park Service. "The core of the experiment" was to see if he could "reinstate the writer as author," activating the appearance of the individual speaking voice in the typically anonymous, diffuse expository field of bureaucratic prose.[89] The "use" of the poet was to perform expressive voice as "the language of Washington"—to proclaim the singular first-person voice in the service of the state.

Whittemore also saw the implications of his role on the geopolitical stage. As national poet, he served on an International Cooperation Year planning committee, a United Nations project commemorating the twentieth anniversary of its founding. A White House Conference on International Cooperation was planned to take place in November and December of 1966. "The difficulties of sponsoring a significant effort in international cooperation while our government deploys and employs military forces all over the world seem very great," he observed. Later that month, Librarian of Congress L. Quincy Mumford wrote to Stephen Spender to make the first international appointment to the poetry office: "Perhaps the time has come to consider the possibility of inviting a distinguished English poet, especially if he could be one who has become almost as much 'at home' in the American scenes as one of our own. It would be particularly appropriate during International Cooperation Year," he wrote. "It seemed appropriate to appoint a citizen of the nation which has been our longtime friend and ally" to the role of the national poetry office,[90] emphasizing the U.S. as the international leader in democratic cooperation. Meanwhile, the library could still claim the poet's apoliticism: when members of Congress protested the appointment of Spender as an "importation of a minor poet with dubious political sentiments," Mumford replied tersely: "the post is not supported by appropriated funds."[91]

Debates about state support for the arts were topical on the eve of the passage of the National Endowment for the Arts. "My own private feelings are that . . . no government program encouraging things as they are would serve any purpose not now being served by private funds," Whittemore reflected after attending a two-day conference titled "What to Do with the New Government Foundation for the Arts and Humanities." Unlike Frost, who advocated for federal support of the arts, Whittemore felt that private support reflected the values of an open society and that "any program encouraging radical changes in the teaching and general promulgation of our humanistic culture would be met with cries of dictatorship." The Association of Literary Magazines of America also witnessed heated debates. Karl Shapiro reminded the symposium of the lesson of the Bollingen Prize: "Institutions, whether the newspaper, the university, the foundation, or the government, can only deaden or paralyze art. . . . No academy should ever be put in the position of having to arbitrate and establish the values of works of art. This great and glorious Library had its knuckles rapped many years ago when it started to give out poetry prizes. And a good thing, too."[92]

Allen Tate, as ALMA honorary president, spoke in favor of foundation subsidies for little magazines. He did, however, "warn against the legislative powers of foundations, excusing the Guggenheim and Bollingen foundations from that vice."[93]

The international focus of the poetry office in the mid-1960s mirrored that of the creative writing industry. Appointed a year before the founding of the International Writing Program at Iowa, and serving during International Cooperation Year, Spender served to highlight the national image of America as an international leader. Spender called himself "unconsciously American," reflecting that he had "acquired rather quickly an American point of view" during the time he spent in the States after the war; he had recorded his poetry with Lowell for the recording archive in 1948 and lectured twice at the library, in 1959 and 1962. The vision of the national poetry office, like Iowa Writers' Workshop, expanded to the political world stage. In the footsteps of Frost, Spender proposed a conference on translation: "Behind the Iron Curtain a new generation of poets is emerging who attach more importance to the appearance of their poems, translated, in other countries than in their own countries, where the intellectual climate is so oppressive and conformist, and there is no vital discussion of poetry except along the lines of whether it is political or anti-political."[94] American poetry, however, was a safe haven for individual expression, supported by the state's "apolitical" ideology of freedom. "The question of translating . . . has become a very living and urgent problem to writers in other languages,"[95] Spender wrote in his proposal, which notably describes a conference on "the translators and the translated," a designation that structures act of translation as an intervention rather than exchange, or indeed as a form of global aid work, in which the poets in "oppressive and conformist" states are rescued by the Western translators. The project's premise that writers from other countries "attach more importance to the appearance of their poems, translated" reflects Engle's claim to American universalism via internationalism.

Spender's proposal did not result in a conference during his term, but instead planted the seed for an International Poetry Festival held two years later. At the White House Conference on International Cooperation, moreover, the Department of State made rare use of the consultant as a laureate, requesting that Spender write an occasional poem: "we all think that a poem written and read by you will adorn the occasion." Spender read "Poem for a Public Occasion" during the opening program of the conference.

In the late 1970s and early 1980s, the Library of Congress became concerned with the ethnic and gender identity of its poetry chair occupants—increasingly considering the national poet as a "representative" American citizen. The library's interest in the identifications of its occupants is reflected in the correspondence of Librarian of Congress Daniel Boorstin (1975–1987), who was especially proactive in soliciting nomination advice for the 1978 post after a "Consultant's Reunion" on March 6. Thirteen of the twenty-four poets who had served as consultants attended the reunion: "In the morning, the poets [met] privately to discuss . . . the present state of poetry, the role of the library in contemporary literature, and the special role of the poetry consultant" and in the evening they gave a public reading.[96] "When you asked my advice about whom to appoint as the next Consultant in poetry, I failed to mention someone who would be an excellent but perhaps unexpected choice," William Jay Smith wrote to Boorstin a week later.

> I refer to N. Scott Momaday, a Professor at Stanford University. He would an excellent choice because his poetry, based largely on the tradition of his Kiowa forebears (he is three-quarters Kiowa), is superb, but unexpected because he is better known as a novelist (his The Way to Rainy Mountain won the Pulitzer Prize for fiction in 1969). But Mr. Momaday's work is truly poetry in the deepest sense. . . . My friend Colonel William F. Odom, the Military Assistant to Dr. Zbigniew Brzezinski at the White House, knew Mr. Momaday some years ago in Moscow and was very impressed by him.[97]

Two phrases are circled in red pencil by library administrators: "N. Scott Momaday" and "three-quarters Kiowa."

Boorstin had also solicited suggestions from Richard Eberhart. After suggesting a few names, Eberhart considered:

> Then there is the quasi-political idea of ethnic groups. I am delighted, as is everybody with Robert and I would not mind seeing him followed by Gwendolyn Brooks, who is I suppose our major black woman poet. I was at Dartmouth last fall, we saw a good bit of her, she is delightful and charming. She would grace the office, but then I thought of Michael Harper, who teaches at Brown and was at the reading, a huge man and old friend, certainly one of the best younger black poets.[98]

Gwendolyn Brooks would not assume the office until 1985. In the meantime, Boorstin would take the advice of Daniel Hoffman, director of the Writing Program at the University of Pennsylvania, who had been in Washington for the consultants reunion reading: "We all looked forward to a stimulating day, but few foresaw that monster turn-out in the evening, or the cheers for the biggest serial poetry reading on record. That crowd certainly gave proof that the public in our most political city really appreciates the poetry programs made available to them over the years by The Library of Congress." Hoffman proposed William Meredith, invoking the posthumous support of Frost: "Robert Frost knew him well and proposed him years ago, when he was unable to take a year or two off, but that impediment no longer obtains." Hoffman also emphasized that Meredith was well-equipped for the consultantship as a *public* figure: "Meredith makes a good public appearance—he'd be a first-rate Consultant in Poetry."[99]

Meredith suggested the subsequent appointment of Maxine Kumin (1981–82), who would call the library a "gentility-ridden, traditional, hidebound place."[100] Kumin diversified the Poetry and Literature Center's reading series, inviting black lesbian feminist Audre Lorde, Marge Piercy, Richard Shelton from Arizona, and the Pueblo poet Leslie Marmon Silko. Adrienne Rich, who had turned down six previous invitations to appear at the library, accepted Kumin's summons and met an at-capacity crowd in the Coolidge Auditorium in April 1981. Kumin held the most politically active consultancy to date: she spoke out against increased military spending and was attacked by the conservative Heritage Foundation. She also held one of the first "activist" or project-based posts, hosting a brown-bag luncheon series for women poets. The scope of subsequent national poets' projects, however, would reflect broader national interests, rather than, as here, an advocacy project of the occupant. Kumin has written that she was accused by Boorstin of "abusing the hospitality of the Library."[101] For the library, the lesson from Kumin's consultancy was that the politics of identity would importantly inform later national poet selections, but that their work must also be appropriately "hospitable" to the state. Her term, however, helped change the way the uses of the office were imagined; several years later, congressional legislation would formalize the position as a representative public figure.

*Rebranding the National Poetry Office:*
*The Creation of the Poet Laureateship*

On December 20, 1985, the United States Congress renamed the poetry chair the poet laureate consultant to the Library of Congress. President Ronald Reagan—who in March would publicly recite from memory Robert Service's "The Cremation of Sam McGee"—signed the act, declaring the laureate's "position of prominence in the life of the Nation," encouraging "each department and office of the Federal Government to make use of the services of the Poet Laureate Consultant in Poetry for ceremonial and other occasions of celebration" and announcing an annual poetry program in cooperation with the National Endowment for the Arts.[102]

Senator Spark M. Matsunaga, a Democrat from Hawaii, was influential in the retitling of the poetry office. In 1963, a year after the National Poetry Festival, Matsunaga had proposed legislation to establish the office of poet laureate of the United States. Unsuccessful, he reintroduced the legislation to each subsequent Congress.[103] Finally, in January 1985, when legislation to reauthorize funding for the NEA and NEH through the National Foundation on the Arts and Humanities Act came up for a vote, Matsunaga added his bill as an amendment. In the original draft of S.213, the poet laureate would have a clearer relationship to federal power: the laureate would be appointed by the president of the United States. The president would also determine the laureate's salary, "not to exceed sixty per cent of the salary of a Federal district court judge." Librarian of Congress Boorstin requested a revision of the amendment so that the laureate would continue to be appointed by him. He also revised the title to bear more continuity with the history of the office: the national poet would be called the "Poet Laureate Consultant in Poetry."

The congressional act did not function merely ceremonially, encouraging "each department and office of the Federal Government to make use of the services of the Poet Laureate . . . for ceremonial and other occasions of celebration." The third section (c) of Public Law 99–194 formalized a partnership between the NEA and the national poetry office at the Library of Congress. When the amendment was discussed by the Senate Committee on Labor and Human Resources, of which Matsunaga was a member, the committee authorized the NEA chairperson to sponsor an annual "Poetry program" in cooperation with the library's poet laureate and under the guidance of the chairperson of the National Endowment for the Arts, with the advice of the National Council on the Arts, "at which the Poet Laureate Consultant in Poetry will present a major work or the work of other distinguished poets."[104] Funds for the program were authorized for fiscal years 1987–1990.

The congressional rebranding of the Library of Congress consultant in poetry as the poet laureate participated in the conscious effort of state arts administrators and politicians to renew the prominence of national poetry in the civic sphere.[105] As we have learned, although supported by the Huntington gift fund, the national poetry office had always been imbricated in other arms of the federal government. And while the Huntington fund continued to support the office after its rebranding as the poet laureateship, the library could no longer claim—as Luther Evans did to angry patriots during the Bollingen affair or to Adrienne Rich when she first refused invitations to read at the library in state protest—that its activities were exclusively "paid for by private funds." But to understand the history of the national poetry office, and especially its operations today, we must also understand the irony of its federalization in the mid-1980s. The Reagan administration had intended to abolish the NEA completely in 1981, and the department's budget was decreased from $158.8 million to $148.5 million that year. Today, the office of the poet laureate no longer supports its activities with NEA funds, according to Robert Casper, head of the Poetry and Literature Center.[106] The state's renewed interest in the uses of the national poetry office reflects its Reagan-era birth and a new era of privatized cultural production: the rebranding of the laureateship tied it to NEA directives, but those achieved through the increasingly regular collaboration of the Library of Congress with private-sector cultural institutions, 501(c)(3) literary organizations that would also increasingly undertake "poetry projects," in particular the Poetry Society of America and the Academy for American Poets and later the Poetry Foundation. At the same time, poetry appeared in federal and state legislation with new frequency in the form of regionalist designations of official cultural poems. These symbolic installments functioned similarly to the ceremonial use of the poet laureate, whose more consequential national service would be expressed through national poetry projects carried out in book clubs, writers' houses, and classrooms.

Gwendolyn Brooks and Robert Penn Warren are, at first glance, an odd pair to represent the redefinition of the national poetry office. Brooks was the last poet and first black woman to hold the title of consultant in poetry in 1985–86. Her successor and the first poet to hold the title of poet laureate was Warren, who had also held the consultant in poetry over forty years earlier in 1944–45. The Library of Congress press release announcing Brooks's appointment celebrated her as the "Pulitzer Prize-winning portrayer of black urban life."[107]

Brooks was unprecedently active as a consultant, using her office more regularly than her predecessors, sponsoring poetry competitions in elementary and high schools, and hosting a luncheon reading series at the library. Like Kumin's brown bag lunch program for women writers in 1981–82,

*Figure 3.2* Gwendolyn Brooks with young fans in Brownie outfits, circa 1985–1986. According to Brooks, who captioned the back of the photograph, "(next to me is Michelle Bebo (daughter of Keith Bebo) who came in Poetry Office for an autograph)." Image courtesy of the Library of Congress, Photographs, Illustrations, and Objects Series.

Brooks's term anticipated the new public responsibilities of the office. Meanwhile, Warren was, from the view of library administrators, a fitting successor to Brooks as the first black female appointee because of his own high profile as a social commentator who had publicly recanted his racist views during the civil rights movement. Warren, famously the coauthor of New Critical cornerstones—*An Approach to Literature* (1938) with Cleanth Brooks and John Thibaut Purser and *Understanding Poetry* (1939) with Cleanth Brooks, instructive books whose legacies are born out in English Department and especially creative writing pedagogies today—also contributed to the Southern Agrarian manifesto *I'll Take My Stand*'s defense of racial segregation ("The Briar Patch," 1930). Warren later recanted his views in an article in *Life* magazine, "Divided South Searches Its Soul," published July 9,

1956—notably in the wake of the 1954 *Brown v. Board of Education* Supreme Court decision. Because of his former views, he was treated as a visible proponent of racial integration. Warren reissued an extended version of the *Life* article as a small book, *Segregation: The Inner Conflict in the South* in 1956 and published an interview collection with Civil Rights movement leaders including Malcolm X and Martin Luther King in *Who Speaks for the Negro?* in 1965.[108] In 1974, Warren was selected to give the National Endowment for the Humanities' Jefferson Lecture, the federal government's "highest honor for achievement in the humanities," and received the Presidential Medal of Freedom in 1980.

In the press release announcing his appointment, Librarian of Congress Boorstin declared Warren to be a "characteristically American man of letters. . . . If there is any person today whose work unites our America in its splendid variety, that person is Robert Penn Warren." Warren's 1944 appointment announcement, meanwhile, bore no trace of his "characteristically American" qualifications.[109] The poet laureate was, finally, the *national* poet. Moreover, the Library of Congress bulletin announcement of his first term as poet laureate emphasized his "numerous books of biography and social commentary" over his "essays and books on literary topics."[110] Warren was not qualified for a second term as a New Critic or Tate's former Fugitive affiliate, but as a purposefully anachronistic national representative. Serving as a counterweight to the national identity represented by Gwendolyn Brooks, Brooks and Warren together represented a multicultural society—and a new public charge to the office.

### *"What does the Consultant in Poetry do?"*:
### *Voicing State Service*

Gwendolyn Brooks, one of Engle's "favorite mentees,"[111] is a case study in how a national poet negotiates their duties in relationship to state power. Her poetry has been historicized as both accommodationist and radical—as Juliana Spahr describes, Brooks was during the 1950s "one of few black poets recognized by Official Verse Culture."[112] However, after attending the second Fisk Black Writers Conference in 1967, Brooks left her publisher Harper and Row to publish *Riot* (1969) with Broadside Press, run by

Dudley Randall "out of his home and [. . .] in the process of becoming one of the most significant publishers of black poetry."[113] Many critics, and Brooks herself, credit a shift in her work and career to the 1967 conference.[114] Spahr suggests that *Riot* represented a short-lived moment in which poetry "put a certain pressure on U.S. literary production," a pressure that would result in subsequent works that "challenged racialized and gendered universalism, were frequently contestatory towards capitalism, and refused accommodationist inclusions."[115] Indeed, on the one hand, Brooks may have been an Engle mentee, but her work often refused state priorities even when acting as a state poet.

Several years before Brooks was appointed consultant in poetry, for example, she attended the Sixth Annual Soviet-American Writers Conference, visiting Kiev, Leningrad, and Moscow alongside prominent Soviet and American writers, including Harrison Salisbury, who organized the trip, Erica Jong, Arthur Schlesinger Jr., Robert Bly, and Susan Sontag. Brooks used the occasion intended for cultural diplomacy to instead draw attention to domestic race relations in the United States.

In a rarely treated travel narrative of the conference, "Black Woman in Russia," Brooks described the cultural tensions between the Soviet and American writers, who sat at "two 'opposing' tables, for two 'opposing' representations, American and Soviet. (At one point . . . Studs Terkel, briskly cheery, urged a shuffling: *Why* should all the Americans be sitting at a table together?—*that* was the trouble in the world today! Let's mix it up a bit!—let's be really *together!* . . . and for the duration of our get-together Studs Terkel [was] at the Soviet table with Russians. The rest of us remain[ed] in our appointed places."[116] At the first dinner of the conference, Brooks and Robert Bly were invited to read. Brooks was "angry," then "angrier and angrier," and then "sorrowful" with the response to her poem "The Life of Lincoln West," which "detail[ed] traumas of a little black boy who, in a roundabout way, begins to recognize and value his identity."[117] "Missing my [Brooks'] point entirely," Nikolai Fedoronko, a large personality among the Russian group, "rhapsodize[d] over little Lincoln" and told a story about how he had encountered a "*touchable* and absolutely *darling*" black boy himself, with "nice white teeth and nice rough hair. Everyone *loved* to pat his nice rough hair." After her reading and Fedoronko's story, Brooks was especially disturbed to find that both tables were "*pleased* with me [Brooks]."[118] Two meetings later, she called for the attention of the entire cultural exchange congregation. Rather than using the platform to represent American racial harmony or the ideals of American life, Brooks challenged both sides of the aisle. Yes, "a nuclear blast would abolish everything, including all aspects of ethnic concern for ethnic bliss," she began her address:

> Nevertheless, I am going to call attention to *blackness*, a matter no one else here feels any reason to cite." (I am, of course, the only black in the room . . .). "No one *else* here feels any *reason* to cite blackness because on the Soviet side there is very little association with blacks. Soviets *see* very few. And on the *American* side there is as little association with blacks as can comfortably be managed, although there is great opportunity in the United States of America, where there are many many many many many MANY blacks. . . . Mr. Fedorenko said something very large: "WE NEVER PAID ANY ATTENTON AT ALL TO THE FACT THAT HE WAS NEGRO."!!!!!!!!! Well, I have to reply to this. *Essential* blacks—by that I mean blacks who are not trying desperately to be white—are happy to have you notice that they do not look like you. *Essential* blacks don't *want* to look like you.[119]

When she assumed the national poetry office, too, Brooks articulated her responsibilities to the state in complex ways. Her "Annual Report of the Poetry Office" stands as an archival record of her year in office, performing expressive voice in the context of administrative labor for the government. Its emphatic opening line, "<u>What</u> does the Consultant in Poetry <u>do</u>?," recalls the annual report of Robert Hayden, the first Black writer to hold the consultantship (1976–78): "What does the Consultant in Poetry *do*?" his report had likewise opened. Brooks's report signals the continuation of Hayden's voice in the state record, the double-underlining acting as a typographical echo of his question. In other respects, the report departs from its predecessors. Reports were historically provided in business letter format; hers is written by hand, in large, loose script on unconventionally sized paper. It stands in stark contrast to Bishop's systematic enumeration of duties in her 1950 report, which was antiexpressive in her adherence to generic normalization, as if to emphasize the performative mastery of an administrative voice—the inverse project of Whittemore's attempt to express creative voice within typically bureaucratic National State Park brochures. Brooks's report, meanwhile, is expressive via individualizing narrative and unique stylistic features. Bishop and Brooks's respective unorthodoxies are functionally strategic, especially where both assert a relationship to secretarial labor that is absent from other annual reports. Bishop had explicitly and repeatedly referred to the poetry office secretary Phyllis Armstrong, acknowledging her work through the narrative use of "we" in tallying the duties completed during the appointment. Brooks, writing her report by hand, forgoes secretarial labor altogether. Bishop had also quantified her own labor through generically standardized features such as the enumerative catalog, minimizing the perception of subjective interference. Brooks, in a lively first-person, takes an opposite approach:

> Well, I have never worked so hard in my life! I have never been so exhausted, but gloriously exhausted, at the end of a day. (Or [double-underlined], at the end of a night, since some [double-underlined] days have been nine a.m. to eleven thirty p.m. "days" If you're puzzled!—some Mondays and Tuesdays I've stayed in my office on the Third Floor until time for a Coolidge Auditorium poet-presentation, meanwhile answering letters, planning my little programs, sorting files, etc. After that 8 p.m. reading or lecture there is, as you know, a reception, from which Nancy, Jenny, myself, Security and the servers are the last to leave.

The report is an opportunity to acknowledge "Security and the servers" as the "last to leave" the working day, but it is equally an opportunity to punch out alongside them on the library's record. Moreover, while her labor is not officially quantified, e.g., by an hourly wage, Brooks suggests ways in which her "flexible" schedule obscures other work she performed. While she was given "choice" about what days she would work and officially only served two days a week, both what appear to be "choice" and a two-day work week turn out not to be:

> I mentioned Mondays and Tuesdays: those are the working days I was allowed to choose [double-underlined]. I myself threw in Wednesdays 9 a.m. to 3:30 p.m. because otherwise I could not have handled the enormous mail that had to be answered nor the many many visitors, local and foreign, I was pleased to receive. (There have been

exceptions, of course: on certain pre-arranged dates I have been out of the office because of campus-visiting in other states.)

While Bishop's report expresses no affective connection to the office, however, Brooks's work is persistently "delicious" and a "pleasure."[120]

Brooks's report, moreover, did not capture the full record of her activities in the office. The "enormous mail that had to be answered" had not been left to the poetry office secretary. She had instead responded to letters herself: to students, prisoners, aspiring poets. "Dear Richard: I received your beautiful letter today, and have to answer right away"[121]; "Dear Sue: Please keep writing! You have a nice sense of rhythm. / Read a lot of poetry (and prose . . .). And keep a journal, for exciting thoughts and impressions! Hold on!";[122] and to one Alfred Cabey she suggested, drawing from her experiences with community-based black publishers like Broadside Press, to "form a little publishing cooperative among people who write poetry—publish each other's work in neat, inexpensive books."[123] To Lloyd Lazard, a prison inmate in New Orleans, she described how "another poet [Etheridge Knight], who had your problems . . . came out to teach at universities and to publish books and to lecture," and had even "read his poetry here [at the Library of Congress on Brooks's invitation] a couple of weeks ago, and [it] was much enjoyed." She also provided critical feedback: "Your poetry needs a little polishing. (I say that because you wanted me to give you an honest opinion.) First, let me tell you the good things: . . . Now, Mr. Lazard, let's talk about clichés . . ." before going on to provide publishing advice: "Then get a pack of envelopes."[124]

I point to these descriptions of work in Brooks's report and to her personal letters to American citizens for multiple reasons. First, they reveal how the bureaucratic burdens of what Evan Kindley calls "poet-administrators" of first-generation modernism had evolved into that of teacher-advisers during the program era. But, more important, they reveal how national poets articulated their relationship to the Library of Congress in distinct ways. Like her surprise address at the Soviet-American Writers Conference, Brooks negotiated new ways to interpret the functions as consultant in poetry, and in turn helped to reimagine the office itself.

When Brooks began a lively lunchtime reading series, for instance, it caused something of a stir among library administrators. "I pay each reading poet $200. It is understood, as you early told me to make it understood,

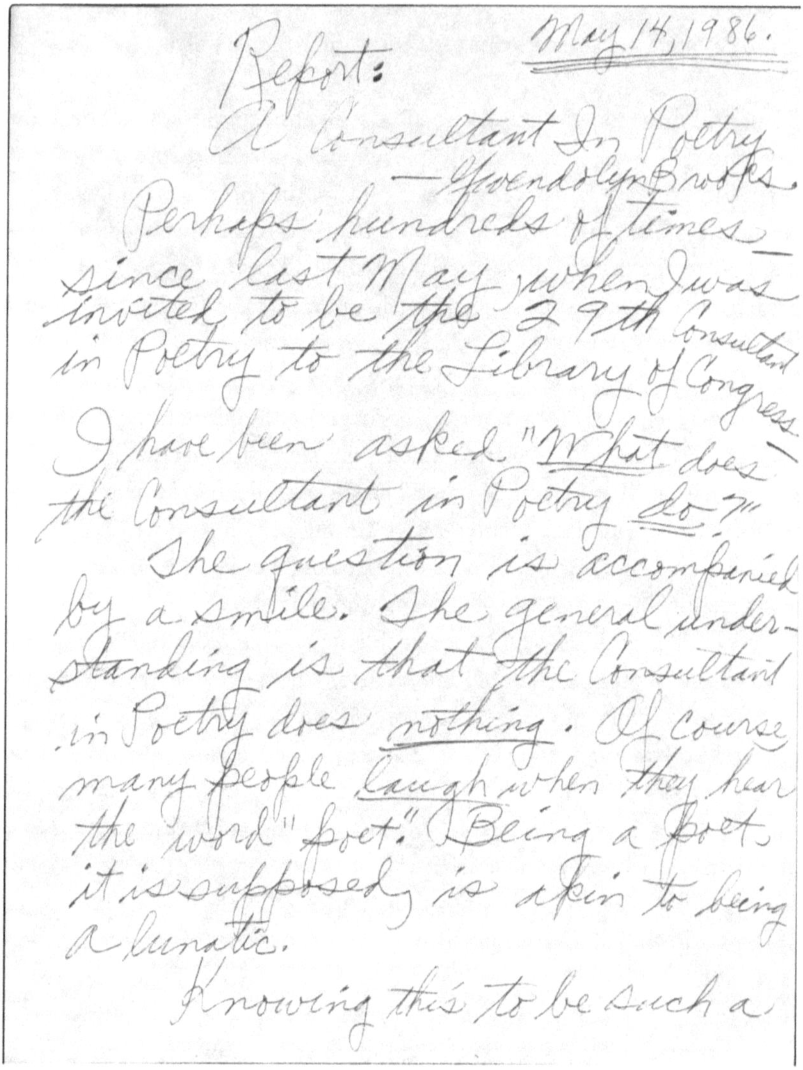

> Report:  May 14, 1986.
>
> A Consultant In Poetry
> — Gwendolyn Brooks.
>
> Perhaps hundreds of times, since last May when I was invited to be the 29th Consultant in Poetry to the Library of Congress I have been asked "What does the Consultant in Poetry do?"
>
> The question is accompanied by a smile. The general understanding is that the Consultant in Poetry does nothing. Of course many people laugh when they hear the word "poet." Being a poet, it is supposed, is akin to being a lunatic.
>
> Knowing this to be such a

*Figure 3.3* The opening page of Gwendolyn Brooks's "Annual Report to the Librarian of Congress, May 14, 1986." The report summarized her work and the activities of the poetry office during her time as consultant. Image courtesy of the Library of Congress Manuscript Division.

when any funds leave my hands, that the Library of Congress is not involved. In no way is the $200 'an honorarium.' I merely wanted to help out," Brooks explained to John Broderick, assistant librarian of Congress for research services.[125] "I recall our talking about the lunchtime series," Broderick wrote to Brooks toward the end of her term, but "what surprised me after the fact was your having given the poets, out of your own pocket, some traveling money":

> This is generous, as is your having treated so large a group at lunch. There is nothing wrong with either step, from the Library's point of view, and that is probably a good use of the honorarium [Brooks's own salary as the national poet]. Nevertheless, I can see why Sam Hazo was confused about the arrangement. Traditionally, we have sought to insulate the Consultant from "arrangements," issuing invitations, making payments, etc. The lunches in the past have been small-scale affairs, manifestly something different from the nighttime program. They have not seemed like rivals to the evening programs, which it is in our interest to cultivate. We [the Library's evening programs] need great audiences too, as Whitman observed.[126]

Brooks's reading series, and her nonbureaucratically sanctioned use of her stipend to support its attendees, apparently threatened the library's more traditional evening programming through the Whittall Fund. But Broderick also acknowledged that "if you [Brooks] have surprised me on occasion, that probably means I was getting set in my ways and in need of a surprise or two."[127] After Brooks, a woman would not hold the office again for the next seven years, nor another black poet for next eight (Mona Van Duyn served in 1992–93, and Rita Dove in 1993–95). Today, however, Brooks's "surprising" work as consultant is remembered admiringly: "When I started at the LOC 11 years ago, staff were still talking about all she [Brooks] did up in the Poetry Office," Casper told me in 2022.[128]

Meanwhile, as Brooks concluded her term, some former national poets, including Whittemore, worried about the implications of the redesignation of the post as the poet laureateship. Would the more official state title impose artistic or ideological limitations on the work of poets who held the office? Was the poet now obligated to perform ceremonially and uncritically at state events? "Those who are concerned with the words 'poet laureate' being added to the title of the Consultantship need not be," Brooks wrote in her report. "The Administration of the Library of Congress in the past has shown great intelligence in selecting sane, talented, and discriminating people for this post—after all, it selected me, didn't it? . . . It will not select people who will consent to write celebrations for sanitary installations. There is nothing to fear."[129] Broderick also attempted to reassure critics, although he did not see a problem with poets performing ceremonially or at what Brooks called "sanitary installations." Incoming poet laureate "Red Warren's schedule will be very much like that of Robert Frost. . . . As for the invitations—and their name is Legion—the Laureate Consultant does not have to accept any of them. Mr. Warren has already declined several, and we have declined others in his name," he wrote. Indeed, Broderick hoped that laureates would follow Frost as a model of a public-facing national poet: "Having said that, I must say that the laureateship is a new ball game—in scale, if nothing else. Frost's appearance at the Kennedy inauguration manifestly secured a hearing for American poetry in ways not institutionalized earlier. I would be very surprised if the Laureate Consultant were not asked to take part in future inaugurals or lesser state occasions. Is that bad? He or she need not accept, but will it be so bad a thing to be asked?"[130]

Richard Wilbur (1987–88), Howard Nemerov (1987–1990), and Mark Strand (1990–91) followed Robert Penn Warren as the first class of poets laureate. Wilbur, Nemerov, and Strand did not perform at state occasions, nor did Nemerov perform at President George H. W. Bush's 1989 inauguration, as Broderick had predicted. But he was right that the transformations to the office helped to "institutionaliz[e] . . . American poetry" before a national audience. With new NEA and growing private institutional cooperation, the office was gradually "professionalized" as a public figure—the poet laureate would no longer be expected to write an Annual Report,[131] for instance, leaving such duties to library administrators to meanwhile focus on their role as an outward-facing national representative. And in the 1990s poets laureate would indeed assume Frost's legacy, undertaking public programming with national reach. By this time, MFA culture was in full force. Two of the first four poets laureate in that decade held MFAs from the Iowa Writers' Workshop; one was an Iowa native who attended the University of Iowa; and the fourth, Joseph Brodsky, was a former Soviet citizen and prisoner who would proclaim the values of "creative writing [as] an essential exercise of individual freedom."[132]

## Manifestos Against Manifest Destiny: Poet-Critics and the Case of Language Poetry

The same year Robert Penn Warren took office as the first poet laureate, *In the American Tree* (1986), an anthology of Language writing edited by Ron Silliman, was published.[133] This anthology rejected the voice-based poem of the 1970s–80s state verse culture, if not, as in Marjorie Perloff's provocation, the entire tradition of lyric poetry:

> For if, as Paul de Man puts it, "The principle of intelligibility, lyric poetry, depends on the phenomenalization of the poetic voice," what do we make of those poems like Lyn Hejinian's or Charles Bernstein's, whose appropriation of found objects—snippets of advertising slogans, newspaper headlines, media cliche, textbook writing, or citation from other poets—works precisely to deconstruct the possibility of the formation of a coherent or consistently lyrical voice, a transcendental ego?[134]

While the anthology constituted a radical departure from the dominant aesthetic values of state verse culture, its publication by the National Poetry Foundation, affiliated with the University of Maine (Orono), suggests its project was *not* anti-institutional or antiestablishment—as many critics have assumed—but an institutionally situated claim to an alternate national tradition.[135]

The anthology did not mean to be neatly retrospective. Two years later, Ron Silliman, Carla Harryman, Lyn Hejinian, Steven Benson, Bob Perelman, and Barrett Watten's coauthored "Aesthetic Tendency and the Politics of Poetry: A Manifesto" appeared in the journal *Social Text*. Locating their work as "a body of writing, predominantly poetry, in what might be called the experimental or avant-garde tradition," the polemic asserts continued "consequential stakes" in the "antagonism between the status quo and work that does not share the canonical norm."[136] The writers situate this body within a U.S.-based poetic lineage: around 1970, a number of writers, adopting the experimental techniques of Gertrude Stein and Louis Zukofsky, began "writing in ways that questioned the norms of persona-centered, 'expressive' poetry." Many of these writers came into contact and dialogue with one another in New York and San Francisco, especially outside of universities; "interaction with others... was exciting and affected the work of all." Silliman and his colleagues compare their collective activity to that of San Francisco Renaissance, Black Mountain, and New York school poetry communities. However, they argue, while recent movements in the visual arts had been met with a largely tolerant response—enjoying gallery patronage, if not rapid integration into institutional frameworks—the reaction to avant-garde poetics had been less embracing:

> The narrowness and provincialism of mainstream literary norms have been maintained over the last twenty years in a stultifyingly steady state in which the personal, "expressive" lyric has been held up as the canonical poetic form. On analogy to the visual arts, where the "avant-garde" is felt to be a virtual commonplace, the situation of poetry is as if the entire history of radical modernism... had been replaced by a league of suburban landscape painters.[137]

Language poets did not restrict their critique of "I"-centered verse to the historically privileged subject. In the creative writing workshop of the 1980s, the individual voice was used to articulate socially marginalized class, race, and gender positions, but with delimiting formal qualifications: poems written from the voice-based subject position still lacked the privilege of formal experimentation and were often viewed as primarily political projects with the implicit obligation to identify the individual self *as* a marginal subject position. "Details of raw particularity" served not merely to authenticate the experience of the individual speaker but now as evidence for an identity label. As such, the political imperative to enlist marginalized subjects in the project of identity-based voice was resisted by many theorists and in the practice of much Language poetry, including Hejinian's *My Life*.

Although sometimes read as a "feminist" work, the text of *My Life* (1987) rejects an identity-based, politically efficacious subjectivity in favor of a nonphonocentric, nonnarrative, and unstable "I." Its title purports autobiographical intent, but *My Life* refuses the autobiographical speaker's conventional rhetoric of self-restoration and self-promotion achieved through chronological progression. *My Life* instead follows a procedural pattern: the first edition, published when Hejinian was thirty-seven years of age, consists of thirty-seven chapters of thirty-seven sentences; and a second edition, published eight years later, reflects a life ongoing in forty-five chapters—adding eight new chapters and eight new sentences to the first thirty-seven.[138] *My Life* opens:

> *A pause, a rose, something on paper* A moment yellow, just as four years later, when my father returned home from the war, the moment of greeting him, as he stood at the bottom of the stairs, younger, thinner than when he had left, was purple—though moments are no longer so colored. Somewhere, in the background, rooms share a pattern of small roses. Pretty is as pretty does. In certain families, the meaning of necessity is at one with the sentiment of pre-necessity. The better things were gathered in a pen. The windows were narrowed by white gauze curtains which were never loosened. Here I refer to irrelevance, that rigidity which never intrudes. Hence, repetitions, free from all ambition.

"I" is free from all narrative ambition. Hejinian's "first year" includes "four years later," rejecting a linear chronology that would narrate the forward-looking progress of a life. Sudden jumps from reminiscent detail to expository abstraction—exhibited in sentences 1–3—are unmediated by transitional links from sentence to sentence, or indeed from clause to clause. Its "raw particulars" form a catalog, rather than authenticate a narrative, of the subject.[139]

Unlike a conventional autobiography, *My Life* lacks specific descriptions of its subject's physical person. While photographs documenting the subject often occupy the middle pages of autobiographies, this centralizing aesthetic representation of identity is absent,[140] avoiding immediate readerly assumptions regarding authorial identity; for example, the poem does not ascribe a singular race or gender to its subject. Hejinian notes the nonassignment of gender, especially, as a self-conscious effort: "As such, a person on paper, I am androgynous."[141] For Hejinian, however, androgyny does not exist in the neutral, genderless pronoun "it." Rather than avoid gendered representations altogether, she genders her persona multiply; throughout the poem, the phrase "I wanted to be" commonly serves as a uniting anaphora: "I wanted to be both the farmer and his horse when I was a child, and I tossed my head and stamped with one foot as if I were pawing the ground before a long gallop" (29); "I wanted to be a brave child, a girl with guts" (32); "If I couldn't be a cowboy, I wanted to be a sailor"

(46). In naming multiple occupational ambitions, Hejinian names multiple gender performances. While she refers to wanting to be "a girl with guts," for instance, the notion of femininity is here doubly undermined: being "brave" and "with guts" are stereotypically masculine qualities; the structure of the sentence, phrased as "I wanted to be" could be posed by either a male or female persona regardless of the specified "want," and the clausal juxtaposition of "child" against "girl" gender neutralizes the latter. The pastoral trope of "the farmer and his horse" is echoed in a subsequent section: "The horse, too, is a farmer."[142] This statement, by grafting the identity of "the horse" onto "the farmer," the latter of which becomes an independent subject in section eight of the text, questions the application of occupational labels, an investigation furthered in Hejinian's musing that "if I couldn't be a cowboy, I wanted to be a sailor."[143] Together, the sentences conflate the roles of the "child," "farmer," and "horse." Hejinian probes not only occupational labels, but categories of human and nonhuman ("child" and "farmer" versus "horse"), implicitly gendered and nongendered ("farmer" is implicitly gendered masculine, while "child" and "horse" remain neutral). Furthermore, by suggesting that she would like to be either "a cowboy" or "a sailor," Hejinian highlights the nonessentiality, even arbitrariness, of occupational labels, and in turn asks us to question the essentiality of other categories troubled in the text (gender, human).

Complicating the identification of speaker and author through the category of female voice, *My Life* asserts theoretical affinity with contemporaneous critiques of gender in the age of identity politics.[144] In Judith Butler's view, "releasing the category of women from a fixed referent"—as seen with Hejinian's troubled subject position—allows "something like 'agency'" to become possible.[145] The multiple subjectivity of *My Life* worries with Butler, Wendy Brown, and other critics of identity politics that uncomplicated access to a stable subject position (i.e., woman) precludes agency by reinforcing the exclusions and normalizations that necessarily constitute its stability. Indeed, like the workshop poem, Language writing understands that "I" functions as a representative citizen—where the agency of the speaker is an analogue for the political agency of the author or reader.[146] But by complicating readerly access to the "I" speaker, Language writing rejects a politics that would seemingly achieve its demands through essentialized representations of its assumed beneficiaries.

This provocation, however, itself solidified as a representative position in the discourse of the "poetry wars." Silliman and his colleagues in "The Politics of Poetry" had worried about the problems with labeling their manifesto's subject: "While we are flagrantly writing this article as a group, the perceptive reader will already have noticed that until this point neither the 'Language School' nor 'Language Poetry' have been named. This is no accident; the politics of group identity are a problem (and challenge) particularly for those alternately identified within and without it."[147] Indeed, voicing an aesthetic politics *against* voice especially posed problems in the genre form of a manifesto.[148] The manifesto typically exercises "wide intelligibility" and "appears to say only what it means, and to mean only what it says," historically relying on a reductive language of dichotomy to forward a transparent public expression of will. The manifesto tends to refuse dialogue or conciliation, instead declaring a position that appears "univocal, unilateral, single-minded."[149] Complicating the most reductive reading of the genre, here the authors nod to those language-oriented writers not subsumed in the "we" and its narrative trajectory, suggesting the subject of the manifesto as something less than unified and monolithic. Interestingly, *Social Text* had suggested the addition of the subtitle "A Manifesto" to the article—an editorial addition that helped to legibly define, if also delimit, Language writing as an aesthetic practice. Moreover, the authors invoke the genre form's signature subject position "we" to ultimately adopt a "rhetoric of exclusivity," even if betraying cognizance of the subject's exclusionary consequences. The manifesto thus advanced a fixed subject position for the sake of political intelligibility, and successfully so. *My Life*, for example, would be canonized as a frequently taught text in university classrooms, and "Language poetry" remembered as a discrete movement in literary history.

Indeed, Language poetry would become the best example of "official verse culture" among peer community-based poetry movements during the 1970s–1990s. Language poetry articulated itself alongside the Black Arts movement; New Narrative; the also San Francisco-based Sister Spit; Kitchen Table: Women of Color Press, the activist feminist press run by and for women of color established by Barbara Smith in response to the suggestion of friend Audre Lorde; June Jordan's Poetry for the People; the Taco Shop Collective (Taco Shop Poets); as well as innumerable other community-based, identity-based, and variously antistate poetry movements, affiliations, and commitments that emerged during this period.[150] Operating largely outside of the creative writing industry, and without the support of government and semiprivate fellowships afforded through the state-private complex, such movements deserve fuller treatment and recognition than a history of state verse culture proper allows. Language poetics, however, unlike many of these movements, acquired traction *within* institutions, with many of its members moving into teaching positions in the academy during the 1990s.

Migrating from salon to seminar, Language poets thus marked an institutional position distinct from the creative writer of the same era—building their careers instead as poet-critics. "The Language poets are taking over the academy," Andrew Epstein proclaimed in 2000, "but will success destroy their integrity?"[151] "What is a poet-critic, or critic-poet, or professor-poet-critic?; which comes first and how can you tell?" Charles Bernstein, who cofounded one of the Language poetry's seminal and movement-defining publications, *L=A=N=G=U=A=G=E* (1978–1981), asked the year before:

> Do the administrative and adjudicative roles of a professor mark the sell-out of the poet?; does critical thinking mar creativity, as so many of the articles in the Associated Writing Program newsletter insist? Can poets and scholars share responsibilities for teaching literature and cultural studies or must poets continue to be relegated to, or is it protected by, creative writing workshops, where, alone in the postmodern university, the expressive self survives?[152]

"Aesthetic Tendency and the Politics of Poetry: A Manifesto" insisted that the aesthetic project of Language poetics was not based in an institution of higher education. Opposing the mainstream to avant-garde poetic traditions, the manifesto suggested that the avant-garde has a necessarily limited relationship to institutions—or, rather, a relationship where institutions serve the project as sites against which to articulate a speaking position. In this context, the move of many prominent Language writers into academic positions in the years following the manifesto's publication might be surprising, or read as a repudiation of their earlier radical and anti-institutional poetics. Hence Bernstein's question: "do the administrative and adjudicative roles of a professor mark the sell-out of the poet?" Ron Silliman, for example, would accuse former affiliates like Bob Perelman of complicity in an academic regime "constitutively hostile to the polysemous presence of radical poetry."[153] If Silliman's accusation, however, can be seen as performative—the public staging of a dialogue between poet-critics who share mutual values—the movement of Language poets into the academy could also be seen as a movement of their poetics outward: a refusal of the coterie enclave, but not of the aesthetic possibilities it had sheltered.

Within the wider field of state verse culture, moreover, Language poetics acquired a complex set of strategies within academic institutions.[154] By emerging as a uniquely coherent challenge to workshop voice in the mid-1980s, Language poetry simultaneously encountered the problem of its own coherence. Stylistically distinct individual texts were more successful in expressing a polysemous poetics than were statements of poetics like "A Manifesto," which purported to reject officialdom through the vehicle of an academic journal—or indeed than admiring critical histories to follow that paradoxically enshrined Language poetry as a voice against voice. Language poetics of the 1990s abandoned reactionary voice against, in favor of critical ventriloquization within, the academy.

In other words, while Language poets effectively presented themselves, and continue to be canonized as "antiestablishment," this "antiestablishment" banner was also copied on English Department Xerox machines, if not on departmental letterhead. In postwar America, *all* verse became establishment verse. But just as earlier creative writing–era fiction presented marginal voices that managed not to be absorbed into the multiculturalist discourse of marginality—McGurl, for example, points to Octavia Butler's disruptive aesthetics within the genre system[155]—so too creative writing–era poetry offered modes of resistance. Because of poetry's historically more dependent relationship with the university, the divide between the programmatic norm and experimental alternatives in poetic production has remained (visibly so since the early 1990s) within the academy. In the 1990s–2000s, the production of Language poetics within the university provided an alternative to the production of workshop voice within the state discourse of multiculturalism and identity politics, reflecting the distinct traditions of the creative writer and of the poet-critic.

In chapter 2, we observed Robert Frost as a central player in an emerging state verse culture and his influence on the consolidating Cold War ideology of poetic voice at the National Poetry Festival in 1962. In this chapter of our history, we saw how this ideology found its most effective and wide-ranging expression in the programmatic workshop norms of the postwar creative writing industry. As the industry's dominant model of voice evolved to advance identity over individuality, the details authenticating narratives of personal experience increasingly functioned as markers of difference to represent the values of a pluralistic society. Community-based movements, as in the case of Language poetry, variously rejected this model—refusing its demands for narrative intelligibility, peppered with voice-authenticating markers of difference—an aesthetic model set out by MFA program founders like Engle as early as the 1960s. Noninstitutionally based poetic affiliations, as in the case of Language poetry, posed figures of alienated or complicated poetic voice resistant not only to the expressive individual but also to the tokenizing politics of identity governing the workshop poem. But we must recognize how this resistance became institutionalized within the academy—hence a feature of what MFA culture today, as with Fenza of the AWP, rejects as "academic" writing—to ultimately bear the "officialdom" it had purported to oppose. Poet-critics, including Language writers and their successors, thus participate ambivalently in official verse culture, though they continue to resist participation in the norms of *state* verse culture shaped by Cold War–era creative writing. Meanwhile, contemporaneous community-based movements were never written into official verse culture, or indeed state verse culture.

The rise of the state-supported creative writing industry during the Cold War has fundamentally changed the public perception of poetry, and in turn of its nationally representative office. From 2012–2022, every poet laureate held an MFA, as do more recent administrators of the office; in 2019, for example, the office was run by three MFA holders. When Casper took on the position, it was the first of a nationwide search—previous administrators of the office had been internal hires, government librarians, or bureaucrats. And the populist, national-reach notions of creative writing's AWP today would begin to dominate the operations of the office in the 1990s and 2000s. In these decades, poets laureate began undertaking large-scale poetry projects "to increase the visibility and appreciation of poetry in the United States."[156] Several national poets, as we have learned, had undertaken more unofficial "outreach projects" previously—Maxine Kumin facilitated brownbag luncheons, a series of poetry workshops for women, during her term in 1981–82, and Gwendolyn Brooks managed popular lunchtime poetry readings and "and actively brought poetry classes and contests to young people in the inner city" in the last year of the consultantship from 1985–86.¹⁵⁷ After the terms of Poets Laureate Robert Penn Warren and Richard Wilbur, Howard Nemerov led poetry seminars for visiting high school classes. With the exception of Brooks, these programs were all held on-site at the Poetry and Literature Center at the Library of Congress.

But Joseph Brodsky, a Russian émigré who assumed the laureateship after Nemerov, introduced a more ambitious vision for poetry office programming: state poetry projects with a "national reach."¹⁵⁸

CHAPTER IV

## Civil Versus Civic Verse

### National Projects of U.S. Poets Laureate, 1990–2022

> Civil poets do not expect to summon sticks, stones, and beasts to a new order. Their language fulfills the idioms shared by contemporary citizens in social, political, economic, legal circumstances; their poems imply not only legitimacy but even hope for the survival of existing social institutions.... Rather than art from the edge, one may prefer poems that engage life at some distance from boundary conditions. The objective, as Arnold said, is to see life steadily and whole. Or is it to change life?
> —ROBERT VON HALLBERG, *LYRIC POWERS*

Joseph Brodsky, a former Soviet citizen, assumed the national poetry office three months before the dissolution of the USSR in December 1991. In his first public lecture on Capitol Hill in October of that year, Brodsky lamented the lack of popular access to poetry in the United States, "the supreme form of locution in any culture," and proposed distributing books of poetry in public places such as airports, supermarkets, and hotel rooms. "There is now an opportunity to turn the nation into an enlightened democracy," Brodsky pronounced. The *Library of Congress Gazette* reported that America's new poet laureate, who had been "sentenced to hard labor in an Arctic gulag for 'social parasitism' and 'decadent poetry' by his government" and immigrated to the United States in 1977, had opened the 1991–92 literary season with "a stinging attack on the token publishing of poetry and the tepid response of literate people to it." Brodsky "praise[d] the English language," but "warned that America is on the verge of a tremendous cultural backslide." Brodsky's former Soviet citizenship and imprisonment made for a compelling platform—indeed, a geopolitical stage—from which to comment on the function of poetry in American national culture. Brodsky's rhetoric was provocative: "*No other language accumulates so much as does English. To be born into it or to arrive in it is the best boon a human can come across. To prevent its keepers from full access to it is an anthropological crime, and that's what the present system of* distribution of poetry boils down to. I don't know what's worse—banning books or not reading them."[1]

Brodsky said he "took the job in the spirit of public service. . . . Maybe I fancied myself as a sort of surgeon general and just wanted to slap a label onto the current packaging of poetry—something like 'This Way of Doing Business Is Dangerous to National Health.'" Brodsky's estimation of the office as a "public service" position alongside elected policy makers explicitly, and self-consciously, recalls Frost's term in the office. He quoted from Frost frequently during his lecture, telling the story of his first encounter with Frost's poetry. Brodsky also closed the lecture by reciting two poems from memory. The first was Frost's "Provide Provide."[2] Frost had read this poem, the last poem that Frost had read publicly during his lifetime, at the 1962 National Poetry Festival during the Cuban Missile Crisis.

Frost's vision of national poetry—which took him from Kennedy's inauguration to a Mission to Moscow—found a fitting inheritor in Brodsky. Both Frost and Brodsky believed that poetry had a unique and consequential role in national culture. Both emphasized the special capacities of the English language, and phonocentrism emblematized by the act of recitation, wherein knowing and saying an English-language poem "by heart" demonstrates that its values have been incorporated into the individual speaking subject. Finally, both professed a populist mission. Brodsky's ideas "for getting poetry into the hands of literate Americans 'age 15 and up'" did not formally coalesce as a national project until after his time in office, when he founded the American Poetry and Literacy Project with Andrew Carroll. The organization produced and distributed a low-cost anthology, *101 Great American Poems*, published by Dover Thrift Editions, but its endeavors were short-lived. Brodsky's explicit linking of poetry to national values, especially where his former Soviet citizenship made him a mouthpiece for America in the ideological contest of the Cold War, was, however, impactful on the office of the poet laureate. The public reach of Brodsky's vision laid the groundwork for the national poetry projects that would come to define the poet laureateship in the mid-1990s.

The projects that followed, supported by a complex of state-private interests, became the central operations of the national poetry office in the second half of the 1990s, the 2000s, and into the present. Poet Laureate Robert Pinsky's Favorite Poem Project was the first of this new breed. The Favorite Poem Project: Americans Saying Poems They Love invited

Americans to "say aloud" a favorite poem at a series of poetry readings and subsequently for national audio and video archives. Pinsky, who served an unprecedented three terms as poet laureate (1997–2000),[3] and is often referred to as a "civic poet," transformed the responsibilities of the office for subsequent national poets, who have since regularly undertaken national poetry projects.[4] Billy Collins's Poetry 180: A Poem a Day for American High Schools project (2001–3) provided a website-based curriculum of 180 poems "designed to make it easy for students to hear or read a poem on each of the 180 days of the school year."[5] Ted Kooser's American Life in Poetry project (2004–6) "provide[d] newspapers and online publications with a free weekly column featuring contemporary American poems."[6] These projects, which aspired to spread poetry across the nation as a kind of public good—poetry, they premised, had the power to transmit cultural values of liberal democracy, neighborly civility, and standard American English at its most elegant and magnanimous—represented a broader shift in the civic function of poetry in the 1990s and 2000s.

The national poets who led them, moreover, represent a category of cultural producers that Robert von Hallberg calls contemporary American "civil verse poets" or "civil poets." For civil poets, poetry has a socially affirmative function: "their poems imply not only legitimacy but even hope for the survival of existing social institutions."[7] Civil verse poets "craft their art from the medium that effectively represents the nation," typically speech-based or phonocentric verse. By "imitat[ing] speech," civil verse poems often "derive the authority of their poems from that of a social class, and beyond that from the premise that civil, secular values properly govern cultural life." Civil verse poets hold to the conviction that "poetic language is not properly separate from ordinary language"—as Frost insisted—to show that "value is to be found within the constraints of recognizable contemporary linguistic and social practice."[8] By elevating what Frost called "ordinary speech" to an urbane style that appeals to the "the college-educated, northern, metropolitan class of the intelligentsia [that] asserts its authority to explain the world," the contemporary civil verse poet affirms that social class and the values that govern it.[9] For von Hallberg, the work of Robert Hass, Robert Pinsky, Jorie Graham, and Louise Glück are chief examples of this project. Their poems "demonstrate the flexibility, exactness, and vitality of standard American English as an artistic medium. If gorgeous or acute art can be made in this medium, one may have faith that just legislation, judicious litigation, and progressive social policy can also be crafted from this general social position."[10]

It is no coincidence that Hass, Pinsky, and Glück all served as poets laureate in the late 1990s and 2000s. Like Frost and Brodsky, Pinsky and other national poets discussed in this chapter fully appreciated the civic power of poetry—promoting "standard American English as an artistic medium" and the social order it affirms not only through their own writing but especially through the projects they undertook as poets laureate. This conviction animated post–Cold War state verse culture more broadly: in 1990, the Library of Congress administered its first poetry prize since 1949; in 1993, an inaugural poem was read at a presidential inauguration for the first time since 1961; and in 1996 the NEA and literary and educational organizations invested in the creation of National Poetry Month and related programming that presupposed the culturally edifying function of civil verse.

Not only did the national poetry projects of the 1990s–2000s share Frost's estimation of poetry as a powerful tool with which to shape civic life, but they drew from Frost's poetics the values of phonocentrism and populist accessibility. Von Hallberg's description of "civil verse," moreover, is helpful in linking the nationalist priority of Frost's poetics and the voice-based model of the workshop poem allied with the national project. Is the purpose of poetry "to see life steadily and whole," von Hallberg asks through Arnold—"Or is it to change life?"[11] For civil verse poets, it is the former. Other poetic communities, including the poet-critics of the Language poetry tradition, have meanwhile interpreted what Pinsky calls "the responsibilities of the poet" differently.[12] Rather than to affirm, poetry should interrogate—even "attack," in the case of Charles Bernstein's *Attack of the Difficult Poems*—existing social structures or dominant forms of national discourse.[13] This poetics, at least philosophically and formally, proposes the "sticks and stones" that von Hallberg speaks of: nonlinear and often nonnarrative structures, often relying on sound rather than the explicit sense of language, as well as on the semantic possibilities of the visual space of the page rather than the directive of the podium. Rather than represent the voice of the citizen, what we can think of in contrast to "civil verse" as *civic* verse represents purposefully alienated figures of voice to consider the noncitizen or alien other. In Frost's politics of poetic form, the checks and balances of a formal order govern the agential speaker. In the Language poetry tradition, too, form and voice are analogues for social structure and for the representational agency of the citizen-subject. But rather than affirm existing social order, purposeful disruptions of form and phonocentric voice represent the incoherence or political illegibility of subjects in the neoliberal discourse of individual agency and identity politics.

National poetry projects initiated in the 1990s and 2000s that meanwhile promoted *civil* verse do not reflect the singular missions of individual poets. While Pinsky's own writings, for example, are in strong ideological alignment with the Favorite Poem Project mission statement, national poetry projects are not only the products of individual initiatives but also carried out in the grip of institutions. These projects represent a complex of state- and private- funded interests and support. This state-private complex, through which the Library of Congress and NEA partner with several mainstay literary organizations in cooperation with mutual patrons, funded the majority of public-facing poetry programming in this period, as it does in the present. National poetry projects also reflect the longer lineage of this complex. Most significantly, a stunning—although, as we know from archival revelations uncovered in chapter 1, foreshadowed—act of patronage seismically transformed one of these organizations, *Poetry*, in 2002. The magazine's parent organization, the Modern Poetry Association, was reborn as the Poetry Foundation the following year. The MPA/*Poetry* had worked with the library since the postwar years, and shared with the library common patrons. But following the controversial $100+ million grant from Ruth Lilly of Lilly Pharmaceutical, the Poetry Foundation became a key—perhaps the singularly most influential—player in state verse culture of the late 2000s and 2010s. National poetry projects not only define the contemporary poet laureateship, then, but reflect the workings of the increasingly privatized institutional complex that motors contemporary American poetic production.

### State Verse Culture After the Cold War: National Poetry Projects in Context

National poetry projects are significant expressions of a broader shift in the civic function of poetry in post–Cold War America. As Brodsky's "poetry for the masses" rhetoric indexes, the early 1990s heralded a second wave of the Frost-Kennedy era national arts vision. The 1990s saw the reintroduction of government poetry prizes, inaugural poetry, and new forms of institutional cooperation between the state and literary organizations.

In 1990, the Library of Congress awarded the inaugural Rebekah Johnson Bobbitt National Prize for Poetry to James Merrill. Merrill, who had previously won the Bollingen Prize, was honored for *The Inner Room* (1988).[14] It was the first prize the library had awarded since the spectacular fiasco of Pound's Bollingen Prize in 1949, after which Congress ruled that a democratic government should not award prizes in "matters of taste." As we have seen, during the Cold War of the 1950s and 1960s the government played arbiter in matters of literary taste often more covertly—through CIA fronts and by building its relationship with private interests. Congress reversed the Bollingen Prize–inspired ruling in 1988, when the Bobbitt family endowed a $10,000 biennial prize to be given every other year in memory of President Lyndon B. Johnson's sister, Rebekah Bobbitt. The Bobbitt Prize was in fact conceived of as "the new Bollingen Prize," according to Robert Casper, who heads the Poetry and Literature Center, which runs the office of the poet laureate at the Library of Congress.[15] Casper recalls that it was the intention of Philip Bobbitt, the son of Rebekah Bobbitt, to establish a prize that mirrored the Bollingen in structure. "The Bobbitt family wishes to endow a national poetry prize . . . in memory of Rebekah Johnson Bobbitt with the Bollingen Award as the model which the Bobbitt Prize might resemble," Librarian of Congress James Billington noted in a memorandum recounting an initiating conversation with Bobbitt.[16] Interestingly, Bobbitt would echo the language of the Library of Congress as it directed the fellows "to be deflected by political considerations" when administering the infamous first Bollingen Prize.[17] In a letter to Nancy Galbraith, then-acting director for the Poetry and Literature Program, Bobbitt wrote that "there ought to be a prize given by the nation and *politics should play no part in it*."[18] But the "new Bollingen," unlike its predecessor, would reflect the interests of a more robust, and mutually imbricated, set of state and state-private interests. "Congress through the distinguished chairman of the Oversight Committee, the White House, the American Academy of Poets, and several distinguished former poetry consultants have all concluded that the Library ought to re-enter the field and that the Rebekah Johnson Bobbitt prize I have discussed is the appropriate way to do this," Bobbitt wrote.[19] Unlike the singular committee of the fellows that awarded Pound the first Bollingen Prize, the Bobbitt Prize mission reflects a nationalized conviction—"the point is for the Library of Congress, home of the U.S. Poet Laureate, to also have a national prize in poetry as part of its efforts to promote the art"[20]—an imperative that now necessarily involves the support of other federal bodies, and of literary institutions, namely the AAP. The prize remembers the Bollingen, then, but records the legacy of the Kennedy-Johnson era of state arts support: not only ceremonially, in honoring President Johnson's sister, but in its administration, which conjoins state and private interests. The AAP had considerable weigh-in when the prize was established, acting in the selection of prize winners. Since 2009, the prize committee has consisted of three judges: one appointed by the poet laureate, one appointed by the librarian of Congress, and one appointed by the Bobbitt family. Betty Sue Flowers has been the Bobbitt family choice on all committees since, and previously in 2008. As with the selection of the poet laureate, formally the librarian of Congress approves the final decision.

In addition to the reintroduction of a government-sponsored poetry prize, poetry was reintroduced at presidential inaugurations in the 1990s. Specifically, Democratic presidents-elect harkened back to Kennedy at their inaugurations with the renewed use of the inaugural poem. Maya Angelou's performance of "On the Pulse of Morning" at the 1993 presidential inauguration of Bill Clinton was the first inaugural poem since Frost's "The Gift Outright" in 1961. Miller Williams performed at the second inaugural of Clinton in 1997. The trend continued into the 2000s, with Elizabeth Alexander and Richard Blanco performing at the 2009 and 2013 inaugurals of Barack Obama, respectively. The role of inaugural poetry in relation to the national poetry office, and as an expression of the consolidation of state verse culture, is discussed in the epilogue.

Through the library, NEA, and Office of the President, the post–Cold War state meanwhile increased visible collaborations with private organizations to promote the place of poetry in national culture. On April 1, 1996, President Clinton announced the celebration of the first annual National Poetry Month: "National Poetry Month offers us a welcome opportunity to celebrate not only the unsurpassed body of literature produced by our poets in the past, but also the vitality and diversity of voices reflected in the works of today's American poetry . . . Their creativity and wealth of language enrich our culture and inspire a new generation of Americans to learn the power of reading and writing at its best."[21] Introduced by the

Academy of American Poets, National Poetry Month—like those of Pinsky, Collins, Kooser, and other laureate-initiated projects through the national poetry office—demonstrates the cooperation of various private and public organizations to define the "vital place" of poetry in American culture. While "National Poetry Month is a trademark of the Academy of American Poets," the AAP "enlisted a variety of government agencies and officials, educational leaders, publishers, sponsors, poets, and arts organizations to help." In 2015, for example, National Poetry Month partners included the American Booksellers Association, the American Library Association, the National Council of Teachers of English, the National Endowment for the Arts, 826 National, New York City Department of Cultural Affairs, New York State Council on the Arts, and Random House; sponsors included Graywolf Press, Papyrus Greeting Cards, the Poetry Foundation, and Random House Children's Books and Scholastic.[22] National Poetry Month calls itself "the largest literary celebration in the world."[23]

The Academy of American Poets provides an instructive proxy for the evolution of state verse culture, as the trajectory of its cultural ambitions parallel that of the national poetry office. It was incorporated as a nonprofit organization in 1936, the same year the national poetry office was endowed at the Library of Congress. Marie Bullock founded the organization, inspired by Joseph Auslander, the first national poet (1937–1941).[24] She would remain president for the rest of her life, and, with Bullock at the helm, the AAP was a regular presence and supporter of library programs. The celebration of the fiftieth anniversary of the AAP, hosted by the Library of Congress in 1983, was the library's "starriest poetic event" since the National Poetry Festival in 1962.[25] The AAP also supported many consultants through prizes and fellowships: at the time of Bullock's death, its fellowship for poetic achievement, for example, had honored consultants including Frost, Williams, Aiken, Bogan, Adams (twice), Tate, Bishop, Kunitz, Eberhart, Hecht, Nemerov, and Hayden.[26] Academy of American Poets activities also paralleled the rise of the creative writing industry, launching a "Poetry-in-the-Schools" program in 1966. Bullock supported library efforts in informal ways, too—in 1973, for example, she helped Consultant in Poetry Daniel Hoffman lobby the United States Post Office to issue a commemorative stamp honoring Robert Frost.[27] Anthony Hecht would say that Bullock did "more for the art of poetry and individual poets over the years than any institution whatever."[28] The AAP founder died in 1986, the same year the title of the national office was changed from the consultant in poetry to the poet laureate. The rebranding of the office was a fitting bookend for the lifelong patron of national poetry: Bullock was instrumental in establishing administrative connections and a shared value of literary populism between the AAP and the library's poetry office over fifty years' time.

National Poetry Month is not only the legacy of an individual patron or the AAP, however, but of NEA efforts to deepen and extend links between public institutions and private industry.[29] From its inception, the NEA understood itself as a "complement" to the more primary "private support of culture." The United States' "system of arts support is different from that of other nations, most of whom rely on government as the primary patron," Chairman Francis Hodsoll affirmed in 1984.[30] National Endowment for the Arts leaders, especially during the Reagan years, emphasized private giving to the arts as "an American tradition." While August Heckscher, Kennedy's original arts consultant, envisaged a more "European model" of federal arts programming, by which the central government would support national theaters, museums, cinema, dance companies, and literary arts academies, the second NEA chairman, Nancy Hanks (1969–1977), "preferred to forge numerous partnerships with nonprofit arts organizations, rather than underwrite the budgets of official state-sponsored arts groups."[31] The Hanks era developed the infrastructure to channel government funding into private organizations; and subsequently Chairman Livingston Biddle (1977–1981) sought to relocate the material and civic impetus for arts organizations more squarely within the private sphere. His threefold provisions for the future of arts funding maintained that 1. "responsibility should be primarily based on private and local initiatives"; 2. "a comprehensive restriction on federal interference in the determination of NEA grantees," which Biddle defined as "a provision basic to freedom of expression and the creative spirit of the arts" should be in place; and 3. "The Endowment must be guided by a council of private citizens."[32] By the time that Biddle's successor Hodsoll (1981–1989) began his term, the Presidential Task Force on the Arts and the Humanities could assess that *"there is no other nation in the world in which the principle of private giving to sustain cultural institutions is so deeply ingrained."*[33]

The federal arts mission of the Reagan era, whereby corporate relationships and individual patronage were "complement[ed]" by federal funds,[34] persists into the present. Like the National Poetry Month, the large-scale arts projects undertaken by U.S. poets laureate, and many projects underwritten by the NEA, are in part and sometimes entirely funded and administrated by private organizations. Indeed, National Poetry Month was established the same year as an infamous NEA budget cut. That the NEA budget would be slashed at the same time as it so visibly invested in the discourse of "national poetry" is telling. The federal government maintains a vested symbolic interest in the arts, but one that it manages through satellite bodies in an increasingly privatized cultural economy.

National Poetry Month, the projects of poets laureate, and other state verse culture programming have received both criticism and praise. For some, the Brodsky- and Pinsky-led era of national poetry programming diluted poetry as what should properly be Poundian "caviar": "The creation of the poet laureateship of the United States is a comical insult to a serious enterprise, and one which ought properly to be mocked every chance one gets," Joseph Epstein wrote in *Poetry* magazine in September 2004.

> Poetry is caviar—an acquired taste, and not for most people, not even for some highly intelligent people—and I happen to believe it demeans it to sell it as if it were hot dogs. Many of the poets laureate have, I fear, seen the job as calling for slapping on the mustard while moving the dogs along . . . [while] the laureates' "projects" usually have had to do with efforts to widen the readership of poetry, the business of the poet is to write as well as possible and leave the job of promoting poetry in a manner sure to vulgarize, if not utterly trivialize, it alone.[35]

Others, like Liam Rector, saw the populist accessibility of national poetry programming as a triumph against elitism of Pound and subsequent generations of academic poet-critics.[36]

This discourse insists on the bifurcated lineages of modernism out of Pound and Frost, which as we have seen would be articulated in the distinct institutional roles of the academic poet-critic and the creative writer of the program era. It understands poetry as either the caviar of difficult elitists or the hot dogs of hospitable Americans. For Charles Bernstein, the debate is not between caviar and hot dogs, but rather about what national poetry programming promotes as "safe" poetry versus poetry that is "difficult":

National Poetry Month is about making poetry safe for readers by promoting examples of the art form at its most bland and its most morally "positive." The message is: Poetry is good for you. But, unfortunately, promoting poetry as if it were an "easy listening" station just reinforces the idea that poetry is culturally irrelevant and has done a disservice not only to poetry deemed too controversial or difficult to promote but also to the poetry it puts forward in this way. "Accessibility" has become a kind of Moral Imperative based on the condescending notion that readers are intellectually challenged, and mustn't be presented with anything but Safe Poetry.[37]

The rhetoric of "moral imperative" and edification ("poetry is good for you") that Bernstein critiqued in 1999, three years after the creation of National Poetry Month, persists in the mission statements of National Poetry Month programming and the national poetry projects of poets laureate today. The assertion that the poems these initiatives promote are "examples of the art form at its most bland," however, like Epstein's division between caviar and hot dogs, takes the limitations of "poems" themselves as objects of critique. But we should equally attend to the discursive and structural limitations of the state-normed projects through which poems circulate and are understood by readers. National Poetry Month does not so much promote "Safe Poems" as define poetry as "safe" or as a mode of cultural production that expresses "civil verse" values that are unthreatening to the interests of the broad swath of private and public players that support them. Rather than enable diverse aesthetic agendas or a diverse range of programming, National Poetry Month and formally privately sponsored national poetry projects are shaped by state involvement. That is, while often only complemented by NEA dollars, they are nonetheless made possible through the agency's bureaucratic reach and, in the case of poets laureate initiatives, centralized by the institutional singularity and symbolic capital of the national poetry office.

This results in a fairly uniform articulation of the possible cultural uses of poetry in national discourse. The Poetry and Literature Center at the Library of Congress, the Poetry Foundation, and poetry-affiliated projects of the National Endowment for the Arts all advocate for a central role for poetry in American culture: National Poetry Month "celebrat[es] poetry's vital place in our culture"; "The Favorite Poem Project is dedicated to celebrating, documenting and encouraging poetry's role in Americans' lives";[38] "The sole mission of this project is to promote poetry: American Life in Poetry seeks to create a vigorous presence for poetry in our culture";[39] "Welcome to Poetry 180. Poetry can and should be an important part of our daily lives."[40]

But what does it mean to promote "poetry?" In the context of these organizations' discourse, "poetry" typically acts as a proxy for a set of loosely defined national values. As many of these projects target K-12 public school classrooms as their mission or a subset of their mission,[41] promoting poetry means promoting those national values. In the case of Pinsky's Favorite Poem Project, for example, poetry is understood to "reflec[t], perhaps concentrate[e], the American idea of individualism";[42] to submit a favorite poem to the Favorite Poem Project is to participate affirmatively in the American idea of individualism. In the introduction to *Poetry 180: A Turning Back to Poetry*, the first published collection of the Poetry 180 project, Collins suggested that there was only a "limited store of smart, clear, contemporary poems"[43]—a rather incredible suggestion, given the enormity and diversity of the American poetic field—demonstrating that as broad and nonpartisan as these projects might appear, being products of multiple institutional agendas, they also make contestable claims about what models of poetic voice are nationally valued. Collins promotes "accessible" poems that are "easy to consume." The "hospitable" poem, written in standard American English, "do[es] not make demands," or by implication political demands, of the reader.[44] At the same time, this preference itself makes a quietly political declaration. In Poetry 180's instructions to teachers, Collins gives an example of a poem that might be read in the classroom—it is written by "John Smith" and entitled "In Memory of My Father."[45] The accessible poem, this example suggests, is especially "hospitable" to an imperialist American history and paternalistic literary canon.

While programs like National Poetry Month systematize the far-reaching interests of the NEA and corporate benefactors through the AAP, the national poetry projects of poets laureate unite institutional players through the office of the poet laureate at the Library of Congress. Pinsky's Favorite Poem Project is a partnership between the library, the Poetry Foundation, and Boston University, with original funding from the National Endowment for the Arts.[46] Random House published Billy Collins's Poetry 180's web-based anthology through the library as a commercially successful anthology.[47] Kooser's American Life in Poetry is a partnership of the Poetry Foundation and the Library of Congress and receives administrative support from the English Department of the University of Nebraska-Lincoln. The most common supporters of National Poetry Month and laureate-sponsored poetry projects include the NEA, AAP, and—most importantly since 2004—the Poetry Foundation.

### *Poetry* and Prozac: The Lilly Donation and the Birth of the Poetry Foundation

In November of 2002, *Poetry* announced the $100 million Ruth Lilly gift, the single largest gift ever donated to a literary group or journal.[48]

The donation came as a shock to the magazine. The reclusive heiress, eighty-seven, was the last surviving great-grandchild of Colonel Eli Lilly, founder of the pharmaceutical giant Eli Lilly and Company. Ruth Lilly's relationship with *Poetry* began in the 1970s, when she submitted poems to the magazine under her former married name of Guernsey van Riper Jr. The poems had been turned down with handwritten notes from the editor. She continued to submit poems, again receiving gentle letters of rejection. "[Your poems] certainly combine many attractive qualities: sensitivity, with a sense of humor, a knowledge of good poetry and the ability to quote aptly, terseness of expression," John Nims wrote to Lilly in 1982. "I'm sorry that none quite worked out for us. We do have a tremendous backlog, and even at best can accept only about 1 poem out of every 300 sent us. Difficult odds."[49] Nims meanwhile thanked Lilly for being a "friend to the magazine." Four years later, and the same year the national poetry office was rebranded the poet laureateship, Lilly endowed *Poetry*'s annual poetry prize: a $25,000 and, as of 2021, a $100,000 award in her name. In addition to the Ruth Lilly Poetry Prize, Ruth Lilly established two fellowships through the magazine in 1989. However, Lilly had not since been in contact with *Poetry* editors or members of its parent organization, the Modern Poetry Association, to suggest a subsequent donation—let alone one of such largesse.

Significant institutional restructuring of the magazine occurred in the wake of the mega-gift, which drew widespread media attention. The *Chicago Tribune* broke the news with a front-page story: "A Billionaire's Ode to Charity: $100 Million to Poetry Journal";[50] by 8:30 a.m. the next day

Joseph Parisi, the editor of the magazine, "had the *New York Times* at one ear and the *Los Angeles Times* at the other, with four other newspapers waiting for callbacks."[51] The gift would also prompt scholarly interest—organizational management literature has used the Lilly donation as a unique case study to understand the impact of large gifts on small non-profit organizations "because of the rareness of the event": mega-gifts are typically given to large organizations. The gift was also unique in that no restrictions were placed on its use.[52] Parisi, who had edited *Poetry* for two decades, resigned shortly after the donation was announced—first as editor, appointing Christian Wiman as his successor, in order to lead a newly established foundation overseeing the MPA board, and a few months later also resigning from the foundation. "Money changes everything," he said.[53]

The Modern Poetry Association became the Poetry Foundation, an independent, 501(c)(3) Chicago-based literary organization and publisher of *Poetry* magazine. The only previous retitling of the magazine or its administrative body occurred after the Bollingen affair, when Shapiro took over editorship and dropped the subtitle from *Poetry: A Magazine of Verse*. John Barr, an investment banker and author of six books of poetry, was appointed its first president in 2004. Barr, who had previously served on the board of the Poetry Society of America and taught in MFA programs,[54] pronounced a new populist vision for the foundation—rather than a grant-providing organization, post-Lilly *Poetry* would invest in joint ventures with other organizations to expand the public audience for the genre. "Poetry's golden age will come when it is in front of a general audience," Barr declared; "by growing the universe of readers who will buy books of poetry, the Foundation hopes to bring economic as well as artistic life to the business of writing poetry."[55] Barr's first visible symbolic action as president was the institution of a new prize, the Mark Twain Award for humor, carrying a $25,000 purse; the inaugural winner was the then best-selling poet in America, Billy Collins, who was poet laureate at the time the Lilly gift was announced. The foundation subsequently embarked on a series of initiatives, including the opening of the Harriet Monroe Poetry Institute, which partnered with the Aspen Institute to "identify ways of strengthening poetry and expanding its audience."[56] The website was restructured and *Poetry*'s mission statement was redrafted, emphasizing a public-minded appeal to wider audiences, mainstream media, and primary school classrooms: "The Poetry Foundation works to raise poetry to a more visible and influential position in American culture. . . . In the long term, the

Foundation aspires to alter the perception that poetry is a marginal art, and to make it directly relevant to the American public."[57]

Ted Kooser, poet laureate from 2004–6, led the first national project to benefit from the new wealth and populist mission of post-Lilly *Poetry*. "It is an honor," said Barr, "to be allied with the Library of Congress. Through the office of Poet Laureate, the Library has done much to celebrate the best poetry and enlarge its audience. We are natural partners in the American Life in Poetry project, which will help get good poetry back into the mainstream."[58]

The Poetry Foundation also found a fast ally in the NEA. Then-chairman Dana Gioia, who had met Barr when they both served on the board of the Poetry Society of America, applauded the Poetry Foundation for "reaching millions of people with poetry."[59] Prior to his NEA appointment by President George W. Bush in 2002, Gioia had reversed an over twenty-year sales decline at General Foods with his alliterative "Jell-O Jigglers" campaign.[60] Barr called himself and the NEA chairman "kindred spirits" because of their shared business background: "we could both read balance sheets and had this love for poetry."[61] The Poetry Foundation joined the NEA in supporting the continuation of national poetry projects, including Pinsky's Favorite Poem Project, and the two would coordinate a series of initiatives, beginning with Poetry Out Loud, a recitation contest for high school students, in subsequent years.

There were vocal critiques of the Poetry Foundation's handling of the Lilly windfall. Despite the foundation's statement that "*Poetry* has always been independent, unaffiliated with any institution or university—or with any single poetic or critical movement or aesthetic school,"[62] Stephen Yenser's indignant charge that "they're funded by drug money—literally—Lilly pharmaceutical!" points to at least one major affiliation.[63] Critics including Juliana Spahr and Steve Evans have suggested that it is an affiliation with consequential bearing on the aesthetic projects favored by the magazine and, moreover, partisan stakes in national economic policy. Evans went so far as to call the Lilly donation a well-timed prop to disguise the collusion of the Bush administration and the pharmaceutical industry.[64] During the same months Lilly made her donation, Evans notes, the Homeland Security Act of 2002 under consideration in Congress was revised to exempt the Lilly Company, a "long-standing supporter of Republican politicians as well as an indirect backer, through the Lilly Endowment, of the usual conservative causes," from lawsuits "related to the manufacture of Thimerosal, a preservative added to vaccines and thought by some to be a cause of autism." Evans maintains that "the heartwarming story of Ruth Lilly's handout to *Poetry* magazine was at least in part timed to draw attention away from the scandalous political payoff that had been snuck into the Homeland Security Bill and hurriedly signed into law by Bush."[65] To Evans, the relationship between Chairman Dana Gioia at the NEA, President John Barr at the Poetry Foundation, and Poet Laureate Kooser at the Library of Congress—"the businessmen poets" or "Poets for Bush"—was a powerful club conspiring "to prescribe Prozac poems" in the service of a broader political agenda.[66]

Whether or not one is persuaded by Yenser's accusation or Evans's incendiary exposé, the NEA, Library of Congress and Poetry Foundation are indeed the nexus between private and state interests that support contemporary national poetry projects. *Poetry*'s relationship with the library and private donors, however—including with the Lilly family—has a longer history.

Despite the "media frenzy" that followed the Lilly donation,[67] what went unmentioned, and what was indeed unknown, is that the Lilly family had ties with *Poetry* long before Ruth Lilly's 1980s bequests. As the Library of Congress archives brought to light, the Lillies communicated with *Poetry* as early as 1949. That year, with increasing urgency in the wake of the Bollingen affair, *Poetry* editor Hayden Carruth had repeatedly implored the Ruth Lilly's brother, Eli Lilly III, to support the faltering magazine. He was denied and shortly thereafter fired. Carruth's ousting initiated an overhaul of the editorial staff at the magazine. This overhaul would be a minor transition, however, compared to wholesale transformation of the magazine that occurred when the Lilly family reemerged to finally grant Carruth's request fifty years later.

That the donation would finally come unsolicited—and with considerable interest—is not the greatest irony of the Lilly patronage. Ruth Lilly's donation secured the death of the Modern Poetry Association; in its place, the Poetry Foundation and the Harriet Monroe Institute revised *Poetry*'s mission nearly wholesale. It is unlikely the Harriet Monroe Institute's namesake, the founding publisher of the magazine, would have approved of the Poetry Foundation's redirection toward a wider national audience. John Barr's "American Poetry in the New Century,"[68] something of a manifesto on the state of poetry in America published in the magazine in September 2006, the same year the institute's first major study was released,[69] laments that "a century ago our newspapers commonly ran poems in their pages," but "today one almost never sees a poem in a newspaper."[70] In 1922, Harriet Monroe had also published an editorial in the magazine that addressed the state of poetry in American culture. She deplored newspaper verse: "These syndicated rhymers, like the movie-producers, are learning that 'it pays to be good,' that one 'gets by by giving the people the emotions of virtue, simplicity and goodness, with this program paying at the box-office.'"[71]

Monroe and Barr nonetheless agreed, in 1922 and 2006, respectively, that "poetry in this country is ready for something new."[72] But, for Barr, the "new" frontier was not aesthetic experimentation as it had been for Monroe. "I believe the next era of poetry will come not from further innovations of form, but from an evolution of the sensibility based on lived experience." What Barr referred to as the dawning of a new "golden age" of poetry—echoing Frost's inaugural poem for President Kennedy, "Dedication," which hailed a "golden age of poetry and power"—celebrates newspaper verse, as with Ted Kooser's American Life in Poetry project, and honors its commercially popular humorists, as with Billy Collins's inaugural humor prize. Poets, held the newly inaugurated Poetry Foundation, must "find their public," reclaiming their position as "unacknowledged legislators of the world" through populist accessibility.[73]

The Lilly donation enabled a new level of coordination of national arts ideology through poetry-based initiatives. As the historical arc of this volume has shown, the missions of the library and *Poetry* have been allied and mediated through common patrons since the postwar period; just as the Mellon Endowment began dividing support between *Poetry* magazine and the Library of Congress in 1946, Lilly's 2002 bequest was divided between *Poetry* magazine and a Washington-based arts education and lobbying group today called Americans for the Arts. *Poetry*, the National Endowment for the Arts, and the Library of Congress were already triangulated through common individuals, mission statement language, and cooperatively undertaken civic initiatives. The balance of this triangle, however, shifted in the wake of the Lilly donation—the Poetry Foundation acquired unprecedented capital to determine the shape of state verse culture. Moreover, the Poetry Foundation adopted, and even exaggerated, the priorities of the early national poetry projects of Poet Laureate Brodsky and his successors. While Brodsky advocated for the dissemination of poetry books in public and commercial spaces, Barr more aggressively held that *"poets should be imperialists"* and *"importers"* of experience.[74]

Before the creation of Lilly-funded the Poetry Foundation, however, the state had already begun cooperating with other institutions on a wider and more public scale than it had in its history. A year after Bill Clinton announced National Poetry Month, Robert Pinsky was appointed poet laureate and initiated the first of the major national poetry projects undertaken at the Library of Congress. In concert with the transformation of the Modern Poetry Association to the Poetry Foundation, these national projects, which would benefit from the Lilly windfall in turn, represented the flowering of an already coherent state verse culture.

## The Advent of Broadly Scaled National Poetry Projects: Pinsky, Collins, Kooser

Following the public-facing imperative of Joseph Brodsky, in the mid-1990s, poets laureate began spearheading broadly scaled national poetry projects through which the Library of Congress collaborated with other public as well as private institutions to promote poetry as a civic good. Robert Pinsky's Favorite Poem Project, Billy Collins's Poetry 180, and Ted Kooser's American Life in Poetry are notable examples, and Kooser's project would benefit from collaboration with the post–Lilly Poetry Foundation. These early projects set a new expectation for the office, whereby two-term poets laureate (referred to at the library as "activist" laureates) now would regularly undertake national initiatives.[75]

### *Robert Pinsky's Favorite Poem Project: Embodying American Voice*

> Poetry reflects, perhaps concentrates, the American idea of independence . . . the art of poetry by its nature operates on a level as profoundly individual as a human voice.
> —ROBERT PINSKY, DEMOCRACY, CULTURE, AND THE VOICE OF POETRY

Robert Pinsky launched the Favorite Poem Project in April 1998, in concert with the third annual National Poetry Month. He was in the first of his unprecedented three consecutive terms as U.S. poet laureate (1997–2000). The "Favorite Poem Project: Americans Saying Poems They Love" invited "Americans from all walks of life, including school children and prominent civic figures" to read, or as Pinsky prefers, to *"say aloud"* a favorite poem at a series of poetry readings, and subsequently for a national audio and video archive. Not only did the Favorite Poem Project set a new precedent for the civic activities of later poets laureate, but Pinsky offered a uniquely developed and ambitious civic pedagogy surrounding the initiative. He is also the clearest inheritor of Frost's phonocentric poetics. Memorizing and "saying aloud" a poem, Pinsky explains, "schools us in the shapes of meaning."[76] "Schools" is no accidental verb choice. If Frost's poetics, emblematized in his inaugural recitation, extended nineteenth- and early twentieth-century curricular traditions of memorization and recitation beyond the classroom, Pinsky's Favorite Poem Project returns his phonocentric nationalism to the classroom proper.

Pinsky introduced the project with five public poetry readings in New York, Washington, Boston, St. Louis, Los Angeles, and at the White House. In Boston, the president of the Massachusetts State Senate read Andrew Marvell's "To His Coy Mistress," a fifth grade public school student read Theodore Roethke's "The Sloth," and "a homeless man" read Robert Frost's "Nothing Gold Can Stay."[77] At the White House, Pinsky and former laureates Robert Hass and Rita Dove read works of "great American poets" Walt Whitman, Emily Dickinson, Edward Arlington Robinson, Langston Hughes, and Wallace Stevens, and President Clinton read Ralph Waldo Emerson and Octavio Paz.[78] The success of the reading series prompted Pinsky to extend the project, "invit[ing] Americans to submit the title and author of a poem they admired enough to say aloud for the national audio and video archive, and to write a few sentences about the poem's personal importance or significance."[79] Something of a franchise developed out of the response—over eighteen thousand entries were received in the first year of open call for submissions—including three anthologies; Pinsky's statement of poetics reflecting on the role of poetry in democratic culture, *Democracy, Culture, and the Voice of Poetry*; and a series of Summer Poetry Institutes and curricula guides that are ongoing today.

While the Favorite Poem Project's archives in bulk, which include original letters and printed email submissions, and raw and edited versions of audio and video recordings, are housed by Boston University's Mugar Library at the Howard Gotlieb Archival Research Center, the core of the project—fifty of the original eighteen thousand Favorite Poem Project videos—was given a permanent home in the Archive of Recorded Poetry and Literature at the Library of Congress. With the selection and addition of the Favorite Poem Project Videos to the archive, Pinsky assumed the role of earlier national poets as archival guardian. Pinsky's project also redefined the archive's function. Video recordings of "individual Americans reading and speaking personally about poems they love" disrupted the traditional content of audio recordings: Mellon's 1946 endowment had intended to support contemporary living poets. We saw, in the postwar period, how poets like Lowell and Bishop exploited the possibilities for individual and collaborative aesthetic decision-making in the process of canon formation, inviting their peers to read for the archive during their time in office. The recitations of Favorite Poem Project contributors, meanwhile, recall Frost's performance of citizenship in the inaugural recitation of "The Gift Outright."

The addition of the video documentaries of "everyday Americans" is striking as a populist or democratizing gesture. The videos offer an expanded interpretation of the archival speaker—including *citizens* who "*say*," not just *poets* who *read*, as participant in the national canon. In other ways, however, the archive describes more limited sources of literary authority and constrained models of poetic voice that are honored in the archive as a reflection of national life. While some Favorite Poem Project videos include poems of contemporary authors, they often reify the status of literary figures from an existing anglophone poetry canon in which American and British authors writing in standard American English or British English are celebrated: Americans read Marvell, Frost, and Roethke for the national camera. Where the project premises that "there are many people for whom particular poems have profound, personal meaning," it also suggests that these poems are not typically authored by contemporary writers. And where the project claims to champion poetry's "vigorous presence in American life," it reveals this as the presence of the canonical past. Moreover, while a historical literary canon supplies the archival content, the symbolic status of that author supplies the source of agency for the archival speaker who recites their "favorite poem." Pinsky describes the act of reading a poem as a transformative experience that provides a sense of increased personal agency— one is lifted into "a different state." In the context of the Favorite Poem

Project, the source of agency is located outside the speaker's body or historical time. The archive does not build a canon, then, but rather uses an existing canon to articulate national values. In the Favorite Poem Project, the transformative speech-act of the poem by an individual is a performance of American citizenship.

The Favorite Poem Project reflects the values of Pinsky's poetics, advanced in *Poetry and the World* and *The Sounds of Poetry*, which, like Frost's poetics, develop an account of poetic voice as the expression of American cultural identity. Pinsky also shares with Frost the values of phonocentrism and individualism, emphasizing emotional restraint and discursive rationality. Moreover, we can see the Favorite Poem Project as a significant touchstone in the development of Pinsky's poetic theory, which motivated his third work, *Democracy, Culture and the Voice of Poetry*.[80] Dedicated "To my colleagues and helpers at / The Favorite Poem Project / Boston University," the slim treatise meditates on the place of poetic voice in the "pluralistic, omnivorous, syncretic" culture of American democracy.[81]

The Favorite Poem Project's "Founding Principles" are effectively threefold: first, and most fundamentally, that poetry is a *vocal* art. "In more than thirty years of teaching poetry, Pinsky has emphasized the bodily, vocal experience of poetry. 'If a poem is written well, it was written with a poet's voice and for a voice,' [Pinsky] says."[82] The project's principle of vocality is explained in *The Sounds of Poetry*: "The theory of this guide is that poetry is a vocal, which is to say a bodily, art. The medium of poetry is a human body: the column of air inside the chest, shaped into signifying sounds in the larynx and the mouth. In this sense, poetry is just as physical or bodily an art as dancing."[83] In the project's "Founding Principles," this analogy is recast to emphasize speaking and hearing: "'Reading a poem silently instead of saying a poem is like the difference between staring at sheet music or actually humming or playing the music on an instrument.'"

The Favorite Poem Project is secondly committed to the *transformative* power of vocal poetry in individual experience:

> [Pinsky] long ago found that when he asks students to read aloud a poem they love *something remarkable happens*—a *discernable change* in their faces and voices that demonstrates their connection to the poem. The Favorite Poem Project grew out of that discovery.
>
> . . .

"There is a *special comfort and excitement* people get from saying aloud words with a certain sound, in a certain order," says Pinsky. "By reading aloud poems we love, we can learn how much pleasure there can be in the sounds of words. It's as though *saying the words of a poem aloud make one feel more able, more capable than in ordinary life*. You can concentrate on the physical sounds of the words to a point where they give you an emotional as well as an intellectual reassurance."

Revisions in 2022 to the website altered the language of the final sentence. The previous version asserted that reading poetry aloud provides "an *emotional or an intellectual relief*. You *enter a different state*."[84]

The language emphasized in Pinsky's account describes a kind of mystical exaltation of the subject. For Pinsky, vocalizing a poem is the gateway to the "remarkable" and "special," a domain outside the bounds of "ordinary" experience. The "discernable change" to the physical body of the reader reflects an inner transformation: a sense of renewed personal agency in which he or she is "more able, more capable than in ordinary life." The hyperattention to the sounds of words—as in the ritual power of prayer—brings "emotional or intellectual relief" or catharsis. Saying a poem aloud is finally an act of conversion, a quasi-spiritual transformation of the subject: "You enter a different state." Moreover, Pinsky and Frost's speech-based poetics emphasizes the power of *individual* vocalization—as opposed to a collective vocalization: group chant, prayer, song, rally—to afford the experience of civic union. Collective uses of oral verse have long knit individuals into a common framework of national community, from Confederate broadside verse during the Civil War to the poetry and song of the civil rights movement. Here, however, the power of the human voice lies principally in its demonstrative recognition of the individual. An individual saying a poem is also a social act with political consequence. For Frost, the poet's speaking voice functioned as a proxy for the American citizen contra Soviet collectivism. With Pinsky, too, the individual voice in poetry is inextricably yoked to individual voice in civic society. He writes that the voice is an index of the nature of both "the art of poetry" and of the American nation. Hence, "poetry reflects, perhaps concentrates, the American idea of individualism as it encounters the American experience of the mass—because the art of poetry by its nature operates on a level as profoundly individual as a human voice."[85]

Pinsky notes that the Favorite Poem Project has been described as an effort to "promote" or "advance" poetry in the United States, to which he offers a modest corrective: "in fact the main idea was in a sense more passive, and in my opinion more profound: to reflect some of the social presence of poetry in the lives of Americans—implicitly, in relation to our cultural anxieties."[86] Because the speaking voice is at the heart of both the art of poetry and the American nation, "poetry and our ideas about it may offer ways to inspect characteristic dramas of our national life."[87] Like Pinsky's book-length poem *An Explanation of America*,[88] the Favorite Poem Project attempts to forge "a common American majority culture and common American identity."[89] "The poet risks speaking for us all here," as Frost biographer Jay Parini wrote of Pinsky's *America*.[90]

### Billy Collins's Poetry 180: A Curricula "Absolutely Unliterary"

Poetry 180: A Poem a Day for American High Schools was founded by two-term Poet Laureate Billy Collins (2001–3) in 2001 to promote poetry in classrooms. "The idea behind Poetry 180 is simple: to have a poem read each day to the students of American high schools across the country." In essence, Poetry 180 is an anthology project: a selection of poems Collins selected with high school-aged readers in mind. On the project site, the full-length project description is addressed "to the high school teachers of America." Participating in the project is "easy"; for a school to participate in Poetry 180, a poem should be printed out from the website and "read to the school in a public forum, such as at the end of the day's announcements."[91] The only requirement is that the poems not be incorporated into academic curricula proper: "Unless students really want to discuss the poem, there is no need to do so. The most important thing is that the poems be read and listened to without any academic requirements."[92] Collins explains: "I wanted teachers to refrain from commenting on the poems or asking students 'literary' questions about them. No discussion, no explication, no quiz, no midterm, no seven-page paper—just listen to a poem every morning and off you go to your first class."[93] The project of Poetry 180 thus follows the phonocentric priority of Frost and Pinsky's poetics, where "poems [should] be read and listened to"—"you do it on your ear."[94] Like Pinsky, Collins describes the speech-act of the poem by an individual as a performance in public space, "read to the school in a public forum, such as at the end of the day's announcements." The poems are "intended to be listened to, and I suggest that all members of the school community be included as readers."[95]

Collins insists on the accessibility of poetic language, where poetry is not a "'literary'" question but nonspecialized discourse or, as Frost called it, a language "absolutely unliterary."[96] Collins is less invested than Pinsky in the speech act of the poem as an experience of transcendence or agency by the individual. In the context of Poetry 180, orality is more primarily a means to clarity and popular accessibility. Under what Collins calls the "Mount Rushmore of modernism," that is, poets including Pound, Eliot, Stevens, and Crane, "difficulty became a criterion for appraising poetic value." Collins links modernist difficulty to the use of the visual field of the page: these poets exploited meaning from "the typographical, graphic appearance of the words in itself, apart from the indication of sound."[97] Reading a poem aloud is a way to avoid ambiguity and "difficulty" of difficult modernist poets: "Clarity is a real risk in poetry. To be clear means opening yourself up to judgment. The willfully obscure poem is a hiding place where the poet can elude the reader and thus make appraisal impossible, irrelevant—a bourgeois intrusion upon the poem. Which is why much of the commentary on obscure poetry produces the same kind of headache as the poems themselves."[98] For Collins, difficulty is elitist, while clarity implies a democratic accessibility and, moreover, the liberal value of "opening yourself up to judgment" in a pluralistic society.

Collins wants to avoid "knotty poems" that invite "the hunt for Meaning" but, evidently, also "kill the poetry spirit."[99] Adapting the web-based anthology to the domain of the printed page, he takes time in the introduction of the Random House anthology to make the point clear: "The idea behind the printed collection, which is a version of the Library of Congress '180' website, was to assemble a generous selection of short, clear, contemporary poems which any listener can basically 'get' on first hearing—*poems whose injection of pleasure is immediate.*"[100]

Finally, Collins, like Frost and Pinsky, hold that poetry has an important role in civic education. Even as Poetry 180 is premised on the educational system—the very structure of the anthology is dictated by the school year calendar—its goal is that poetry "will become a part of the daily life of students" *separately* from "literary" subjects or any other "subject that is part of the school curriculum."[101] As such, Collins likens the website anthology to the fun of a jukebox—"The website itself has movable parts; it is a kind of poetry jukebox where the songs can be changed and updated to keep the offerings fresh"[102]—and the print edition of the catalog to a deck of cards: "I know every one is an ace, or at least a face card, because I personally rigged the deck." The educational quality of poetry is also likened to an "injection," or an otherwise medicinal intervention: "with *Poetry 180*, there is something to be said for starting at the beginning and reading just a poem or two each day. Like pills, for the head and the heart."[103] In other words, a little bit of sugar (injection of pleasure) makes the medicine (cultural education) go down. While poetry need not be considered a literary question or academic subject, it does have an edifying or salubrious effect; hence it can be considered an educational project: not an academic subject, but a civics lesson. Poetry 180 is not about critically analyzing a poem, learning its history, or otherwise engaging with difficulty, but about moving poetry off the curricula and into the daily habits of students as citizens-in-training. Von Hallberg says civil verse poets "teach us manners." As Collins puts it, the anthology models "taste": "Apart from any educational value the '180' collections may have, they can be viewed more simply as expressions of my taste in poetry"; the anthology provides the right "menu."[104]

What civic values will "reading just a poem or two each day" help to cultivate? Collins suggests liberalism and tolerance: "I like poems that have a speculative feel to them rather than poems that seem to have their minds already made up." He also suggests emotional restraint or ease, prizing poems that feel "light-handed" and begin as "naturally as a conversation."[105] These poems do not model a civic society in which the speaker-citizen is disruptive, inaccessible, or difficult, or makes explicit political demands. Poetry 180 rejects "unnatural" speech acts, which might mean, given the content of the anthology, the use of language other than standard American English. The program's instructional guide, too, implicitly values certain forms of voice and speaker over others. In instructions to high school teachers for implementing Poetry 180 in classrooms addressed to high school teachers—"How should the poems be presented?"—Collins explains that "whoever is going to read the poem can simply say, for example": "Today's poem is by John Smith and it is titled 'In Memory of

My Father.'" For the sake of clarity, some of the poems on the website will come with brief introductory comment, which should be read first. Afterward, the reader might close by saying, "That was a poem by John Smith called 'In Memory of My Father.'"[106]

The program's dicta, then, suggest that the civic value of poetry is in "John Smith" reading a poem in remembrance of his paternal heritage. No other examples of poem titles or authors are provided. According to Casper, who has run the office of the poet laureate since 2011, the Center of Poetry and Literature at the Library of Congress has since sought to diversify and expand the Poetry 180 selections.[107]

### *American Life in Poetry: Ted Kooser's "Everyman" Column*

Poet Laureate Ted Kooser, a retired insurance executive from the Great Plains, launched the American Life in Poetry: A Project for Newspapers project in April 2005 to coincide with National Poetry Month. A partnership between the library and the Poetry Foundation, American Life in Poetry provided newspapers and online publications with a free weekly column featuring contemporary American poems. Kooser's project was not the first collaboration of the Library of Congress and the Poetry Foundation, but it was one of the first in name: the Modern Poetry Association had just been overhauled with the creation of the Poetry Foundation following the Lilly donation. The organization's recalibrated mission statement, championing a newly public-facing and populist directives, allied with Kooser's vision: "The sole mission of this project is to promote poetry: American Life in Poetry seeks to create a vigorous presence for poetry in our culture."[108]

When Kooser was appointed in August 2004, Librarian of Congress James Billington highlighted the representational charge to the office, whereby the national poet represents a component cultural identity within a pluralistic society. In Kooser's case, this identity was his regional heritage: "the first Poet Laureate chosen from the Great Plains." Kooser is "a major poetic voice for rural and small-town America. . . . His verse reaches beyond his native region to touch on universal themes in accessible ways."[109] Billington's statement also exploited the connection between rural regional identity and national values observed in Frost's self-promotion to American publishers and in Engle's fundraising campaign for the Iowa Writers'

Workshop: Frost had convinced the then-nationalist Poetry Society of America of his patriotism by using the money from his first book to buy farm and would later become "*the* national poet"; Engle had appealed to the imagery of Iowan cornfields and tractors in his approaches to Midwestern businessmen. For both poets, veritable giants within state verse culture, the rural, pastoral, or small-town geographical region symbolizes "American" values.

Kooser's project, too, capitalized on this discursive tradition. The homepage of the website features a solitary image of Kooser, who stands, grimly smiling, in front of a wooden shed flanked by rusted tools (saws, chains, etc.).[110] The American poet conveys rugged individualism through a regionalist idiom, wherein "the toolshed" stands in for "the creative writing workshop." Here, poetic expression is cast as productive labor accomplished through individual acts of will. This do-it-yourself ethos is reflected also in Kooser's instructional guide to writing poetry, *The Poetry Home Repair Manual: Practical Advice for Beginning Poets*, which opens "You'll never be able to make a living writing poems."[111] Notably, this instructional guide also stresses the use of judicious and culturally specific details in the tradition of program-era voice.

Whereas Pinsky's *Democracy, Culture, and the Voice of Poetry* represented the urbane style of "the college-educated, *northern*, metropolitan class of the intelligentsia [that] asserts its authority to explain the world," Kooser's *The Poetry Home Repair Manual* represents the "honest, ordinary" rhetoric Frost exploited to cultivate his image as a rural, and thereby authentically national, poet. Kooser's project also prioritizes "everyday speech" to the exclusion of phonocentrism proper. As the Poetry Foundation holds that "'poetry' or 'poems' refer to verses intended to be understood as poems, *not as part of something else such as rap, song lyrics, Bible verses, or greeting card messages*," American Life in Poetry requires the printed page, in a way the Favorite Poem Project and Poetry 180 do not, to solidify the generic purity of its content. "Saying aloud" a poem in the idiom of the northern managerial elite stages the accessibility and universality of the values of the social class it represents. For Kooser, the visual domain of newspaper verse circumvents the misrecognition of "poetry as ordinary speech" as simply "ordinary speech." By the same token, however, Kooser's newspaper column does not feature rap, song lyrics, or other forms that others may consider poetry.

While all three of these foundational poets laureate projects seek to promote the "present vitality" of poetry as an art form in American culture, all also refer to a national past as the source of this vitality. With Barr, Kooser, and Collins, this takes the form of a revivalist narrative of bringing poetry "back into the mainstream." Given the increased readership and increased numbers of self-identified poets in twentieth- and twenty-first-century America, this is a notable and surprising consensus. It suggests, again, that these projects have more specialized cultural values than the broad language of their mission statements might superficially suggest. The Project for Newspapers provides a nostalgic mission, the attempt to revive a form that "was long a popular staple in the daily press" against changing reading habits of "recent years."[112] Poetry 180 also casts poetry more abstractly as a retrospective engagement. The 180-poem list offers a poem for every day of the approximately 180-day school year, but "there is another reason [Collins] chose that name. A 180-degree turn implies a *turning back*—in this case, to poetry."[113] While Collins endeavored to include contemporary poems—"textbooks and anthologies typically lag behind the times"—he described having difficulty in selecting over 100 contemporary poems for the first anthology, suggesting that this difficulty likely reflected a "limited store of smart, clear, contemporary poems" in contemporary America.[114] The Favorite Poem Project videos, meanwhile, turn back to the authority of the historical canon within a recording archive previously purposed for contemporary poets.

Moreover, all three draw from elements of Frost's poetics, prioritizing the expressive voice of the poetic speaker—this is especially phonocentricism for Pinsky, accessibility for Collins, and regionalist authenticity and populism for Kooser. All share a civic charge: poetry as category of cultural production is uniquely tasked to perform national identity. The poem as object—stowed away in the archive or bounded as a newspaper column—acts as a repository for American values; saying or speaking the poem expresses them. Whereas, for these projects, the voice of the citizen-poet is rooted in a national past, the civic poetics proposed by poets working out of the state verse network proper have imagined alternative models of voice, often working outside standard American English or traditional lyric strategies to reflect a historical present and speculate about the future. More recent poets laureate have pointed to this. The terms of Poets Laureate Juan Felipe Herrera and Tracy K. Smith, among their more recent predecessors, undertook national poetry programming that has in many important ways departed from the civil verse projects of the 1990s and 2000s.

### The Evolution of National Poetry Projects: Ryan, Trethewey, Herrera, Smith, and Harjo

Since the tenures of Pinsky, Collins, and Kooser, poets laureate now regularly undertake national projects during office. The activities of one-year term laureates have been quieter, and the Library of Congress does not recognize them among the "Past Poet Laureate Projects" that began with Pinsky.[115] When Charles Wright (2014–15), for example, was asked what he wanted his role as poet laureate to be in light of his predecessors—"Billy Collins tried to bring poems into high school classrooms. Ted Kooser wrote a weekly column for newspapers. What do you think you might do?"—Wright offered: "Well, I'll probably stay here at home and think about things. . . . I will not be an activist laureate, I don't think, the way Natasha [Trethewey] was . . . and certainly not the way Billy Collins was, or Bob Hass, or Rita Dove, or Robert Pinsky, you know, they had programs. I have no program. I have been deprogrammed, as it were."[116] The Library of Congress now typically alternates between one-term poets laureate, more honorific appointees who assume more passive duties, and, increasingly, two-term poets laureate, often younger appointees who Poetry and Literature Center administrators describe within the office as "activist Poets Laureate."[117]

Substantive projects undertaken by poets laureate serving two-term tenures include Kay Ryan (2008–10), Natasha Trethewey (2012–14), Juan Felipe Herrera (2015–17), Tracy K. Smith (2017–19), and Joy Harjo (2019–22). This more recent poets laureate–led programming, while also viewing poetry as a civic tool, has adjusted the notions of voice and the goals of civic engagement as understood by national poetry projects of the 1990s and 2000s. In particular, the projects have often interacted in community spaces outside the reach of previous projects and revised the values of phonocentricism, individualism, regionalist authenticity, and populist accessibility. Recent projects undertaken by Juan Felipe Herrera and Tracy K. Smith are particularly notable in this respect, respectively incorporating nonphonocentric and nonanglophone-centered verse and engaging with rural communities.

Prior to Herrera and Smith, Kay Ryan's "Poetry for the Mind's Joy" (2008–10) sought to "promote the hard work of the staffs and students in American community colleges," including a poetry contest and video conference with Ryan and community college students across the nation, and designated April 1, during National Poetry Month, "Community College Poetry Day." Cooperative with the AAP in making the designation Poetry for the Mind's Joy was sponsored by the library in collaboration with the Community College Humanities Association. Prior to her laureateship, Ryan had been awarded a National Humanities Medal, fellowships from the National Endowment for the Arts and the Guggenheim Foundation, and a Poetry Foundation Ruth Lilly Poetry Prize.[118] After the nonproject, single-year terms of W. S. Merwin (2010–11) and Philip Levine (2011–12), Natasha Trethewey (2012–14) held office hours open to the public in her first term—in part as a nod to Gwendolyn Brooks, who had opened the poetry office to the public in unprecedented ways in the mid-1980s. In her second term, Trethewey expanded the scope of this work and initiated the project "Where Poetry Lives," traveling across the country to highlight the unique ways various communities engage with poetry. Through this project, Trethewey participated in reports for the Poetry Series with PBS NewsHour Senior Correspondent Jeffrey Brown and focused, according to the library, on "societal issues through poetry's focused lens."[119] The Where Poetry Lives reports focused on civil rights history as well as contemporary issues related to racial injustice, including youth incarceration.[120] Trethewey, a past recipient of NEA, Guggenheim, and Rockefeller Foundation funding, also served as the poet laureate of Mississippi from 2012–16, becoming the first national poet laureate to concurrently serve as a state laureate. "[Trethewey's] projects," as Casper has suggested, began a trend in the office of the poet laureate focused "toward championing poetry as community-building and not just an expression of individual voice."[121]

Indeed, the two terms that followed Trethwey's tenure suggest a shift in programming values. Herrera and Smith were more active than previous laureates in explaining and contextualizing their projects' priorities, which marked an even more decisive turn away from the "civil verse" imperatives of their predecessors of the late 1990s and early 2000s. In addition to engaging with geographical spaces and populations outside the scope of previous projects, Herrera and Smith's initiatives did not claim to "promote" poetry as a kind of good in and of itself, but rather, more precisely, to engage poetry within communities as a mode of experience. They also departed from the phonocentric priority of the Favorite Poem Project and Poetry 180—rather than individual recitations for the national archive or a classroom, poetry was shared in online-based formats and participatory and discussion-based formats. Lastly, they abandoned the "retrospective" or "revivalist" rhetoric of Barr and Kooser, involving collaborative authorship and increased numbers of contemporary poets and poems. In 2019, Smith explicitly remarked in a public forum that she viewed her project as distinct from her predecessors in its political commitments.[122] Smith was succeeded by Joy Harjo, whose inaugural reading at the Library of Congress the same year suggested that calibrated political commentary or critique may not be fully outside of the role of the poet laureate as a state official.

### *Juan Felipe Herrera's La Casa de Colores, "The Technicolor Adventures of Catalina Neon," and Wordstreet Champions and Brave Builders of the Dream*

Juan Felipe Herrera was appointed to office by Librarian of Congress James Billington in 2015, and to a second term by acting Librarian of Congress David Mao in 2016.[123] The first Hispanic national poet, Herrera had previously been appointed California poet laureate in 2012. During his tenure, Herrera engaged in multiple community-engaged projects as poet laureate: La Casa de Colores, "The Technicolor Adventures of Catalina Neon," and Wordstreet Champions and Brave Builders of the Dream. Herrera described La Casa de Colores, undertaken in his first 2015–16 term, as a "house for all voices"; the project included "La Familia," a crowdsourced epic poem, in which contributors submitted writing on monthly themes, which ranged from "Migrants: Portraits and Friends" and "Thank-You Poems to Our Vets."[124] The initiative was notable in departing from the anglophone-based projects of its predecessors, as well as in departing from previous projects' phonocentric priority and prizing of singular authorship. Rather than asking participants to read aloud or to listen to a poem read aloud during the school day, as in the case of the Favorite Poem Project and Poetry 180, La Familia segments collated the invited contributions of writers through the project's website. La Casa de Colores also included "El Jardín," a project that invited participants to "get inspired by primary resources from the Library [of Congress]'s collections."[125] The webcast series featured Herrera's discussions with curators from collections including graphic art from Asamblea de Artistas Revolucionarios de Oaxaca as well as from his *Automatika* series and intergenre drawing/artist book from the Prints and Photographs Division, from the Hispanic Law Collection, and the Rare Book and and Special Collections Division; his poem-responses to each exhibit and discussion; and the curator's response. It also prompted participant viewers to create their own "word-art" response, for example, "*You can write a portrait-poem. One scene. Let us know this person as intimately as possible.*"[126] Emphasizing poetic creation as a process rooted in historical and cultural material rather than the internal lyric subject, the project also destabilizes the generic stability of the poem as object. Poetry is iteratively constructed, participant in multiple genres or artistic fields—a conviction distinct from laureate programming that promoted "poetry" as a discrete category and civic imperative. Herrera's own career, too, insists on the values of La Casa de Colores. His poetry collections frequently include text in both Spanish and English (as in *187 Reasons Mexicanos Can't Cross the Border: Undocuments 1971–2007*);[127] he is not known singularly as a "poet," but as a performance artist and activist, cartoonist, and fiction author; and his work crosses generic borders, understanding poetry as a hybrid art form, and regularly models co- or multiple authorship.

Herrera's second-term online project "The Technicolor Adventures of Catalina Neon" (2016–17) extended the values of nonanglophone writing, collaborative authorship, and nonphonocentric practice. A bilingual illustrated poem created by Herrera and artist Juana Medina, "The Technicolor Adventures of Catalina Neon" featured the contributions of elementary school students, teachers, and librarians.[128] Also during his second term, Herrera and the Library of Congress partnered with the Poetry Foundation and Chicago Public Schools on Wordstreet Champions and Brave Builders of the Dream. Through the yearlong project, Herrera worked with ninth-grade teachers at the Poetry Foundation offices to develop teaching strategies for poetry.[129] The Poetry Foundation, rather than the Library of Congress, issued the press release for the program.[130]

Herrera's laureateship further established the contemporary national poetry office as a public-facing, civic position. However, it departed from the first of the library's formal laureate projects, which inherited the anglophone and phonocentric values of Frost's poetics, suggesting an expanded scope of poets laureate programming. Meanwhile, Herrera's projects point to a narrowing gap between the institutional missions of the poet laureateship at the Library of Congress and private organizations like the Poetry Foundation.

## *Tracy K. Smith's American Conversations*

Tracy K. Smith was the first appointee of fourteenth librarian of Congress Carla Hayden, the first woman and first Black person to lead the nation's oldest federal cultural institution. Under Hayden, Rob Casper, who had served as the head of the Poetry and Literature Center since 2011, actively revised the selection process for poets laureate—"institutionalizing" the procedure to include nominations from a broad swath of individuals and institutions. The internal recommending committee to the librarian considered ninety-one nominations from seventy-two nominators, including academics, bookstore owners, former poets laureate, conference directors, editors, and private literary organizations across twenty-six states.[131]

During her 2017–19 term, Smith worked in rural communities to "take[e] poetry to audiences outside places where poets typically present their work": "If writers and scholars are only talking to each other, we're missing out on a huge part of the story," Smith explained in 2018.[132] Smith traveled to New Mexico, South Carolina, and Kentucky that year, where she gave readings and hosted workshops at Air Force bases, schools, churches,[133] and local cultural centers. The project was variously referred to as the "National Project Rural Tour and as Smith's "rural communities project,"[134] and it was eventually formalized by the Library of Congress as American Conversations: Celebrating Poems in Rural Communities. Like Collins's Poetry 180, which led to the publication of his two anthologies, American Conversations led to *American Journal: Fifty Poems for Our Time* (2018), jointly published by Graywolf Press and the Library of Congress.[135] The Library of Congress distributed free copies of *American Journal* to attendees at Smith's second-term events, and discussions with participants focused on the poems in the anthology.[136]

When asked in 2019 how she understood American Conversations in relation to Billy Collins's Poetry 180 and Pinsky's Favorite Poem Project, Smith explicitly differentiated her goals from those of her predecessors: "Yes, I do [see my project as different]." In contrast to Pinsky's project, "I

*Figure 4.1* Tracy K. Smith speaking with a service member at the Cannon Air Force Base near Clovis, New Mexico, January 11, 2018. Credit Shawn Miller/Library of Congress.

am teaching people who don't have favorite poems," Smith explained. She also described her project as "more sociological" and as "responding to the current political landscape." By crossing urban and rural divides,[137] Smith's work stands in striking contrast to the tour stops of Pinsky's Favorite Poem Project in New York, Washington, Boston, St. Louis, Los Angeles, and at the White House.

In some ways, Smith does not reject, even as she adjusts, the poetics of her predecessors. In particular, she is optimistic about the political potential of the lyric voice. In an editorial for the *New York Times*, "Political Poetry Is Hot Again," written in her second term as laureate, Smith acknowledged that "perhaps America's individualism predisposed its poets toward the lyric poem, with its insistence on the primacy of a single speaker whose politics were intimate, internal, invisible." But she suggests that this has changed after 9/11, and that the "I" can propel political action and not only engage in acts of internal reflection. For Smith, faith in the lyric "I" is not an insistence on phonocentric voice or populist accessibility, but in a range of formal strategies that may be tied to various political commitments. Smith asked readers to consider the work of more experimental, if lyrically driven, contemporary poets, including the somatic poetics of

C. A. Conrad and Jos Charles's *feeld* (2018). Reading Charles's poetry, for example—"'i care so / much abot the whord i cant / reed / it marks mye bak /wen I pass'"—requires a "strange labor of deciphering the text." "I'm made to realize that the vernacular of the poems," Smith writes, "tampers with history; it announces a continuum where Chaucer and 19th-century enslaved blacks and a 21st-centry white trans woman seem quite effortlessly to share a lexicon." Smith also asked readers to consider Evie Shockley's poem "semiautomatic," which suggested to the poet laureate "the absurdity of merely *thinking* about outrageous injustice."[138] Smith's syllabus for Americans is civic verse, rather than civil verse. These are not poems that are typically "light-handed" or "hospitable," as preferred by Collins in Poetry 180; rather, these examples of politically engaged poetics may indeed "make demands" of the reader.[139] They are more "difficult" than "safe." Rather than promoting poems whose conversational "injection of pleasure is immediate," as Collins would have it,[140] Smith used her role as poet laureate to call attention to poets—and models of voice—that the office has been traditionally reluctant to acknowledge as representative.

Moreover, while Smith's statements defend the political potential of lyric voice-based poetry, much of her own work of the same year in fact turned to *non*lyric strategies—including the use of found texts and erasure as techniques in what she has called "more public-facing poem[s]." Published in *Wade in the Water*,[141] this series of poems, which marks an important new direction in Smith's work, are based in historical documents including letters that Black soldiers wrote to their families and to Abraham Lincoln during the Civil War, correspondence between slave owners, and reports of recent immigrants and refugees. Rather than writing from "private experience," Smith refers to the authors of these source texts as "example[s] of people who belong to this country but are not claimed by it."[142] A poem like "The United States Welcomes You" is what Smith calls "public-facing," and not only a reflection of voices or injustices in a historical record: "I was also thinking [when I wrote the poem] about all of the ongoing, unarmed black victims of police violence."[143] "Why and by whose power were you sent?" the poem opens. Structured as a series of questions, it asks in conclusion "What if we / Fail? How and to whom do we address our appeal?"[144] If understood as a lyric poem, it proposes voice as a choral arrangement of multiple voices rather than a representative "I" speaker. By using nonphonocentric or voice-based compositional strategies,

*Figure 4.2* Tracy K. Smith reading from *Wade in the Water*, February 24, 2018, at the James E. Clyburn Wiltown Community Center near Adams Run, South Carolina. Credit Shawn Miller/Library of Congress.

Smith suggests, as she does in her *New York Times* opinion essay, that we can hold onto the communicative resources of lyric poem, but it must be based in historical as well as contemporary political awareness. If *Wade in the Water* tests the politically representative capacity of the lyric voice, it also marks Smith's meanwhile negotiation of her representative capacity and the political responsibilities of the office of the poet laureate.

Smith ended her term on April 15, 2019, with an "American Celebration" in the library's Coolidge Auditorium that featured Smith in discussion with Brooklyn Poet Laureate Tina Chang, Hawaii Poet Laureate Kealoha, Indiana Poet Laureate Adrian Matejka, Oklahoma State Poet Laureate Jeanetta Calhoun Mish, and Clark County, Nevada, Poet Laureate Vogue Robinson.[145] Reflecting on her outreach to rural communities, as well as the roles of state, city, and county poets laureate, Smith suggested poetry was a resource that reminds us of "the things we share" while "highlighting the differences between us." As with predecessor national poetry projects, poetry makes a claim to, and functions as a proxy for, national values, here most centrally democratic plurality: poems "advocat[e] implicitly for the validity of differing perspectives." Additionally, however, Smith insisted on poetry as a mode of questioning or critique—poetry as a practice that can "jostle us out of a rote engagement with the world."[146]

### Joy Harjo's Living Nations and the Future of Laureate Programming

Two months later, Librarian of Congress Carla Hayden announced the appointment of Joy Harjo as the twenty-third poet laureate. The June 19, 2019, press release celebrated Harjo, a member of the Mvskoke Creek Nation, as the first Native American poet laureate.[147] "Joy Harjo has championed the art of poetry—'soul talk' as she calls it—for over four decades. To her, poems are 'carriers of dreams, knowledge and wisdom,' and through them she tells an American story of tradition and loss, reckoning and myth-making. Her work powerfully connects us to the earth and the

*Figure 4.3* Joy Harjo with Librarian of Congress Carla Hayden, September 19, 2019, in the librarian's ceremonial office in the Jefferson Building, Library of Congress. Credit Shawn Miller/Library of Congress.

spiritual world with direct, inventive lyricism that helps us reimagine who we are," Hayden stated in the press release.[148] At the time of the appointment, Harjo did not have plans for a national project during her term as poet laureate. "I don't have a defined project right now, but I want to bring the contribution of poetry of the tribal nations to the forefront and include it in the discussion of poetry," she told the Associated Press.[149] Like Smith, her immediate predecessor, Harjo situated her office and its mission as responsive to the political moment: "This country is in need of deep healing. We're in a transformational moment in national history and earth history, so whichever way we move is going to absolutely define us."[150]

Media coverage noted that that Harjo publicly expressed views unsupportive of then President Donald J. Trump, but that Harjo declined to speak about him during her appointment interviews. "Everything is political," she suggested instead. Rob Casper affirmed to reporters that the poet laureate is not a political position and that poets laureate are encouraged to focus on "poems and the way they work."[151] In a personal interview, he elaborated that he sees the position as fundamentally nonpartisan: the Library of Congress "is for Congress, to provide information, knowledge (and creative programming) for a Congress and public that includes all political persuasions and voices that aren't our own."[152] He sees this nonpartisan commitment as a special feature of the poet laureate being housed under the legislative branch, whereas the NEA is run through the executive branch, of federal government.

In other words, Casper draws a stark distinction between the expression of political beliefs by poets and the expression of political beliefs in the poetry that they write: "there is room for U.S. Poets Laureate to express political beliefs *through their poems and the poems they champion*."[153] Outside of their poems, however, Casper "strongly believe[s] a Poet Laureate who would use the position to express political beliefs outside of poems would do a disservice to the both position and the art. She or he would run the risk of drawing attention away from, and even undermine, their work in support of poetry."[154] Casper moreover sees his role in running the office of the poet laureate as a kind of translator between the government and the poet: to coordinate with the librarian and the legislative branch, but also to ensure that "the federal government does not impinge on the laureate's activities."[155]

Like Herrera's projects, in which poetry interacted with other art forms, Harjo inaugurated her tenure as poet laureate as an artist of multiple mediums with an evening of poetry and music at the Library of Congress on September 19, 2019. Harjo read poetry and played the saxophone, accompanied by musicians Howard Cloud, Larry Mitchell, and Robert Muller, to an overflowing Coolidge Auditorium. Some of the new laureate's remarks to the audience suggested that she saw spaces in her representative position for playfully calibrated political commentary. "So rabbit is our trickster figure," Harjo said, introducing the poem "Rabbit Is Up to Tricks." "Every human culture has trickster figures. [For] some the coyote, some have jesters—and often, you find that trickster figures sit close to the person in power . . . until, in some instances, they take over the seat of power." The crowd laughed. "And that's all I'm going to say," Harjo laughed in response—though she would also address the removal of her people, the Mvskoke Nation, from their territory seven generations ago, and ongoing events "that [are] happening right now at the [U.S.-Mexico] border."[156]

Harjo was reappointed to second term in April 2020, and in November 2020 to a rare third term as the poet laureate of the United States—serving as the twenty-third poet laureate of the United States from 2019–2022.

Robert Pinsky (1997–2000) is Harjo's only poet laureate predecessor to have previously served three terms. Her second- and third-term project, Living Nations, Living Words: A Map of First Peoples Poetry, officially launched to the public to coincide with her third-term appointment in November 2020,[157] is a primarily web-based project, curating work by forty-seven Native Nations poets through an interactive ArcGIS Story Map and a new Library of Congress audio collection. This library project continues the work of Harjo's more immediate predecessors, including Herrera and Smith. Unlike Pinsky and the 1990s–2000s projects, Living Nations does not promote poetry as such, but instead focuses on its role across American communities, and, as the plural term *nations* in the project title suggests, this Library of Congress archive advances a newly multiple conception of American "nation."

The legacy of the civic—or, as I have argued, more accurately civil—verse initiatives of 1990s–2000s were revised or reimagined in many important respects in the 2010s. The conflation of accessibility and clarity with writing in standard American English, and nationalist interpretations of American citizenship based in regional, rural or nonurban communities, have

*Figure 4.4* Joy Harjo dancing with Arielle Lowe, Poetry Coalition fellow for In-Na-Po: Indigenous Nations Poets, in the Jefferson Building's Neptune Plaza on April 29, 2022. Sponsored by the Library of Congress, the dance party celebrating Harjo's three years as poet laureate featured DJ Tnyce (Haliwa-Saponi) and showcased songs selected by Harjo. Credit Shawn Miller/Library of Congress.

been recalibrated through the projects of Poets Laureate Herrera and Smith. These projects represent broader changes to the office of the poet laureate. The last decade has witnessed increased diversity in representatives of the national poetry office and more politically engaged uses of the platform through project programming. Since 2008, it has seen its first active representative of LGBTQ+ populations, the first Chicano, and, most recently, the first Native American poet laureate. In 2011, the Library of Congress ran its first national search for a new Poetry and Literature Center director, who runs the poet laureateship, and Rob Casper would become the first MFA holder and noninternal hire to hold the position. The appointment of Carla Hayden as librarian of Congress in 2016, and the coinciding revision of the selection process of the poet laureate by Casper, suggests that the priorities of the poets laureate projects will continue to evolve.

But Pinsky, Collins, and Kooser's foundational civic programming—drawing from the more nationalist strands of Frost's poetics and the politically catalyzing "spark" of Joseph Brodsky—cast a long shadow. Throughout

Smith's term, and following Harjo's appointment, the United States Poet Laureate Web Guide at the Library of Congress featured only one photo of a poet laureate: not of the current laureate but of a preeminent former laureate: "Billy Collins, U.S. Poet Laureate, 2001–3."[158] Pinsky's, Collins's, and Kooser's projects not only helped to recast the contemporary poet laureateship as a public-facing civic position but also reflected an increasingly institutionally imbricated system of state-private support for the uses of poetry as a civic tool. The Poetry Foundation, following the Lilly windfall that guaranteed its operations in perpetuity and reengineered its mission under the populist rhetoric of John Barr, remains a hugely influential player in this nexus. When its offices were opened, the celebration included former poets laureate, and Barr christened one office that of the poet laureate, showing it to Billy Collins—who, humorously, "wanted to move the furniture around."[159] The office is primarily symbolic, although was used recently by Herrera when his third project as poet laureate was undertaken at the Poetry Foundation.

While the Poetry Foundation is cooperative in the production of civil verse through national poetry projects, the organization also participates in the circulation of verse that falls outside of this category: the poetic traditions, institutions, and audiences it attempts to represent are broad and often internally contradictory. The same is true of the individual poets, if less so the initiatives, who have historically received NEA support. Just as important as those individual poets and poems, however, are the values of the projects through which they circulate. Within a complex of institutional limitations, it may be difficult to engage in "civic" poetics without becoming merely "civil"—that is, critical or resistant writing risks being normed through a generalizing mission of "promoting poetry" rather than articulating a more discrete political goals or aesthetic ambitions. At the same time, the values of poets laureate projects have varied, more clearly prizing phonocentrism, individuality, and accessibility in the 1990s and early 2000s. While both the Pinsky-Collins-Kooser and Herrera-Smith-Harjo generations of national poetry projects sought to promote poetry to Americans, the latter generation more actively engaged with various types of communities. In this sense, there is an important distinction between the general public outreach model initiated by Brodsky and Pinsky and the particularistic community support model initiated earlier by Brooks and then carried on by Herrera and Smith.

As products of a collaborative institutional network, the administration of multiple organizations critically impacted the missions of both generations of projects, especially the ambitious, broadly scaled projects of the first generation—which reflected the values of John Barr at the Poetry Foundation and Dana Gioia at the NEA as much as the values of any one individual poet laureate. Administrative changes continue to shape national poetry projects, as with the appointment of a new director of the Poetry and Literature Center in 2011 and of a new librarian of Congress in 2016. Under newer library administration, recent poets laureate have continued the public-facing responsibilities of the national poet while maintaining a more interrogative, albeit negotiated, relationship to state interests than the civil verse projects of the 1990s and early 2000s.

# Epilogue

## "An Invisible Berlin Wall," the U.S. Inaugural Poem, and the Future of State Verse

> The land was ours before we were the land's.
> She was our land more than a hundred years
> Before we were her people. She was ours
> In Massachusetts, in Virginia,
> But we were England's, still colonials,
> Possessing what we still were unpossessed by,
> Possessed by what we now no more possessed.
> —ROBERT FROST, "THE GIFT OUTRIGHT"

> One sun rose on us today, kindled over our shores,
> peeking over the Smokies, greeting the faces
> of the Great Lakes, spreading a simple truth
> across the Great Plains, then charging across the Rockies...
> —RICHARD BLANCO, "ONE TODAY"

"The land was ours before we were the land's," Robert Frost proclaimed at the inauguration of John F. Kennedy in 1961. The imperialist and nationalist vision of the first poem ever read at a U.S. presidential inauguration would, as we have seen, be expressed in the dominant values of state verse culture during the Cold War. The inaugural poem delivered by Richard Blanco at the second inauguration of Barak Obama in 2013 suggests this Cold War legacy lives on in the present.

The U.S. inaugural poem has a short and discontinuous history: Blanco was only the fourth poet to read at a presidential inauguration since Frost's recitation of "The Gift Outright." Frost and Blanco delivered inaugural poems—and, later, Blanco would deliver a State Department–commissioned occasional poem at the reopening of the U.S. Embassy in Cuba—at key moments in the national project. Frost's performance had staged the voice of the poet as the expressive agency of the individual citizen. This model of voice served instrumentally in the project of midcentury American nationalism and, as inherited by Blanco, in the longer project of neoliberal identity formation. Both poets projected the poetic speaker as an individual convinced of his continuity with history and his agency with respect to a national future. Unlike Frost, however, Blanco also claimed to speak on behalf of marginalized subjects. Blanco, born in Spain to Cuban parents who "fled the Castro regime,"[1] read a poem entitled "One Today," which celebrated "diverse individual histories and cultural backgrounds" and "reconfirmed the collective identity" of the American nation.[2] The Cold War legacy of both models of voice demands a critical evaluation of the role that Blanco was positioned to play when a voice for the nation in January 2013, as well as when a state poet at the reopening of the Cuban embassy two years later. Bookending the history of the U.S. inaugural poem until the 2021 performance of Amanda Gorman at the inauguration of President Joseph Biden,[3] Frost and Blanco not only point to the political imperatives of the Cold War in the formation of American poetic culture but also dramatize the ways in which poetry, modeling the voice of the citizen and processes of national identity formation, is called on to serve the project of American empire in the present.

*Blanco in Washington and Havana: "One Today" and "Matters of the Sea / Cosas del mar": A Poem Commemorating a New Era in US-Cuba Relations*

"To this day, I don't know exactly how I was chosen as inaugural poet. I asked committee staff, but no one seemed to know the details. . . . In fact, I believe I am the only inaugural poet in history who didn't have some kind of personal connection to the administration that chose him or her," Blanco explains in the opening of a memoir of his experience as the inaugural poet.[4]

The memoir concludes in homage to Robert Frost. Flying home from the inauguration of President Barack Obama in 2013, "the plane taxies down the runway without my knowing that in July I'll read my poetry at the Robert Frost farm in Derry, New Hampshire":

> I will walk through his home, sit in his chair at the kitchen table where he wrote, and feel the ghost of his words at my fingertips as I lay my hands over the typewriter keys. Suddenly I will understand why Frost was *Frost*—arguably our country's most celebrated, honored, popular,

*Figure 5.1* Inaugural Poet Richard Blanco visiting Poet Laureate Natasha Trethewey in the library's Poetry Room, January 23, 2013. Credit Abby Brack Lewis/Library of Congress.

and remembered poet—because he wrote about (and for) the things and people right before him, *his* America, plain and true. His work was embedded in folklore, sprung from the very pastures and pleasures, snows and sorrows of the people—including himself—in his own backyard, so to speak. Inspired and possessed, I'll feel reborn into yet another story—the story Frost began for America.⁵

Staged in an allusive future tense, the passage plays on the last line of what the nation "*will* become" in Frost's "The Gift Outright" and echoes the language of colonial possession of its sixth and seventh lines ("Possessing what we still were unpossessed by, / Possessed by what we now no more possessed"). Despite the prospective insertion into Frost's legacy, Blanco's "One Today" had already marked itself in the tradition of "The Gift Outright"—inheriting its blank verse meter, representative anglophone speaker, and description of U.S. land holdings—to charismatically restage the expressive agency of the individual citizen as "American voice."

Like "The Gift Outright," "One Today," a sixty-nine-line poem in unrhymed iambic pentameter, focuses centrally on the relationship of the speaker with American geographical territory. It begins with a description of land as a blank canvas: "One sun rose on us today, kindled over our shores, / peeking over the Smokies, greeting the faces / of the Great Lakes, spreading a simple truth / across the Great Plains, then charging across the Rockies." These lines reanimate Frost's vision of "the land vaguely realizing westward / But still unstoried," progressing from the geographical features of Eastern to Midwestern to Western American states and naturalizing the relationship of the speaker as "possessing" or "possessed by" an expanding American continent. It is a decidedly dehistoricized trajectory. While Frost's land was always already American through a temporal paradox—in his narrative of colonial possession, "the land was ours before we were the land's"—Blanco's American geography has *no* past. All nine stanzas unfold in the eternal present tense of an ahistorical "*one today.*"

While "The Gift Outright" speaks from the common "we" and "our," "One Today" slips between the singular first-person "I" and common "we" and "our," as well as "one" and "all"—foregrounding the individuality of the speaking subject, and through its slippage into "we," "our," "one," and "all," staging the individual speaking subject as the universally representative American citizen. This is an important gesture in the context of Blanco's own identity. When questioning why he was selected as the inaugural poet, Blanco suggests that "I *did* fill a lot of 'boxes.'" "I was the youngest, first openly gay, first immigrant, and first Latino inaugural poet." Alongside the oft-cited Cold War–era narrative of Blanco's family fleeing communist rule, these categories of identity were the focus of media coverage of Blanco's selection as the inaugural poet and of his performance. Blanco is fond of saying that he was "made in Cuba, assembled in Spain and imported to the USA."[6] But if in Blanco's self-objectification as a commodity ("made, assembled, imported") we hear a trace of satire about the categories of identity he might feel compelled to represent, this satire is absent from his inaugural poem.

In "One Today," markers of multicultural identity authenticate, rather than disrupt, the anglophone speaking subject. Its use of multilingualism, for instance, provides an exemplary instance of high cultural pluralism—an aesthetic, as we saw McGurl describe in chapter 3, that joins "the values of literary modernism with a fascination with the experience of cultural difference and the authenticity of the ethnic voice,"[7] which has been useful to developing critiques of how features of program–era writing risk commodifying or fetishizing racial and ethnic difference for white audiences. A multilingual catalogue of greetings in the sixth stanza, "*hello / shalom / buon giorno / howdy / namaste / or buenos días*," ostensibly represents the diverse language traditions in American society:

> Hear: squeaky playground swings, trains whistling,
> or whispers across café tables, Hear: the doors we open
> for each other all day, saying: *hello / shalom /
> buon giorno / howdy / namaste / or buenos días*
> in the language my mother taught me—in every language
> spoken into one wind carrying our lives
> without prejudice, as these words break from my lips.[8]

The egalitarian possibility of representing "every language" (6:5), however, is here refused by "one" (6:6) language of neoliberal multiculturalism. The anglophone "hello" functions as the ur-greeting, the template for subsequent translations—rendering them comprehensible to monolingual American English speakers. All nonanglophone variants that follow "hello," the governing signifier, are substitutable as synonyms: rather than stand for a specific language tradition, each greeting stands in for difference. That is, the poem does not depend on the semantic distinction between "shalom" and "buon giorno"; "buon giorno" could have been replaced with "bonjour." The catalogue stages the notion of linguistic diversity without actually achieving differential linguistic signification. The inclusion of "howdy," a regional variant of the standard American English hello, makes this point yet more starkly. If Frost's blank verse modeled democracy's "checks and balances," Blanco's catalogue models a neoliberal logic of substitution—reducing multiple language traditions to the adjectival color of standard American English.

The risk of representing marginality—especially on a national stage—is the appropriation of marginal experience into legible claims of dominant state interest. Performing uncertain intelligibility, then, would seem an ethical response to the representational project of the inaugural poem. "One Today" did not pursue other ways in which poetry's formal and discursive resources could have been activated: a multilingual poetics that does not reduce multiple language traditions to a singular signifying practice might have alternately included an entire stanza in Spanish that was not a translation of a preceding stanza in English. At the very least, it would have perhaps included a single word that is not a synonym or subsidiary to its anglophone equivalent. Words that are not understood in standard American English, less legible to a monolingual anglophone audience, would index the exclusions and innate opacities of a poem that speaks for "all Americans." Instead, "One Today" asserts that the expressive agency of the individual, claiming that "every language / spoken" is distributed "without prejudice."[9] By performing an uncertain or conditionally intelligible speaking voice, the inaugural poem would have instead questioned the presumed distributive equality of expressive agency.

Certainly, the mere reference to non-English language speakers could be seen as a departure from Frost's narrative of colonial possession and expansion. But the poem's central project sought to reconfirm the nationalist values of Frost's nationalist poetics, safely adapting them to the current moment. Precisely by "giving a voice" to disenfranchised constituencies, Blanco's poem risked attributing agency where it does not exist—obscuring the ongoing structural deprivations of those subjects it does not identify and representing, for those subjects it does identify, a false fulfillment of their political resources by the state.

The Office of the President, and popular media coverage, considered "One Today" a triumph. The next year, on December 17, 2014, President Barack Obama announced an initiative to begin the normalization of relations between the United States and Cuba; when diplomatic relations were officially reestablished in July of 2015, the State Department commissioned Richard Blanco to read an occasional poem at the reopening of the American embassy in Havana. The poet read "Matters of the Sea / Cosas del mar": A Poem Commemorating a New Era in US-Cuba Relations" at the ceremonial flag-raising on August 14—in which the "sea of silence that has divided one people, one culture for decades" is figured as an unnavigable wall. "In my lifetime I've witnessed and experienced the metaphorical equivalent of a Berlin Wall—the ninety miles of ocean (that might as well be nine-thousand miles) between 'us,' as well as between the two halves of myself, many of my generation, and so many exiles," Blanco explained.[10] The poem seeks to mend this wall: in the final lines of the third and last stanza, the U.S. and Cuban citizen are finally united by "the sea still telling us the end / to our doubts and fears is to gaze into the lucid blues / of our shared horizon, breathe together, heal together."[11]

Like "One Today," the speaking voice of "Matters of the Sea" alternates between the individual "I" and collective "we and "our." The poem prefers a unified notion of self, rejecting a divided or fragmented identity—the sea heals by dissolving or erasing the illusory appearance of multiple selves: "a mirage of selves vanished / in waves."[12] Yet tucked into the encompassing "we" and "our" of the poem is a series of binary oppositions representing Cuba and the United States: fathers are either "cutting sugarcane" or "clocking-in at factories"; children are scouting stars above either "palms" or "skyscrapers"; mothers are "teaching us how to read in Spanish / or English."[13] While the identity of the poet himself promises the progressive symbol of a multicultural society, the speaker of these lines naturalizes traditional notions of a nuclear, heterosexual, and single-income family as the cultural common ground between Cuba and the United States. He also maintains essentialized economic, geographical, and linguistic binaries dividing them—factories or fieldwork, city or country, Spanish or English. Most notably, by using two languages as placeholders for two nations, Cuba is presumed as "Spanish speaking" and the United States as "English speaking."

Because languages are presented as national placeholders, moreover, it is important to note that although the word *Spanish* appears first in the poem—"Our mothers teaching us how to read in Spanish / or English" (2:8–9)—English is otherwise prioritized in the poem's performative as well as textual contexts. Blanco had apparently "insisted [the poem] had to be in both languages,"[14] but at the ceremony he read the poem only in English. The reading was subtitled with a Spanish translation for televised audiences in Cuba. When poem was released as a commemorative bilingual chapbook by the University of Pittsburgh Press in September 2015, including a Spanish translation by Ruth Behar, English was also prioritized in its print layout: the texts of the "Preface" and "Matters of the Sea" are followed, respectively, by the texts of "Prefacio" and "Cosas del mar." America is represented as "English," and the United States governs "Matters of the Sea."

Blanco is a demonstrative point of intersection as a contemporary state poet: his ceremonial verse representing the values of individual voice and pluralistic inclusion as dominant values in American poetic culture and how these values have been shaped by state interests. His 2013 and 2015 performances staged voice in the tradition of Frost as the national poet and model citizen (chapter 2), as well as in the tradition of the creative writing workshop poet (chapter 3). Indeed, Blanco, an MFA holder, has spoken against the "academicization" of poetry, rejecting poetic projects that cast poetry as a "high form of art,"[15] preferring the aesthetic values that defined creative writing since its professionalization in the 1960s and the populist civil verse initiatives of state verse culture in the 1990s and 2000s. Blanco's inaugural and state-commissioned poetry not only suggests the Cold War as a still-active framework through which the state engages with poetry, then, but the dominance of the creative writer, in expressed contrast to the poet-critic or community-based or coterie writer, as a Cold War legacy in the United States.

This legacy also defines how the office of the poet laureate imagines itself in the present. A 2019 promotion of the Archive of Recorded Poetry and Literature at the Library of Congress, for example, highlights a 1992 reading by Joseph Brodsky in the Montpelier Room as a "particularly powerful" example of the work of the office. Noting Brodsky's former Soviet citizenship and time in a labor camp as the backdrop for his U.S. poet laureateship in 1991, the library notes how Brodsky had bookended the reading by reciting the poetry of Robert Frost. Brodsky's own poems "about exile and displacement" stand in contrast to Frost's apparently American assertion that "there is no one I / Am put out with / Or put out by."[16] Frost, Brodsky, and the national poetry projects that these poets helped to motivate in the 1990s and 2000s offer civil verse assurances—modeling an America of individual expression, plural inclusivity, and democratic magnanimity against alternative models of voice and state.

Blanco, however, was selected to perform in 2013 and 2015 not by the Library of Congress but by the Office of the President and the Department of State. The Library of Congress praised Blanco's inaugural poem, affirming that the multicultural identity of the speaker in "One Today" represented the values of a democratic and pluralistic society: "'One Today' was and is a celebration of the shared American experience, an experience made possible not despite but because of our diverse individual histories and cultural backgrounds."[17] But the selection process that led to Blanco's invitation was opaque to legislative branch administrators at the Library of Congress,[18] which meanwhile was developing an increasingly participatory and transparent selection process for its poets laureate. In this sense, poets laureate are less direct mouthpieces of state power than inaugural or ceremonially designated poets. Instead, they represent how state power expresses its interests in increasingly privatized networks of literary production. Although Blanco's poems may be the last explicitly Cold War expressions of the national poet as representative citizen—the specter of Russian election interference in the United States and territorial aggression in the years that followed notwithstanding—that model has proven a durable template for state interests concerned to legitimize a triumphalist American vision of neoliberal multiculturalism and diversity.

## The Future of State Verse: Aesthetic Consolidation and Local Resistance

Initially privately endowed, today the U.S. national poetry office is the only federally funded position for a literary artist in the country—and the most visible public position for a poet in the United States. Yet our history of the position, the consultant in poetry from 1937 until 1985 and since 1986 the U.S. poet laureate, has often focused on individuals and institutions beyond consultants and poets laureate proper. I argue that this is the most accurate way to understand their work and its cultural impact. The poet laureateship is a lens to understand the evolving, and increasingly public and popularized, place of poetry in American culture—and to understand the ways that the state has expanded its reach in processes of cultural production in the field of American poetry in a neoliberal economy. If the Library of Congress, which remains an underexplored body in literary studies, and its laureates have shaped American poetry as we know it—and I argue that it has—it has done so by constellating a network of privatized players, thus ably yoking historically disparate aesthetic traditions into common cultural priorities.

When the position consultant in poetry was founded, it was one post among many other new administrative roles in an increasingly institutionalized, but aesthetically fragmented, literary field: the prewar period was still the era of the "little magazine," defined by the warring factions of international modernisms and reactionary—in the case of the Poetry Society of America, sometimes explicitly nationalist—poetry groups in the United States. *Poetry*, for example, was explicitly aligned with the fellows of the Library of Congress during the postwar period—sharing a common patron and publishing a defense of the fellows' decision to award Ezra Pound the Bollingen Prize—while a veritable public enemy of the Poetry Society of America, whose president, Robert Hillyer, decried the decision, and whose cofounder had come to love Frost only after determining he was "American to the core." The poetic field expressed discrete, often tentative, and diverse aesthetic projects. When Karl Shapiro assumed editorship of *Poetry* in the wake of the Bollingen affair, T. S. Eliot wrote to him observing that the scene was changing. Eliot believed that a little magazine does and should *not* hold a "broa[d] base" of support, as its distinguishing characteristics are its short-lived subsistence under a single editor and by extension subsistence under a singular guarantor or patron (or guarantors and patrons) who was singular in intention with the purpose of the experiment. Even though *Poetry* had been floundering, that was not a symptom of failure—a "little magazine" was ideally purposed as one project and therefore *should* end abruptly before suffering symptoms of "decay." But by 1950, under multiple editors and patrons, and thus straddling multiple reading publics and literary projects, "'Poetry,' in fact, [was] not a little magazine but an INSTITUTION."[19] Eliot's diagnosis, like Shapiro's predecessor's correspondence with Eli Lilly III several months earlier, was prescient.

What was once a little magazine proposing a distinct aesthetic directive is today a public-facing and multipurposed cultural organization, or mega "INSTITUTION." Guaranteed to exist in perpetuity since 2002 following the beneficence of the very same pharmaceutical fortune, the Poetry Foundation has remained an important partner of the Library of Congress and national poets—symbolized by the "Poet Laureate" office at foundation headquarters. But it is also allied with the PSA and a broad array of other poetry organizations across the nation, now formally through the Poetry Coalition administered by the latter.

The consolidation of state with private agendas is a victory for the library in many respects, enabling its expanded programming since the national poetry project of Ted Kooser, the first poet laureate to directly benefit from the post–Lilly Foundation, and continuing through the projects of Ryan, Trethewey, Herrera, and Smith. But it is important to observe that this consolidation is concomitant with directives toward populist accessibility tied to cultural imperialism, as in the "make American poetry great again" rhetoric of Poetry Foundation president John Barr in the early aughts—"Poetry needs to find its public again . . . before the largest possible audience;" "poets should be imperialists and importers of experience"[20]—moreover, with the aesthetic norming of tastes and missions of previously diverse players in the literary field.

In the last several years, internal state bodies have also consolidated, so that poets laureate stand for a more multifaceted complex of institutional agendas than they ever have before. In fiscal year 2020, the Poetry and Literature Center at the Library of Congress, which ran the office of the poet laureate, was absorbed into the Literary Initiatives Office, known as LIT, which did not exist before 2019; the LIT also absorbed National Book Festival programming. Rob Casper, whose title remains head of the Poetry and Literature at the Library of Congress, continues to run the office of the poet laureate, now as an LIT employee. Casper acknowledges the "tricky business of the federal government or government agencies of any sort celebrating and championing artists" today,[21] just as it did during the postwar period.

But this business is less "tricky" today than in the early years of the Cold War, when a government prize stood clearly as a government prize. Now, state interests are expressed, and standardized, through a wider network of institutions and are not as visibly politicized or socially controversial. While during the postwar years the state shied away from promoting the arts after the fiasco of awarding a "government prize," however, poetry later became an important tool in cultural diplomacy initiatives and indeed on the cultural front of the Cold War. We have seen this most visibly in the "golden age" of "poetry and power" of the 1960s, when the nation celebrated its first inaugural poet, Kennedy sent Frost on a Mission to Moscow, and the CIA alongside other state agencies and quasi-private organizations funded the Iowa Writers' Workshop—and in the first "National Poetry Festival," which united poets and, even more importantly, poetry patrons and organizations under the auspices of the state during the Cuban Missile Crisis. But, in the increasingly privatized cultural economy of the 1980s and 1990s,[22] poetry could even more readily serve dominant state interests through the increased cooperation of federal bodies with private enterprise. As such, even as literary criticism of postwar and contemporary American poetry has attended to institutions, the role of the state in poetic production more broadly has remained revealingly underexplored: *it is hidden in plain sight.*

In other words, the increasing privatization of the arts during the 1980s and 1990s—or, more exactly, the increasingly complex imbrication of the state arts agenda within semiprivate literary organizations—often, and effectively, obscures the role of the U.S. federal government in poetic production. In 2011, Juliana Spahr reflected on the "intensification of interest in literature's possible nationalism during the Bush years," during which the Department of State and other federal bodies, including the National Endowment for the Arts, collaborated in new ways with private literary organizations like the Poetry Foundation and with corporate sponsors to support national poetry projects. In addition to the new era of national poetry projects of poets laureate, for example, the NEA launched Operation Homecoming in 2004, a writing workshop program for veterans, funded by the arms and energy company Boeing,[23] a project Eleanor Wilner criticized as an "unholy alliance" between poetry and the Pentagon. What Spahr more broadly describes as "oxymoronic synergies between privatization and nationalism, the same oxymoron that so defines contemporary capitalism,"[24] indeed characterizes national poetry programming, only now more visibly. The groundwork for this synergy was laid by the early Cold War state, and in the 2000s—what Barr called, following Frost, poetry's new "golden age"—the federal government actively *re*invested in poetry as a nationalist resource.

This is also the difference between what Charles Bernstein articulated as "official verse culture" and the cultural transformation of the American poetic field that I argue should be described as the development of state verse culture. In one sense, my argument is that we must understand just how murky this distinction is: it is only through the state's collaboration with private interests, i.e., the "official" outlets of literary culture, that nationalist projects have and continue to influence dominant streams of poetic production. But I also hope to point to this as an intentionally *quiet* role, so that we can understand "official verse culture" not simply as the dominant values of mainstream poetic production shaped by conservative instincts of literary gatekeepers at traditional publications. Rather, the poetic values of those gatekeepers are products of state interest in the era of late capitalism and neoliberal governance in an ongoing Cold War. Official verse culture, put simply, was *always undergirded by the state.*

A term like *official verse culture* also suggests active aesthetic divisions in the poetic field—between the official and unofficial or otherwise fragmented interests. While such divisions still exist, *state* verse culture is now a more accurate description of how diverse aesthetic traditions have been institutionally unified to represent shared cultural priorities within a state-private complex.

Still, even within this process of cultural norming, poets who inevitably participate in the operations of official verse culture can, and do, resist or contradict the dominant values of state verse culture. Moreover, the expanded selection process for poets laureate, and changing values of national poetry projects, suggest that the boundaries of what constitute voice and models of citizenship within state verse culture are not as finite as they were in when it emerged in the 1960s or flowered in the late 1990s and early 2000s. Tracy K. Smith's closing event as poet laureate in 2018, for example, which included ten local poets laureate from across the country, points toward the various ways in which American poets might understand their role as public servants—and how they develop various strategies of relating to state power.

The offices of city and state poet laureateships are, on the one hand, knitted to the national poetry office: many past national poets laureate had previously served as local laureates, including Gwendolyn Brooks and Juan Felipe Herrera. Notably, both Brooks and Herrera also used the national office to advance more community-based projects, distinct from the "civil verse" poets laureate projects that defined the late 1990s and 2000s. Practically, their appointments suggest that their nominations by the Library of Congress were encouraged by their success in previous posts as civic representatives. But it also points to the expanded potential, especially more recently, of the city and state laureateships—which, though they share the title of poet laureate, more often engage with organizations outside the dominant state verse culture matrix, i.e., the Library of Congress with the NEA, their private patrons, and the Poetry Foundation.

In Philadelphia, for example, the poet laureate program, previously administered by the City of Philadelphia, moved to a new Center for Public Life at the Free Library of Philadelphia in late 2017. According to Raquel Salas Rivera, the poet laureate of Philadelphia from 2018–19, the position enjoys considerable "freedom" under the Free Library.[25] The contract for the position requires only that the laureate give two public events or readings during a two-year term; the only ceremonial functions Salas Rivera was asked to attend included an LGBTQ+ flag-raising and the inauguration of new youth poets laureate. During their term, Salas Rivera, a queer Puerto Rican poet and translator who writes in both Spanish and English, launched the 2018 summer poetry festival We (Too) Are Philly.

Taking its name from Langston Hughes's famous poem "I, Too," the festival hosted "a line-up of poets of color who have a strong commitment to fighting white supremacy and collaborating with local communities to create shared creative spaces."[26] Each event featured a poet from Philadelphia and at least one poet who writes in multiple languages. This programming, supported by an honorarium from the Free Library, funds from the Kelly Writers House at the University of Pennsylvania, and Salas Rivera's own contributions, did not seek to "promote poetry" as a de facto good—the mission of state projects homogenized by crowded institutional interests—but rather the political ambitions of the poet laureate's own poetry and related community initiatives. The We (Too) project followed the publication of Salas Rivera's *lo terciario/the tertiary*, a bilingual collection released written in 2016 as an aggrieved response to the Puerto Rican bond devaluation crisis and the controversial Puerto Rico Oversight, Management, and Economic Stability Act (PROMESA) Bill, passed July 1 of that year. Much as *lo terciario/the tertiary* was a response to PROMESA, the We (Too) Are Philly festival undertaken in Salas Rivera's position as Philadelphia's poet laureate was a response to "ICE and fascism," insisting on Philadelphia's continued status as a sanctuary city for immigrant and refugee populations.

The political activism of a poet laureate like Raquel Salas Rivera suggests that civic-minded or public-facing projects of local laureates depart from, or provide new models for, the projects of national poets laureate. Rather than promoting "poetry" as a placeholder for generic national values, local projects are more likely to participate in a politically defined or potentially antistate messages. City and state poet laureateships have more local and community-based ties that enable them to operate outside the paradigm of state verse culture more effectively, albeit to smaller audiences. The expanded political engagement of their offices results not only from the expressive freedom afforded by their more modest platforms but also the more diffuse—and limited—institutional partners that fund them.

At the same time, however, nonnational poets laureate also reflect the consolidation of state-private interests in the field of American poetry, most visibly in the appearance of nongovernment-appointed laureates. The U.S. "Young People's Poet Laureate," for instance, is a position awarded by the Poetry Foundation.[27] And the Youth Poets Laureate program, founded in 2008 in New York City by the literary arts organization Urban Word, created the position of a "National Youth Poet Laureate" when it began

*Figure 5.2* Amanda Gorman recites her inaugural poem, "The Hill We Climb," during the 59th U.S. presidential inauguration ceremony, January 20, 2021. Credit Navy Petty Officer 1st Class Carlos M. Vazquez II; courtesy of the chairman of the Joint Chiefs of Staff, Washington, D.C.

partnering with the Poetry Foundation in 2017.[28] The first poet to be named national youth poet laureate was Amanda Gorman, who later served as the 2021 inaugural poet at the inauguration ceremony of President Joe Biden.

The youngest-ever inaugural poet, twenty-two-year-old Gorman's performance of "The Hill We Climb" examined themes of racial identity and racial justice and was widely lauded.[29] In the weeks that followed, the poet signed with IGM Models, who would represent her for fashion and beauty endorsements; and Gorman also performed her poetry at the preshow of the National Football League Super Bowl LV.[30] As Gorman's multiple public roles suggest, the relationship between state and private interests will continue to define the field of American poetry. The history of that relationship provided by this study will, I hope, instruct our understanding of the role of poetry in civic life going forward.

The relationships of city, locality and state-based poet laureateships and civic-minded poetry programming with government entities, and the partnerships of these government entities with private institutions—as well as with community-based initiatives—remain an important avenue for future study. Primarily, they point to the ways that contemporary state verse culture is more multifaceted than a singular nationalist program—even though, as the history of the national poetry office has shown, it has historically prioritized a model of individual, expressive voice that acted as a proxy for the values of American citizenship in projects of Cold War–driven imperialism and cultural showmanship. Because of the massive networks with multiple institutions it assumes, state verse culture is most dominantly expressed in "civil verse" projects that reaffirm the earlier Cold War legacy of poetry that supports existing national values, but also, if more recently, in projects that promote civic engagement that do not always assume political neutrality.

Since its postwar origins, expressions of state verse culture—national poetry projects and the more public-facing missions of major literary organizations—have been increasingly successful at absorbing poetic production into a unified institutional and discursive system. That is not to say all state poetry is "pro-state" or nationalist: many poets, from Bishop and Lowell to Brooks, Herrera, and Smith, occupied their positions with self-conscious ambivalence. Rather, the success of state verse culture is that by linking diverse public and private interests through patron endowments and federal legislation, it has also been able to yoke disparate aesthetic traditions into a common national project.

Likewise, the lesson of the history of the national poetry office is not that state support of poetry—or civic-minded poetry programming—is necessarily or inherently problematic. In fact, increased and more explicit forms of state support for the arts would surely enable poets and poetry organizations to articulate more distinct aesthetic commitments and political motivations.

But understanding the complex nature of the interests that create public-facing poets is increasingly important. Within a nationalist and privatized cultural economy, the commitments of individual poets laureate will be important to follow, now even more consequentially than in the first decades of the national poetry office. With public-facing reach and, today, an explicitly civic charge, the programs they lead—and the poems that they read—on the national stage teach us not about poetry but how we should be citizens.

APPENDIX I

# Occupants of the U.S. National Poetry Office

Poet Laureate Consultants in Poetry to the
Library of Congress (1986–2022)

Ada Limón (2022– )
Joy Harjo (2019–2022)
Tracy K. Smith (2017–2019)
Juan Felipe Herrera (2015–2017)
Charles Wright (2014–2015)
Natasha Trethewey (2012–2014)
Philip Levine (2011–2012)
W.S. Merwin (2010–2011)
Kay Ryan (2008–2010)
Charles Simic (2007–2008)
Donald Hall (2006–2007)
Ted Kooser (2004–2006)
Louise Glück (2003–2004)
Billy Collins (2001–2003)
Stanley Kunitz (2000–2001)
Special Bicentennial Consultants (1999–2000)
    Rita Dove
    Louise Glück
    W.S. Merwin

Robert Pinsky (1997–2000)
Robert Hass (1995–1997)
Rita Dove (1993–1995)
Mona Van Duyn (1992–1993)
Joseph Brodsky (1991–1992)
Mark Strand (1990–1991)
Howard Nemerov (1988–1990)
Richard Wilbur (1987–1988)
Robert Penn Warren (1986–1987)

## Consultants in Poetry to the Library of Congress (1937–1985)

Gwendolyn Brooks (1985–1986)
Reed Whittemore (Interim Consultant in Poetry, 1984–1985)
Robert Fitzgerald (appointed but unable to serve, 1984–1985)
Anthony Hecht (1982–1984)
Maxine Kumin (1980–1982)
William Meredith (1978–1980)
Robert Hayden (1976–1978)
Stanley Kunitz (1974–1976)
Daniel Hoffman (1973–1974)
Josephine Jacobsen (1971–1973)
William Stafford (1970–1971)
William Jay Smith (1968–1970)
James Dickey (1966–1968)
Stephen Spender (1965–1966)
Reed Whittemore (1964–1965)
Howard Nemerov (1963–1964)
Louis Untermeyer (1961–1963)
Richard Eberhart (1959–1961)
Robert Frost (1958–1959)
Randall Jarrell (1956–1958)
William Carlos Williams (appointed in 1952 but did not serve)
Conrad Aiken (1950–1952)
Elizabeth Bishop (1949–1950)
Léonie Adams (1948–1949)

Robert Lowell (1947–1948)
Karl Shapiro (1946–1947)
Louise Bogan (1945–1946)
Robert Penn Warren (1944–1945)
Allen Tate (1943–1944)
Joseph Auslander (1937–1941)

## APPENDIX II

# Fellows in American Letters at the Library of Congress

Léonie Adams (served 1949–1956)
Conrad Aiken (1947–1954)
Wynstan Hugh Auden (1947–1954)
Elizabeth Bishop (1952–1956)
Richard P. Blackmur (1952–1956)
Louise Bogan (1946–1951)
Cleanth Brooks (1952 -1956)
Van Wyck Brooks (1944–1946)
Katherine Garrison Chapin (1944–1953)
Thomas Stearns Eliot (1947–1954)
Paul Green (1944–1953)
Robert Lowell (1949–1956)
Archibald MacLeish (1949–1956)[1]
Samuel Eliot Morison (1950–1956)
Katherine Anne Porter (1944–1953)
John Crowe Ransom (1950–1956)
Carl Sandburg (1944–1946)
Karl Shapiro (1947–1953)
Theodore Spencer (1947–1949)[2]
Allen Tate (1944–1951)
Willard Thorp (1944–1951)
Mark Van Doren (1944–1945)
Robert Penn Warren (1945–1953)
Thornton Wilder (1950–1956)
William Carlos Williams (1949–1956)

APPENDIX III

## U.S. Inaugural Poets

Robert Frost, "The Gift Outright," inauguration of President John F. Kennedy (1961)

Maya Angelou, "On the Pulse of Morning," inauguration of President Bill Clinton (1993)

Miller Williams, "Of History and Hope," inauguration of President Bill Clinton (1997)

Elizabeth Alexander, "Praise Song for the Day," inauguration of President Barack Obama (2009)

Richard Blanco, "One Today," inauguration of President Barack Obama (2013)

Amanda Gorman, "The Hill We Climb," inauguration of President Joe Biden (2021)

# Notes

## Introduction

1. Robert Casper, head of the Poetry and Literature Center, Library of Congress, interview by author, August 2, 2019.
2. Gwendolyn Brooks, "Annual Report to the Librarian of Congress from the Chair of Poetry," 5, William McGuire Papers, Manuscript Division, Library of Congress.
3. Archer M. Huntington executed a deed of trust providing perpetuity to the Library for the maintenance of a chair of poetry of the English language in November 1936; Joseph Auslander was the first to hold the post in 1937. G. Forrest Butterworth Jr. to Herbert Putnam, president, Library of Congress, November 19, 1936, Library of Congress Trust Funds, 1928, 1936–44, 1956–59, 1971, 1985, William McGuire Papers, Manuscript Division, Library of Congress.
4. "The Poetry and Literature Center at the Library of Congress: About the Position of Poet Laureate Consultant in Poetry," Library of Congress, https://www.loc.gov/poetry/about_laureate.html (accessed May 15, 2019).
5. Elizabeth Bishop, "View of the Capitol from the Library of Congress," *New Yorker*, July 7, 1951, 17.
6. "Udall Report on Robert Frost Trip to USSR, April 1963," April 10, 1963, President's Office Files: Department of the Interior, Papers of John F. Kennedy, John F. Kennedy Presidential Library.
7. Edward Ohnemus, "Brodsky Urges Publishers to Distribute Poetry to the Masses," *Library of Congress Gazette*, October 11, 1991, 9.
8. Ohnemus.

9. Brooks, "Annual Report," 1.
10. "Annual Report of the Consultant in Poetry for the Fiscal Year Ending September 30, 1977," 1, William McGuire Papers. Manuscript Division, Library of Congress.
11. Gwendolyn Brooks, "Black Woman in Russia," in Elaine Lee, ed., *Go Girl!: The Black Woman's Book of Travel and Adventure* (Portland: Eighth Mountain, 1997), 237.
12. Brooks, 237–38.
13. Gwendolyn Brooks to John C. Broderick, March 26, 1986; Broderick to Brooks, April 3, 1986, William McGuire Papers, Manuscript Division, Library of Congress.
14. Casper, email message to author, August 21, 2020.
15. David Mearns to Archibald MacLeish, "Duties of Allen Tate as Consultant in Poetry," April 27, 1943, Archibald MacLeish Papers, Manuscript Division, Library of Congress.
16. Mearns.
17. "The Poetry and Literature Center at the Library of Congress: About the Position of Poet Laureate Consultant in Poetry," Library of Congress. This slightly adjusts the 2015 description of the office, when the official duties of the poet laureate were kept "to a minimum" (accessed May 2, 2015).
18. L. Quincy Mumford to W. Sterling Cole, House of Representatives (New York). Roy Basler, chief of the Manuscript Division, Burton W. Adkinson, and Verner Clapp, previously the acting librarian, assisted in the drafting of the letter. Quoted in William McGuire, *Poetry's Catbird Seat: The Consultantship in Poetry in the English Language at the Library of Congress, 1937–1987* (Washington, D.C.: Library of Congress, 1988), 196.
19. Elizabeth Bishop to Robert Lowell, April 22, 1960, in Thomas Travisano and Saskia Hamilton, eds., *Words in Air: The Complete Correspondence Between Elizabeth Bishop and Robert Lowell* (New York: Farrar, Straus and Giroux, 2008), 316 (210).
20. "'Dedication,' Robert Frost's Presidential Inaugural Poem, 20 January 1961: Typescript with Frost's Holograph Script Corrections in Ink and Stewart Udall's Holograph Clarifications in Pencil on the Last Page," Stewart L. Udall Papers, Manuscript Division, Library of Congress.
21. National Foundation on the Arts and the Humanities Act of 1965 (Pub. L. 89-209).
22. "Gwendolyn Brooks Is Named as Next Library Poetry Consultant," *Library of Congress Information Bulletin*, May 20, 1985, 106.
23. Casper, interview by author, August 2, 2019.
24. Ohnemus, "Brodsky Urges Publishers to Distribute Poetry to the Masses."
25. Joseph Parisi and Stephen Young, eds., *Between the Lines: A History of Poetry in Letters, 1962–2002* (Chicago: Dee, 2006), 6.

26. Stephen Young, program director, the Poetry Foundation, interview by author, August 8, 2019.
27. "Poetry Coalition," Academy of American Poets, https://poets.org/academy-american-poets/poetry-coalition (accessed August 20, 2019).
28. Sarah Aridi, "Mellon Foundation Grants $2.2 Million to Academy of American Poets," *New York Times*, January 15, 2019, https://www.nytimes.com/2019/01/15/arts/mellon-foundation-poetry.html (accessed August 9, 2021).
29. Hayden Carruth to Ernest Brooks Jr., secretary of the Bollingen Foundation, August 26, 1949, Bollingen Foundation Records, Manuscript Division, Library of Congress.
30. Yale University Librarian James T. Babb to Gwendolyn Brooks, August 30, 1949, Bollingen Foundation Records, Manuscript Division.
31. Ruth Lilly also received letters of rejection from later editors, including John Nims and Joseph Parisi. Stephen Young, email message to author, September 21, 2019. Also see *Poetry*: History of Poetry Magazine," Poetry Foundation, https://www.poetryfoundation.org/poetrymagazine/history (accessed September 21, 2019); and Parisi and Young, *Between the Lines*, 241–42, 7.
32. Léonie Adams to Luther Evans, April 19, 1949, William McGuire Papers, Manuscript Division.
33. Richard Eberhardt to Daniel Boorstin, March 16, 1978, William McGuire Papers, Manuscript Division.
34. Casper, interview by author, August 2, 2019.
35. The categories used in the twenty-third poet laureate selection process in full included 1. Academic; 2. Bookstore Owner; 3. Director; 4. Conference Director; 5. Distributor Director; 6. Festival Director; 7. Funder Director; 8. Media Member; 9. Membership Organization Director; 10. Poet Laureate (former); 11. Poetry Coalition Member; 12. Presenter Director—National; 13. Presenter Director—Regional; 14. Publication Editor; 15. Residency Director. Casper, "PL Appointment Process," email message to author, August 1, 2019.
36. "If a nominator only nominated one poet, their choice received six points; if a nominator nominated two poets, their first choice received four points and their second choice received two points; if a nominator nominated three poets, their first choice received three points, their second choice received two points, and their third choice received one point." Casper.
37. Casper, interview by author, August 2, 2019; Casper.
38. Casper. Casper has arranged such a call for each of the poets laureate appointed during his time at the library.
39. William McGuire, *Poetry's Catbird Seat: The Consultantship in Poetry in the English Language at the Library of Congress, 1937–1987* (Washington: Library of Congress, 1988).

40. Kamran Javadizadeh, "The Institutionalization of the Postwar Poet," *Modernism/Modernity* 23, no. 1 (January 2016): 113–39; also see Kamran Javadizadeh, *Institutionalized Lyric: American Poetry at Midcentury* (New York: Oxford University Press, forthcoming).
41. Much of this literature follows the work of Terry Eagleton, Jonathan Culler, Stanley Fish, and Jane Tompkins, where an institutional approach to literary study disrupts notions of literary individuation, e.g., authorial genius. This study, meanwhile, follows scholarship that retains the notion of individual agency *within* institutions. Lawrence Buell, for example, holds that "at the heart of the Houghton Mifflin institutional juggernaut, the discretionary role of the (well-placed) individual actor was crucial" in the canonization of Thoreau, providing an institutional account of canon formation where individuals act not as passive functionaries but agentive and ideologically endowed actors. Lawrence Buell, "Henry Thoreau Enters the American Canon," in Robert F. Sayre, ed., *New Essays on Walden* (New York: Cambridge University Press, 1992), 37–38.
42. Christopher Kempf, *Craft Class: The Writing Workshop in American Culture* (Baltimore: Johns Hopkins University Press, 2022).
43. Michael Davidson, *The San Francisco Renaissance: Poetics and Community at Mid-Century* (Cambridge: Cambridge University Press, 1989).
44. This study especially follows D. G. Myers, *The Elephants Teach: Creative Writing Since 1880* (Chicago: University of Chicago Press, 2006); and Mark McGurl, *The Program Era: Postwar Fiction and the Rise of Creative Writing* (Cambridge, Mass.: Harvard University Press, 2009).
45. Consider, for example, the legacy of dueling anthologies since 1960, when Donald Allen's *New American Poetry* championed the "new avant-garde" against the traditional verse of mainstream collections such as Hall, Pack, and Simpson's *New Poets of England and America*. Even more recent critical anthologies like *American Hybrid: A Norton Anthology of New Poetry* retain this division, here through the very promise to hybridize the two spheres of American postwar poetry. Donald Allen, ed., *The New American Poetry, 1945–1960* (Berkeley: University of California Press, 1960); Donald Hall, Robert Pack, and Louis Simpson, eds., *New Poets of England and America* (New York: Meridian, 1957); Cole Swenson and David St. John, eds., *American Hybrid: A Norton Anthology of New Poetry* (New York: Norton, 2009).
46. "Let me be specific as to what I mean by 'official verse culture'—I am referring to the poetry publishing and reviewing practices of the *New York Times*, the *Nation*, *American Poetry Review*, the *New York Review of Books*, the *New Yorker*, *Poetry* (Chicago), *Antaeus*, *Parnassus*, Atheneum, all the major trade publishers, the poetry series of almost all of the major university presses (the university of California Press being a significant exception at present)."

Charles Bernstein, "The Academy in Peril: William Carlos Williams Meets the MFA," in *Content's Dream: Essays, 1975–1984* (Evanston: Northwestern University Press, 2001), 247.

47. The role of the private-state network in soft diplomacy initiatives during the Cold War has been discussed importantly in Kenneth Osgood's *Total Cold War: Eisenhower's Secret Propaganda Battle at Home and Abroad* (Lawrence: University Press of Kansas, 2006); Laura Belmonte, *Selling the American Way: U.S. Propaganda and the Cold War* (Philadelphia: University of Pennsylvania Press, 2008); and Amanda Laugesen, *Taking Books to the World: American Publishers and the Cultural Cold War* (Amherst: University of Massachusetts Press, 2017).

48. See Serge Guilbaut, *How New York Stole the Idea of Modern Art: Abstract Expressionism, Freedom, and the Cold War* (Chicago: University of Chicago Press, 1983) on avant-garde painting. More recent scholarship has explored the role of the arts in Cold War cultural diplomacy and propaganda across artistic fields, including film, in Peter Decherney, *Hollywood and the Culture Elite: How the Movies Became American* (New York: Columbia University Press, 2005); dance in Clare Croft, *Dancers as Diplomats: American Choreography and Cultural Exchange* (New York: Oxford University Press, 2015); music in Danielle Forster-Lussier, *Music in America's Cold War Diplomacy* (Berkeley: University of California Press, 2015); and the publishing industry in Amanda Laugesen, *Taking Books to the World: American Publishers and the Cultural Cold War* (Amherst: University of Massachusetts Press, 2017).

49. Juliana Spahr, *Du Bois's Telegram: Literary Resistance and State Containment* (Cambridge, Mass.: Harvard University Press, 2018).

50. T. S. Eliot, "The Social Function of Poetry" in *On Poetry and Poets* (New York: Farrar, Straus and Giroux, 1943), 8.

51. Spahr, *Du Bois's Telegram*, 142.

52. Robert von Hallberg, *American Poetry and Culture, 1945–1980* (Cambridge, Mass.: Harvard University Press, 1988), 2.

53. von Hallberg, 4.

54. Quoted in Dana Goodyear, "The Moneyed Muse," *New Yorker*, February 19, 2007.

55. Ron Silliman et al., "Aesthetic Tendency and the Politics of Poetry: A Manifesto," *Social Text*, nos. 19/20 (Autumn 1988): 265.

56. Piotr Gwiazda, *US Poetry in the Age of Empire, 1979–2012* (New York: Palgrave MacMillan, 2014), 1–2.

57. Paul Jay, *Global Matters: The Transnational Turn in Literary Studies* (Ithaca, N.Y.: Cornell University Press, 2010), 118 (emphasis in the original), quoted in Gwiazda, 9.

58. Gwiazda, 4.

59. Robert Pinsky, *An Explanation of America* (Princeton, N.J.: Princeton University Press, 1979).
60. Tyler Hoffman, *Robert Frost and the Politics of Poetry* (Hanover, N.H.: Middlebury College Press, 2001), 44.
61. Roberg von Hallberg, *Lyric Powers* (Chicago: University of Chicago Press, 2008), 90.
62. Yet even the Language poets, who posted the most coherent challenge to the representative voice of the national poetry project during the age of identity politics, leave difficulties unresolved. Their own movement-defining manifestos—as well as most recent literary-critical narratives of avant-garde practice—assert their "marginalization" in the American canon, staging a conflict between the institutional norm and the utopian open text. The practical transparency of voice in these narratives yields a fascinating aesthetic inconsistency and testament to the pervasiveness of identity-based politics in the 1980s. Even the most radical poetics—where "the self as the central and final term of creative practice is being challenged and exploded"—adopts a visible, legible subject position to represent political demands. Silliman et al., "Aesthetic Tendency and the Politics of Poetry," 263.
63. Louise S. Robbins, "The Library of Congress and Federal Loyalty Programs, 1947–1956: No 'Communists or Cocksuckers,'" *Library Quarterly* 64, no. 4 (October 1994): 367. Robbins confirmed this quotation in a telephone conversation with an interviewer of Shapiro; also see Natalie Robins, *Alien Ink: The FBI's War Against Freedom of Expression* (New York: William Morrow, 1992).
64. Paul Mariani, *William Carlos Williams: A New World Naked* (San Antonio: Trinity University Press, 2016), 651.
65. "'Dedication,' Robert Frost's Presidential Inaugural Poem."
66. "History and Mission," Poetry Foundation, http://www.poetryfoundation.org/foundation/history-and-mission (accessed March 2, 2015).
67. Tracy K. Smith, "Why Poetry? Why Now?" presented at the Philomathean Society 2019 Annual Oration, Q & A with author, University of Pennsylvania, Philadelphia, March 28, 2019.
68. Young, interview by author, August 8, 2019.

# 1. State Verse Scandals

1. Bishop to Lowell, January 21, 1949 in Thomas Travisano and Saskia Hamilton, eds., *Words in Air: The Complete Correspondence Between Elizabeth Bishop and Robert Lowell* (New York: Farrar, Straus and Giroux, 2008), 81–82 (70). Hereafter *WIA*.

2. Other possibilities discussed at the November 19 meeting included Marianne Moore, Randall Jarrell, Delmore Schwartz, and Richard Eberhart. William McGuire Papers, Manuscript Division, Library of Congress. The post would be formally offered to Williams, Moore, Adams, and finally to Bishop.
3. Lowell to Bishop, December 18, 1948, *WIA* 70 (63).
4. Lowell to Bishop, January 14, 1949, *WIA* 79 (69).
5. "They can't 'change their minds,' poor souls! Dr. Evans has to OK our choice, but he always does. Nor can we re-consider." Lowell to Bishop, January 24, 1949, *WIA* 83 (71).
6. December 18, 1948, *WIA* 70 (63).
7. "I think I'll write to Mrs. Ames right now and ask about July." January 21, 1949, *WIA* 82 (70).
8. December 24, 1948, *WIA* 72 (65).
9. January 31, 1949, *WIA* 84–5 (72).
10. "Pound, in Mental Clinic, Wins Prize For Poetry Penned in Treason Cell: PRIZE VOTED POUND FOR PRISON POETRY," *New York Times*, February 20, 1949.
11. "The Pisan Cantos Wins for Ezra Pound First Award of Bollingen Prize in Poetry," Library of Congress press release no. 542, February 20, 1949.
12. Lowell to the Yaddo Board, February 26, 1949. On February 11, 1949, *The New York Times* reported that according to U.S. Army intelligence, former Yaddo writer-in-residence Agnes Smedley was in league with a Soviet spy ring. Three days later, FBI investigators arrived in Saratoga Springs. See Micki McGee, ed., *Yaddo: Making American Culture* (New York: Columbia University Press, 2008); Hugh Stevens, "Confession, Autobiography, and Resistance: Robert Lowell and the Politics of Privacy," in Douglas Field, ed., *American Cold War Culture* (Edinburgh: Edinburgh University Press, 2005); Carla Blumenkranz, "'Deeply and Mysteriously Implicated': Communist Sympathies, FBI Informants, and Robert Lowell at Yaddo," *Poetry*, December 18, 2006.
13. Quoted in Paul Mariani, *Lost Puritan: A Life of Robert Lowell* (New York: Norton, 1996), 175.
14. The Yaddo trial, a prescient controversy on the eve of the the "Bollingen Affair," is often referred to by literary historians as the "Lowell Affair."
15. Luther Evans to Bishop, April 19, 1949, William McGuire Papers, Manuscript Division, Library of Congress.
16. "With what I've saved from the Library and Yaddo and my Guggenheim, I can easily last two years before I have to think of teaching," Lowell wrote to the Tates after his year in Washington. Quoted in William McGuire, *Poetry's Catbird Seat: The Consultantship in Poetry in the English Language at the Library of Congress, 1937–1987* (Washington, D.C.: Library of Congress, 1988), 107.

17. The sheer number of government employees increased from 953,891 in 1939 to almost 3 million shortly after the war, for example; Pentagon expenditures quadrupled between 1948 and 1953. Field, *American Cold War Culture*, 5.

    Although technically privately endowed, Lowell's salary reflected the 14 percent increase applied to all government employee salaries per congressional vote that year. McGuire, *Poetry's Catbird Seat*, 102.
18. The CIA was founded on September 18, 1947. A day later, Lowell wrote his first letter to Bishop from the Jefferson Building: "when [I] look up I see the dome of our capitol." *WIA* 8 (5).
19. Tadd Fisher to Bishop, "Department of State Information Request: Survey of National Interest in American Poetry," August 17, 1950, William McGuire Papers, Manuscript Division, Library of Congress.
20. Thomas Travisano, *WIA* 96.
21. Elizabeth Bishop, "Annual Report to the Librarian of Congress from the Chair of Poetry 1949–1950," William McGuire Papers, Manuscript Division, Library of Congress.
22. Paul Mellon's wife, Mary Conover Mellon, named the foundation for Carl Jung's country retreat, Bollingen Tower, in the eponymous Swiss village. Princeton University Press assumed the series in 1969, and today cites Mellon's vision for the now over 250-volume collection: "Jung might be considered the central core, the binding factor, not only of the Foundations' general direction but also of the ultimate intellectual temper of Bollingen Series as a whole." Mellon quoted in "Bollingen Series (General)," Princeton University Press, http://press.princeton.edu/catalogs/series/bollingen-series-(general).html.
23. Paul Mellon to Huntington Cairns, January 1946, Bollingen Foundation Records, Manuscript Division, Library of Congress.
24. Quoted in McGuire, *Poetry's Catbird Seat*, 93–94.
25. The Woodberry Poetry Room at Harvard University developed a collection in the 1930s, but early collaborative recordings were made in conjunction with the British Council. The recordings did not project a national archive, as did the library, which partnered with NBC to release high-production quality tapes for public consumption.
26. The first organizational meetings were held on May 26–27, 1944, Bollingen Foundation Records, Manuscript Division, Library of Congress. See appendix 2 for a list of the Fellows in American Letters and their terms served.
27. January 23, 1948, Bollingen Foundation Records, Manuscript Division, Library of Congress.
28. Jed Rasula, *The American Poetry Wax Museum: Reality Effects, 1940–1990* (Urbana: National Council of Teachers of English, 1995), 101–2.

29. Verner Clapp to the Fellows in American Letters, Bollingen Foundation Records, Manuscript Division, Library of Congress.
30. It is unclear in archival documentation if this vote was recorded at the first (November 19) or second meeting, Bollingen Foundation Records, Manuscript Division, Library of Congress.
31. Quoted in McGuire, *Poetry's Catbird Seat*, 112–3. Shapiro would not follow the liberal aesthetic of Tate's "objective critic," reasoning in the *Partisan Review*: "I am a Jew and I cannot honor anti-Semites;" and that Pound's "moral and political philosophy ultimately vitiates the Cantos and lowers the literary quality of the work." Karl Shapiro, "The Question of the Pound Award," *Partisan Review* 16, no 5 (May 1949): 518–19.
32. Andrew Gross, "Liberalism and Lyricism, or Karl Shapiro's Elegy for Identity," *Journal of Modern Literature* 34, no. 3 (Spring 2011), 2. See Shapiro, *Reports of My Death* (Chapel Hill: Algonquin, 1990), 43.
33. Gross.
34. "I simply observe that you are in great distress, and the result is confusion." Allen Tate to Karl Shapiro, quoted in McGuire, *Poetry's Catbird Seat*, 113.
35. Given what McGuire calls "profuse an often confusing convolutum of letters among the Fellows" in November 1948–February 1949, "the documentation to be found in the Library archives is not altogether clear" (*Poetry's Catbird Seat*, 113). I agree.
36. Theodore Spencer had passed away several weeks before, but, as he had nominated *The Pisan Cantos* in November, his vote counted for Pound.
37. Rasula writes that the fellows' collectively signed rebuttal to the *Saturday Review* "sounds uncannily like the voice of Tate" (*American Poetry Wax Museum*, 106). His authorship is likely considering the special committee's request that he write the original press release addendum; it is also implied in MacLeish's exhortations to Tate on the eve of the statement's publication in a letter of October 15, discussed in more depth shortly. Formally, the cosignatories were Adams, Bogan, Shapiro, and Thorp.
38. "The Pisan Cantos Wins for Ezra Pound First Award of Bollingen Prize in Poetry."
39. See Al Filreis, *Counter-revolution of the Word: The Conservative Attack on Modern Poetry, 1945–1960* (Chapel Hill: University of North Carolina Press, 2008) and Rasula for more comprehensive catalogues of "pro-Pound," "anti-Pound," or neutral publications.
40. Bollingen Foundation Records, Manuscript Division, Library of Congress.
41. Frost in a memorandum to his secretary, Kay Morrison, quoted in McGuire, *Poetry's Catbird Seat*, 115. Frost's reaction to the award is not well known, as he would later famously assist in Pound's release. As I will discuss in chapter 2,

Pound's release was symbolic of a new state investment in the arts to project a free and rational society during the Cold War.
42. Bollingen Foundation Records, Manuscript Division, Library of Congress.
43. Robert Hillyer, "Treason's Strange Fruit: The Case of Ezra Pound and the Bollingen Award" and "Poetry's New Priesthood," *Saturday Review of Literature*, June 11 and 18, 1949.
44. Luther Evans, "A Letter from the Librarian of Congress," *Saturday Review of Literature*, July 2, 1949, 20–21.
45. Hillyer, "Treason's Strange Fruit," 9.
46. Norman Cousins and Harrison Smith, "Editor's Note," *Saturday Review of Literature*, June 18, 1949, 7.
47. Norman Cousins and Harrison Smith, "More on Pound," *Saturday Review of Literature*, July 30, 1949, 22.
48. The committee's chairman, Senator Theodore F. Green, of Rhode Island, in an announcement to the press, quoted in McGuire, *Poetry's Catbird Seat*, 121.
49. Congress reversed the 1949 decision in 1988, after the Bobbitt family endowed a $10,000 poetry prize to be awarded every other year. Modeled after the Bollingen Prize and administered by the Library of Congress, the Bobbitt Prize is further discussed in chapter 4.
50. "In 1946, when it became evident that publication costs were rising very rapidly." Hayden Carruth and Thomas C. Lea to J. K. Lilly, November 11, 1949, Bollingen Foundation Records, Manuscript Division, Library of Congress.
51. The Bollingen Foundation first donated to the Modern Poetry Association of Chicago to support *Poetry* in 1946; the continuing grant provided $82,500 over eight years. "Bollingen Foundation Data Sheet For Contributions," Bollingen Foundation Records, Manuscript Division, Library of Congress.
52. Thomas C. Lea to Huntington Cairns, November 27, 1946, Bollingen Foundation Records, Manuscript Division, Library of Congress.
53. Huntington Cairns to Paul Mellon, November 27, 1946, Bollingen Foundation Records, Manuscript Division, Library of Congress.
54. "In recognition of the decision of your board to discontinue further financial help at present, we are hard at work searching for replacement funds, as without them, publications sometime in 1950 will be impossible. The spiraling costs of printing, paper, etc. these days make it very difficult for enterprises such as ours and our only hope is that we shall discover an individual or foundation, that, like the Bollingen Foundation, are vitally interested in the advancement of outstanding letters, in our time." Geraldine Udell to Ernest Brooks, January 13, 1949, Bollingen Foundation Records, Manuscript Division, Library of Congress.

55. Hayden Carruth to Ernest Brooks, August 26, 1949, Bollingen Foundation Records, Manuscript Division, Library of Congress.
56. Emphasis mine. This letter formalized a conversation Carruth apparently had with Brooks a few days earlier and anticipated a visit in person to his offices in hopes of securing the prize. In an accompanying note, Carruth wrote to Brooks: "Following your suggestion in our phone conversation the other day, I have prepared a letter containing my suggestions. Here it is; I hope it will receive favorable attention from the directors." Carruth to Brooks, August 26, 1949.
57. James T. Babb to Ernest Brooks, August 30, 1949, Bollingen Foundation Records, Manuscript Division, Library of Congress.
58. Ernest Brooks, memorandum "Re: Poetry Prize—Phone with Mr. Babb to Board of Trustees," December 21, 1949, Bollingen Foundation Records, Manuscript Division, Library of Congress. Moreover, Babb and other administrators felt "at least some of the Fellows of the Library of Congress in American Letters should serve on the jury."
59. Babb to Brooks, December 22, 1949, Bollingen Foundation Records, Manuscript Division, Library of Congress. The proposed committee of award was drawn up by the new executive committee, composed of James Babb as chairman, Professor Cleanth Brooks, and Donald Gallup as secretary. Yale president Charles Seymour sent sixteen letters of invitation to Léonie Adams, Conrad Aiken, W. H. Auden, Elizabeth Bishop, Louise Bogan, Katherine Garrison Chapin, T. S. Eliot, Robert Lowell, Archibald MacLeish, Katherine Anne Porter, Karl Shapiro, Willard Thorp, Robert Penn Warren, William Carlos Williams, Paul Green, and Allen Tate. Williams, MacLeish, and Bishop had become fellows after the Pound ballot; Spencer had passed away. As signatories to the fellows' statement against the *Saturday Review*, after all, MacLeish and Williams had already in effect been added to the Bollingen's jury of selection in the public eye.
60. "In discussing with Babb the form of the letter to be sent by President Seymour to each individual invited to serve on the Committee of Award, I emphasized that the prize should be referred to as having been established by Yale University, not by [the] Bollingen Foundation." Brooks, memorandum "Re: Poetry Prize to Bollingen Foundation Board of Trustees," January 19, 1950, Bollingen Foundation Records, Manuscript Division, Library of Congress.
61. James Babb to Brooks, December 22, 1949, Bollingen Foundation Records, Manuscript Division, Library of Congress.
62. Ernest Brooks, "Publicity Release Draft Material," January 19, 1950, Bollingen Foundation Records, Manuscript Division, Library of Congress.

63. Brooks, memorandum "Re: Poetry Prize—Phone with Mr. Babb to Bollingen Foundation Board of Trustees," December 21, 1949.
64. J. K. Lilly III to the Modern Poetry Association, quoted by Hayden Carruth to Ernest Brooks, November 11, 1949, Bollingen Foundation Records, Manuscript Division, Library of Congress.
65. Carruth to Brooks.
66. Carruth to Brooks.
67. Carruth to Brooks.
68. J. K. Lilly III to the Modern Poetry Association.
69. Hayden Carruth to Ernest Brooks, December 10, 1949, Bollingen Foundation Records, Manuscript Division, Library of Congress.
70. Carruth to Brooks.
71. Carruth was fired at the general meeting of the board of the Modern Poetry Association on January 9, 1950. Julia Bowe to Ernest Brooks, January 11, 1950; Carruth to Brooks, January 10, 1949 [sic 1950], Bollingen Foundation Records, Manuscript Division, Library of Congress.
72. Per Yale librarian James Babb's facetious self-characterization in his bid to administer the Bollingen Prize. Babb to Brooks, August 30, 1949, Bollingen Foundation Records, Manuscript Division, Library of Congress.
73. The committee of award during its first year at Yale included Léonie Adams, Conrad Aiken, W. H. Auden, Katherine Garrison Chapin, T. S. Eliot, Robert Lowell, Archibald MacLeish, Elizabeth Bishop, Katherine Anne Porter, Karl Shapiro, Willard Thorp, Robert Penn Warren, William Carlos Williams, Paul Green, and Allen Tate. Enclosure in Babb to Brooks, May 14, 1951, Bollingen Foundation Records, Manuscript Division, Library of Congress.
74. Norman Cousins and Harrison Smith, "Ezra Pound and the Bollingen Award," *Saturday Review of Literature*, June 11, 1949, 20.
75. Rasula, *American Poetry Wax Museum*, 113–4.
76. Scandal also worked as a mechanism for the solidification of the ideological program. The Bollingen Affair, through public news media, magnetized aesthetic and social differences into party lines: genres of the poetic manifesto, postwar social criticism, and the book review were instrumentally entangled as the op-ed statement; a critic commandeered the byline and poets were rounded up as signatories. Rasula suggests how the affair might have productively proliferated discourse, but the complex of aesthetic and social concerns that the Bollingen initially animated settled into two balkanized party sides, e.g., for the purposes of institutional codification of an interpretive methodology in English Department classrooms and a clean bifurcation of two modernist lineages in literary canon-formation. The pro-Pound Bollingen discourse would be a resource plumbed by both sides, however—as in

the exemplary case of Frost's defense of Pound a decade later—in the service of Cold War nationalism.
77. Carruth to Brooks, January 10, 1949 [sic 1950], Bollingen Foundation Records, Manuscript Division, Library of Congress.
78. There were not many at the time. In June 1958, the Poet's House in New Harmony, southern Indiana, received a trust in memory of Robert Lee Blaffer, and five trustees oversaw applications for "temporary citizens" of the unique "living community," dedicated to "reanimating in Mid-America the attributes of individual religious faith, intellect, imagination and creative industry that, together, have made and will sustain our national character." Jane Blaffer Owen to Gustav Davidson, September 17, 1958, Gustav Davidson Papers, Manuscript Division, Library of Congress. In the decades that followed, the number of university teaching positions, artists' residencies, and other means of institutional support for poets proliferated dramatically.
79. "At its annual meeting on January 9, the Board of Trustees of the Modern Poetry Association considered the reappointment of Mr. Hayden Carruth as editor of POETRY. The board very regretfully decided that it could not meet the conditions set by Mr. Carruth for his continued services. It was therefore unable to renew his appointment, which will end on February 1st." Julia Bowe to Ernest Brooks, January 11, 1950, Bollingen Foundation Records, Manuscript Division, Library of Congress.
80. Karl Shapiro to Ernest Brooks, February 22, 1950, Bollingen Foundation Records, Manuscript Division, Library of Congress.
81. Today, the Poetry Foundation's public history provides an altogether different account: "Carruth wanted to print more and longer works by established poets, reducing the number of new voices that appeared. He also continued to tilt the balance of the magazine toward prose, at one point going so far as to include only eight pages of poetry in an issue. Not surprisingly, perhaps, Carruth lasted only a year in the job." "*Poetry*: A History of the Magazine," Poetry Foundation, September 21, 2019, http://www.poetryfoundation.org/poetrymagazine/history (accessed January 12, 2015).
82. Gross, "Liberalism and Lyricism," 2. See Shapiro, *Reports of My Death*, 43.
83. Karl Shapiro to Ernest Brooks, February 22, 1950, Bollingen Foundation Records, Manuscript Division, Library of Congress.
84. Bowe preemptively corrected any political awkwardness between the new editor and the Bollingen Trustees: "Mr. Shapiro is aware that POETRY continues through the generosity of the Bollingen Foundation, and he will be happy to consult with you whenever there may be an occasion to do so." Julia Bowe to Ernest Brooks, January 11, 1950, Bollingen Foundation Records, Manuscript Division, Library of Congress.
85. Shapiro to Brooks, February 22, 1950.

86. "Miss Moore has written that 'she can't in conscience digress [from her current translation project],'" as Léonie Adams quoted to Lowell, who in turn quoted Adams's Moore to Bishop, January 14, 1949, *WIA* 79 (69).
87. Thomas Travisano writes that the fellows elected Marianne Moore as the next consultant, and the post would be offered to Bishop if Moore declined (*WIA* 69). But, as my archival research reveals, in fact the library next sought Adams to stay on another year. Léonie Adams to Luther Evans, April 19, 1949, William McGuire Papers, Manuscript Division, Library of Congress. In *WIA* (6), Travisano also incorrectly states that MacLeish created the national poetry office during World War II. The office was created under Librarian of Congress Herbert Putnam (1899–1939) in conversation and with the funding of Archer Huntington in 1937.
88. William Carlos Williams to Luther Evans, March 3, 1948, William McGuire Papers, Manuscript Division, Library of Congress.
89. After declining the post, Williams accepted a meantime appointment as a fellow but did not participate in the Bollingen Prize ballot. He attended his first fellows meeting in January 1950, and, by the time Aiken wrote to him about the 1953 post, Williams had attended several meetings and considered them a "good gang." William Carlos Williams to Conrad Aiken, January 1950, quoted in Reed Whittemore, *William Carlos Williams: Poet from Jersey* (New York: Houghton-Mifflin, 1975), 308.
90. William Carlos Williams to Conrad Aiken, March 12, 1952, quoted in McGuire, *Poetry's Catbird Seat*, 149.
91. Williams had been recently appointed as a fellow, and some constituents apparently confused this with an appointment to the national poetry office, prompting their outrage. Harrison Smith of the *Saturday Review* also wrote to Librarian of Congress Luther Evans after Williams's review.
92. However, many accounts of the Williams imbroglio obscure its politics, explaining that Williams was unable to accept the post due to illness. Mary Lethbridge's "Poets in Washington: The Consultants in Poetry to the Library of Congress" for *Records of the Columbia Historical Society, Washington, D.C.* (1969/70), for example, claims that Dr. Williams "relinquished the [1949–50 term] appointment because of ill health," (473); he "was again appointed in 1952, but illness again intervened, and the Consultantship remained vacant until Randall Jarrell came to the Library in September 1946" (476). The Library of Congress states simply that "Williams was named Consultant in Poetry in 1952, but did not serve." "Poet Laureate Consultant in Poetry: Past Poets Laureate, 1937–1960," Poetry and Literature Center at the Library of Congress, 2019. https://www.loc.gov/poetry/laureate-1937-1960.html.
93. McGuire, *Poetry's Catbird Seat* 151.

94. Robert Hillyer in a letter to the *New York Herald Tribune*, quoted in McGuire, *Poetry's Catbird Seat* 115.
95. *Lyric*'s editor letter, reported in the *Washington Times Herald*, October 20, 1952. *Lyric* was a publication of Virginia Kent Cummins's Lyric Foundation. Quoted Whittemore, *William Carlos Williams*, 309.
96. "Should we not ask Dr. Williams to fill out Standard Form 85 now?" Verner Clapp to Luther Evans, October 15, 1952, quoted McGuire, *Poetry's Catbird Seat* 152.
97. Fulton Lewis Jr., *New York Journal-American*, November 21, 1952, quoted in McGuire, *Poetry's Catbird Seat* 152.
98. The Williamses had planned to visit Washington in early December, and the letter reached Flossie before they departed. They met with Clapp in person on December 8.
99. As early as 1950, an internal Bollingen Foundation memorandum records that the fellows were considering resigning as a body, feeling that the library had not fully supported them during the controversy. "Allen Tate said that the Fellows of the Library of Congress in Americal [penciled over N] Letters are planning to resign as a body." "Tate is also annoyed because Evans never issued a statement expressing approbation of Yale's taking over the award. . . . Tate told me on December 5, 1949 when I asked him what the attitude of Luther Evans would be to the Fellows individually continuing as jurors, and he phoned me back after talking on the telephone with Evans. At that time we were thinking of Poetry magazine as the most likely new sponsor of the award." Ernest Brooks Jr., Memorandum for File, March 30, 1950, Bollingen Foundation Records.
100. "This change in the situation results not only from our view of the present state of your health, but also from the new elements introduced into the relationship between yourself and the Library in letters recently addressed by your attorney to various members of my staff. . . . I wish to make it very clear that the above action has nothing to do with any allegations regarding your loyalty which may have been published in various places. . . . All further investigation is being stopped, and the case removed from the Board's docket. . . . Perhaps I can put the loyalty aspect of your case in proper perspective by saying that if the aforesaid allegations were completely disposed of as of now in a manner completely favorable to you, I would nevertheless revoke the aforesaid offer of appointment." Luther Evans to William Carlos Williams, January 13, 1953, quoted in McGuire, *Poetry's Catbird Seat* 155. Williams's attorney James F. Murray Jr. responded with "a mixture of disgust and incredulity" to the letter Whittemore called "uncivil and dictatorial." Murray reported that Williams was offended by Evans's "self-appointment

as an expert" on his health and resented the "inference that you [Evans] are doing him a favor by suggesting that such investigation [the FBI investigation] be not completed. . . . Steps are now underway not only to clear Dr. Williams' status at the highest possible level but also fully to investigate within Washington and elsewhere the sources of the attacks against him." McGuire, *Poetry's Catbird Seat*, 155.

101. Evans wrote to Williams conditionally reinstating the appointment on April 24, 1953, to begin May 15 after Williams fulfilled loyalty and security procedures. But the full loyalty investigation from the Civil Service commission did not arrive at the Library until June 26, 1953, at which point the library's loyalty board sat on it, effectively allowing it to lapse. Evans was meanwhile preparing to leave the librarianship, resigning July 1, 1953, to serve as the head of the UNESCO. By the time Williams heard the investigation had been received, it had been returned, unevaluated, to the FBI. The appointment expired in September 1953, and Williams did not hear from the library for a year. A new librarian of Congress was also not appointed until April of the following year.

102. Robert Lowell to L. Quincy Mumford, November 7, 1955 (received November 14, 1955), William McGuire Papers, Manuscript Division, Library of Congress.

103. Conrad Aiken in conversation with Roy Basler, April 1953, quoted in McGuire, *Poetry's Catbird Seat*, 162.

104. Archibald Huntington, whose endowment, alongside the funding of Gertrude Whittall, funded the operations of the poetry office at the library, wrote to Mumford with "one piece of advice: if you are going to liquidate the Fellows, as you imply, do by all means call a meeting of the present and immediately past members and give them a chance to be heard [on the selection of the new Consultant in Poetry]. I urge this for the sake of the Library not for the sake of the Fellows." Quoted in Roy Basler, *The Muse and the Librarian* (Westport, Conn.: Greenwood, 1974), 39. Although the fellows declined to meet, many did write in with suggestions. Lowell, for example, in his letter to Mumford, suggested Randall Jarrell, Richard Wilbur, or William Meredith. "But first [in hand] I think the position should again [be] offered to Dr. Williams and an apology made for his treatment in 1952 [in type]," Lowell wrote to Mumford on November 7, 1955. William McGuire Papers, Manuscript Division.

105. McGuire, *Poetry's Catbird Seat*, 136.

106. May 6, 1950, *WIA* 99 (89).

107. When in 1954 the recordings "came to a standstill with the depletion of the Bollingen Foundation grant which made this recording program possible," the library "reissued the T. S. Eliot and Robert Frost albums on long-playing

records and is presently engaged in transferring the complete series of forty-two poets to long-playing records." Roy P. Basler, "Annual Report of the Poetry Office for the Fiscal Year Ended June 30, 1954," excerpted from the Annual Report of the General Reference and Bibliography Division, Library of Congress, July 15, 1954, 2–3, William McGuire Papers, Manuscript Division, Library of Congress.

108. Lowell's letters referring to their own librariness ("these bulky envelopes were the Library's idea, not mine") could be considered instances of what Michel de Certeau calls "an enunciative practice through which "the worker's own work [is] disguised as work for his employer.... La perruque may be as simple a matter as a secretary's writing a love letter on 'company time.'" Michel de Certeau, *The Practice of Everyday Life*, trans. Steven Rendell (Berkeley: University of California Press, 1984), 25. As poets for pay, however, Bishop and Lowell's expressions of resistance are necessarily more playful and complex than this example: writing a poem, e.g., "View of the Capitol from the Library of Congress," would not recuperate but be an appropriate use of "company time."

109. September 19, 1947, *WIA* 8 (5).

110. In another typographical intimation of mutual confidence, Lowell scare-quotes the "fellows," i.e., the Fellows in American Letters of the Library of Congress, to signal critical distance from their bureaucratic officialdom. September 19, 1947, *WIA* 8 (5).

111. September 22, 1947, *WIA* 9 (6).

112. April 27, 1948, *WIA* 52 (47).

113. A later version of the poem makes the reproving relationship of the poet to the state performance even more pronounced. In Bishop's *Complete Poems*, we do not observe the "Air Force Band / in uniforms of *brilliant* blue," but more insistently the "Air Force Band / in uniforms of *Air Force* blue." The revised "View of the Capitol" also dispenses with three commas, leaving conversational pauses and lilt behind in favor of mimicry of militaristic consistency. Elizabeth Bishop, "View of the Capitol from the Library of Congress," in *The Complete Poems, 1927–1979* (New York: Noonday, 1979), 69.

114. Robert Lowell, "Memories of West Street and Lepke," in *Life Studies* (Farrar, Straus and Giroux, 1959), 85–86, 2:3–5.

115. "The papers were full of headlines such as *poet snubs President*." Robert Lowell to Elizabeth Bishop, June 15 1965, *WIA* 575 (319).

116. Quoted in McGuire, *Poetry's Catbird Seat*, 135.

117. "Reference work assigned to this office by the Library has gone on more or less continuously, by telephone and letter, and usually been taken care of either by Miss Armstrong or myself"; "From time to time . . . we have sent [letters of inquiry] on to be attended to by the General Reference and

Bibliography Division"; "There was no stenographer at [the Fellows meeting of January 20, 1950], but from Miss Armstrong's and my own notes I drew up a report of the proceedings." Bishop, "Annual Report to the Librarian of Congress from the Chair of Poetry."

118. Elizabeth Bishop to Tadd Fisher, "Response to State Department Survey Request," August 23, 1950, William McGuire Papers, Manuscript Division, Library of Congress.
119. Bishop and Armstrong's reports detail the scheduling of a second recording session that would be more to his satisfaction, e.g., Adams wrote to Frost saying nothing about the Bollingen affair and only talks about his archival recordings (June 3, 1949).
120. McGuire, *Poetry's Catbird Seat*, 137.
121. "The stiff spokes of this wheel / touch the sore spots of the earth." Robert Lowell, "July in Washington," in *For the Union Dead* (New York: Farrar, Straus and Giroux, 1964), 58–99, 1:1–2.
122. The Bollingen affair hosted not only a debate about the aesthetic autonomy, or attempt to define the relationship of poetry to the U.S. state, but reveals the institutional locations of this debate. Through the lens of the poetry office at the Library of Congress, the Bollingen affair illuminates the role of national government and private patronage in the discursive formation of aesthetic positions, which subsequently calcified as critical affiliations proper to the academy. In other words, what we now see as a properly academic debate, i.e., New Criticism as a disciplinary tradition of the English Department, was complexly institutionally entangled at the time, and its subsequent location in the academy is more properly its outcome.
123. April 22, 1960, *WIA* 316 (210).
124. "Dinner in Honor of André Malraux, Minister of State for Cultural Affairs of France, 8:00 p.m.," May 11, 1962, John F. Kennedy Presidential Library.
125. Robert Lowell to Elizabeth Bishop, May 15, 1962, *WIA* 416 (251).
126. January 13, 1962, *WIA* 383 (242).
127. April 4, 1962, *WIA* 398 (247).

## 2. Inaugurating National Poetry

1. "Poetry Office Press Conference Transcript," December 8, 1958, folder 44, Robert Frost Papers, Manuscript Division, Library of Congress.
2. Lawrance Thompson and R. H. Winnick, *Robert Frost, a Biography: The Authorized Life of the Poet Condensed Into a Single Volume*, ed. Edward Connery Lathem (New York: Holt, Rinehart and Winston, 1981), 474–75. Hereafter TWL.

3. "Poetry Office Press Conference Transcript."
4. Robert Frost to John T. Bartlett, Fourth of July [1913], Beaconsfield, in Lawrance Thompson, ed., *The Selected Letters of Robert Frost* (New York: Holt, Rinehart and Winston, 1964), 80 (53). Hereafter *SL*.
5. Sherman Adams to Robert Frost, February 15, 1958, *SL* 572.
6. "Some of us think Eisenhower should continue to be President, and most of us are confident he will be able to. We thought you might like to lend your moral strength to a group which we call Committee of Artists & Scientists for Eisenhower, which you will see spelled CASE. You would not have to do any more than give it a blessing." Sherman Adams to Robert Frost, July 3, 1956, *SL* 559.
7. *SL* 558 and TWL 460.
8. When Frost uncharacteristically declined participation in the essay series, the secretary of state reiterated the invitation, expressing "importance of such visits by prominent literary figures" in a letter that "help[ed] [Frost] to a decision." John Foster Dulles to Robert Frost, February 12, 1957; Frost to Dulles, February 26, 1957, *SL* 562. Frost likely saw the venture as "small potatoes class," and, indeed, more prestigious opportunities to export the values of American life would follow.
9. Frost to Dulles.
10. Harold E. Howland to Robert Frost, December 10, 1956, *SL* 560.
11. Dwight D. Eisenhower to Robert Frost, February 16, 1958, 6:41 p.m.; Sherman Adams to Robert Frost, February 15, 1958; Frost to Adams, February 12, 1958, *SL* 572–73.
12. Adams asked Mumford to appoint Frost; Mumford's letter was a formality: "our understanding [is] that you will make definite plans to be at the Library of Congress next October 13–18." L. Quincy Mumford to Robert Frost, May 2, 1958, *SL* 578–79 (449-a).
13. "I don't want to run for office, but I want to be a politician," Frost declared at the December Library of Congress press conference in December, half-jesting that he hoped "some good Senator would resign about six months before the end of his term and let me finish it out." "Poetry Office Press Conference Transcript," December 8, 1958, folder 44, Robert Frost Papers, Manuscript Division, Library of Congress.
14. "Poetry Office Press Conference Transcript," "Within a few minutes, the scope of the Consultantship in Poetry at the Library of Congress had expanded beyond anything heretofore contemplated, by anyone other than Frost, at least. The questions, answers, and badinage continued for an hour, covering the Pound case [and] such divergent topics as socialism [and] the need for more study of humanities as opposed to science." Roy Basler, *The Muse and the Librarian* (Westport, Conn.: Greenwood, 1974), 59.

15. "The Poetry Office has become increasingly concerned with the preparation and presentation of the programs under the Gertrude Clarke Whittall Poetry and Literature Funds. . . . For the first time this year we have been unable to record new poets for the Library's archives due to lack of funds." Roy Basler, "Annual Report of the Poetry Office for the Fiscal Year Ended June 30, 1954," excerpted from the Annual Report of the General Reference and Bibliography Division, July 15, 1954, 1–2, William McGuire Papers, Manuscript Division, Library of Congress.
16. Marlene Morrissey, special assistant to Librarian of Congress Luther Evans, quoted in William McGuire, *Poetry's Catbird Seat: The Consultantship in Poetry in the English Language at the Library of Congress, 1937–1987* (Washington, D.C.: Library of Congress, 1988), 139.
17. L. Quincy Mumford to W. Sterling Cole, William McGuire Papers, Manuscript Division, Library of Congress. Archival documentation suggests the letter was drafted by Roy Basler, Burton W. Adkinson, and Verner Clapp.
18. "Robert Frost Appointment Press Conference, Wilson Room, Library of Congress," transcript, May 21, 1958, Robert Frost Papers, Manuscript Division, Library of Congress.
19. Anthony Lewis, "Court Drops Charge Against Ezra Pound," *New York Times*, April 19, 1958. Frost was at the Poetry Center in New York City the day of the announcement: "This morning's paper said I took two years to get Ezra Pound out of jail, but the truth is, I did it all in just one week" (*SL* 575). Although Frost felt his role had been decisive, in fact Archibald MacLeish was at the "self-effacingly active" (*SL* 563) helm of the campaign for Pound's release, as Jed Rasula and Al Filreis have demonstrated. MacLeish did, however, invoke Frost's support strategically, "aware of the influence a conservative 'poet of the people' like Frost might wield" (*SL* 575). In February 1957, for example, MacLeish drafted an appeal to the attorney general on letterhead of the American Academy of Arts and Letters—a Huntington-funded arts organization—and acquired three cosignatories "whose reputations were calculated to have a good deal of weight with the Republican Party members of the Eisenhower regime": Ernest Hemingway in Cuba, T. S. Eliot in England, and Frost in England (Herbert Brownell Jr. to Robert Frost, February 28, 1957, Washington D.C., *SL* 563). Frost met MacLeish and agreed to the appeal during his State Department-sponsored goodwill mission in London, where he also met and discussed it with Eliot (Archibald MacLeish to Kathleen Morrison, June 17, 1957, *SL* 568). Back in Ripton, however, Frost would cite his "misgivings" about the "bad business" to MacLeish—"the affair might better wait until the Fall" when more influential government officials would be in Washington (Frost to MacLeish, June 24, 1957 [transcribed from first draft of, typewritten, revised in ink, and unsigned], *SL* 569).

Frost finally agreed unable to "bear that anyone's fate should hang too much on mine . . . you go ahead and make an appointment with the Department of Justice" (*SL* 563). After the announcement of Pound's release, however, Frost would clutch the symbolic figure of high literary modernism like an Oscar, claiming victory by way of extending "thanks . . . all you did to make simple and easy for me my first raise on the Capital City. . . . Things are shaping up to turn me into something Washingtonian right now" (*SL* 577).

20. L. Quincy Mumford to Robert Frost, May 2, 1958, *SL* 578–9 (4409-a).
21. *SL* 577.
22. "I wouldn't have much confidence in myself in that way [consulting in all matters of politics] if I hadn't been so successful in Washington lately in a law case. But, I surprised myself." "Robert Frost Conference, Wilson Room, Library of Congress," transcript, May 21, 1958, Robert Frost Papers, Manuscript Division, Library of Congress.
23. "Robert Frost Conference."
24. Interview with Rose Feld, *New York Times Book Review*, October 21, 1923 reprinted in Edward Connery Lathem and Lawrance Thompson, eds., *The Robert Frost Reader: Poetry and Prose* (New York: Holt, 1972), 330. Hereafter *RFR*.
25. "I like the middle way, as I like to talk to the man who walks the middle way with me. . . . I write blank verse. I must have the pulse beat of rhythm, I like to hear it beating under the things I write." Robert Frost, interview with Feld, *RFR*, 331.
26. Tyler Hoffman, *Robert Frost and the Politics of Poetry* (Hanover, N.H.: Middlebury College Press, 2001), 10, 202.
27. Frost's poetics did not represent dissent that threatened social order but a discourse of individuality in the service of the politics of freedom during the Cold War. One of Frost's most frequently anthologized poems, "The Road Not Taken," in which the speaker "took the road less traveled by, / And that has made all the difference," was used to analogize the American way contra Soviet conformity by the secretary of the interior during the Kennedy Administration. "Udall Report on Robert Frost Trip to USSR, April 1963," Papers of John F. Kennedy, John F. Kennedy Presidential Library.
28. Serge Guilbaut, *How New York Stole the Idea of Modern Art: Abstract Expressionism, Freedom, and the Cold War* trans. Arthur Goldhammer (Chicago: University of Chicago Press, 1983).
29. Eric Bennett, *Workshops of Empire: Stegner, Engle, and American Creative Writing During the Cold War* (Iowa City: University of Iowa Press, 2015); Juliana Spahr, *Du Bois's Telegram: Literary Resistance and State Containment* (Cambridge, Mass.: Harvard University Press, 2018). Also see Frances Stonor Saunders's foundational *The Cultural Cold War: The CIA and the World of Arts and Letters*

(New York: New Press, 2000) and the wider body of literature describing Cold War cultural diplomacy and propaganda across various artistic fields noted in the introduction.
30. "'Dedication,' Robert Frost's Presidential Inaugural Poem, January 20, 1961: Typescript with Frost's Holograph Script Corrections in Ink and Stewart Udall's Holograph Clarifications in Pencil on the Last Page," Stewart L. Udall Papers, Manuscript Division, Library of Congress.
31. "'Dedication.'"
32. Robert Frost to Sidney Cox, January 2, 1915 [The Gallows], *SL* 146–49.
33. *SL* 162.
34. Quoted in TWL 224.
35. Robert Frost to William Stanley Brathwaite, March 22, 1915, *SL* 159.
36. Edward Garnett, "A New American Poet," *Atlantic Monthly*, August 1915.
37. Jessie Rittenhouse, "North of Boston; Robert Frost's Poems of New England Farm Life," *New York Times*, May 16, 1915.
38. "The only nastiness in Jessie B's article is the first part where she speaks of the English reviews as fulsome. There she speaks dishonestly out of complete ignorance—out of some sort of malice or envy I should infer." Robert Frost to Sidney Cox, May 16, 1915, *SL* 173.
39. Quoted in TWL 224.
40. Frost to Amy Lowell, May 14, 1916, *SL* 203.
41. Frost was announced as honorary president in 1940, and ostensibly remained the masthead of the PSA until his death in 1963. I have found no record of a subsequent poet holding the title.
42. *The Letters of Robert Frost to Louis Untermeyer*, ed. Louis Untermeyer (New York: Holt, Rinehart and Winston, 1963), 24.
43. Jessie B. Rittenhouse, *My House of Life* (New York: Houghton Mifflin, 1934), 240. The College Poetry Society of America's first president was Robert Hillyer, the author of the *Saturday Review* polemics against the awarding of the Bollingen Prize to Pound. Hillyer was also president of the PSA during the Bollingen affair.
44. The Eisenhower telegram conveyed warm wishes to the Poetry Society of America, joining the national tribute to Frost: "It is fortunate that our Nation is blessed with citizens like Robert Frost who can express our innermost feelings and speak so clearly to us of our land and life." January 16, 1958, *SL* 571.
45. "The Society . . . ought to be along national lines, and should meet in a public rather than a private place." Rittenhouse, *My House of Life*, 223.
46. Robert Hillyer, "Treason's Strange Fruit," *Saturday Review of Literature*, June 11, 1949, 10–11.
47. Rittenhouse, *My House of Life*, 222.

48. Rittenhouse, 223.
49. Rittenhouse, 226–27 (emphasis mine).
50. Rittenhouse, 227.
51. Robert Frost to John T. Bartlett, c. November 5, 1913, SL 98.
52. Frost to Barlett.
53. Robert Frost to Thomas B. Mosher, July 17, 1913, Beaconsfield, SL 83–84 (55) (emphasis in the original).
54. TWL 164.
55. Frost to Bartlett.
56. TWL 165. Frost also tells this story in a *Paris Review* interview later in life.
57. TWL.
58. "The more I think of it the less I like the connection he sees between me and the Irishman who could sit on a kitchen-midden and dream stars. It is so stupidly wide of the mark. And then his inaccuracies about my family affairs!" Frost to Mosher.
59. Frost to Mosher.
60. Frost to Bartlett, Fourth of July [1913], SL 79.
61. Robert Frost to Ezra Pound, [c. July 20, 1913, Beaconsfield], SL 85–86 (57).
62. Frost to Mosher.
63. Frost to Bartlett, c. November 5, 1913, SL 98; "Now who will have the better claim to the title of People's Poet?," Robert Frost to Harold Monro, December 1914 [The Gallows], SL 142 (94).
64. Frank S. Flint to Robert Frost [July 26, 1913] [London], SL 86–87 (57a).
65. Ezra Pound, "Modern Georgics," *Poetry: A Magazine of Verse* (December 1914): 127. Other reviews of *North of Boston* referred to Frost's theory of the sound of sense as he had advertised it to them through correspondence, including Georgian poets Lascelles Abercrombie in the *Nation*, Wilfrid Gibson in the *Bookman*, and Edward Thomas in the *English Review*. See Lascelles Abercrombie, "A New Voice," *Nation* 15, July 13, 1914.
66. Pound, 129.
67. Robert Frost to Sidney Cox, January 2, 1915 [The Gallows], SL 147 (97).
68. Frost, 148.
69. Frost, 149.
70. Alfred Harcourt wrote an editorial for the *New York Times* in turn: "That Mr. Frost's volume of poems, 'North of Boston,' made its first appearance under the imprint of an English instead of an American publisher has disturbed some of our reviewers. . . . But now Mr. Frost comes to the rescue with the explanation the simplicity of which should allay at once any international jealousies or suspicions. . . . He happened to be in England when the idea came to him of collecting his poetry manuscripts into a volume. . . . He

declares he 'didn't cross the water seeking a British publisher.' The thing 'just happened.' And, so, there is not 'another case of American inappreciation' to record" (TWL 220).

71. TWL 199.
72. TWL.
73. Alfred Harcourt knew about the incident at Ellis Island, and sent Robert Haven Schauffler, author of "Scum o' the Earth"—a widely praised poem celebrating the plight of industrious immigrants—to escort Frost to the PSA meeting (TWL 199). This was an ill-conceived match; Schauffler had criticized Frost's poetry at the previous PSA meeting.
74. Frost would give a talk on his prosodic theory at the annual PSA dinner in winter 1916; his solemnity fell flat, followed by Untermeyer's parody of his and other contemporary poetic polemics.
75. "Another experience I cant [sic] seem to get over is Ellis Island. I dreamed last night that I had to pass a written examination in order to pass the inspection there" (SL 162).
76. Frost was cunning about presenting his loyalties—desperate to disaffiliate from Pound's "party of London refugees" in view of New York publishers, he would meanwhile call England "half my native land" privately in a good-bye letter to Monro: "England the victorious. Good friends I have had here and hope to keep." Robert Frost to Harold Monro, [c. 13 February 1915] [Liverpool], SL 152 (100).
77. Jessie B. Rittenhouse, "The New Poetry and Democracy," stenographic report of an extemporaneous address at the Asbury Park Conference, Annual Meeting of the American Library Association (July 1916), 137.
78. Rittenhouse, 142 (earlier emphasis mine).
79. Rittenhouse, 143.
80. Interview with Feld, RFR, 331.
81. Robert Frost to John T. Bartlett, December 8, 1913, SL 102 (67).
82. Frost to Bartlett, c. November 5, 1913, SL (98).
83. Frost to Bartlett, Fourth of July [1913], SL 79–81:80 (53).
84. SL 141.
85. Principally through conversations with T. E. Hulme. Frost would later own a copy of Bergson's "Theory of Art" published in *Speculations* in 1924. Richard Poirier and Tyler Hoffman have also noted the influence of James on Frost's conceptions of personal and political sovereignty. Hoffman, *Robert Frost and the Politics of Poetry*, 238.
86. T. E. Hulme, *The Collected Writings of T. E. Hulme*, ed. Karen Csengeri (Oxford: Clarendon, 1994), 163.
87. Frost to Bartlett, Fourth of July [1913], SL 80 (53).

88. Hoffman, *Robert Frost and the Politics of Poetry*, 7; 44.
89. Robert Frost to Sidney Cox, December 1914 [The Gallows], *SL* 140 (93).
90. Frost.
91. Frost to Bartlett, December 8, 1913, *SL* 102 (67).
92. Frost.
93. "Mr. Frost has dared to write, and for the most part with success, in the natural speech of New England; in natural spoken speech, which is very different from the 'natural' speech of the newspapers, and of many professors." Pound, "Modern Georgics," 127–28.
94. Robert Frost, "How Hard It Is to Keep Being King," in *Robert Frost: Collected Poems, Prose, and Plays*, ed. Richard Poirier and Mark Richardson (New York: Library of America, 1995), 469. Hereafter *CPPP*.
95. Robert Frost, interview with Feld, *RFR*, 336. In "How Hard It Is," he who "writes free verse . . . He'll tell you about Freedom," where it turns out "Freedom is slavery." Metrical form as a stay against social chaos appears throughout Frost's writings and poetry—"Let chaos storm! / Let cloud shapes swarm! / I wait for form." "Pertinax" (1936), *CPPP* 281. In "Dedication," composed for Kennedy's inauguration, "how seriously the races swarm / In their attempts at sovereignty and form."
96. Hoffman, *Robert Frost and the Politics of Poetry*, 10, 202.
97. "I like the middle way, as I like to talk to the man who walks the middle way with me. . . . Men have told me, and perhaps they are right, that I have no 'straddle.' That is the term they use: I have no straddle. That means that I cannot spread out far enough to live in filth and write in the treetops. I can't . . . I write blank verse. I must have the pulse beat of rhythm, I like to hear it beating under the things I write." Frost, interview with Feld, *RFR*, 331, 336.
98. Stephen Cushman's term for "an imaginative creation that imbues aesthetic ideology with a sense of national significance," quoted in Hoffman, *Robert Frost and the Politics of Poetry*, 171.
99. Katherine Kearns, *Robert Frost and a Poetics of Appetite* (Cambridge: Cambridge University Press, 1994), 138.
100. Hoffman, *Robert Frost and the Politics of Poetry*, 190.
101. "'Dedication.'"
102. Telegram, December 14, 1960, Special Correspondence: Robert Frost, May 1961-April 1962, Papers of John F. Kennedy, John F. Kennedy Presidential Library.
103. Frost to Dulles, February 26, 1957, *SL* 562 (436).
104. George Monteiro, "Frost's Politics and the Cold War," in *The Cambridge Companion to Robert Frost*, ed. Robert Faggen (Cambridge: Cambridge University Press, 2001), 226.

105. SL 536.
106. In March 1950 speech, Senator William Benton of Connecticut advocated for a "Marshall Plan in the field of ideas," a phrase that became widely applied to describe U.S. cultural missions during the Cold War. "Benton Is Honored for Stressing Ideas," *New York Times*, April 21, 1950, 14.
107. At the same time that Frost was planning his trip to the USSR, for example, the Congress for Cultural Freedom was expanding its activities in South America. "The Cultural Congress is going to back our trip," Lowell wrote to Bishop on March 18, 1962. *WIA* 395 (246).
108. "May I suggest that possibly the best thing *you* could do for the cause would be to keep on magnifying me the way you have been ever since you descended in state on us that night at the St. Botolph Club," Frost wrote to Adams after the meeting. Robert Frost to Sherman Adams, June 21, 1956, 558–59 (443).
109. SL 558 and TWL 460.
110. "It is fortunate that our Nation is blessed with citizens like Robert Frost who can express our innermost feelings and speak so clearly to us of our land and life. It is a pleasure to join in tribute to the great gifts of Robert Frost." Quoted in *SL* 571.
111. Robert Frost to Sherman Adams, February 12, 1958, South Miami, *SL* 571–72 (443).
112. Eisenhower called Frost to an "INFORMAL STAG DINNER AT THE WHITE HOUSE" almost certainly at the behest of Adams ("I understand that through some circuitous means you have been invited to come and spend the evening with the President," Adams wrote to Frost a day before Frost received the president's invitation by telegram) given Frost's wheedling. Lawrance Thompson has described Frost's "epistolary tactics" (158) with literary notables in his early career; this chapter bears out his reading, showing that Frost applied these same tactics with political notables in his late career. Dwight D. Eisenhower to Robert Frost, February 16, 1958, 6.41 p.m., *SL* 572–3 (443-b); Sherman Adams to Robert Frost, February 15, 1958, *SL* 572 (443-a).
113. See more on Adams and the Eisenhower administration's political investment in Frost in Thomas Smith, "Robert Frost, Stewart Udall, and the 'Last Go-Down,'" *New England Quarterly* 70, no. 1 (March 1997): 3–32.
114. "Not many lobbyists have ever achieved more for whatever cause, and none, so far as I know, has ever achieved a comparable national public image in the process. It is no denigration of the cause of the arts and the humanities at large, in my book at least, to recognize that Frost's ego was his primary motivation." Basler, *The Muse and the Librarian*, 76–77.
115. TWL 478.

116. Frost's remarks on May 21, 1959, recorded stenographically during his talk and quoted in his annual report assembled by the poetry office, William McGuire Papers, Manuscript Division, Library of Congress.
117. TWL 475.
118. TWL 477. After the remark won the front page of the *New York Times* ("Robert Frost, on 85th Birthday, Romps Through Interview Here: Predicts Election of Kennedy and Gives Poetry's Case with Equal Agility"), Kennedy sent Frost a warm note and met him for a "get-acquainted conversation" at the Library of Congress. This meeting, and the fact that Kennedy often quoted lines from Frost's "Stopping By Woods" in his closing remarks on the campaign trail—"But I have promises to keep / And miles to go before I sleep"—prompted Udall to suggest to Kennedy that he invite Frost to participate in the inaugural program. Stewart Udall, "Robert Frost, Kennedy and Khrushchev: A Memoir of Poetry and Power," *Shenandoah* 26, no. 2 (1975): 53–54.
119. Mark Bauerlein and Ellen Grantham, eds., *National Endowment for the Arts: A History, 1965–2008* (Washington, D.C.: National Endowment for the Arts, 2008), 13.
120. Bauerlein and Grantham, 7.
121. Bauerlein and Grantham, 5.
122. National Foundation on the Arts and the Humanities Act of 1965 (Pub. L. 89-209).
123. Kay Morrison described "Dedication" as "rather editorial in tone"; Louis Untermeyer, consultant in poetry, 1960–61, would call it "the worst thing he ever wrote." See Kay Morrison, undated, handwritten letter to Udall, and Untermeyer, quoted in Udall, "Robert Frost, Kennedy, and Khrushchev," 55.
124. Frost delivered his first public reading of the poem at a Phi Beta Kappa annual meeting at the College of William and Mary on December 5, 1941, two days before Japan's attack on Pearl Harbor, which prompted the entrance of the U.S. in World War II (TWL 417).
125. Stewart L. Udall Oral History Interview—JFK #3, John F. Kennedy Library Oral History Program, interview by W. W. Moss, 16 pp., March 12, 1970, John F. Kennedy Presidential Library, JFKOH-SLU-03.
126. Frost had been invited to read "The Gift Outright" by Udall and Kennedy and only announced to Udall on the way to the inauguration that he planned to preface it with the occasional piece (Smith, "Robert Frost, Stewart Udall, and the 'Last Go-Down,'" 6–7). But for viewers, that Frost "botched his surprise" (Udall, "Robert Frost, Kennedy and Khrushchev," 55) before the more confident delivery of "The Gift Outright" effected spontaneity; Frost's "natural" performance "stole the hearts of the Inaugural crowd," as the *Washington Post* would report the next day (quoted in Thompson 282).

127. Robert Frost, "The Gift Outright," in *The Poetry of Robert Frost*, ed. Edward Connery Lathem (New York: Holt, Rinehart and Winston 1969). Copyright © 1923, 1969 by Henry Holt and Company. Copyright © 1951 by Robert Frost. Reprinted by permission of Henry Holt and Company. All rights reserved.
128. Jay Parini, *Robert Frost: A Life* (New York: Holt, 2015), 336.
129. Derek Walcott, "The Road Taken," in *Homage to Robert Frost*, ed. Joseph Brodsky, Seamus Heaney, and Derek Walcott (New York: Farrar, Straus and Giroux, 1996), 93–94. Marit MacArthur has argued that while the poem has been widely read as an expression of "triumphant nationalism" and "celebration of colonialism" since its inaugural performance, the poem in fact expresses only a "measured contempt" for its narrative of colonial possession. Marit MacArthur, *The American Landscape in the Poetry of Frost, Bishop, and Ashbery: The House Abandoned* (New York: Palgrave, 2008), 63, 69. Raphael Allison grants that, while in the context of its initial publication—a 1942 issue of *Virginia Quarterly Review* on the progress of war—the poem may have meant to express a less "sure-footed patriotism," Frost's live readings, and his treatment of readings "as opportunities to politicize his poems . . . ensure that [his] poems remain interpretively labile . . . absorbing and recirculating the timely inflections at the Kennedy inauguration." Ralph Allison, "Robert Frost, Live: Authenticity and Performance in the Audio Archive," *Twentieth-Century Literature* 58, no. 4 (2012): 607–8.
130. Robert Frost, *A Witness Tree* (New York: Holt, 1942), 41.
131. In its initial publication in the *Virginia Quarterly Review*, the last line read "such as she might become." Stephen Gould Axelrod points to the evolution from *might* to *would* to *will* as an evolution in the poem's political meaning, where its ultimate ending "now unambiguously predicts white male dominance in an era of national greatness." Stephen Gould Axelrod, "Frost and the Cold War," in Mark Richardson, ed., *Robert Frost in Context* (Cambridge: Cambridge University Press, 2014), 210. Udall showed "The Gift Outright" to Kennedy on December 7 as a possibility for the inaugural reading, to which the president-elect suggested the poem, though fitting for the occasion, needed a different ending; after a second reading, he suggested substituting "would" for "will." Udall, Notes for Journal, December 7, 1960, box 80, Udall Papers, quoted in Smith, "Robert Frost, Stewart Udall, and the 'Last Go-Down,'" 6–7.
132. See Charles Taylor, "The Politics of Recognition," in Amy Gutmann, ed., *Multiculturalism: Examining the Politics of Recognition* (Princeton, N.J.: Princeton University Press, 1994), 30–31.
133. Kenneth Hopkins, *The Poets Laureate* (London: Bodley Head, 1954).
134. Joshua Freeman, *American Empire: The Rise of a Global Power, the Democratic Revolution at Home, 1945–2000* (New York: Viking, 2012), 163.
135. Udall oral history interview by Moss.

136. "Udall Report on Robert Frost Trip to USSR."
137. The plan was hatched for what would become known as Frost's Mission to Moscow over dinner in May 1962, when Frost and Soviet Ambassador to the U.S. Anatoly Dobrynin were guests at the home of Secretary of the Interior Stewart Udall. F. D. Reeve, *Robert Frost in Russia* (Boston: Little, Brown, 1963), 3.
138. Robert Frost to John F. Kennedy, July 24, 1962, Special Correspondence: Robert Frost, May 1961–April 1962, Papers of John F. Kennedy, John F. Kennedy Presidential Library. Received by the White House July 26, 1962.
139. Frost to Kennedy. Frost would echo his view of this world order in his meeting with Khrushchev, to whom he "insisted on a distinction between European civilization on the one hand, and Asian and African on the other. To his impassioned plea for recognition of common European cultural values, shared by Russia and the United States, too, in contradistinction to what he called the absence of culture in Africa and the impossible foreignness of China, the Premier was restrained." Reeve, *Robert Frost in Russia*, 115.
140. For a thorough chronological record of the trip, see Reeve.
141. Reeve, 21–22. In Udall's accounts, Frost repeated this line to Khrushchev in their meeting. See Udall, "Robert Frost, Kennedy and Khrushchev," 62; "Udall Report on Robert Frost Trip to USSR."
142. *CPPP* 39:23, 27/45.
143. "'Mending Wall' in Moscow," *New York Times Magazine*, September 16, 1962, 34.
144. Reeve, *Robert Frost in Russia*, 92.
145. Reeve, 93.
146. Frost to Kennedy, July 24, 1962.
147. Frost saw competition as the "main dynamo" of life, and the USSR and U.S. as "laid out for rivalry all the time—in sports, in art, in science." "Udall Report on Robert Frost Trip to USSR," 14. "Let's hope we can take it out in sports, science, arts, business, and politics before ever we have to take it out in the bloody politics of war." Frost quoted in Reeve, *Robert Frost in Russia*, 123.
148. "To Premier Khrushchev / from his rival in friendship / Robert Frost // Gagra / Sept 7 1962." Reeve, 117.
149. Udall, "Robert Frost, Kennedy and Khrushchev," 63.
150. "Professor Reeve was present during the entire conversation between Frost and Khrushchev, and he has advised me in a letter that he did not hear Khrushchev make a "Too liberal to fight" statement." "Udall Report on Robert Frost Trip to USSR."
151. Udall, "Robert Frost, Kennedy and Khrushchev," 65.
152. Smith, "Robert Frost, Stewart Udall, and the 'Last Go-Down,'" 25.
153. Smith, 20.

154. "Udall Report on Robert Frost Trip to USSR," 13.
155. Quoted in Reeve, *Robert Frost in Russia*, 131.
156. Robert Lowell to Elizabeth Bishop, May 15, 1962, *WIA* 415 (251).
157. Elizabeth Bishop to Robert Lowell, April 4, 1962, *WIA* 398 (247).
158. Elizabeth Bishop to Robert Lowell, October 28, 1962, *WIA* 422 (258); April 13, 1964, *WIA* 531 (293). In the latter, Bishop remarked on Lowell's "Colloquy on Mount Kisco" having been honored in the Congress for Cultural Freedom's *Congress News* (Winter 1964).
159. See Gilles Scott-Smith and Charlotte Lerg, eds., *Campaigning Culture and the Global Cold War: The Journals of the Congress for Cultural Freedom*, vol 1. (London: Palgrave MacMillan, 2017).
160. Elizabeth Bishop to Robert Lowell, May 9, 1962, *WIA* 415 (250).
161. Estimates of the number of viewers of the inauguration vary. The first of Kennedy's news conferences, less than a week after his inauguration, was viewed by an estimated 65 million people. "John F. Kennedy and the Press," John F. Kennedy Presidential Library, https://www.jfklibrary.org/learn/about-jfk/jfk-in-history/john-f-kennedy-and-the-press (accessed July 17, 2019). Meanwhile, almost 1 million people gathered at the Capitol for Kennedy's inauguration. "The Inauguration of John F. Kennedy," John F. Kennedy Presidential Library, https://www.jfklibrary.org/visit-museum/exhibits/permanent-exhibits/the-inauguration-of-john-f-kennedy (accessed July 17, 2019).
162. Quoted in McGuire, *Poetry's Catbird Seat*, 247.
163. Huntington Cairns proposed the festival to the trustees in December 1961. The Bollingen Foundation Trustees approved a $15,000 grant for the festival budget in March, as well as a $5,000 grant to *Poetry* for festival expenditures. William McGuire Papers, Manuscript Division, Library of Congress.
164. Reeve, *Robert Frost in Russia*, 18.
165. McGuire, *Poetry's Catbird Seat*, 236.
166. McGuire, 139–40.
167. I use this term, referring to and following Whittall, to indicate the bureaucratically unmediated power of a patron as tastemaker, e.g., control over the literary content of supported programming. Independent wealthy patrons will reemerge in our story, but the new state arts imperative effectively phased out hatbox patronage-style philanthropy. In the case of individual patron Ruth Lilly's donation to *Poetry* magazine, for instance, a considerable number of public and private organizations determined the uses of the gift.
168. Untermeyer, quoted in McGuire, *Poetry's Catbird Seat*, 246–47.
169. William McGuire Papers, Manuscript Division, Library of Congress.
170. "Radio and Television Address to the American People on Soviet Arms Build-up in Cuba, 22 October 1962," White House Audio Recordings,

1961–1963, White House Audio Collection, John F. Kennedy Presidential Library.
171. Quoted in McGuire, *Poetry's Catbird Seat*, 242.
172. Quoted in McGuire, 243.
173. Quoted in McGuire, 247 (emphasis mine).
174. Roy Basler, "Yankee Vergil—Robert Frost in Washington," in Basler, *The Muse and the Librarian*, 76. Frost concluded his reading with "Provide, Provide," which former Soviet citizen Joseph Brodsky would also recite from memory at the press conference where he took office as poet laureate in 1991.
175. "Remarks Upon Presenting a Congressional Award to Robert Frost, 26 March 1962," White House Audio Recordings, 1961–1963, White House Audio Collection, John F. Kennedy Presidential Library.
176. Basler, *The Muse and the Librarian*, 76–77.

## 3. The Politics of Voice

1. Horace Gregory, "The Postwar Generation in Arts and Letters: Poetry," *Saturday Review*, March 1953. The poet-in-uniform took his place within a broader class of "professional creative" types or "creative laborers" that emerged after World War II. See Alan McKinlay and Chris Smith, eds., *Creative Labour: Working in the Creative Industries* (New York: Palgrave Macmillan, 2009).
2. John Berryman, "Dream Song 354," in *The Dream Songs* (New York: Farrar, Straus and Giroux, 1969), 376, 1:3.
3. Charles Pritchard, "Inaugural Poet Richard Blanco Talks America and Poetry at Sherrill-Kenwood Library," *Oneida Dispatch*, June 18, 2019, https://www.oneidadispatch.com/news/local-news/inaugural-poet-richard-blanco-talks-america-and-poetry-at-sherrill/article_840270ca-91d0-11e9-ad42-5fcbb18ecaf6.html.
4. Berryman, "Dream Song 354," 376, 7–8; 13–16.
5. See Anis Shivani, *Against the Workshop: Provocations, Polemics, Controversies* (Huntsville: Texas Review Press, 2011).
6. Shivani.
7. David O. Dowling, *A Delicate Aggression: Savagery and Survival in the Iowa Writers' Workshop* (New Haven: Yale University Press, 2019), 125.
8. An act to amend the National Foundation on the Arts and the Humanities Act of 1965, and for other purposes (Pub. L. 99-194, Title VI, Sec. 601, Dec. 20, 1985, 99 Stat. 1347).

9. Maria Damon, "Poetic Canons: Generative Oxymoron or Stalled-out Dialectic?" *Contemporary Literature* 39 (Autumn 1998), 468. "Poetry, as any quick survey of literary nationalism will reveal, is far more easily pressed into the service of national identity formation than other forms of writing and seems to carry a symbolic weight in the national Imaginary that makes such civic service important. Almost every era and nation has a national poet, a representative poet, a poet laureate, et cetera, whether by popular acclaim, self-appointment, or official decree; no such office, formal or informal, exists for more narrative forms of imaginative writing, though the latter is far more often studied in such contexts."
10. Robert Casper, interview by author, August 2, 2019.
11. William McGuire, *Bollingen: An Adventure in Collecting the Past* (Princeton, N.J.: Princeton University Press, 1989).
12. The first writing programs were created at the University of Iowa, Stanford University, Johns Hopkins University, the University of Denver, and Cornell University.
13. Donald Sears, ed., *Directory of Creative Writing Programs* (Fullerton, Cal.: College English Association, 1970). Notably, 42 percent of these were *new* institutions, established during or just after the war—and as such generally fleet rather than flagship state universities: land-grant institutions, new campus branches, commuter schools, and former teachers colleges. D. G. Myers, *The Elephants Teach: Creative Writing Since 1880* (Chicago: University of Chicago Press, 2006), 164.
14. Myers, 163.
15. Myers, 166.
16. The AWP apparently consisted of thirteen programs at twelve member institutions: "AWP was established as a nonprofit organization in 1967 by fifteen writers representing thirteen creative writing programs;" "From twelve member colleges and universities in 1967 to over 500 today, AWP's membership has grown with the expansion of creative writing programs and with AWP's growing number of partnerships with allied literary organizations." "Our History and the Growth of Creative Writing Programs," Association of Writers and Writing Programs, https://www.awpwriter.org/about/our_history_overview (accessed February 9, 2015).
17. The rise of the postwar creative writing industry was virtually unacknowledged until McGurl's *The Program Era: Postwar Fiction and the Rise of Creative Writing*, save Eric Bennett's dissertation of the same year, "Creative Writing and the Cold War." Earlier studies, such as D. G. Myers's *Elephants Teach*, did not seek to place the creative writing within the broader field of American literature and cultural production. Mark McGurl, *The Program Era: Postwar*

Fiction and the Rise of Creative Writing (Cambridge, Mass.: Harvard University Press, 2009); Eric Bennett, "Creative Writing and the Cold War," PhD diss., Harvard University, 2009.

18. "Our History and the Growth of Creative Writing Programs."
19. David Fenza, "From Our Executive Director," Association of Writers and Writing Programs 2013 Annual Report, 5.
20. Charles Pritchard, "Inaugural Poet Richard Blanco Talks America and Poetry at Sherrill-Kenwood Library," *Oneida Dispatch*, https://www.oneidadispatch.com/news/local-news/inaugural-poet-richard-blanco-talks-america-and-poetry-at-sherrill/article_840270ca-91d0-11e9-ad42-5fcbb18ecaf6.html (accessed July 27, 2019).
21. Piotr K. Gwiazda, *US Poetry in the Age of Empire, 1979–2012* (New York: Palgrave MacMillan, 2014), 15.
22. Paul Engle, "The Writer and the Place," in Robert Dana, ed., *A Community of Writers: Paul Engle and the Iowa Writers' Workshop* (Iowa City: University of Iowa Press, 1999), 9.
23. On the longer history of rhetoric, composition, literary study as disciplinary formations, see Myers, who traces their evolution from the mid-nineteenth century to the birth of "New English" and "English composition" in the 1880s and 1890s and to the twentieth-century debates from which creative writing emerged. Also see Evan Watkins, *Work Time: English Departments and the Circulation of Cultural Value* (Stanford: Stanford University Press, 1989), which argues that the disciplinary entangling of composition and literary study functioned to endow students with increasingly compound skill sets as managerial workers in a postindustrial economy.
24. Myers, *The Elephants Teach*, 8.
25. Both Myers and Bennett use the two-generation timeline.
26. Myers, *The Elephants Teach*, 6–7.
27. When courses in creative writing—"Writing Fiction" and "Writing Poetry"—were first introduced under the "Writers' Workshop" heading in the 1939–40 University of Iowa *Catalogue*, Foerster's term "Imaginative Writing" was dropped as a prefix to course titles. Stephen Wilbers, *The Iowa Writers' Workshop: Origins, Emergence, and Growth* (Iowa City: University of Iowa Press, 1980), 52. Some histories date the birth of creative writing at Iowa from the formalization of "Imaginative Writing" as field of literary study in 1931. Although I prefer to mark the emergence of workshop writing from the appearance of "creative writing" in Iowa's course catalog, it is worth noting that university president Walter Jessup also successfully urged Foerster to organize the first national "Conference on Creative Writing" in order to bring publicity to Iowa's innovative doctoral program in 1931.

28. "Iowa's School of Letters Admits Imaginative, Critical Writing for Ph.D. Thesis," *Daily Iowan*, March 26, 1931.
29. In the next years, Foerster sponsored a series of readings by nationally recognized writers on campus. Tellingly, "[he] proposed Robert Frost as the first visitor, remembering his long service in various institutions, especially Amherst." Letter to John Gerber, quoted in Wilbers, *The Iowa Writers' Workshop*, 47. Frost and Engle were the headliners at the summer workshop of 1941, Iowa's last major prewar event. During the war, the workshop would scale back its activities (53).
30. Myers, *The Elephants Teach*, 148. Also see Eric Bennett's dissertation chapter "Creative Writing and the New Humanism: Teaching the Soul," which describes how new humanist conceptions of "integrated individuality" and personal responsibility, espoused most influentially by Irving Babbitt, Paul Elmer More, and Norman Foerster, laid the philosophical foundations for creative writing pedagogy in the 1940s. Bennett's telling is more continuous genealogy, where Foerster's pupils, notably Wilbur Schramm, Paul Engle, and Wallace Stegner, formed "a visionary conviction that literature mattered not only to the academy but to the nation and the world" (28). In both Bennett and Myers's accounts, early creative writing develops as a rejection of New Critical autonomy of the literary object. Like national poet Robert Frost, creative writing program founders grew increasingly convicted of the civic responsibility of literature.
31. Between 1933 and 1941, 620,000 students received federal support for college education through the Federal Emergency Relief Administration and National Youth Administration. At the end of World War II, half of American college students were in private colleges; subsequently, private colleges lost 1 percent enrollment annually. Myers, *The Elephants Teach*, 165.
32. Myers, 160–61.
33. See Clark Kerr, *The Uses of the University* (Cambridge, Mass.: Harvard University Press, 1963), based on the Godkin Lectures Kerr delivered April 23–25, 1963 at Harvard University.
34. Allen Tate, "What Is Creative Writing?" *Wisconsin Studies in Contemporary Literature* 5, no. 3 (1964): 182.
35. Wilbers, meanwhile, is reluctant to overestimate Engle's influence in the development of creative writing. "Although the emphasis of the program under Engle's direction changed from treating creative writing as part of a broader scholarly discipline to viewing scholarship as an activity beneficial to the writer, the basic premise was the same: the creation of literature is academically as respectable and important as the study of literature." Wilbers, *The Iowa Writers' Workshop*, 83. Engle's correspondence, however, casts creative writing as antithetical to scholarship proper. While Engle perhaps

strategically emphasized this division to potential funders, it was nonetheless operative in Iowa's rise to national eminence.

36. "Those who went through Iowa went out and took part in other writing programs—a kind of pyramid scheme, it seems now, looking back." Donald Justice in 1984, "An Interview with Donald Justice," quoted in Myers, *The Elephants Teach*, 164.

37. Myers, 183.

38. Paul Engle to the Rockefeller Foundation, February 19, 1952, quoted in Bennett, "Creative Writing and the Cold War," 97.

39. Paul Dawson has baldly contended that "the [creative writing] workshop developed because of the influence of the New Criticism," for example (Bennett 99–100). McGurl likewise calls the success of the creative writing workshop "the achievement of the New Critics," based on their prominence in the postwar university—New Criticism was "lodged at the core of American literary studies in the postwar period. In this [New Critics' ideas] can be taken as emblematic of American writers more broadly"—and retroactively drawn discursive homologies: "the practice of close reading of literary texts in the classroom would harmonize conspicuously well with the obsessive concern for "craft" that began to define writing programs at roughly the same time" (McGurl, *The Program Era*, 22–23). This study aligns itself with Bennett's corrective. As observed in chapter 1, New Critical discourse valued the aesthetic autonomy of the literary object, even in the case of *The Pisan Cantos*; workshop founders, by contrast, championed the civic responsibility of creative expression.

40. Bennett, "Creative Writing and the Cold War," 28.

41. Bennett, 97–99.

42. Bennett, 84. The Rockefeller Foundation, working in conjunction with the State Department and other intelligence agencies, supported ideologically motivated projects across artistic fields. As Peter Decherney has shown in the case of film, the foundation focused on "educational, documentary films and their potential use in advancing democratic societies." Peter Decherney, "The Politics of Patronage," in *Hollywood and the Culture Elite: How the Movies Became American* (New York: Columbia University Press, 2005), 168.

43. Bennett, "Creative Writing and the Cold War," 96. The foundation pledged $40,000 to support three years of fellowships (four to be awarded each year) in fiction, poetry, and drama, selected by a committee of Karl Shapiro, Robert Lowell, Charles Shattuck, Hansford Martin, and Thomas Mabry. Moreover, the Rockefeller Foundation had a vested interest in the field of creative writing since 1944: the *Kenyon Review*, the *Sewanee Review*, the *Hudson Review*, the *Partisan Review*, and the State University of Iowa, which in total had received $385,300 from the foundation between 1947–1957, in turn provided

fellowships to fifty-eight writers—many of whom were graduates of Iowa, and many of whom were among the first set of NEA grantees in 1967.

44. March 16, 1960, in cover letter of "Proposal for Travel in Asia and Europe" to the Rockefeller Foundation. Quoted in Bennett, "The Pyramid Scheme," in Chad Harbach, ed., *MFA vs. NYC: The Two Cultures of American Fiction* (New York: n + 1/Faber and Faber, 2014), 51.

45. Engle also wrote copy for Hallmark, slogans for Nissen and a trampoline manufacturer, and Hall of Fame Christmas operas on NBC (Bennett 133–34), not unlike poet Dana Gioia, who at General Foods reversed an over twenty-year sales decline with his alliterative "Jell-O Jigglers" campaign before acting as NEA chairman (2002–2009). Dana Gioia, "A Poet in the Supermarket," *New York Times*, October 28, 2007.

46. Bennett, "The Pyramid Scheme," 53.

47. In Engle's "To Praise a Man," Frost is "Unhurried, free, with steady gait / He is our greatest, final state. / In him these crooked times provide / A straight astonishment of pride / In such a country, when it can / Bear such a poet, such a man." Paul Engle, "To Praise a Man," in the feature "Paean for a Poet by a Poet," *Life*, June 15, 1959, 65.

48. Paul Engle, "Dedication," in *On Creative Writing* (New York: Dutton, 1964), vii.

49. "In an open society such as ours, writer, businessman and university can join to make an environment which is useful to the writer, friendly for the businessman, and healthy for the university. The following believed this: Northern Natural Gas Company of Omaha; Reader's Digest Foundation; The Fisher Foundation of Mashalltown, Iowa; W. Averell Harriman of Washington, D.C.; The Maytag Co. Foundation, Newton, Iowa; U.S. Steel Foundation; the John D. Rockefeller III Fund; Time Inc.; The Louis W. and Maud Hill Family Foundation of St. Paul; The Cowles Charitable Trust; The New York Foundation; The Fred Maytag Family Foundation; Quaker Oats Co.; Amana Refrigeration; Gardner Cowles, Jr.; Miss Lillian Gish; H.J. Sobiloff, New York; Mrs. John P. Marquand, *Esquire*; J. Patrick Lannan, Chicago; The Robert R. McCormick Foundation; Mrs. Loyal L. Minor, Mason City, Iowa; Mr. Joseph Rosenfield, Mr. Ed Burchette, and Iowa Power and Light Co., all of Des Moines; WMT-TV and Radio, Iowa Electric Light and Power Co., Iowa Manufacturing Co., Merchants National Bank, Iowa Steel and Iron Works, May Drug Co., John B. Turner and Sons, and Iowa National Mutual Insurance Co., all of Cedar Rapids, Iowa, that remarkable city." Engle, "Dedication," vii–viii.

50. Bennett, "Creative Writing and the Cold War," 136–37.

51. Bennett, "The Pyramid Scheme," 54.

52. Richard McCarthy, July 2, 1962 quoted in Bennett, "Creative Writing and the Cold War," 150.
53. T. J. Reardon, Jr. to Engle, January 11, 1962 quoted in Bennett, 151.
54. Bennett, 152.
55. William McGuire Papers, Manuscript Division, Library of Congress.
56. Bennett, "Creative Writing and the Cold War," 150–52.
57. Bennett, 153–54.
58. Engle, *On Creative Writing*, vii.
59. Bennett, "Creative Writing and the Cold War," 156.
60. In September 1964, the passage of the National Arts and Cultural Development Act established a council with twenty-four members to "recommend ways to maintain and increase the cultural resources of the nation and to encourage and develop greater appreciation and enjoyment of the arts by its citizens." A $50,000 budget was approved in October; Paul Engle was chosen as the council's representative from the field of poetry. Mark Bauerlein and Ellen Grantham, eds., *National Endowment for the Arts: A History, 1965–2008* (Washington, D.C.: National Endowment for the Arts, 2008), 15–16.
61. National Foundation on the Arts and the Humanities Act of 1965 (Pub. L. 89-209).
62. Also in 1965, the Higher Education Act (Pub. L. 89-329) offered millions secure federal grants and loans for college; and the National Defense Education Act of 1958 (Pub. L. 85-864) was expanded to include English and the social sciences. The successful launching of Sputnik 1 by the USSR in October 1957 helped to catalyze the passage of the NDEA, which provided funding to reform the national educational system to meet national defense priorities.
63. Bennett, "Creative Writing and the Cold War," 164.
64. According to Bennett, this was another channel for CIA money.
65. Eric Bennett, "Creative Writing and the Cold War University," in *A Companion to Creative Writing* (Hoboken, N.J.: Wiley-Blackwell, 2013), 382.
66. Bauerlein and Grantham, *National Endowment for the Arts*, 25–26.
67. The spread of the workshop as a cultural phenomenon can be observed in the Poetry Society of America's 1966 bulletin announcing its first Round Table Workshop: "(Group limited to 10 members (enrollees) . . . Each to pay $15 for 10 sessions)." Entrepreneurial executive secretary Gustav Davidson was excited by the moneymaking opportunities of the workshop format: "Some months ago I offered 3 proposals to the Board by way of putting PSA back on the poetic map. One of those [sic] 3 proposals was a live, roundtable Poetry Workshop, which became a reality recently with 10 weekly evening sessions operating from this Library. The Workshop proved extremely successful . . .

I am therefore encouraged to revive mention of my 2nd proposal—which was, and is, the launching under PSA sponsorship and support of a Poetry Quarterly . . . a first-class typographer . . . might sell at $1.00 or $1.25 the copy and by annual subscription. As a further source of income it might run paid advertisements pertaining to poetry. I figure that the cost of the venture, for the first 5 years, could be borne by the cash reserves we have built up in the di Castagnola Trust Fund." Davidson understood that the business of poetry was growing: "the Society can ill afford to be constantly lagging behind because of inaction or inertia. That is why other poetry organizations have taken the lead out of our hands. I say, let's get started!" "Proposal submitted by Gustav Davidson to the PSA Governing Board," February 6, 1967, Gustav Davidson Papers, Manuscript Division, Library of Congress.

68. "Men Walk on the Moon: Astronauts Land on Plain; Collect Rocks, Plant Flag" the front page proclaimed. It was more fitting for MacLeish than the current national poet, William Jay Smith, to write a poem commemorating the event. As the wartime librarian of Congress (1939–1944), MacLeish was the key actor in establishing the poetry office as a national institution: he instituted the first national public poetry readings, appointed Allen Tate as the national poet, and formed the fellows. MacLeish was instrumental in solidifying a national canon for poetry by providing institutional centrality through the library.

69. Archibald MacLeish Papers, Manuscript Division, Library of Congress.
70. Jameson, "Dirty Little Secret" in Harbach, *MFA vs. NYC*, 271.
71. Bennett, "Creative Writing and the Cold War University," 386.
72. Paul Engle and Warren Carrier, eds., *Reading Modern Poetry* (Glenview, Ill.: Foresman, 1968), 75.
73. Bennett, "Creative Writing and the Cold War University," 387.
74. The concrete particular or sensory detail is an important thread through twentieth-century American poetics, from William Carlos Williams's "no ideas but in things" ("Paterson," 1927) and Louis Zukofsky's "the detail, not the mirage of seeing" ("An Objective") to Allen Ginsberg's "What did I notice? Particulars!" ("Wales Visitation"). The writing workshop blended these formulations: the detail now served chiefly to authenticate the voice of the individual speaking voice.
75. Paul Engle to Chadbourne Gilpatric, associate director for the Humanities Division at the Rockefeller Foundation, March 22, 1963, quoted in Bennett, "Creative Writing and the Cold War University," 153.
76. Paul Engle to Chadbourne Gilpatric, October 9, 1963, quoted in Bennett.
77. Engle to Gilpatric, quoted in Bennett.
78. McGurl theorizes "high cultural pluralism" as one of the dominant modes of program era fiction, alongside what he calls "lower-middle-class

modernism" and "technomodernism," theorizing these as principally genre-based modalities as autopoetic processes that reflect the conditions of their production. McGurl, *The Program Era*, 32–34.

79. Engle to Gilpatric, March 22, 1963, quoted in Bennett, "Creative Writing and the Cold War," 154 (emphasis mine).

80. "High cultural pluralism enacts a layering of positively marked differences: in the modernist tradition, it understands its self-consciously crafted and/or intellectually substantial products as importantly distinct from mass culture or genre fiction, although in practice . . . [e.g.,] when Toni Morrison's *Beloved* (1987) is read by Oprah's Book Club—this distinction is often blurred or intentionally put at risk." McGurl, *The Program Era*, 57. In creative writing workshop poetry, three correlate modes unfold more or less chronologically: 1. individual voice that stands for expressive, democratic values; 2. increasingly in the 1970s and 1980s, unique identities of a plural society; and 3. the formal experiments of poet-critics. These are not neat parallels, but they do help to highlight the compatibility between the speaking subject of "high cultural pluralism" in McGurl's account of creative writing fiction and of the creative writing industry's model of poetic voice by the mid-1980s and 1990s.

81. McGurl, 58–59.

82. Bennett, "Creative Writing and the Cold War University," 383.

83. Fenza, "From Our Executive Director," 5.

84. From Reed Whittemore, *The Feel of Rock: Poems of Three Decades* (Takoma Park, Md.: Dryad, 1982), which originally appeared in *An American Takes a Walk* (Minneapolis: University of Minnesota Press, 1956).

85. Gwendolyn Brooks, "Black Woman in Russia, in *Go Girl!: The Black Woman's Book of Travel and Adventure*, ed. Elaine Lee (Portland: Eighth Mountain, 1997), 235, 237.

86. Reed Whittemore, *The Past, the Future, the Present: Poems Selected and New* (Fayetteville: University of Arkansas Press, 1990), 40. "Notes on a Certain Terribly Critical Piece" originally appeared in Whittemore, *The Self-Made Man* (New York: Macmillan, 1959).

87. "Consultant in Poetry Named for 1964–5," *Library of Congress Information Bulletin*, May 4, 1965, 200–1.

88. McGuire, *Poetry's Catbird Seat*, 279.

89. McGuire.

90. McGuire, 291.

91. McGuire. Archival records suggest Basler drafted the letter. William McGuire Papers, Manuscript Division, Library of Congress.

92. The symposium was held April 2–3, 1965. *The Little Magazine and Contemporary Literature, A Symposium Held at the Library of Congress* (published for the

Reference Department at the Library of Congress by the Modern Language Association of America, 1966), 20.
93. *The Little Magazine.*
94. McGuire, *Poetry's Catbird Seat*, 280.
95. The project evolved from a conversation with Russian poet Anna Akhmatova, who had told Spender several years earlier while visiting London that she found English translations of her poem "Requiem" inaccurate, but her interpreter's accurate translation publishable.
96. "News Information Office from the Library of Congress Press Release," March 2, 1978, William McGuire Papers, Manuscript Division, Library of Congress.
97. William Jay Smith to Daniel Boorstin, March 16, 1978, William McGuire Papers, Manuscript Division, Library of Congress.
98. Richard Eberhart to Daniel Boorstin, March 13, 1978, William McGuire Papers, Manuscript Division, Library of Congress. Along with Brooks, Eberhart suggested James Wright, Donald Hall, and Maxine Kumin in a ranked list of twenty-two suggestions: "You realize of course that in naming names it is all a matter of taste . . . I wouldn't mind seeing Allen Ginsberg in the office. Unlike at least one of my colleagues at the meeting, I think his poetry is historical and important. He is 52. I think of the work of Anthony Hecht, 55, an opposite kind of a poet, lapidary [circled in red pencil], perfectionist."
99. Daniel Hoffman to Daniel Boorstin, March 20, 1978, William McGuire Papers, Manuscript Division, Library of Congress. One week later, Boorstin wrote to Elizabeth Bishop, who despised public readings, not to solicit advice for the next appointment but to thank her for her attendance at the recent poetry consultants' reunion. During the reunion roundtable, which focused on the recording archive and literacy initiatives in schools, she contributed to the discussion only once, and then at the prodding of the moderator: "Oh . . . I'm rather out of it. I don't like video tapes and recordings. More important to sit home and read a book or write a poem than see any of these things in the classroom. . . . I can't stop progress whatever that is." Bishop's attitude shows how the emphasis on the "public appearance" of the national poetry office had evolved since her appointment in 1949. "Poetry Consultants' Reunion Transcript Notes," March 6, 1978, William McGuire Papers, Manuscript Division, Library of Congress.
100. Dan Vera, "The Library and Its Laureates: The Examples of Auslander, Williams, Dickey, and Kumin," *Beltway Poetry Quarterly* 10, no. 4 (Fall 2009).
101. Vera.
102. An act to amend the National Foundation on the Arts and the Humanities Act of 1965, and for other purposes (Pub. L. 99-194, Title VI, Sec. 601, Dec. 20, 1985, 99 Stat. 1347), effective January 3, 1986.

103. McGuire, *Poetry's Catbird Seat*, 425–26.
104. "Poetry program / (1) The Chairperson of the National Endowment for the Arts, with the advice of the National Council on the Arts, shall annually sponsor a program at which the Poet Laureate Consultant in Poetry will present a major work or the work of other distinguished poets. (2) There are authorized to be appropriated to the National Endowment for the Arts $10,000 for the fiscal year 1987 and for each succeeding fiscal year ending prior to October 1, 1990, for the purpose of carrying out this subsection." Pub. L. 99-194, title VI, Sec. 601, Dec. 20, 1985, 99 Stat. 1347.
105. The library was in a timely position to rebrand the office on the eve of its fiftieth anniversary. Meanwhile, while Senator Spark M. Matsunaga (HI) was pitching his bill to retitle the Consultant in Poetry as the Poet Laureate, "The Library of Congress—specifically, John Broderick—has commissioned [William McGuire] to write a book about the Consultantship in Poetry, which will be fifty years old in 1986 or 1987, the dates respectively of the endowment and the first appointment." William McGuire to Edward D'Alessandro, March 25, 1985, William McGuire Papers, Manuscript Division, Library of Congress.
106. Casper, interview by author.
107. "Gwendolyn Brooks Is Named as Next Library Poetry Consultant," *Library of Congress Information Bulletin*, May 20, 1985, 106.
108. Robert Penn Warren, *Segregation: The Inner Conflict in the South* (New York: Vintage, 1956); Robert Penn Warren, *Who Speaks for the Negro?* (New York: Random House, 1965).
109. Special Order No. 102, "Appointment of Robert Penn Warren as the Library of Congress Consultant in Poetry and editor of the Quarterly Journal of Current Acquisitions for 1944–45," Office of the Librarian, Library of Congress, May 9, 1944, container 953, Archibald MacLeish Papers, Manuscript Division, Library of Congress.
110. "Robert Penn Warren Is Named First Poet Laureate, Poetry Consultant," *Library of Congress Information Bulletin*, March 10, 1986, 78–9.
111. Eric Bennett, *Workshops of Empire: Stegner, Engle, and American Creative Writing During the Cold War* (University of Iowa Press, 2015), 199n.
112. Juliana Spahr, *Du Bois's Telegram: Literary Resistance and State Containment* (Cambridge, Mass.: Harvard University Press, 2018), 121.
113. Spahr, 122.
114. For an earlier account of this watershed moment in Brooks's career, see Don L. Lee, "The Achievement of Gwendolyn Brooks," *Black Scholar* 3, no. 10 (Summer 1972): 32.
115. Spahr, *Du Bois's Telegram*, 125–26.
116. Brooks, "Black Woman in Russia," 236–37.

117. Brooks, 237.
118. Brooks.
119. Brooks, 238.
120. Gwendolyn Brooks, "Annual Report to the Librarian of Congress from the Chair of Poetry," William McGuire Papers, Manuscript Division, Library of Congress.
121. Gwendolyn Brooks to Richard Shaffer, November 5, 1985, William McGuire Papers, Manuscript Division, Library of Congress.
122. Gwendolyn Brooks to Sue Federico, October 28, 1985, William McGuire Papers, Manuscript Division, Library of Congress.
123. Gwendolyn Brooks to Alfred Cabey, November 12, 1985, William McGuire Papers, Manuscript Division, Library of Congress.
124. Gwendolyn Brooks to Lloyd Lazard, March 11, 1986, William McGuire Papers, Manuscript Division, Library of Congress. The poetry office received Lazard's letter to Brooks only a four days earlier: "I, Lloyd E. Lazard am writing to you as a fellow poet. I am presently confine in Orleans Parish Prison, and as an inmate my dormant talent as a poet have manifest it self to me. I am a victim of the economic repression of 1983, in which I lost my business at New Orleans International Airport, because of renovation which displaced me the only Black owned concessionaire." Lloyd E. Lazard to Brooks, February 24, 1986, stamped received March 7, 1986, William McGuire Papers, Manuscript Division, Library of Congress.
125. Gwendolyn Brooks to John Broderick, March 26, 1986, William McGuire Papers, Manuscript Division, Library of Congress.
126. John Broderick to Gwendolyn Brooks, April 3, 1986, William McGuire Papers, Manuscript Division, Library of Congress.
127. Broderick to Brooks.
128. Robert Casper, email message to the author, May 25, 2022.
129. Brooks, "Annual Report to the Librarian of Congress," 15–16.
130. Quoted in McGuire, *Poetry's Catbird Seat*, 429.
131. Casper, interview by the author.
132. From Joseph Brodsky, "Uncommon Visage," published in *Poets and Writers*, quoted in "Joseph Brodsky," Poetry Foundation, https://www.poetryfoundation.org/poets/joseph-brodsky (accessed July 28, 2019).
133. Ron Silliman, ed., *In the American Tree: Language, Realism, Poetry* (Orono, Me.: National Poetry Foundation, 1986).
134. Marjorie Perloff, "Ca(n)non to the Right of Us, Ca(n)non to the Left of Us: A Plea for Difference," *New Literary History* 18, no. 3 (Spring 1987): 633–56.
135. "Established in 1971 by Carroll F. Terrell (1917–2003) as a center for Pound scholarship, our mission was expanded by Burton Hatlen (director from 1990 until his death in 2008) to include the entire tradition of innovative poetry

from modernism to the present day." "About Us," National Poetry Foundation, http://www.nationalpoetryfoundation.org/about-us/ (accessed May 12, 2015).
136. Ron Silliman, Carla Harryman, Lyn Hejinian, Steve Benson, Bob Perelman, and Barrett Watten, "Aesthetic Tendency and the Politics of Poetry: A Manifesto," *Social Text* 19/20 (Autumn 1988): 262.
137. Silliman, 261–62.
138. Here I refer to the later edition. Lyn Hejinian, *My Life* (Providence: Sun and Moon, 1987).
139. The opening line of *My Life*, "A pause, a rose, something on paper," importantly recalls Gertrude Stein's iconic "rose is a rose is a rose is a rose" (1913). Hejinian's "rose" as a commercialized trope of femininity and romantic love is displaced by her professed aesthetic forbear's signature exercise in repetition. Through repetition, Stein demonstrates the multiplicity of meanings that a singular word can produce. *Rose* can connote a flower, an action ("to rise") or a proper feminine name; when verbally uttered, it suggests "rows," adding a second, discreet semantic category with its own set of possible significations. Moreover, the geometric, structural connotation of "rows" would act as a foil to the archetype of the soft, pliant bloom of a "rose." The combinatory possibilities further reveal a "rose" is never just a "rose." Notably, Stein also appears in "Aesthetic Tendency and The Politics of Poetry: A Manifesto," which writes Language poetry within a progressive literary genealogy. While *My Life* recalls Stein repeatedly and variously, "The Politics of Poetry" invokes Stein as a birthmother in a linearly unfolding project. Just as Stein's "rose" asks to be repeated infinitely, the phrase "A pause, a rose, something on paper" is repeated throughout *My Life*. While this repetition acts as an ordering device, orienting the reader around a familiar phrase, so too it deritualizes and disorients meaning—each distinct context bears with it a new set of semantic associations, releasing writer and reader from narrative and interpretive authority. The repetition of "I" throughout the text and across editions of *My Life* achieves a similar effect, but if the repetition of "A pause, a rose, something on paper" records the unfixable nature of language, "I" foregrounds the unfixable nature of identity.
140. Unlike the 1980 edition published by Burning Deck, the 1987 edition features a photographic portrait of Hejinian on its cover. This reprint, issued by Sun and Moon Press, raises a new set of questions: Does the cover photograph foreground the disparity between author and persona? Or does this new legibility compromise the antigeneric or anti-identitarian project? To my mind, the photograph works cooperatively with the title to recall the conventional autobiography, demarcating a sharper, perhaps more ironic contrast between readerly expectations dictated by genre and the text itself.

141. Hejinian, *My Life*, 105. Additionally, in an early version of "The Rejection of Closure," Hejinian posits language as inherently genderless: "The desire that is stirred by language seems to be located more interestingly within language, and hence it is androgynous." Lyn Hejinian, *Writing/Talks*, ed. Bob Perelman (Carbondale: Southern Illinois University Press, 1985), 283.

142. Hejinian, *My Life*, 34.

143. Hejinian, 46.

144. This literature argues that by participating in the discourse of representation governed by identity politics, feminism undercuts its own emancipatory project; the construction of woman as a stable subject reifies the structures of power that feminism would seek to dismantle. See, for example, Judith Butler, *Gender Trouble* (New York: Routledge, 1990); Wendy Brown, *States of Injury: Power and Freedom in Late Modernity* (Princeton: Princeton University Press, 1995).

145. Judith Butler, "Contingent Foundations: Feminism and the Question of the 'Postmodern,'" in *Feminists Theorize the Political* (New York: Routledge, 1992), 19.

146. In "The Rejection of Closure," the text that rejects the authority of the writer over the reader "thus, by analogy, [rejects] the authority implicit in other (social, economic, cultural) hierarchies." Lyn Hejinian, *The Language of Inquiry* (Berkeley: University of California Press, 2000), 134.

147. Silliman et al., "Aesthetic Tendency and the Politics of Poetry," 272–73.

148. Perelman, in conversation with author.

149. Janet Lyon, *Manifestoes: Provocations of the Modern* (Ithaca, N.Y.: Cornell University Press, 1999), 9.

150. Thanks to Sarah Dowling, Julia Bloch, Ted Rees, Maria Damon, SaraEllen Strongman, and others for conversations that contributed to this brief survey.

151. Andrew Epstein, "Verse vs. Verse," *Lingua Franca* (September 2000): 45–54, 45.

152. Charles Bernstein, "Revenge of the Poet-Critic," in *My Way: Speeches and Poems*, 5.

153. Libbie Rifkin, *Career Moves: Olson, Creeley, Zukofsky, Berrigan, and the American Avant-Garde* (Madison: University of Wisconsin Press, 2000), 140.

154. For example, the institutional strategies of hybrid poetry-criticism or "talk." What McGurl calls more widely "autopoetics" is a means to objectify the institutional frame governing the production of poetry and academic criticism for the poet-critic in the English Department. In *Career Moves*, Libbie Rifkin reads Bob Perelman's staging of a "'double personnage' [sic] as avant-garde participant and academic professional"—"the stance of being both inside and outside" (Perelman, "Counter-Response," 43)—as the central

tension of *The Marginalization of Poetry: Language Writing and Literary History* (1996). The "double personnage" was also performed at an event staged in response to the book in an "East Village performance space on March 22, 1997, and published two months later as an installment in *The Impercipient Lecture Series*," where Perelman's "talk" recalled "Olson's on-air crisis at Berkeley . . . in both theme and social context." While deploying "talk" as an "institutional strategy," Perelman departed from the "vatic singularity" of Olson's declaration that "'I am now publishing tonight . . . because I'm talking writing' . . . Whereas Olson's performance worked to collapse realms of individual impulse and institutional codification into a single revolutionary event, *The Impercipient* event and publication suggest that at least one branch of the avant-garde is . . . replacing the hero-poet with a more diversified cadre of players" (*Career Moves*, 141). See Bob Perelman, "A Counter-Response," in *The Impercipient Lecture Series: Readings and Responses to Bob Perelman's "The Marginalization of Poetry"* by Ron Silliman, Ann Lauterbach, Juliana Spahr, and Steve Evans; with a Counter-Response by Bob Perelman, repr. in *Jacket 2* 1, no. 4 (May 1997), http://jacketmagazine.com/02/perel.html.

155. While "high cultural pluralist" fiction reductively voiced identity positions through the programmatic norming of multiculturalist sensibilities, there are many breakout acts of literary diversity. For McGurl, Octavia Butler provides an instructive instance: as a graduate of the Clarion Workshop (the Clarion Workshops do not occupy the regular academic calendar year, structurally embedding the "liminal status of creative writing as a scholarly pursuit"), she was "well placed to perceive how the formation of our individuality in and by the otherness of institutional relations could easily be radicalized in our relation to the truly alien." Her Xenogenesis trilogy of the 1980s, collected in *Lilith's Brood* (2000), presents a heroine who "overcomes her nostalgia for the old wholeness and her disgust for the new hybrid on behalf of a paradoxically posthuman human survival through the Ooloi. . . . This, seen through the visionary magnifying glass of genre fiction, is what it really means to accept the necessity of the otherness of institutionality and of system." McGurl, *The Program Era*, 396–97.

156. "The Poetry and Literature Center at the Library of Congress: Poetry Resources," Library of Congress, http://www.loc.gov/rr/program/bib/lcpoetry/poetry.html (accessed February 1, 2015).

157. "The Poetry and Literature Center at the Library of Congress: Past Poets Laureate: 1981–1990," Library of Congress, http://www.loc.gov/poetry/laureate-1981-1990.html (accessed February 1, 2015).

158. "Since 1991, following the lead of Joseph Brodsky, the Poets Laureate have frequently designed programs with a national reach." "The Poetry and

Literature Center at the Library of Congress: About the Poetry and Literature Center," Library of Congress, http://www.loc.gov/poetry/about.html (accessed February 1, 2015).

## 4. Civil Versus Civic Verse

1. Edward Ohnemus, "Brodsky Urges Publishers to Distribute Poetry to the Masses," *Library of Congress Gazette*, October 11, 1991, 9 (emphasis mine).
2. Ohnemus.
3. Prior to Pinsky, and later Harjo, no poet laureate served more than two successive years after the position was retitled in 1985. Joseph Auslander, who was appointed in 1937 when the position of consultant in poetry position was first created, occupied it for four years (1937–1941), but all consultants in poetry and poets laureate subsequently served one-year or two-year terms.
4. According to the Library of Congress as of July 2019, notable poetry projects began with Pinsky, and include successive projects undertaken by Collins, Kooser, Kay Ryan, Natasha Trethewey, and Juan Felipe Herrera. "Past Poet Laureate Projects," Poetry and Literature Center at the Library of Congress, https://www.loc.gov/poetry/laureate-projects.html (accessed July 19, 2019).
5. "Poetry 180: A Poem a Day for American High Schools," Library of Congress, http://www.loc.gov/poetry/180 (accessed March 2, 2015).
6. "American Life in Poetry," American Life in Poetry: A Project for Newspapers by Ted Kooser, Poet Laureate of the United States 2004–2006, http://www.americanlifeinpoetry.org/ (accessed March 2, 2015).
7. von Hallberg, *Lyric Powers*, 233.
8. von Hallberg, 103.
9. von Hallberg argues that the authority of the lyric has three sources: "first, traditions of religious affirmation; second, the social status of those who speak the idioms from which particular poems are made; third, extraordinary cognition produced by the formal, and in particular musical, resources of some poems" (7). He also draws a broader distinction between *orphic* (vatic) versus *rhetorical* (speech-based) poetics, calling these two "rival families" of poetry in U.S. literary culture (1–2). In his reading, "civil poets" Pinsky, Hass, Graham, Glück fall into the second category in both breakdowns as rhetoricians who "ground their art in the imitation of speech" and draw authority from civil, secular values. However, von Hallberg does not account for the ways in which civil poets also draw from a "musicality that seems mysterious, or seems to symbolize a transcendent order." In civil verse projects, most notably Pinsky's Favorite Poem Project, orphic power helps to authorize the speech idioms of a

social class, and to impute transcendent significance to those "secular values [that] properly govern cultural life." In short, civil poets who are rhetorical, "who ground their art in the imitation of speech" also draw on the orphic (vatic) tradition, where the authority of "social class" and the authority of "religious belief or experience" are rendered indistinguishable through the speech-act of the poem to elevate the values of the managerial elite. We will see this in Pinsky's language of transcendence—the way something beyond "ordinary life" happens when one recites a poem written in "ordinary language." "About the Favorite Poem Project: Founding Principles: Giving Voice to the American Audience," Favorite Poem Project: Americans Saying Poems They Love, http://www.favoritepoem.org/about.html.

10. von Hallberg, 90.
11. von Hallberg, 233.
12. Robert Pinsky, "Responsibilities of the Poet," *Critical Inquiry* 13, no. 3 (April 1987): 421–33.
13. Charles Bernstein, *Attack of the Difficult Poems: Essays and Inventions*. Chicago: University of Chicago Press, 2011.
14. Amy Clampitt, who served as a judge on the committee, was uneasy about the government-issued prize given the active fights over federal arts funding especially through the NEA. Elizabeth Kastor, "James Merrill Is Winner of Bobbitt Poetry Prize," *Washington Post*, October 28, 1990, https://www.washingtonpost.com/archive/politics/1990/10/28/james-merrill-is-winner-of-bobbitt-poetry-prize/33cb27bb-e6e8-4a01-b926-0f10b8bc51c0/.
15. Casper, interview by author, August 2, 2019.
16. Memorandum for file with carbon copy of James Billington to Philip Bobbitt, September 14, 1989, Records of the Poetry and Literature Center at the Library of Congress, quoted by Rob Casper in an email message to author, August 2, 2019.
17. Verner Clapp to the Fellows in American Letters, Bollingen Foundation Records.
18. Philip Bobbitt to Nancy Galbraith, December 2, 1988, Records of the Poetry and Literature Center at the Library of Congress, quoted by Rob Casper in an email message to author. "I also strongly agree with Bobbitt, in both the prize and in the center's work in general, that "politics should play no part in it," Casper affirmed in 2019. Casper, email message to author, August 2, 2019.
19. Casper, email message to author, August 2, 2019.
20. Casper.
21. "National Poetry Month: Proclamations," Academy of American Poets, http://www.poets.org/national-poetry-month/national-poetry-month-proclamations (accessed March 2, 2015).

22. This list reflects the primary supporters of the 2015 National Poetry Month. Contributors that year included Alfred A. Knopf, Inc.; Hamline University; Houghton Mifflin Harcourt; Penguin Books; W. W. Norton and Company; supporters included Columbia University School of the Arts; Consortium Book Sales and Distribution; Copper Canyon Press; Farrar, Straus and Giroux; HarperCollins Publishers; Marsh Hawk Press; Milkweed Editions; the Graduate Center at Seattle Pacific University; University of Notre Dame Press; Wake Forest University Press and Wayne State University Press. "National Poetry Month: Sponsors and Partners," Academy of American Poets, http://www.poets.org/national-poetry-month/sponsors-partners (accessed March 10, 2015).
23. "National Poetry Month: About the Celebration."
24. Marie Bullock attended Joseph Auslander's lectures at Harvard. The figure of a winged horse, which honors Auslander's history of poetry *The Winged Horse* (1927) and *Winged Horse Anthology* (1929), remains the logo of the AAP today. The AAP was founded in 1934 in New York and incorporated as a nonprofit in 1936.
25. William McGuire, *Poetry's Catbird Seat: The Consultantship in Poetry in the English Language at the Library of Congress, 1937–1987* (Washington, D.C.: Library of Congress, 1988), 404.
26. The AAP was key in promoting "prize culture" in the field of postwar American poetry. See James English, *The Economy of Prestige: Prizes, Awards, and the Circulation of Cultural Value* (Cambridge, Mass.: Harvard University Press, 2005). From 1954–1985, the AAP expanded $200,000 in sponsoring annual $100 poetry prizes at 130 colleges and universities and issuing anthologies of winning poems. With the help of A.W. Mellon Foundation grants, the AAP invited poetry societies nationwide to become AAP affiliates.
27. McGuire, *Poetry's Catbird Seat*, 338.
28. McGuire, 405–6.
29. Early state arts councils and business initiatives helped forge these relationships in previous decades. In the fall of 1967, David Rockefeller and corporate leaders formed the Business Committee for the Arts to devise "strategies to bring the business and arts communities into partnerships and more effective forms of mutual support." Mark Bauerlein and Ellen Grantham, eds., *National Endowment for the Arts: A History, 1965–2008* (Washington, D.C.: National Endowment for the Arts, 2008), 17.
30. Francis S. M. Hodsoll, "Supporting the Arts in the Eighties: The View from the National Endowment for the Arts," *Annals of the American Academy of Political and Social Science* 471, no. 1 (January 1984): 85.
31. Bauerlein and Grantham, *National Endowment for the Arts: A History*, 36.
32. Bauerlein and Grantham, 55.

33. Presidential Task Force on the Arts and the Humanities, Report to the President (Washington, DC: Government Printing Office, 1981), 3, quoted in Hodsoll, "Supporting the Arts in the Eighties," 85 (emphasis mine).
34. Hodsoll, 85.
35. Joseph Epstein, "Thank You, No," Poetry 184 (September 2004): 373–74.
36. Liam Rector, "Elitism, Populism, Laureates, and Free Speech," *American Poetry Review* 32, no. 1 (January/February 2003): 9–13.
37. Charles Bernstein, "Against National Poetry Month as Such," in *My Way: Speeches and Poems* (Chicago: University of Chicago Press, 1999), 28.
38. "About the Favorite Poem Project."
39. "American Life in Poetry."
40. "Poetry 180: A Poem A Day for American High Schools."
41. The Academy of American Poets, for example, offers lesson plans and instructional articles and guides "on teaching poetry" in connection with National Poetry Month: "[The AAP] presents lesson plans most of which align with Common Core State Standards, and all of which have been reviewed by our Educator in Residence with an eye toward developing skills of perception and imagination. We hope they will inspire the educators in our community to bring even more poems into your classrooms!" "Lesson Plans," Academy of American Poets, http://www.poets.org/poetsorg/lesson-plans (accessed March 11, 2015).
42. Robert Pinsky, *Democracy, Culture, and the Voice of Poetry* (Princeton, N.J.: Princeton University Press, 2002), 18.
43. Billy Collins, ed., *Poetry 180: A Turning Back to Poetry* (New York: Random House, 2003), xxiii.
44. Collins, xvi.
45. Collins, "To the high school teachers of America: Poetry 180: A Poem a Day for American High Schools," Library of Congress, http://www.loc.gov/poetry/180 (accessed March 2, 2015).
46. "About the Favorite Poem Project."
47. Collins, *Poetry 180*. A second anthology sought to widen the project's audience, exposing not only high school students but "readers of all ages to the best of today's poetry." Billy Collins, *180 More: Extraordinary Poems for Every Day* (New York: Random House, 2005), dust jacket.
48. The amount of the donation is contested. It has been reported as ranging from $100 million to $200 million. Between January and December 2002, 3.8 million shares of Lilly stock declined in value by 36 percent; Americans for the Arts and *Poetry* later sued National City Bank of Indiana for negligence and breach of fiduciary duty after a "botched" sell-off of the stock. See Steve Evans, "Free (Market) Verse," in Craig Dworkin, ed., *The Consequence of Innovation: Twenty-first-Century Poetics* (New York: Roof, 2008), 27; and Juliana

Spahr, "Contemporary U.S. Poetry and Its Nationalisms," *Contemporary Literature* 52, no. 4 (Winter 2011): 684–715. In 2007, the *New York Times* reported that the gift was then estimated to be worth $200 million. Julia Klein, "A Windfall Illuminates the Poetry Field, and Its Fights." *New York Times*, November 12, 2007.

Editor Joseph Parisi announced the gift at *Poetry*'s ninetieth-anniversary dinner on November 15, 2002, but the magazine learned of the gift the fall of 2001. Stephen Kinzer, "Lilly Heir Makes $100 Million Bequest to Poetry Magazine," *New York Times*, November 19, 2002; Dana Goodyear, "The Moneyed Muse," *New Yorker*, February 19, 2007. Joseph Parisi and Stephen Young, eds., *Between the Lines: A History of Poetry in Letters, 1962–2002* (Chicago: Dee, 2006), 6.

49. Parisi and Young, 242.
50. James Warren, "A Billionaire's Ode to Charity: $100 Million to Poetry Journal," *Chicago Tribune*, November 17, 2002. Also see Nick Paumgarten, "A Hundred Million." *New Yorker*, December 2, 2002.
51. Parisi and Young, *Between the Lines*, 8.
52. Max Stephenson Jr., Marcy Schnitzer, and Verónica Arroyave, "Nonprofit Governance, Management, and Organizational Learning: Exploring the Implications of One 'Mega-Gift,'" *American Review of Public Administration* 39, no. 1 (January 2009): 43. A "mega-gift" is defined as a gift of $1 million or more to a single entity. Jerold Panas, *Mega Gifts: Who Gives Them, Who Gets Them* (Chicago: Pluribus, 1984), 201.
53. Judy Valente with Parisi, "The Well-Endowed 'Poetry' Magazine," *National Public Radio*, May 22, 2005.
54. Barr had been on the boards of the Poetry Society of America, Bennington College, and Yaddo, and had taught for three terms in the MFA program at Sarah Lawrence. Barr's individual trajectory from the Poetry Society of America to the creative writing workshop to the Poetry Foundation usefully highlights the trajectory of aesthetic values through institutions.
55. John Barr, "Foundation Release Letter from John Barr, President," Poetry Foundation, September 2004, http://www.poetryfoundation.org/foundation/release_letter.html.
56. Foundation spokesperson Annie Halsey quoted in Julia Klein, "A Windfall Illuminates the Poetry Field, and Its Fights," *New York Times*, November 12, 2007, 8.
57. "History and Mission," Poetry Foundation, http://www.poetryfoundation.org/foundation/history-and-mission (accessed March 2, 2015).
58. "Project Description," American Life in Poetry: A Project for Newspapers.
59. Klein, "A Windfall."

60. Dana Gioia, "A Poet in the Supermarket," *New York Times*, October 28, 2007.
61. Heidi Benson, "Poet Wants to Write Verse into Everyone's Daily Requirements," *San Francisco Gate*, June 27, 2004.
62. "History and Mission."
63. Quoted in Goodyear, "The Moneyed Muse."
64. Spahr, "Contemporary U.S. Poetry and Its Nationalisms," 692–93; Evans, "Free (Market) Verse," 25–36. Also see an earlier version of Evans's essay in the *Baffler*, no. 17 (June 2006).
65. Evans, "Free (Market) Verse," 26–27.
66. Evans, 32.
67. Parisi and Young, *Between the Lines*, 7.
68. John Barr, "American Poetry in the New Century," *Poetry* 188, no. 5 (September 2006): 433–41.
69. *Poetry in America: Review of the Findings* echoes the language and cultural ambitions of the Poetry Foundation's mission statement and of financially allied institutional players. To diagnose the current "state of poetry in America," the Foundation commissioned the National Opinion Research Center at the University of Chicago to determine poetry's current audiences, factors that contribute to ongoing participation with poetry, perceptions of poetry, poets and poetry readers, obstacles to engagement with poetry, and recommendations for broadening the audience for poetry in the United States. The report is less valuable for its findings than for its stated objectives, motivating assumptions, operational definitions, and the extent to which the ideological vision these summarize is institutionally unique or similar to other national poetry projects. For instance, the report sets out a working "definition" of poetry to all survey respondents: "Poetry is unique because it uses rhythm and language in verses to create images in the mind of the reader. Sometimes poetry rhymes, but not always . . . the words 'poetry' or 'poems' refer to verses intended to be understood as poems, not as part of something else such as rap, song lyrics, Bible verses, or greeting card messages." The report explicitly assumes poetry's social function ("poetry and other literary forms serve important purposes—they celebrate our culture, create economic opportunities, educate our citizenry, and enhance our lives"), and implicitly assumes poetry as an inherent good a priori of form, content and affiliation—that is, poetry is a genre with quasi-spiritual value, i.e., the power to humanize and edify. *Poetry in America: Review of the Findings*, prepared by Lisa K. Schwartz, Ph.D., Lisbeth Goble, Ned English, and Robert F. Bailey at the National Opinion Research Center (Chicago: Poetry Foundation and the National Organization for Research at the University of Chicago, January 2006).
70. Barr, "American Poetry in the New Century," 434.

71. Harriet Monroe, "Newspaper Verse," *Poetry: A Magazine of Verse* 19, no. 6 (March 1922): 329.
72. Barr, "American Poetry in the New Century," 433.
73. Barr, 438.
74. "Poetry and Investment Banking: It's All About Risk," Knowledge@Wharton, January 26, 2005, http://knowledge.wharton.upenn.edu/article/poetry-and-investment-banking-its-all-about-risk (accessed July 8, 2015; emphasis mine).
75. Casper, interview by author, August 2, 2019.
76. Pinsky, *Democracy, Culture, and the Voice of Poetry*, 48.
77. The Boston reading (April 8, 1998) was sponsored by the Library of Congress, the Boston Public Library, and Boston University. The New York reading (April 1, 1998) was hosted by the Academy of the American Poets and sponsored by the *New York Times* advertising department.
78. "About the Favorite Poem Project."
79. Pinsky, *Democracy, Culture, and the Voice of Poetry*, 49.
80. Robert Pinsky, *Poetry and the World* (New York: Ecco, 1988); *The Sounds of Poetry* (New York: Farrar, Straus and Giroux, 1998); *Democracy, Culture, and the Voice of Poetry* (2002). *Democracy, Culture, and the Voice of Poetry* is the published version of four Tanner Lectures delivered at the Princeton University Center for Human Values, "approach[ing] its subject partly through the Favorite Poem Project, which has depended upon the vision and support provided by Boston University, the Carnegie Education Foundation, and The National Endowment for the Arts." Pinsky, *Democracy, Culture, and the the Voice of Poetry*, ix.
81. Pinsky, *Democracy, Culture, and the Voice of Poetry*, 15.
82. "About the Favorite Poem Project: Founding Principles."
83. While "other conceptions of poetry might include flamboyantly expressive vocal delivery, accompanied by impressive physical presence, by the poet or performer; or the typographical, graphic appearance of the words in itself," those conceptions "are not part of this book's conception." Pinsky, *The Sounds of Poetry*, 8.
84. "About the Favorite Poem Project: Founding Principles" (emphases mine). Annette Frost, the director of the Favorite Poem Project, provided me with the revised language to appear in a new website for the project, forthcoming as of July 2022.
85. Pinsky, *Democracy, Culture, and the Voice of Poetry*, 17–18.
86. Pinsky, 49–50.
87. Pinsky, 16.
88. Robert Pinsky, *An Explanation of America* (Princeton, N.J.: Princeton University Press, 1979).

89. "[*An Explanation of America*] is an ideal poem for a national poet to have written, and the very stuff of which laureateships are made." Pinsky read from this poem—"The Founders made / A Union mystic yet rational"—at a news conference shortly after taking office as Poet Laureate in October 1997. Robert Archambeau, *Laureates and Heretics. Six Careers in American Poetry: Yvor Winters, Robert Pinsky, James McMichael, Robert Hass, John Matthias, John Peck* (Notre Dame: University of Notre Dame Press, 2010), 66–67.
90. Quoted in Archambeau, 81.
91. "Poetry 180: More About This Program," Library of Congress, http://www.loc.gov/poetry/180/p180-more.html (accessed March 2, 2015).
92. "Poetry 180."
93. Collins, *Poetry 180*, xvi.
94. "In 'North of Boston' you are to see me performing in a language absolutely unliterary. What I would like is to get so I would never use a word or combination of words that I hadn't heard used in running speech.... You do it on your ear." Robert Frost to John T. Bartlett, December 8, 1913, *SL* 102. For more on Frost's poetics, see chapter 2.
95. "Poetry 180: A Poem a Day for American High Schools."
96. "Poetry 180."
97. Collins, *Poetry 180: A Turning Back to Poetry*, xviii.
98. Collins, xix.
99. Collins.
100. Collins, xvi (emphasis mine).
101. "Poetry 180: More About This Program."
102. Collins, *Poetry 180*, xxii.
103. Collins, xxiii.
104. Collins, *180 More*, xix; xviii.
105. Collins, xx.
106. "Poetry 180: A Poem a Day for American High Schools, a Project from Poet Laureate Billy Collins: More About this Program," Poetry and Literature Center at the Library of Congress," https://www.loc.gov/poetry/180/p180-more.html (accessed August 1, 2019).
107. Casper, interview by author, August 2, 2019.
108. "American Life in Poetry."
109. Quoted in "The Poetry Foundation and the Library of Congress Cosponsor Poet Laureate's Newspaper Project," Library of Congress Press Release 05-052, March 24, 2005.
110. "American Life in Poetry."
111. Ted Kooser, *The Poetry Home Repair Manual: Practical Advice for Beginning Poets* (Lincoln: University of Nebraska Press, 2005), 1.

112. "The Poetry Foundation and the Library of Congress Cosponsor Poet Laureate's Newspaper Project," Press Release 05-052.
113. "Poetry 180: More About This Program" (emphasis mine).
114. Collins, *Poetry 180: A Turning Back*, xxiii.
115. "Past Poet Laureate Projects," Poetry and Literature Center at the Library of Congress, https://www.loc.gov/poetry/laureate-projects.html (accessed July 19, 2019).

    Kay Ryan's two-year term, for instance, was sandwiched by four one-year posts: she was preceded by Donald Hall (2006–7), who during his term collaborated with the Poetry Foundation in a "American poets" podcast, and Charles Simic (2007–8). W. S. Merwin held the laureateship from 2010–11, and Philip Levine from 2011–12. Unlike Ryan, none of these one-term laureates undertook a substantive project. Moreover, the Library of Congress does not include Hall's podcast with the Poetry Foundation in its history of past poets laureate projects.
116. "New Poet Laureate: 'The Meaning Has Always Stayed the Same,'" *National Public Radio*, June 12, 2014.
117. Casper, interview by author, August 2, 2019.
118. "More About Kay Ryan: Poet Laureate Consultant in Poetry, 2008–2010," Poetry and Literature Center at the Library of Congress, https://www.loc.gov/poetry/more_ryan.html (accessed July 19, 2019).
119. "Past Poet Laureate Projects," Poetry and Literature Center at the Library of Congress, https://www.loc.gov/poetry/laureate-projects.html (accessed July 19, 2019).
120. "Where Poetry Lives," PBS NewsHour, https://www.pbs.org/newshour/tag/where-poetry-lives (accessed July 20, 2019).
121. Casper, email message to author, November 7, 2019.
122. Tracy K. Smith, in Q&A with author following "Why Poetry? Why Now?" Philomathean Society 2019 Annual Oration, University of Pennsylvania, Philadelphia, March 28, 2019.
123. "Librarian of Congress Appoints Juan Felipe Herrera Poet Laureate," Library of Congress Press Release No. 15-096, June 10, 2015; "Juan Felipe Herrera Named Poet Laureate for Second Term," Library of Congress Press Release No. 16-068, April 13, 2016.
124. "La Familia (The Familia): La Casa de Colores, Hosted by Juan Felipe Herrera, U.S. Poet Laureate," Poetry and Literature Center at the Library of Congress, https://www.loc.gov/poetry/casadecolores/familia/index.html (accessed July 24, 2019).
125. "El Jardín (The Garden): La Casa de Colores, Hosted by Juan Felipe Herrera, U.S. Poet Laureate," Poetry and Literature Center at the Library of

Congress," https://www.loc.gov/poetry/casadecolores/jardin/index.html (accessed July 24, 2019).

126. "Graphic Art by Asamblea de Artistas Revolucionarios de Oaxaca and Herrera's Automatika Series: El Jardín (The Garden), La Casa de Colores, Hosted by Juan Felipe Herrera, U.S. Poet Laureate, 2015- | The Poetry and Literature Center at the Library of Congress," https://www.loc.gov/poetry/casadecolores/jardin/herrera-blood3.html (accessed July 24, 2019).

127. Juan Felipe Herrera, *187 Reasons Mexicanos Can't Cross the Border: Undocuments, 1971–2007* (San Francisco: City Lights, 2007).

128. "The Technicolor Adventures of Catalina Neon," Library of Congress, http://read.gov/catalinaneon/ (accessed July 24, 2019).

129. "Wordstreet Champions and Brave Builders of the Dream: A Poet Laureate Project of Juan Felipe Herrera and the Poetry Foundation," The Poetry and Literature Center at the Library of Congress, https://www.loc.gov/poetry/wordstreet/ (accessed July 24, 2019).

130. "United States Poet Laureate Works on Yearlong Project with Chicago Public Schools," Poetry Foundation press release, November 9, 2016, https://www.poetryfoundation.org/foundation/press/91329/united-states-poet-laureate-works-on-yearlong-project-with-chicago-public-schools-.

131. The 2017 poet laureate selection process is described in detail in the introduction.

132. "Poet Laureate Tracy K. Smith," Library of Congress Bibliographies, Research Guides, and Finding Aids (Virtual Programs & Services)," Library of Congress, https://www.loc.gov/rr/program/bib/smith/ (accessed July 24, 2019).

133. Mary Hudetz, "US Poet Laureate Starts Rural Reading Tour in New Mexico," *US News & World Report*, January 12, 2018, https://www.usnews.com/news/best-states/new-mexico/articles/2018-01-12/us-poet-laureate-starts-rural-reading-tour-in-new-mexico; Shamira McCray, "U.S. Poet Laureate Makes Stop in Lake City," *SCNow Morning News*, February 23, 2018, https://www.scnow.com/townnews/poetry/article_7500d220-191c-11e8-853b-979f9551f792.html.

134. McCray.

135. "U.S. Poet Laureate Tracy K. Smith to Launch Fall Tour with New Anthology 'American Journal: Fifty Poems for Our Time," press release 18-100, Library of Congress, August 9, 2018. Tracy K Smith, ed., *American Journal: Fifty Poems for Our Time* (Minneapolis: Graywolf, 2018).

136. Tracy K. Smith, email message to author, July 25, 2019.

137. Tracy K. Smith, in Q&A with author following "Why Poetry? Why Now?" (Philomathean Society 2019 Annual Oration, University of Pennsylvania, Philadelphia, PA, March 28, 2019).

138. Tracy K. Smith, "Political Poetry Is Hot Again: The Poet Laureate Explores Why, and How," *New York Times*, December 14, 2018.
139. Collins, *180 More*, xx, xvi.
140. Collins, *Poetry 180*, xvi.
141. Tracy K. Smith, *Wade in the Water: Poems* (Minneapolis: Graywolf, 2018).
142. Tracy K. Smith, "Why Poetry? Why Now?" presented at the Philomathean Society 2019 Annual Oration, Q & A with author, University of Pennsylvania, Philadelphia, PA, March 28, 2019.
143. Smith.
144. Smith, *Wade in the Water*, 41.
145. "About the Position of Poet Laureate Consultant in Poetry," Poetry and Literature Center at the Library of Congress, https://www.loc.gov/poetry/about_laureate.html (accessed May 28, 2019).
146. Tracy K. Smith, "Poet Laureate Closing Lecture," Library of Congress, April 15, 2019. Transcript shared in correspondence with author.
147. "Librarian of Congress Names Joy Harjo the Nation's 23rd Poet Laureate," Library of Congress, https://www.loc.gov/item/prn-19-066/librarian-of-congress-names-joy-harjo-the-nations-23rd-poet-laureate/2019-06-19/ (accessed September 15, 2019).
148. Peter Armenti, "Research Guides: Joy Harjo, U.S. Poet Laureate: A Resource Guide: Introduction," https://guides.loc.gov/poet-laureate-joy-harjo (accessed July 17, 2019).
149. Hillel Italie, "Joy Harjo Is First Native American Named US Poet Laureate," *AP News*, June 19, 2019.
150. Italie.
151. Italie.
152. Casper, interview by the author, August 2, 2019.
153. Casper, email message to author, November 7, 2019 (my emphasis).
154. Casper.
155. Casper, interview by the author, August 2, 2019.
156. "Poet Laureate Inaugural Reading Celebrating Joy Harjo, 23rd Poet Laureate Consultant in Poetry joined by musical guests Howard Cloud, Larry Mitchell, Robert Muller; presented by the Poetry and Literature Center in association with National Book Festival Presents," Coolidge Auditorium, Thomas Jefferson Building, Library of Congress, September 19, 2019, event transcription by author.
157. Cheryl Lederle, "Poet Laureate Joy Harjo Gets a Third Term; Launches 'Living Nations, Living Words.'" Library of Congress, Teaching with the Library of Congress, November 24, 2020.
158. "United States Poets Laureate: A Guide to Online Resources," Library of Congress Bibliographies, Research Guides, and Finding Aids: Virtual

Programs and Services, https://www.loc.gov/rr/program/bib/poetslaureate (accessed July 17, 2019).
159. Stephen Young, interview by the author, August 8, 2019.

## Epilogue

1. This phrase was used in the majority of media reports surrounding Blanco's inaugural poem, e.g., the BBC, the *Atlantic*, and the *Daily Beast*.
2. Peter Armenti, "Richard Blanco's Inaugural Poem: 'One Today,'" *From the Catbird Seat: Poetry and Literature at the Library of Congress*, January 28, 2013. Mainstream media coverage received Blanco warmly; I am not aware of sustained critical appraisals of Blanco's inaugural poem to date.
3. Alexandra Alter, "Amanda Gorman Captures the Moment, in Verse." *New York Times*, January 19, 2021.
4. Blanco, *For All of Us*, 11.
5. Blanco, 106–7.
6. See, for example, Richard Blanco, "Bio," accessed October 1, 2019, https://richard-blanco.com/bio/. This phrase was also quoted widely in news media coverage surrounding the inaugural poem.
7. Mark McGurl, *The Program Era: Postwar Fiction and the Rise of Creative Writing* (Cambridge, Mass.: Harvard University Press, 2009), 32.
8. Richard Blanco, "One Today," in *For All of Us*, 87–91, 6:1–7.
9. Blanco, 6:5–7.
10. Richard Blanco, *Matters of the Sea / Cosas Del Mar: A Poem Commemorating a New Era in US-Cuba Relations, August 14, 2015, United States Embassy, Havana, Cuba* (Pittsburgh: University of Pittsburgh Press, 2015),viii–ix.
11. Richard Blanco, "Matters of the Sea," in *Matters of the Sea / Cosas Del Mar*, 3:9–10.
12. Blanco, 1:6–7.
13. Blanco, 2:8–9.
14. Quoted in Mimi Whitefield, "Poet Richard Blanco Speaks of the Sea and Hope in Cuba," *Miami Herald*, August 14, 2015, http://www.miamiherald.com/news/nation-world/world/americas/cuba/article31164290.html.
15. Charles Pritchard, "Inaugural Poet Richard Blanco Talks America and Poetry at Sherrill-Kenwood Library," *Oneida Dispatch*, https://www.oneidadispatch.com/news/local-news/inaugural-poet-richard-blanco-talks-america-and-poetry-at-sherrill/article_840270ca-91d0-11e9-ad42-5fcbb18ecaf6.html (accessed July 27, 2019).
16. Anne Holmes, "Literary Treasures: Joseph Brodsky Reads His Poetry at the Library of Congress, 1992," *From the Catbird Seat: Poetry and Literature at*

*the Library of Congress,* July 16, 2019, //blogs.loc.gov/catbird/2019/07/literary-treasures-joseph-brodsky-reads-his-poetry-at-the-library-of-congress-1992/.

17. Armenti, "Richard Blanco's Inaugural Poem."
18. Robert Casper, interview by author, August 2, 2019.
19. T. S. Eliot to Karl Shapiro, March 6, 1950, Bollingen Foundation Records.
20. Barr, "American Poetry in the New Century," 440, "Poetry and Investment Banking: It's All About Risk," Knowledge@Wharton, January 26, 2005.
21. Robert Casper, head, Poetry and Literature Center, Library of Congress, interview by the author, August 2, 2019.
22. George Yúdice, "The Privatization of Culture," *Social Text* 59 (Summer 1999): 17–34.
23. Eleanor Wilner, "Poetry and the Pentagon: Unholy Alliance?" *Poetry* 185, no. 1 (October 2004): 37–42.
24. Juliana Spahr, "Contemporary U.S. Poetry and Its Nationalisms," *Contemporary Literature* 52, no. 4 (Winter 2011): 685.
25. Raquel Salas Rivera, personal interview, July 17, 2019.
26. Raquel Salas Rivera, "We (Too) Are Philly Festival," January 29, 2018. https://raquelsalasrivera.com/we-too-are-philly/.
27. "Awarded by the Poetry Foundation for a two-year term, the Young People's Poet Laureate aims to raise awareness that young people have a natural receptivity to poetry and are its most appreciative audience, especially when poems are written specifically for them." "Young People's Poet Laureate," Poetry Foundation, https://www.poetryfoundation.org/learn/young-peoples-poet-laureate (accessed July 2, 2019).
28. "National Youth Poet Laureate Finalists Read with Jacqueline Woodson at the Poetry Foundation," Poetry Foundation, February 23, 2017, https://www.poetryfoundation.org/foundation/press/92567/the-poetry-foundation-hosts-the-finalists-of-the-national-youth-poet-laureate-reading-and-workshop-featuring-jacqueline-woodson-.
29. Alter, "Amanda Gorman Captures the Moment."
30. Sandra E. Garcia, "Amanda Gorman, Poet, Gets Modeling Agent and a Stage at the Super Bowl," *New York Times,* January 27, 2021.

# Appendix 2: Fellows in American Letters at the Library of Congress

Adapted from the most comprehensive account of the fellows' membership diaries provided by Roy Basler, *The Muse and the Librarian* (Westport, Conn. Greenwood, 1974), 43.

1. Joined the fellows after the selection of the first Bollingen Prize at the Library of Congress.
2. Spencer died before completing the term (January 18, 1949), but was a member when the fellows acted as the jury of selection for the Bollingen Prize.

# Bibliography

Abercrombie, Lascelles. "A New Voice." *Nation* 15, July 13, 1914.
"About the Favorite Poem Project." Favorite Poem Project: Americans Saying Poems They Love, July 6, 2022. http://www.favoritepoem.org/about.html (accessed March 12, 2015).
"About the Poetry and Literature Center." Poetry and Literature Center at the Library of Congress. http://www.loc.gov/poetry/about.html (accessed May 15, 2019).
"About the Position of Poet Laureate Consultant in Poetry." Poetry and Literature Center at the Library of Congress. http://www.loc.gov/poetry/about_laureate.html (accessed May 15, 2019).
"About Us." National Poetry Foundation. www.nationalpoetryfoundation.org/about-us (accessed May 12, 2015).
Allen, Donald, ed. *The New American Poetry, 1945–1960*. Berkeley: University of California Press, 1960.
Allison, Raphael. "Robert Frost, Live: Authenticity and Performance in the Audio Archive." *Twentieth Century Literature* 58, no. 4 (2012): 606–39.
Alter, Alexandra. "Amanda Gorman Captures the Moment, in Verse." *New York Times*, January 19, 2021. https://www.nytimes.com/2021/01/19/books/amanda-gorman-inauguration-hill-we-climb.html.
"American Conversations | Read.Gov." Library of Congress. http://read.gov/americanconversations/index.html (accessed August 4, 2019).
"American Life in Poetry." American Life in Poetry: A Project for Newspapers by Ted Kooser, Poet Laureate of the United States, 2004–2006. http://www.americanlifeinpoetry.org/ (accessed March 2, 2015).

Archambeau, Robert. *Laureates and Heretics. Six Careers in American Poetry: Yvor Winters, Robert Pinsky, James McMichael, Robert Hass, John Matthias, John Peck.* Notre Dame, In.: University of Notre Dame Press, 2010.

Archibald MacLeish papers, 1907–1981. Collection ID No. MSS30932. Manuscript Division, Library of Congress, Washington, D.C.

Aridi, Sarah. "Mellon Foundation Grants $2.2 Million to Academy of American Poets." *New York Times*, January 15, 2019. https://www.nytimes.com/2019/01/15/arts/mellon-foundation-poetry.html (accessed August 9, 2021).

Armenti, Peter. "Research Guides: Joy Harjo, U.S. Poet Laureate: A Resource Guide: Introduction." Library of Congress. https://guides.loc.gov/joy-harjo (accessed July 17, 2019).

———. "Richard Blanco's Inaugural Poem: 'One Today.'" *From the Catbird Seat: Poetry and Literature at the Library of Congress* (blog), January 28, 2013. http://blogs.loc.gov/catbird/2013/01/richard-blancos-inaugural-poem-one-today/.

"Association of Writers and Writing Programs 2013 Annual Report." Fairfax, Va.: Association of Writers and Writing Programs, 2013. https://www.awpwriter.org/application/public/pdf/AWPAnnualReport13.pdf.

Auden, W. H., William Barrett, Robert Gorham Davis, Clement Greenberg, Irving Howe, George Orwell, Karl Shapiro, and Allen Tate. "The Question of the Pound Award." *Partisan Review* 16, no. 5 (May 1949): 512–22.

Axelrod, Steven Gould. "Frost and the Cold War." In *Robert Frost in Context*, edited by Mark Richardson, 207–13. Cambridge: Cambridge University Press, 2014.

Barr, John. "American Poetry in the New Century." *Poetry* 188, no. 5 (September 2006): 433–41.

———. "Foundation Release Letter from John Barr, President." Poetry Foundation, September 2004. http://www.poetryfoundation.org/foundation/release_letter.html.

Basler, Roy P. "Annual Report of the Poetry Office, 1953." Library of Congress Reference Department, April 28, 1953. William McGuire Papers. Manuscript Division, Library of Congress, Washington, D.C.

———. "Annual Report of the Poetry Office for the Fiscal Year Ended June 30, 1954." Excerpted from the Annual Report of the General Reference and Bibliography Division. Library of Congress, July 15, 1954. William McGuire Papers. Manuscript Division, Library of Congress, Washington, D.C.

———. *The Muse and the Librarian.* Westport, Conn.: Greenwood, 1974.

———. "Robert Frost: Lobbyist for the Arts." *Quarterly Journal of the Library of Congress* 31, no. 2 (April 1974): 108–15.

Bauerlein, Mark, and Ellen Grantham, eds. *National Endowment for the Arts: A History, 1965–2008.* Washington, D.C.: National Endowment for the Arts, 2008.

Bawer, Bruce. *The Middle Generation: The Lives and Poetry of Delmore Schwartz, Randall Jarrell, John Berryman, and Robert Lowell.* Hamden, Conn.: Archon, 1986.

Beach, Christopher. *Poetic Culture: Contemporary American Poetry Between Community and Institution.* Evanston: Northwestern University Press, 1999.

Belmonte, Laura A. *Selling the American Way: U.S. Propaganda and the Cold War.* Philadelphia: University of Pennsylvania Press, 2008.

Bennett, Eric. "Creative Writing and the Cold War." PhD diss., Harvard University, 2009.

———. "Creative Writing and the Cold War University." In *A Companion to Creative Writing.* Hoboken, N.J.: Wiley-Blackwell, 2013.

———. "How Iowa Flattened Literature." *Chronicle of Higher Education*, February 10, 2014. https://www.chronicle.com/article/How-Iowa-Flattened-Literature/144531.

———. "The Pyramid Scheme." In *MFA vs. NYC: The Two Cultures of American Fiction*, edited by Chad Harbach, 51–72. New York: n + 1/Faber and Faber, 2014.

———. *Workshops of Empire: Stegner, Engle, and American Creative Writing During the Cold War.* Iowa City: University of Iowa Press, 2015.

Benson, Heidi. "Poet Wants to Write Verse Into Everyone's Daily Requirements." *San Francisco Gate*, June 27, 2004. http://www.sfgate.com/books/article/Poet-wants-to-write-verse-into-everyone-s-daily-2711084.php.

"Benton Is Honored for Stressing Ideas." *New York Times*, April 21, 1950, 14.

Bernstein, Charles. "The Academy in Peril: William Carlos Williams Meets the MFA." In *Content's Dream: Essays, 1975–1984*, 244–51. Evanston: Northwestern University Press, 2001.

———. "Against National Poetry Month as Such." In *My Way: Speeches and Poems.* Chicago: University of Chicago Press, 1999. http://www.press.uchicago.edu/Misc/Chicago/044106.html.

———. *Attack of the Difficult Poems: Essays and Inventions.* Chicago: University of Chicago Press, 2011.

———, ed. *The Politics of Poetic Form: Poetry and Public Policy.* New York: Roof, 1990.

Bernstein, Charles, and Bruce Andrews, eds. *The L=A=N=G=U=A=G=E Book: Poetics of the New.* Carbondale: Southern Illinois University Press, 1984.

Berryman, John. *The Dream Songs.* New York: Farrar, Straus and Giroux, 1969.

———. *Selected Poems.* Edited by Kevin Young. New York: Library of America, 2004.

Bishop, Elizabeth. "Annual Report to the Librarian of Congress from the Chair of Poetry, 1949–1950." William McGuire Papers. Manuscript Division, Library of Congress, Washington, D.C.

———. *The Complete Poems, 1927–1979.* New York: Noonday, 1979.

———. "View of the Capitol from the Library of Congress." *New Yorker*, July 7, 1951.

Blanco, Richard. *For All of Us, One Today: An Inaugural Poet's Journey.* Boston: Beacon, 2013.

———. *Matters of the Sea / Cosas Del Mar: A Poem Commemorating a New Era in US-Cuba Relations, August 14, 2015, United States Embassy, Havana, Cuba.* Translated by Ruth Behar. Pittsburgh: University of Pittsburgh Press, 2015.

Blumenkranz, Carla. "'Deeply and Mysteriously Implicated': Communist Sympathies, FBI Informants, and Robert Lowell at Yaddo." *Poetry*, December 18, 2006. http://www.poetryfoundation.org/article/178893.

Bollingen Foundation Records, 1927–1981. Collection ID No. MSS50567. Manuscript Division, Library of Congress, Washington, D.C.

Bourdieu, Pierre. *The Field of Cultural Production: Essays on Art and Literature.* Edited by Randal Johnson. New York: Columbia University Press, 1993.

Brooks, Gwendolyn. "Annual Report to the Librarian of Congress from the Chair of Poetry." May 14, 1986. William McGuire Papers. Manuscript Division, Library of Congress, Washington, D.C.

———. "Black Woman in Russia." In *Go Girl!: The Black Woman's Book of Travel and Adventure,* ed. Elaine Lee. Portland: Eighth Mountain, 1997).

Brown, Wendy. *States of Injury: Power and Freedom in Late Modernity.* Princeton, N.J.: Princeton University Press, 1995.

———. "Wounded Attachments." *Political Theory* 21, no. 3 (August 1993): 390–410.

Brunner, Edward. *Cold War Poetry.* Urbana: University of Illinois Press, 2001.

Buell, Lawrence. "Henry Thoreau Enters the American Canon." In *New Essays on Walden,* edited by Robert F. Sayre, 23–52. New York: Cambridge University Press, 1992.

Butler, Judith. "Contingent Foundations: Feminism and the Question of the 'Postmodern.'" In *Feminists Theorize the Political.* New York: Routledge, 1992.

———. *Gender Trouble.* New York: Routledge, 1990.

Carruth, Hayden. "An Editorial. The Bollingen Award: What Is It?" *Poetry* 74, no. 3 (June 1949): 154–56.

Coles, Katharine, ed. *Blueprints: Bringing Poetry Into Communities.* Salt Lake City and Chicago: University of Utah Press, Harriet Monroe Poetry Institute, Poetry Foundation, 2011.

Collins, Billy. *The Art of Drowning.* Pittsburgh: University of Pittsburgh Press, 1995.

———, ed. *180 More: Extraordinary Poems for Every Day.* New York: Random House, 2005.

———, ed. *Poetry 180: A Turning Back to Poetry.* Random House, 2003.

"Consultant in Poetry Named for 1964–5." *Library of Congress Information Bulletin,* May 4, 1964.

Cousins, Norman, and Harrison Smith. "Ezra Pound and the Bollingen Award." *Saturday Review of Literature,* June 11, 1949.

Cowley, Malcolm. "The Battle Over Ezra Pound, *The New Republic,* October 3, 1949." In *The Case Against the Saturday Review of Literature,* 31–38. Chicago: Modern Poetry Association, 1949.

Croft, Clare. *Dancers as Diplomats: American Choreography in Cultural Exchange.* New York: Oxford University Press, 2015.

"Current State Poets Laureate." Main Reading Room, Researcher and Reference Services Division, Library of Congress. https://www.loc.gov/rr/main/poets/current.html (accessed May 28, 2019).

Damon, Maria. "Poetic Canons: Generative Oxymoron or Stalled-out Dialectic?" *Contemporary Literature* 39, no. 3 (Autumn 1998): 468–74.

Davidson, Michael. *The San Francisco Renaissance: Poetics and Community at Mid-Century.* Cambridge: Cambridge University Press, 1989.

de Certeau, Michel. *The Practice of Everyday Life.* Translated by Steven Rendell. Berkeley: University of California Press, 1984.

Decherney, Peter. *Hollywood and the Culture Elite: How the Movies Became American.* New York: Columbia University Press, 2005.

Dowling, David O. *A Delicate Aggression: Savagery and Survival in the Iowa Writers' Workshop.* New Haven: Yale University Press, 2019.

"El Jardín (The Garden): La Casa de Colores, Hosted by Juan Felipe Herrera, U.S. Poet Laureate, 2015– (Poetry and Literature Center at the Library of Congress)." Webpage. https://www.loc.gov/poetry/casadecolores/jardin/index.html (accessed July 24, 2019).

Eliot, T. S. "The Social Function of Poetry," 3–16. In *On Poetry and Poets.* New York: Farrar, Straus and Giroux, 1943.

Engle, Paul. "Dedication." In *On Creative Writing,* ed. Paul Engle, vii. New York: Dutton, 1964.

——, ed. *On Creative Writing.* New York: Dutton, 1964.

——. *Poems in Praise.* New York: Random House, 1959.

——. "To Praise a Man." In "Paean for a Poet by a Poet." *Life,* June 15, 1959, 65–66.

——. "The Writer and the Place," 1–10. In *A Community of Writers: Paul Engle and the Iowa Writers' Workshop,* ed. Robert Dana. Iowa City: University of Iowa Press, 1999.

Engle, Paul, and Warren Carrier, eds. *Reading Modern Poetry: A Critical Anthology.* Glenview, Ill.: Foresman, 1968.

English, James. *The Economy of Prestige: Prizes, Awards, and the Circulation of Cultural Value.* Cambridge, Mass.: Harvard University Press, 2005.

Epstein, Andrew. "Verse vs. Verse." *Lingua Franca* (September 2000): 45–54.

Epstein, Joseph. "Thank You, No." *Poetry*, September 2004.
Evans, Luther. "A Letter from the Librarian of Congress." *Saturday Review of Literature*, July 2, 1949.
Evans, Steve. "Free (Market) Verse." In *The Consequence of Innovation: Twenty-first-Century Poetics*, edited by Craig Dworkin, 25–36. New York: Roof, 2008.
Fenza, D. W. "Creative Writing and Its Discontents." Association of Writers and Writing Programs, March 1, 2000. https://www.awpwriter.org/magazine_media/writers_news_view/2871/creative_writing_its_discontents.
Field, Douglas, ed. *American Cold War Culture*. Edinburgh: Edinburgh University Press, 2005.
Filreis, Alan. *Counter-Revolution of the Word: The Conservative Attack on Modern Poetry, 1945–1960*. Chapel Hill: University of North Carolina Press, 2008.
Fineberg, Gail. "A Poem a Day: Laureate Launches 'Poetry 180 Web Site for High Schools.'" *Library of Congress Information Bulletin* 61, no. 1 (January 2002). http://www.loc.gov/loc/lcib/0201/poems180.html.
Fosler-Lussier, Danielle. *Music in America's Cold War Diplomacy*. Oakland: University of California Press, 2015.
"Founding Principles: Giving Voice to the American Audience for Poetry." Favorite Poem Project. http://www.favoritepoem.org/principles.html (accessed May 29, 2012).
Freedlander, David. "Richard Blanco, Obama's Historic Inauguration Poet." *Daily Beast*, January 21, 2013. http://www.thedailybeast.com/articles/2013/01/21/richard-blanco-obama-s-historic-inauguration-poet.html.
Freeman, Joshua B. *American Empire: The Rise of a Global Power, the Democratic Revolution at Home, 1945–2000*. New York: Viking, 2012.
French, Jackson. "Poets Laureate Share Writing with Glasgow." *Bowling Green Daily News*, March 16, 2018. https://www.bgdailynews.com/news/poets-laureate-share-writing-with-glasgow/article_56c5ccdc-ef1c-5e4f-a14d-559f63b343ec.html.
Frost, Robert. "'Dedication,' Robert Frost's Presidential Inaugural Poem, 20 January 1961: Typescript with Frost's Holograph Script Corrections in Ink and Stewart Udall's Holograph Clarifications in Pencil on the Last Page." Stewart L. Udall Collection. Manuscript Division, Library of Congress, Washington, D.C.
———. "The Gift Outright." American Treasures of the Library of Congress. http://www.loc.gov/exhibits/treasures/trio50.html (accessed June 7, 2011).
———. "The Gift Outright." In *The Poetry of Robert Frost*, edited by Edward Connery Lathem. New York: Holt, Rinehart and Winston, 1969.
———. "On Being Appointed Consultant to the Library of Congress." In *Robert Frost: Collected Poems, Prose and Plays*, edited by Richard Poirier and Mark Richardson, 845–46. New York: Library of America, 1958.

———. *Robert Frost: Collected Poems, Prose and Plays*. Edited by Richard Poirier and Mark Richardson. New York: Library of America, 1995.

———. *A Witness Tree*. New York: Holt, 1942.

Furr, Derek. *Recorded Poetry and Poetic Reception from Edna Millay to the Circle of Robert Lowell*. New York: Palgrave Macmillan, 2010.

Garcia, Sandra E. "Amanda Gorman, Poet, Gets Modeling Agent and a Stage at the Super Bowl." *New York Times*, January 27, 2021. https://www.nytimes.com/2021/01/27/style/amanda-gorman-img-super-bowl.html.

Garnett, Edward. "A New American Poet." *Atlantic Monthly*, August 1915.

Gifford, Sally. "National Endowment for the Arts Helps U.S. Troops Write About Their Wartime Experiences," April 20, 2004. http://www.nea.gov/news/news04/OHAnnounce.html.

Gioia, Dana. "A Poet in the Supermarket." *New York Times*, October 28, 2007. http://www.nytimes.com/2007/10/28/jobs/28boss.html?_r=0.

Goffman, Erving. *Frame Analysis: An Essay on the Organization of Experience*. Cambridge, Mass.: Harvard University Press, 1974.

Golding, Alan. *From Outlaw to Classic: Canons in American Poetry*. Madison: University of Wisconsin Press, 1995.

Goodyear, Dana. "The Moneyed Muse." *New Yorker*, February 19, 2007.

"Graphic Art by Asamblea de Artistas Revolucionarios de Oaxaca and Herrera's Automatika Series: El Jardín (The Garden), La Casa de Colores, Hosted by Juan Felipe Herrera, U.S. Poet Laureate, 2015." Poetry and Literature Center at the Library of Congress. Accessed July 24, 2019. https://www.loc.gov/poetry/casadecolores/jardin/herrera-blood3.html.

Gregory, Horace. "The Postwar Generation in Arts and Letters: Poetry." *Saturday Review*, March 1953.

Gross, Andrew. "Liberalism and Lyricism, or Karl Shapiro's Elegy for Identity." *Journal of Modern Literature* 34, no. 3 (Spring 2011): 1–30.

Grossman, C. O., and Juliana Spahr. "The Lives of the Most Eminent State Department Poets." *n+1*, December 11, 2015.

"Growth of Creative Writing Programs, 1975–2012." Association of Writers and Writing Programs, January 2012. https://www.awpwriter.org/application/public/pdf/AWP_GrowthWritingPrograms.pdf.

Guilbaut, Serge. *How New York Stole the Idea of Modern Art: Abstract Expressionism, Freedom, and the Cold War*. Translated by Arthur Goldhammer. Chicago: University of Chicago Press, 1983.

Gustav Davidson papers, 1909–1992. Collection ID No. MSS84137. Manuscript Division, Library of Congress, Washington, D.C.

"Gwendolyn Brooks Is Named as Next Library Poetry Consultant." *Library of Congress Information Bulletin*, May 20, 1985, 106–7.

Gwiazda, Piotr K. *US Poetry in the Age of Empire, 1979–2012*. New York: Palgrave Macmillan, 2014.

Hall, Donald, Robert Pack, and Louis Simpson, eds. *New Poets of England and America*. New York: Meridian, 1957.

Harbach, Chad, ed. *MFA vs NYC: The Two Cultures of American Fiction*. New York: n + 1/Faber and Faber, 2014.

Harriet Monroe Poetry Institute. "Best Practices for Fair Use in Poetry: The Poetry Foundation," 2011. http://www.poetryfoundation.org/foundation/best practices.

———. "Blueprints: Bringing Poetry Into Communities: The Poetry Foundation," 2010. http://www.poetryfoundation.org/foundation/blueprints.

———. Poetry and New Media: The Poetry Foundation," 2009. http://www.poetryfoundation.org/foundation/poetry-and-new-media.

Hejinian, Lyn. *The Language of Inquiry*. Berkeley: University of California Press, 2000

———. *My Life*. Rev. ed. Providence: Sun and Moon, 1987.

———. *Writing/Talks*. Ed. Bob Perelman. Carbondale: Southern Illinois University Press, 1985.

Henderson, Alice Corbin. "American Verse and English Critics." *Poetry: A Magazine of Verse*, January 1918.

Herrera, Juan Felipe. *187 Reasons Mexicanos Can't Cross the Border: Undocuments, 1971–2007*. San Francisco: City Lights, 2007.

Hillyer, Robert. "Poetry's New Priesthood." *Saturday Review of Literature*, June 18, 1949.

———. "Treason's Strange Fruit: The Case of Ezra Pound and the Bollingen Award." *Saturday Review of Literature*, June 11, 1949.

"History and Mission." Poetry Foundation. http://www.poetryfoundation.org/foundation/history-and-mission (accessed March 2, 2015; July 1, 2019).

"History of Poetry Magazine." Poetry Foundation. https://www.poetryfoundation.org/poetrymagazine/history (accessed September 21, 2019).

Hodsoll, Francis S. M. "Supporting the Arts in the Eighties: The View from the National Endowment for the Arts." *Annals of the American Academy of Political and Social Science* 471, no. 1 (January 1984): 84–88.

Hoffman, Tyler. *Robert Frost and the Politics of Poetry*. Hanover, N.H.: Middlebury College Press, 2001.

Holmes, Anne. "Literary Treasures: Joseph Brodsky Reads His Poetry at the Library of Congress, 1992. *From the Catbird Seat: Poetry and Literature at the Library of Congress*." July 16, 2019. https://blogs.loc.gov/catbird/2019/07/literary-treasures-joseph-brodsky-reads-his-poetry-at-the-library-of-congress-1992/.

Hopkins, Kenneth. *The Poets Laureate*. London: Bodley Head, 1954.

Hudetz, Mary. "US Poet Laureate Starts Rural Reading Tour in New Mexico." *US News & World Report*. January 12, 2018. https://www.usnews.com/news/best-states/new-mexico/articles/2018-01-12/us-poet-laureate-starts-rural-reading-tour-in-new-mexico.

Hulme, T. E. *The Collected Writings of T.E. Hulme*. Edited by Karen Csengeri. Oxford: Clarendon, 1994.

"Inaugural Address, 20 January 1961: Drafts and Press Releases, 20 January 1961." Theodore C. Sorensen Personal Papers. JFK Speech Files, 1961–1963. John F. Kennedy Presidential Library.

"Iowa's School of Letters Admits Imaginative, Critical Writing for Ph.D. Thesis." *Daily Iowan*, March 26, 1931.

Italie, Hillel. "Joy Harjo Is First Native American Named US Poet Laureate." *AP News*, June 19, 2019. https://apnews.com/a71dbd5172d545788eb8b2842b03e169.

Jameson, Frederic. "Dirty Little Secret." In *MFA vs. NYC: The Two Cultures of American Fiction*, edited by Chad Harbach, 263–80. New York: n + 1, 2014.

———. *Postmodernism: The Cultural Logic of Late Capitalism*. Duke University Press, 1991.

Javadizadeh, Kamran. "The Institutionalization of the Postwar Poet." *Modernism/Modernity* 23, no. 1 (January 2016): 113–39.

———. *Institutionalized Lyric: American Poetry at Midcentury*. New York: Oxford University Press, forthcoming.

Jay, Paul. *Global Matters: The Transnational Turn in Literary Studies*. Ithaca, N.Y.: Cornell University Press, 2010.

"John F. Kennedy and the Press." John F. Kennedy Presidential Library and Museum. https://www.jfklibrary.org/learn/about-jfk/jfk-in-history/john-f-kennedy-and-the-press (accessed July 17, 2019).

"Joseph Brodsky." Poetry Foundation. https://www.poetryfoundation.org/poets/joseph-brodsky (accessed July 28, 2019).

"Joy Harjo Appointed to Third Term as U.S. Poet Laureate." Press Release 20-075. November 19, 2020. Library of Congress, Washington, D.C. https://www.loc.gov/item/prn-20-075/joy-harjo-appointed-to-third-term-as-u-s-poet-laureate/2020-11-19/.

"Juan Felipe Herrera Named Poet Laureate for Second Term." Press Release 16-068. April 13, 2016. Library of Congress, Washington, D.C.

Karl Jay Shapiro papers, 1947–1964. Collection ID No. MSS15099. Manuscript Division, Library of Congress, Washington, D.C.

Kastor, Elizabeth. "James Merrill Is Winner of Bobbitt Poetry Prize." *Washington Post*, October 28, 1990. https://www.washingtonpost.com/archive/politics/1990/10/28/james-merrill-is-winner-of-bobbitt-poetry-prize/33cb27bb-e6e8-4a01-b926-0f10b8bc51c0/.

Kearns, Katherine. *Robert Frost and a Poetics of Appetite*. Cambridge: Cambridge University Press, 1994.
Kempf, Christopher. *Craft Class: The Writing Workshop in American Culture*. Baltimore: Johns Hopkins University Press, 2022.
Kerr, Clark. *The Uses of the University*. Cambridge, Mass.: Harvard University Press, 1963.
Kindley, Evan. *Poet-Critics and the Administration of Culture*. Cambridge, Mass.: Harvard University Press, 2017.
Kinzer, Stephen. "Lilly Heir Makes $100 Million Bequest to Poetry Magazine." *New York Times*, November 19, 2002, E8.
Klein, Julia M. "A Windfall Illuminates the Poetry Field, and Its Fights." *New York Times*, November 12, 2007. https://www.nytimes.com/2007/11/12/giving/12POETRY.html.
Kooser, Ted. *The Poetry Home Repair Manual: Practical Advice for Beginning Poets*. Lincoln: University of Nebraska Press, 2005.
"La Familia (The Familia): La Casa de Colores, Hosted by Juan Felipe Herrera, U.S. Poet Laureate, 2015." Poetry and Literature Center at the Library of Congress. https://www.loc.gov/poetry/casadecolores/familia/index.html (accessed July 24, 2019).
Lathem, Edward Connery, ed. *The Poetry of Robert Frost*. New York: Holt, Rinehart and Winston, 1969.
Lathem, Edward Connery, and Lawrance Thompson. "Interview with Rose C. Feld, *New York Times Book Review*, October 21, 1923." In *The Robert Frost Reader: Poetry and Prose*, 329–37. New York: Holt, 1972.
——, eds. *The Robert Frost Reader: Poetry and Prose*. New York: Holt, 1972.
Laugesen, Amanda. *Taking Books to the World: American Publishers and the Cultural Cold War*. Amherst: University of Massachusetts Press, 2017.
Lederle, Cheryl. "Poet Laureate Joy Harjo Gets a Third Term: Launches 'Living Nations, Living Words.'" Library of Congress. Teaching with the Library of Congress, November 24, 2020. https://blogs.loc.gov/teachers/2020/11/poet-laureate-joy-harjo-gets-a-third-term-launches-living-nations-living-words/.
Lee, Don L. "The Achievement of Gwendolyn Brooks." *Black Scholar* 3, no. 10 (Summer 1972): 32–41.
Lethbridge, Mary C. "Poets in Washington: The Consultants in Poetry to the Library of Congress." *Records of the Columbia Historical Society* 69/70: 466–88.
Lewis, Anthony. "Court Drops Charge Against Ezra Pound." *New York Times*, April 19, 1958.
"Librarian of Congress Appoints Juan Felipe Herrera Poet Laureate." Press Release 15-096. June 10, 2015. Library of Congress, Washington, D.C.

"Librarian of Congress Appoints Tracy K. Smith to Second Term as Poet Laureate." Press Release 18-034. March 22, 2018. Library of Congress, Washington, D.C.

"Librarian of Congress Names Joy Harjo the Nation's 23rd Poet Laureate." Press Release 19-066. July 19, 2019. Library of Congress, Washington, D.C.

"Librarian of Congress Names Tracy K. Smith Poet Laureate." Press Release 17-083. June 14, 2017.

Lowell, Robert. *Collected Poems.* New York: Farrar, Straus and Giroux, 2007.

———. *For the Union Dead.* New York: Farrar, Straus and Giroux, 1964.

———. "July in Washington." In *For the Union Dead.* New York: Farrar, Straus and Giroux, 1964.

———. *Life Studies.* New York: Farrar, Straus and Giroux, 1959.

———. "Memories of West Street and Lepke." In *Life Studies.* New York: Farrar, Straus and Giroux, 1959.

Lyon, Janet. *Manifestoes: Provocations of the Modern.* Ithaca, N.Y.: Cornell University Press, 1999.

MacArthur, Marit. *The American Landscape in the Poetry of Frost, Bishop, and Ashbery: The House Abandoned.* New York: Palgrave, 2008.

MacLeish, Archibald. Letter to Allen Tate, October 15, 1949. William McGuire Papers. Manuscript Division, Library of Congress, Washington D.C.

———. Letter to Allen Tate, February 15, 1950. William McGuire Papers. Manuscript Division, Library of Congress, Washington D.C.

Mariani, Paul. *Lost Puritan: A Life of Robert Lowell.* New York: Norton, 1996.

———. *William Carlos Williams: A New World Naked.* San Antonio: Trinity University Press, 2016.

McCray, Shamira. "U.S. Poet Laureate Makes Stop in Lake City." *SCNow.* February 23, 2018. https://www.scnow.com/townnews/poetry/article_7500d220-191c-11e8-853b-979f9551f792.html.

McGee, Micki, ed. *Yaddo: Making American Culture.* New York: Columbia University Press, 2008.

McGrory, Mary. "Library Sends Regrets to Those Poet 'Fellows.'" *Sunday Star,* November 6, 1955.

McGuire, William. "Annals of American Poetry: Pound and the Bollingen Prize of '49," October 23, 1988, Letters to the Editor. http://www.nytimes.com/1988/10/23/opinion/l-annals-of-american-poetry-pound-and-the-bollingen-prize-of-49-565588.html.

———. *Bollingen: An Adventure in Collecting the Past.* Princeton, N.J.: Princeton University Press, 1989.

———. *Poetry's Catbird Seat: The Consultantship in Poetry in the English Language at the Library of Congress, 1937–1987.* Washington, D.C.: Library of Congress, 1988.

McGurl, Mark. *The Program Era: Postwar Fiction and the Rise of Creative Writing.* Cambridge, Mass.: Harvard University Press, 2009.

McKinlay, Alan, and Chris Smith, eds. *Creative Labour: Working in the Creative Industries.* Critical Perspectives on Work and Employment. New York: Palgrave Macmillan, 2009.

"'Mending Wall' in Moscow." *New York Times Magazine,* September 16, 1962, 34.

"Mission and History." Academy of American Poets. http://www.poets.org/academy-american-poets/mission-history (accessed March 2, 2015).

Monroe, Harriet. "Newspaper Verse." *Poetry: A Magazine of Verse* 19, no. 6 (March 1922): 324–30.

Monteiro, George. "Frost's Politics and the Cold War." In *The Cambridge Companion to Robert Frost,* edited by Robert Faggen, 221–39. Cambridge: Cambridge University Press, 2001.

"More About Kay Ryan: Poet Laureate Consultant in Poetry, 2008–2010." Poetry and Literature Center at the Library of Congress. https://www.loc.gov/poetry/more_ryan.html (accessed July 19, 2019).

"More About This Program: Poetry 180: A Poem a Day for American High Schools, a Project from Poet Laureate Billy Collins." Poetry and Literature Center at the Library of Congress. https://www.loc.gov/poetry/180/p180-more.html (accessed August 1, 2019).

Mumford, L. Quincy. Letter to T. S. Eliot, May 16, 1955. William McGuire Papers. Manuscript Division, Library of Congress, Washington, D.C.

Myers, D. G. *The Elephants Teach: Creative Writing Since 1880.* Chicago: University of Chicago Press, 2006.

———. "The Rise of Creative Writing." *Journal of the History of Ideas* 54, no. 2 (April 1993): 277–97.

"National Poetry Month: About the Celebration." Academy of American Poets. http://www.poets.org/national-poetry-month/about-celebration (accessed March 2, 2015).

"National Poetry Month: Proclamations." Academy of American Poets. http://www.poets.org/national-poetry-month/national-poetry-month-proclamations (ccessed March 2, 2015).

"National Poetry Month: Sponsors and Partners." Academy of American Poets. http://www.poets.org/national-poetry-month/sponsors-partners (accessed March 10, 2015).

"National Youth Poet Laureate Finalists Read with Jacqueline Woodson at the Poetry Foundation." Poetry Foundation, February 23, 2017. https://www.poetryfoundation.org/foundation/press/92567/the-poetry-foundation-hosts-the-finalists-of-the-national-youth-poet-laureate-reading-and-workshop-featuring-jacqueline-woodson-.

"New Poet Laureate: 'The Meaning Has Always Stayed the Same.'" National Public Radio, June 12, 2014. http://www.npr.org/2014/06/12/321383934/new-poet-laureate-the-meaning-has-always-stayed-the-same.

Ohnemus, Edward. "Brodsky Urges Publishers to Distribute Poetry to the Masses." *Library of Congress Gazette*, October 11, 1991. http://www.loc.gov/rr/program/bib/brodsky/brodsky.pdf.

Osgood, Kenneth. *Total Cold War: Eisenhower's Secret Propaganda Battle at Home and Abroad*. Lawrence: University Press of Kansas, 2006.

O'Shea, Heather Eileen. "Suitable Poets in Brook Brothers Suits: Allen Tate, the New Critics, and the American Poets Laureate." Ph.D. diss., University of New Mexico, 2002.

"Our History and the Growth of Creative Writing Programs." Association of Writers and Writing Programs. https://www.awpwriter.org/about/our_history_overview.

Padgett, Ron. *Collected Poems*. Minneapolis: Coffee House, 2013.

Panas, Jerold. *Mega Gifts: Who Gives Them, Who Gets Them*. Chicago: Pluribus, 1984.

Papers of John F. Kennedy. Presidential Papers, President's Office Files. Special Correspondence: Frost, Robert, May 1961–April 1962.

Parini, Jay. *Robert Frost: A Life*. New York: Holt, 2015.

"'Paris Review Interview.'" In *Robert Frost: Collected Poems, Prose and Plays*, 873–93. New York: Library of America, 1960.

Parisi, Joseph, and Stephen Young, eds. *Between the Lines: A History of Poetry in Letters, 1962–2002*. Chicago: Dee, 2006.

"Past Poet Laureate Projects." Poetry and Literature Center at the Library of Congress. https://www.loc.gov/poetry/laureate-projects.html (accessed May 15, 2019).

"Past Poets Laureate: 1981–1990." Poetry and Literature Center at the Library of Congress. http://www.loc.gov/poetry/laureate-1981-1990.html (accessed February 1, 2015).

Paumgarten, Nick. "A Hundred Million." *New Yorker*, December 2, 2002.

Perelman, Bob. "A Counter-Response." *The Impercipient Lecture Series: Readings and Responses to Bob Perelman's "The Marginalization of Poetry" by Ron Silliman, Ann Lauterbach, Juliana Spahr, and Steve Evans; with a Counter-Response by Bob Perelman*, repr. in *Jacket* 2 1, no. 4 (May 1997). http://jacketmagazine.com/02/perel.html.

——. *The Marginalization of Poetry: Language Writing and Literary History*. Princeton, N.J.: Princeton University Press, 1996.

——, ed. *Writing/Talks*. Carbondale: Southern Illinois University Press, 1985.

Perloff, Marjorie. "Ca(n)non to the Right of Us, Ca(n)non to the Left of Us: A Plea for Difference." *New Literary History* 18, no. 3 (Spring 1987): 633–56.

Pinsky, Robert. *Democracy, Culture, and the Voice of Poetry.* Princeton, N.J.: Princeton University Press, 2002.

———. *An Explanation of America.* Princeton, N.J.: Princeton University Press, 1979.

———. *Poetry and the World.* New York: Ecco, 1988.

———. "Responsibilities of the Poet." *Critical Inquiry* 13, no. 3 (April 1, 1987): 421–33.

———. *The Sounds of Poetry.* New York: Farrar, Straus and Giroux, 1998.

Pinsky, Robert, and Maggie Dietz, eds. *Americans' Favorite Poems: The Favorite Poem Project Anthology.* New York: Norton, 2000.

"Poet Laureate Consultant in Poetry: Current Poet Laureate, Juan Felipe Herrera." Poetry and Literature Center at the Library of Congress. https://www.loc.gov/poetry/laureate.html (accessed May 15, 2019).

"Poet Laureate Consultant in Poetry: Past Poets Laureate, 1937–1960." Poetry and Literature Center at the Library of Congress. https://www.loc.gov/poetry/laureate-1937-1960.html (accessed September 7, 2019).

"Poet Laureate Juan Felipe Herrera: Online Resources." Library of Congress Bibliographies, Research Guides, and Finding Aids. Virtual Programs and Services, Library of Congress. https://www.loc.gov/rr/program/bib/herrera/ (accessed July 19, 2019).

"Poet Laureate Tracy K. Smith: Online Resources." Library of Congress Bibliographies, Research Guides, and Finding Aids. Virtual Programs and Services, Library of Congress. https://www.loc.gov/rr/program/bib/smith/?loclr=eadrs (accessed July 17, 2019).

"Poetry 180: A Poem a Day for American High Schools." Library of Congress. http://www.loc.gov/poetry/180/ (accessed March 2, 2015).

"Poetry 180: More About This Program." Library of Congress. http://www.loc.gov/poetry/180/p180-more.html (accessed March 2, 2015).

"*Poetry*: A History of the Magazine." Poetry Foundation. http://www.poetryfoundation.org/poetrymagazine/history (accessed January 12, 2015; September 21, 2019).

"Poetry and Investment Banking: It's All About Risk." Knowledge@Wharton, University of Pennsylvania, January 26, 2005. http://knowledge.wharton.upenn.edu/article/poetry-and-investment-banking-its-all-about-risk/.

"Poetry Foundation Builds a Home in Chicago." Poetry Foundation, April 21, 2010. http://www.poetryfoundation.org/foundation/announcement/042110.

"Poetry in America: Review of the Findings." Poetry Foundation: The National Opinion Research Center, January 2006.

"Poetry in New Media: A Users' Guide." Poetry Foundation: The Poetry and New Media Working Group, Harriet Monroe Institute, 2009.

"Poetry Office Press Conference Transcript." December 8, 1958. Frost, Robert 1874–1963, Folder 44. Library of Congress Archives, Library of Congress, Manuscript Division, Washington, D.C.

"Poets and Poems: Richard Blanco." Poetry Foundation, May 4, 2015. http://www.poetryfoundation.org/bio/richard-blanco.

"Poetry Coalition." Academy of American Poets. https://poets.org/academy-american-poets/poetry-coalition (accessed August 20, 2019).

"Poetry Consultants' Reunion Transcript Notes," March 6, 1978. William McGuire Papers, Manuscript Division, Library of Congress.

Pound, Ezra. "Modern Georgics." *Poetry: A Magazine of Verse*, December 1914, 127–30.

"Pound, in Mental Clinic, Wins Prize For Poetry Penned in Treason Cell: PRIZE VOTED POUND FOR PRISON POETRY." *New York Times*, February 20, 1949. https://www.nytimes.com/1949/02/20/archives/pound-in-mental-clinic-wins-prize-for-poetry-penned-in-treason-cell.html.

"Press Release: National Recording Registry Includes Three National Archives Sound Recordings." *U.S. National Archives and Records Administration*, March 23, 2004. http://www.archives.gov/press/press-releases/2004/nr04-39.html.

Pritchard, Charles. "Inaugural Poet Richard Blanco Talks America and Poetry at Sherrill-Kenwood Library." *Oneida Dispatch*, June 18, 2019. https://www.oneidadispatch.com/news/local-news/inaugural-poet-richard-blanco-talks-america-and-poetry-at-sherrill/article_840270ca-91d0-11e9-ad42-5fcbb18ecaf6.html.

Pritchard, William H. *Frost: A Literary Life Reconsidered*, 2nd ed. Amherst: University of Massachusetts Press, 1993.

"Program to Bicentennial Celebration, Poetry Society of America," April 24, 1975. Papers of Gustav Davidson. Manuscript Division, Library of Congress, Washington, D.C.

"Project Description." American Life in Poetry: A Project for Newspapers by Ted Kooser, Poet Laureate of the United States, 2004–2006 http://www.americanlifeinpoetry.org/description.html (accessed March 2, 2015).

"Project Description: American Life in Poetry." http://www.americanlifeinpoetry.org/description.html (accessed May 21, 2011.).

Rasula, Jed. *The American Poetry Wax Museum: Reality Effects, 1940–1990*. Urbana: National Council of Teachers of English, 1995.

"Rebekah Johnson Bobbitt National Prize for Poetry: Prizes and Fellowships." Poetry and Literature Center at the Library of Congress. https://www.loc.gov/poetry/prize-fellow/bobbitt.html (accessed August 1, 2019).

Rector, Liam. "Elitism, Populism, Laureates, and Free Speech." *American Poetry Review* 32, no. 1 (January/February 2003): 9–13.

Reeve, F. D. *Robert Frost in Russia*. Boston: Little, Brown, 1963.

"Remarks Upon Presenting a Congressional Award to Robert Frost, March 26, 1962." White House Audio Recordings, 1961–1963. White House Audio Collection, John F. Kennedy Presidential Library.

"Revitalizing Poetry in the Classroom." Favorite Poem Project. http://www.favoritepoem.org/forTeachers.html (accessed May 29, 2012).

"Richard Blanco: Bio." Richard Blanco. http://richard-blanco.com/bio/ (accessed October 1, 2019).

"Richard Blanco Will Be First Latino Inaugural Poet." *National Public Radio*, January 9, 2013. http://www.npr.org/2013/01/09/168899347/richard-blanco-will-be-first-latino-inaugural-poet.

Rifkin, Libbie. *Career Moves: Olson, Creeley, Zukofsky, Berrigan, and the American Avant-Garde*. Madison: University of Wisconsin Press, 2000.

Rittenhouse, Jessie B. *My House of Life*. New York: Houghton Mifflin, 1934.

———. "The New Poetry and Democracy." *Papers and Proceedings of the Thirty-Eighth Annual Meeting of the American Library Association* 10, no. 4 (July 1916): 137–43.

———. "North of Boston; Robert Frost's Poems of New England Farm Life." *New York Times*, May 16, 1915.

———. "The Poetry Society of America." *Poetry* 1, no. 5 (February 1913): 166–68.

Robbins, Louise S. "The Library of Congress and Federal Loyalty Programs, 1947–1956: No 'Communists or Cocksuckers.'" *Library Quarterly* 64, no. 4 (October 1994): 365–85.

"Robert Casper Named Head of the Poetry and Literature Center." Library of Congress, Washington, D.C. https://www.loc.gov/item/prn-11-065/casper-to-head-poetry-center/2011-03-23/ (accessed July 25, 2019).

"Robert Frost Appointment Press Conference, Wilson Room, Library of Congress." Library of Congress, May 21, 1958. Collection ID: 001625; 1/40. Library of Congress Archives, Central File: Frost, Robert 1874–1963, Library of Congress, Manuscript Division, Washington, D.C.

"Robert Hillyer Papers: Overview of the Collection." Special Collections Research Center, Syracuse University Library. http://library.syr.edu/digital/guides/h/hillyer_r.htm#d2e51 (accessed September 23, 2012).

"Robert Penn Warren Is Named First Poet Laureate, Poetry Consultant." *Library of Congress Information Bulletin* 45, no. 10 (March 10, 1986): 78–79.

Robins, Natalie. *Alien Ink: The FBI's War Against Freedom of Expression*. New York: William Morrow, 1992.

Roman, Camille. *Elizabeth Bishop's World War II—Cold War View*. New York: Palgrave Macmillan, 2004.

"Ruth Lilly Dies at 94; Philanthropist and Heir to Eli Lilly Fortune." *Los Angeles Times*, January 1, 2010. https://www.latimes.com/entertainment/arts/la-xpm-2010-jan-01-la-me-ruth-lilly1-2010jan01-story.html.

Saunders, Frances Stonor. *The Cultural Cold War: The CIA and the World of Arts and Letters*. New York: New Press, 2000.
———. *Who Paid the Piper? The CIA and the Cultural Cold War*. London: Granta, 1999.
Schmidt, Elizabeth Hun, ed. *The Poets Laureate Anthology*. New York: Norton, 2010.
Scott-Smith, Gilles, and Charlotte Lerg, eds. *Campaigning Culture and the Global Cold War: The Journals of the Congress for Cultural Freedom*, vol. 1. London: Palgrave MacMillan, 2017.
Sears, Donald, ed., *Directory of Creative Writing Programs*. Fullerton, Cal.: College English Association, 1970.
Shapiro, Karl. "The Question of the Pound Award." *Partisan Review* 16, no 5 (May 1949): 518–19.
———. *Reports of My Death*. Chapel Hill: Algonquin, 1990.
———. *Trial of a Poet*. New York: Reynal and Hitchcock, 1947.
———. "Why Out-Russia Russia?" *New Republic*, June 9, 1958.
Shivani, Anis. *Against the Workshop: Provocations, Polemics, Controversies*. Huntsville: Texas Review Press, 2011.
Silliman, Ron, ed. *In the American Tree: Language, Realism, Poetry*. Orono, Me.: National Poetry Foundation, 1986.
———. "The Marginalization of Poetry by Bob Perelman." *The Impercipient Lecture Series*, Reprinted in *Jacket 2*, 1, no. 4 (May 1997). http://jacketmagazine.com/02/silliman02.html.
Silliman, Ron, Carla Harryman, Lyn Hejinian, Steve Benson, Bob Perelman, and Barrett Watten. "Aesthetic Tendency and the Politics of Poetry: A Manifesto." *Social Text*, nos. 19/20 (Autumn 1988): 261–75.
Smith, Thomas G. "Robert Frost, Stewart Udall, and the 'Last Go-Down.'" *New England Quarterly* 70, no. 1 (March 1997): 3–32.
Smith, Tracy K, ed. *American Journal: Fifty Poems for Our Time*. Minneapolis: Graywolf, 2018.
———. "Poet Laureate Closing Lecture." Library of Congress, April 15, 2019.
———. "Political Poetry Is Hot Again. The Poet Laureate Explores Why, and How." *New York Times*, December 14, 2018. https://www.nytimes.com/2018/12/10/books/review/political-poetry.html.
———. *Wade in the Water: Poems*. Minneapolis: Graywolf, 2018.
———. "Why Poetry? Why Now?" presented at the Philomathean Society 2019 Annual Oration, Q & A., University of Pennsylvania, Philadelphia, March 28, 2019.
Spahr, Juliana. "Contemporary U.S. Poetry and Its Nationalisms." *Contemporary Literature* 52, no. 4 (Winter 2011): 684–715.
———. *Du Bois's Telegram: Literary Resistance and State Containment*. Cambridge, Mass.: Harvard University Press, 2018.

"Special Progress Report for Fiscal Year 1956, Chair of English Poetry (Annual Report)." Library of Congress Reference Department, October 3, 1956. William McGuire Papers. Manuscript Division, Library of Congress, Washington D.C.

"Special Progress Report for Fiscal Year 1956–October 3, 1956: Chair of English Poetry." Library of Congress, 1956. William McGuire Papers. Manuscript Division, Library of Congress, Washington, D.C.

Stephenson, Jr., Max, Marcy Schnitzer, and Verónica Arroyave. "Nonprofit Governance, Management, and Organizational Learning: Exploring the Implications of One 'Mega-Gift.'" *American Review of Public Administration* 39, no. 1 (January 2009): 43–59. https://doi.org/10.1177/0275074007311888.

Stevens, Hugh. "Confession, Autobiography and Resistance: Robert Lowell and the Politics of Privacy." In *American Cold War Culture*, edited by Douglas Field, 164–84. Edinburgh: Edinburgh University Press, 2005.

Swenson, Cole, and David St. John, eds. *American Hybrid: A Norton Anthology of New Poetry*. New York: Norton, 2009.

Tate, Allen. "What Is Creative Writing?" *Wisconsin Studies in Contemporary Literature* 5, no. 3 (1964): 181–84. https://doi.org/10.2307/1207355.

Taylor, Charles. "The Politics of Recognition." In Amy Gutmann, ed., *Multiculturalism: Examining the Politics of Recognition*, 25–73. Princeton, N.J.: Princeton University Press, 1994.

*The Letters of Robert Frost to Louis Untermeyer*. Ed. Louis Untermeyer. New York: Holt, Rinehart and Winston, 1963.

*The Little Magazine and Contemporary Literature, A Symposium Held at the Library of Congress*. Washington, D.C.: Reference Department at the Library of Congress, Modern Language Association of America, 1966.

"The Pisan Cantos Wins for Ezra Pound First Award of Bollingen Prize in Poetry." Press release no. 542. Library of Congress, February 20, 1949.

"The Poetry Foundation and the Library of Congress Cosponsor Poet Laureate's Newspaper Project." Press release 05-052. Library of Congress, March 24, 2005.

"The Technicolor Adventures of Catalina Neon (Read.Gov)." Library of Congress. http://read.gov/catalinaneon/ (accessed July 24, 2019).

Thompson, Lawrance, ed. *The Selected Letters of Robert Frost*. New York: Holt, Rinehart and Winston, 1964.

Thompson, Lawrance, and R. H. Winnick. *Robert Frost, a Biography: The Authorized Life of the Poet Condensed Into a Single Volume*. Edited by Edward Connery Lathem. New York: Holt, Rinehart and Winston, 1981.

Travisano, Thomas, and Saskia Hamilton, eds. *Words in Air: The Complete Correspondence Between Elizabeth Bishop and Robert Lowell*. New York: Farrar, Straus and Giroux, 2008.

Udall, Stewart L. "Robert Frost, Kennedy and Khrushchev: A Memoir of Poetry and Power." *Shenandoah* 26, no. 2 (1975): 53–54.

———. "Udall Report on Robert Frost Trip to USSR, April 1963," April 10, 1963. Papers of John F. Kennedy. Presidential Papers. President's Office Files. Departments and Agencies: Interior. John F. Kennedy Presidential Library. JFKPOF-080-003.

"United States Poets Laureate: A Guide to Online Resources." Bibliographies, Research Guides, and Finding Aids (Virtual Programs and Services), Library of Congress. https://www.loc.gov/rr/program/bib/poetslaureate/ (accessed July 17, 2019).

"United States Poet Laureate Works on Yearlong Project with Chicago Public Schools." Poetry Foundation press release, November 9, 2016. https://www.poetryfoundation.org/foundation/press/91329/united-states-poet-laureate-works-on-yearlong-project-with-chicago-public-schools-.

"U.S. Poet Laureate Tracy K. Smith to Launch Fall Tour with New Anthology 'American Journal: Fifty Poems for Our Time.'" Library of Congress. Press Release 18-100. August 9, 2018.

Valente, Judy, with Joseph Parisi. "The Well-Endowed 'Poetry' Magazine." *National Public Radio*, May 22, 2005.

Vera, Dan. "The Library and Its Laureates: The Examples of Auslander, Williams, Dickey, and Kumin." *Beltway Poetry Quarterly* 10, no. 4 (Fall 2009). http://washingtonart.com/beltway/fourlaureates.html.

von Hallberg, Robert. *American Poetry and Culture, 1945–1980.* Cambridge, Mass.: Harvard University Press, 1988.

———. *Lyric Powers.* Chicago: University of Chicago Press, 2008.

———. "Poetry, Politics, and Intellectuals," In *The Cambridge History of American Literature*, vol. 8: *Poetry and Criticism, 1940–1995*, ed. Sacvan Bercovitch, 9–260. Cambridge: Cambridge University Press, 1996.

Walcott, Derek. "The Road Taken." In *Homage to Robert Frost*, ed. Joseph Brodsky, Seamus Heaney, and Derek Walcott, 93–94. New York: Farrar, Straus and Giroux, 1996.

Warren, James. "A Billionaire's Ode to Charity: $100 Million to Poetry Journal." *Chicago Tribune*, November 17, 2002.

Warren, Robert Penn. *Segregation: The Inner Conflict in the South.* New York: Vintage, 1956.

———. *Who Speaks for the Negro?* New York: Random House, 1965.

"Watch Poet Richard Blanco Read the Inaugural Poem." PBS News Hour, 2013. http://www.youtube.com/watch?v=AkSRy8SGTEE.

Watkins, Evan. *Work Time: English Departments and the Circulation of Cultural Value.* Stanford: Stanford University Press, 1989.

"We (Too) Are Philly Festival." Raquel Salas Rivera. https://raquelsalasrivera.com/we-too-are-philly/ (accessed January 29, 2019).

"Where Poetry Lives." PBS News Hour. https://www.pbs.org/newshour/tag/where-poetry-lives (accessed July 20, 2019).

Whitefield, Mimi. "Poet Richard Blanco Speaks of the Sea and Hope in Cuba." *Miami Herald*, August 14, 2015. http://www.miamiherald.com/news/nation-world/world/americas/cuba/article31164290.html.

Whittemore, Reed. *The Feel of Rock: Poems of Three Decades*. Takoma Park, Md.: Dryad, 1982.

———. *The Past, the Future, the Present: Poems Selected and New*. Fayetteville: University of Arkansas Press, 1990.

———. *The Self-Made Man*. New York: Macmillan, 1959.

———. *William Carlos Williams: Poet from Jersey*. New York: Houghton Mifflin, 1975.

Wilbers, Stephen. *The Iowa Writers' Workshop: Origins, Emergence, and Growth*. Iowa City: University of Iowa Press, 1980.

William McGuire papers, 1868–1998. Collection ID No. MSS82545. Manuscript Division, Library of Congress, Washington, D.C.

Wilner, Eleanor. "Poetry and the Pentagon: Unholy Alliance?" *Poetry* 185, no. 1 (October 2004): 37–42.

"Wordstreet Champions and Brave Builders of the Dream: A Poet Laureate Project of Juan Felipe Herrera and the Poetry Foundation." Poetry and Literature Center at the Library of Congress). https://www.loc.gov/poetry/wordstreet/ (accessed July 24, 2019).

"Young People's Poet Laureate." Poetry Foundation. https://www.poetryfoundation.org/learn/young-peoples-poet-laureate (accessed July 2, 2019).

Yúdice, George. "The Privatization of Culture." *Social Text* 59 (Summer 1999): 17–34.

# Index

Abercrombie, Lascelles, 237, 275
Abstract Expressionism, 67, 112, 219, 235, 281
academicization of poetry, 16, 22–23, 47, 100–8, 122, 145–48, 159, 199, 232, 248, 258
Academy of American Poets, The (AAP), 6, 11–12, 104, 156–58, 161–62, 179, 217, 261–63, 276, 286, 289
Adams, Frederick, 93
Adams, Léonie, 13, 28, 32, 35–36, 50, 210, 212, 217, 225–26, 228
Adams, Sherman, 68, 86, 233, 240
Adkinson, Burton W., 216, 234
Advisory Council on the Arts, 68, 88, 115
Aiken, Conrad, 35, 37, 50, 53–54, 58–60, 157, 210, 212, 225–26, 228, 230
Akhmatova, Anna, 254
Alexander, Elizabeth, 156, 213; "Praise Song for the Day," 213
Allen, Donald, 218, 275
Allison, Raphael, 242, 275

American Booksellers Association, 157
American Conversations: Celebrating Poems in Rural Communities, 23, 182, 275
*American Journal: Fifty Poems for Our Time*, 182, 269, 291, 293
American Life in Poetry: A Project for Newspapers, 23, 152, 161–62, 164, 166–67, 175–76, 260, 263–64, 267, 275, 289
American Poetry and Literacy Project, 151
*American Poetry Review*, 218, 263, 289
*Amerika*, 31
Ames, Elizabeth, 28, 30–31, 50, 221
Andrew W. Mellon Foundation, 11, 217, 262, 276
Angelou, Maya, 156, 213; "On the Pulse of Morning," 156, 213
Annual Report to the Librarian of Congress from the Chair of Poetry, 1, 3, 12, 32, 53, 56, 58, 135–36, 138, 140, 215–16, 222, 231–32, 234, 241, 256, 276–78; Basler's, 231, 234, 276;

Annual Report to the Librarian of
  Congress from the Chair of Poetry
  (*continued*)
  Bishop's, 33, 53–54, 58, 135–37, 222,
    232, 277; Brooks's, 1, 3–4, 12–13,
    135–40, 215–16, 256, 278; Hayden's,
    3–4, 135; Kumin's, 12–13
*Antaeus*, 218
anticommunism, 8, 21, 30, 33, 50–51, 67,
  96, 99, 102, 112, 118, 211, 236, 221,
  278, 290
antilaureate, 60, 66
antitotalitarianism, 9, 24, 39, 85, 95–96,
  110–12, 122–23
Archambeau, Robert, 267, 276
Aridi, Sarah, 217, 276
Armenti, Peter, ix, 270–72, 276
Armstrong, Phyllis, 12, 33–35, 58–59, 65,
  136, 231–32
Arroyave, Verónica, 264, 292
Asamblea de Artistas Revolucionarios
  de Oaxaca, 181, 269, 281
Asia Foundation, The, 117
Aspen Institute, The, 163
Associated Writing Programs (AWP),
  100, 106–9, 114, 118, 148, 246, 276,
  280–81. See also Association of
  Writers and Writing Programs
  (AWP)
Association of Literary Magazines of
  America, 126
Association of Writers and Writing
  Program (AWP), 9, 106–9, 114, 118,
  148, 246–47, 276, 280–81. See also
  Associated Writing Programs
  (AWP)
Atheneum Press, 218
Auden, W. H., 35, 37, 212, 225–26, 276
Auslander, Joseph, 157, 211, 215, 254,
  260, 262, 293
Axelrod, Stephen Gould, 242, 276

Babb, James, 12, 41–43, 217, 225–26
Babbitt, Irving, 248
Bailey, Robert F., 265
Bair, Barbara, ix
Barr, John, 11, 163–167, 177, 180,
  190–91, 201, 203, 264–66, 272, 276;
  "American Poetry in the New
  Century," 165–67, 265–66, 272, 276
Bartlett, John T., 76–77, 81, 233, 237–39
Basler, Roy, 52, 65, 87, 99, 216, 230–31,
  233–34, 240, 245, 253, 272
Battle, Lucius D., 115–16
Bauerlein, Mark, 241, 251, 262
Beach, Christopher, 16, 277
Behar, Ruth, 198, 278
Belmonte, Laura, 219, 277
Bennett, Eric, 15, 18, 67, 106, 110–11,
  115–16, 119–20, 235, 246–53, 255
Benson, Steve, 141, 257, 291; "Aesthetic
  Tendency and the Politics of Poetry:
  A Manifesto," 141, 257, 291
Benton, Senator William, 240, 277
Bernstein, Charles, x, 18, 103–4, 141,
  146, 153, 159–60, 203, 219, 258, 261;
  *Attack of the Difficult Poems: Essays and
  Inventions*, 153, 261, 263, 277;
  *Content's Dream: Essays, 1975–1984*,
  219, 277
Berryman, John, 100–3, 245, 276–77
*Better Homes and Gardens*, 113
*Between the Lines: A History of Poetry in
  Letters, 1962–2002*, 25, 217, 264–65,
  287
Biddle, Francis, 36, 38
Biddle, Livingston, Jr., 158
Biden, President Joseph R., 26, 193,
  206, 213
Billington, James, 14, 155, 175, 180, 261
Bishop, Elizabeth, 2–4, 7, 9, 13, 21,
  27–28, 30–32, 49, 53–61, 96, 103–4,
  135–37, 157, 169, 207, 210, 212,

215–16, 220–22, 225–26, 228, 231–32, 240, 242, 244, 254, 277, 285, 290, 292; "One Art," 56; "View of the Capitol from the Library of Congress," 2–4, 31, 56, 59, 215, 231; versions of "View of the Capitol," 56, 231, 278
Black Arts Movement, 9, 145
Black Mountain School, 142
Blackmur, R. P., 35, 212
Blaffer, Robert Lee, 227
Blanco, Richard, 25, 107, 122, 156, 192–200, 213, 245, 247, 271–72, 276, 278, 280, 289–90, 293; *For All of Us*, 271, 278; "One Today," 25, 192–99, 213, 271, 276, 278; "Matters of the Sea / *Cosas del mar*," 193, 197–98, 271, 278
Bloch, Julia, 258
Blumenkranz, Carla, 221, 278
Bly, Robert, 134
Bobbitt, Philip, 155–56, 224, 261
Bobbitt, Rebekah Johnson, 155
Boeing, 203
Bogan, Louise, 34–38, 157, 211–12, 223, 225
Bollingen affair, 21, 29–40, 44–47, 49–53, 59–62
Bollingen Prize, 8, 11, 21, 29–30, 32, 36–54, 60, 72, 101, 107, 126, 155, 201, 221, 223, 224, 226, 228, 236, 273, 285
*Bookman, The*, 237
Boorstin, Daniel, 13, 127–30, 133, 217, 254
Boston University, 161, 169–70, 266; Howard Gotlieb Archival Research Center, 169
Bourdieu, Pierre, 19, 278
Bowe, Julia, 226–27
Brathwaite, William Stanley, 236
British Council, The, 222

Broadside Press, 133, 137
Brodsky, Joseph, 3–4, 10, 104, 140, 149–51, 153–54, 159, 167, 189, 190, 199, 210, 215–16, 242, 245, 256, 259–60, 271–72, 282, 283, 287, 293
Broderick, John C., 139–40, 216, 255–56
Brooks, Cleanth, 132, 212, 225; *An Approach to Literature*, 132; *Understanding Poetry*, 132
Brooks, Ernest, Jr., 12, 40, 217, 224–27, 229
Brooks, Gwendolyn, 1, 3–4, 7, 10, 13, 105, 123, 128, 131–40, 148–49, 179, 190, 204, 207, 210, 212, 215–17, 253, 256, 278, 281, 284; "Black Woman in Russia," 123, 134, 216, 253, 278; correspondence with inquiries to national poetry office, 137, 256; as host of luncheon reading series at Library of Congress, 131–32, 148–49; "The Life of Lincoln West," 4, 123, 134; *Riot*, 133–34; at Sixth Soviet-American Writers Conference, 4, 134–35
Brooks, Van Wyck, 212
Brown, Jeffrey, 179
Brown, Wendy, 144, 258, 278
Brownell, Herbert, Jr., 234
Buell, Lawrence, 218, 278
Bullock, Marie, 12, 157–58, 262
Burning Deck Press, 257
Bush, George H. W., 140
Bush, George W., 164–65, 203
Butler, Judith, 144, 258, 278
Butler, Octavia, 147, 259; *Lilith's Brood*, 259
Butterworth, G. Forrest, Jr., 215

Cabey, Alfred, 137, 256
Cairns, Huntington, 34–35, 40, 44, 97–98, 222, 224

Carrier, Warren, 119, 252, 279
Carroll, Andrew, 151
Carruth, Hayden, 12, 19, 40–42, 44–46, 48–49, 117, 165, 217, 224–27, 278
*Case Against "The Saturday Review of Literature," The*, 38, 41, 45, 279
Casper, Robert, ix, xi, 13, 131, 155, 182, 187, 189, 202, 215, 246, 256, 261, 272
Central Intelligence Agency (CIA), 6, 9, 31, 61, 67, 85, 102–3, 110, 112, 117, 222, 235, 251
Chang, Tina, 185
Chapin, Katherine Garrison, 35–38, 212, 225–26
Charles, Jos, 184; *feeld*, 184
Chicago Public Schools, 181, 269, 293
*Chicago Tribune*, 162, 264, 293
civil verse poets, 20, 23, 152–54, 160, 174, 177–79, 184, 188, 190–91, 199, 204, 207, 260
Clampitt, Amy, 261
Clapp, Verner, 36, 51–52, 216, 223, 229, 234
Clarion Workshop, 259
Clinton, William Jefferson, 156, 167–68, 213
Cloud, Howard, 188, 270
Cole, W. Sterling, 65, 216, 234
Coleman, Elliott, 108
College of William and Mary, 241
College Poetry Society of America, 72, 236
Collins, Billy, 7, 17, 23, 104, 152, 157, 161, 163, 166–67, 172–75, 177–78, 182, 184, 189–90, 209, 260, 263, 267, 286
Columbia University School of the Arts, 262
Committee of Artists and Scientists for Eisenhower, 64

Community College Humanities Association, 179
Community College Poetry Day, 179
Congress for Cultural Freedom, 61, 96, 102, 117, 244, 291; *Congress News*, 244
Congressional Joint Committee on the Library of Congress, 39
Conrad, C. A., 184
Consortium Book Sales and Distribution, 262
Coordinating Council of Literary Magazines, 117
Copper Canyon Press, 262
Cornell University, 108, 219, 246, 258, 283, 285
*Counterattack: Facts to Combat Communism*, 50–51
Cousins, Norman, 39, 224, 226, 279
Cowles, Gardner, Jr. 113, 250
Cox, Sidney, 70, 76–78, 236–37, 239
creative writing industry, 61–62, 67, 100–8; role of Iowa Writers' Workshop, 108–18; workshop poem, 9, 20, 101–3, 122, 144, 148, 153
Croft, Clare, 219, 279
Culler, Jonathan, 218
Cummins, Virginia Kent, 229
Cushman, Stephen, 239

Damon, Maria, 246, 258, 279
Davidson, Gustav, 227, 251–52, 281, 289
Davidson, Michael, 16, 218
Dawson, Paul, 249
de Certeau, Michel, 231, 279
Decherney, Peter, 219, 249, 279
de Man, Paul, 141
Department of Justice, 235
Deutsch, Babette, 98
Dickey, James, 210, 254, 293
Dickinson, Emily, 168
Dove, Rita, 139, 168, 178, 209, 210

Dover Thrift Editions, 151
Dowling, David O., 104, 245, 279
Dowling, Sarah, 258
*Du Bois's Telegram: Literary Resistance and State Containment*, 18–19, 67, 219, 235, 255, 291
Dulles, John Foster, 233, 239
Duncan, Robert, 117

Eagleton, Terry, 218
Eberhart, Richard, 128, 157, 210, 221, 254
826 National, 157
Eisenhower administration, 8, 10, 61, 64, 85–86, 88, 91, 219, 234, 240, 287
Eisenhower, Dwight D., 65, 66, 72, 84, 86–88, 233, 236, 240
Eliot, T. S., 1, 18, 35, 37–39, 72, 173, 201, 212, 219, 225–26, 230, 234, 272, 279, 286
Emerson, Ralph Waldo, 168
Emre, Merve, 15
Engle, Paul, 9, 69, 101, 104, 108–17, 119–21, 127, 133–34, 148, 175–76, 235, 247–53, 277, 279; *On Creative Writing*, 113, 250; regional promotion, 112–14; relations with federal arts programs, 114–18; "To Praise a Man," 250; views on cultural difference, 120–22; world recruiting tour, 116–17, 120–23
English, James, x, 16, 262, 279
English, Ned, 265, 288
*English Review, The*, 237
Epstein, Andrew, 146, 258, 280
Epstein, Joseph, 159–60, 263, 280
Evans, Luther, 21, 31, 34, 36, 41–43, 50–51, 65, 131, 217, 221, 224, 228–29, 234, 280
Evans, Steve, 164, 259, 263, 287
Executive Order 9835, 51

expressive agency, 7, 22, 68, 192, 195, 197

Farfield Foundation, 61–62, 102, 117
Farrar, Straus and Giroux, 262
Favorite Poem Project: Americans Saying Poems They Love, The, 20, 23, 55, 151, 154, 160–61, 164, 167–72, 176–77, 180, 182–83, 260–61, 263, 266, 275, 280, 288, 290; "Founding Principles," 170, 261, 266, 280
Federal Emergency Relief Administration, 248
Federico, Sue, 256
Fedoronko, Nikolai, 134
Feld, Rose, 235, 238–39, 284
Fellows in American Letters, vii, 27, 29, 33–34, 54, 212, 222–23, 231, 261, 272
Fenza, David, 107, 122, 148, 247, 253, 280
Field, Douglas, 221, 280, 292
Filreis, Al, x, 223, 234, 280
Fish, Stanley, 218
Fisher, Tadd, 222, 232, 250
Fisk Black Writers Conference, 133
Fitzgerald, Robert, 210
Flint, F. S., 74–75, 77, 237
Flowers, Betty Sue, 156
Foerster, Norman, 109, 112, 247–48
Forster-Lussier, Danielle, 219
Ford Foundation, 11
Fox, Cheryl, ix
Free Library of Philadelphia, 204–5; Center for Public Life, 204
Freeman, Joshua, 242, 280
Frost, Robert, vii, 3, 4, 7, 9–12, 20–23, 25–26, 37, 54–55, 59, 63–97, 99–101, 106, 110, 112–14, 116, 118, 125–28, 140, 147, 151–54, 156–57, 159, 166, 168–73, 175–76, 181, 189, 192–99, 201–3, 210, 213, 215, 216, 220, 223,

Frost, Robert (*continued*)
227, 230, 232–45, 248, 250, 266–67, 275–76, 280–82, 284–87, 289–93; *A Boy's Will*, 75; "Dedication," 89, 166, 216, 220, 236, 239, 241, 280; "The Gift Outright," 22, 26, 68, 84, 89, 90, 96–97, 156, 169, 192, 194–95, 213, 241–42; "How Hard It Is," 239; *In the Clearing*, 94; Mission to Moscow, 3, 22, 63, 85, 92–96, 151, 202, 243; *North of Boston*, 71, 77, 81, 83, 112, 236–37, 267, 290; "Pertinax," 239; relations with Eisenhower, 64–66, 72, 84–88, 233, 236, 240; relations with Kennedy, 3, 9–10, 15, 22, 25–26, 54, 68–70, 83–84, 89–99, 101–3, 114–16, 118, 140, 151, 154, 166, 192, 202, 213, 215, 232, 235, 239, 241–45, 283, 287, 290, 293; relations with the Truman administration, 85; "The Road Not Taken," 235; *A Witness Tree*, 90, 242, 281

Fugitives, The, 133

Galbraith, Nancy, 155, 261
Gallup, Donald, 225
Garnett, Edward, 71, 77–78, 236, 281
General Foods, 164, 250
Gerber, John, 248
G.I. Bill, 8, 61, 100, 109
Gibson, Wilfrid, 237
Gilpatric, Chadbourne, 252–53
Ginsberg, Allen, 13, 104, 252, 254
Gioia, Dana, 164–65, 191, 250, 265, 281
Glück, Louise, 20, 152, 209
Goble, Lisbeth, 265, 281
Goldhammer, Arthur, 235, 281
Golding, Alan, 16, 281
Goodyear, Dana, 219, 264–65, 281
Gorman, Amanda, 25, 193, 206, 213, 271–72, 275, 281; "The Hill We Climb," 25, 193; as inaugural poet, 25, 206; as model, 206; as national youth poet, 206; responses to inaugural reading, 206; at Super Bowl LV, 206

Graham, Jorie, 152, 260
Grantham, Ellen, 241, 251, 262, 276
Graywolf Press, 157, 182
Green, Paul, 35, 37, 212, 225–26
Green, Theodore F., 224
Gregory, Horace, 245, 281
Gross, Andrew, 223, 281
Guggenheim Foundation, 110, 126, 179, 221
Guilbaut, Serge, 67, 219, 235
Gutmann, Amy, 242, 292
Gwiazda, Piotr, 20, 108, 219, 247, 282

Hall, Donald, 13, 104, 209, 218, 254, 268, 282
Hallmark, 250
Hamilton, Saskia, 216, 220, 292
Hamline University, 262
Hanks, Nancy, 158
Harbach, Chad, 250, 252, 277, 282–83
Harcourt, 78–79
Harcourt, Alfred, 237–38
Harjo, Joy, xi, 7, 13–14, 24, 178, 180, 186–90, 209, 260, 270, 276, 283–85; *Living Nations, Living Words: A Map of First Peoples Poetry*, 186, 188, 270, 284
Harper, Michael S., 128
Harper and Row, 133
HarperCollins, 262
Harriet Monroe Poetry Institute, 163, 278, 282
Harryman, Carla, 141, 257, 291; "Aesthetic Tendency and the Politics of Poetry: A Manifesto," 141, 257, 291

Harvard University, 222, 248, 262;
    Woodberry Poetry Room, 222
Hass, Robert, 20, 152–53, 168, 178, 210,
    260, 267, 276
Hathaway, Baxter, 108
Hatlen, Burton, 256
Hayden, Carla xi, 14, 24, 182, 186, 189
Hayden, Robert, 3, 135, 157, 210
Hazo, Sam, 139
Heaney, Seamus, 242, 293
Hecht, Anthony, 13, 157, 210, 254
Heckscher, August, 88, 95–96, 99, 158
Hejinian, Lyn, 103, 141–44, 257–58, 282;
    "Aesthetic Tendency and the Politics
    of Poetry: A Manifesto," 141, 146,
    219–20, 257–58, 291; *The Language of
    Inquiry*, 258, 282; *My Life*, 142–45,
    257–58, 282; *Writing/Talks*, 252, 282,
    287
Hemingway, Ernest, 89, 234
Henry Holt, 78, 88
Heritage Foundation, 129
Herrera, Juan Felipe, 7, 14, 23–24,
    177–82, 187–90, 201, 204, 207, 209,
    260, 268–69, 279, 281–84, 288, 294;
    *Automatika*, 181, 269, 281; Brave
    Builders of the Dream, 180–81, 269,
    294; California laureateship, 180; "El
    Jardín," 180, 268–69, 279, 281; La
    Casa de Colores, 180–81, 268–69,
    279, 281, 284; "La Familia," 180, 268,
    284; *187 Reasons Mexicanos Can't Cross
    the Border: Undocuments 1971–2007*,
    181, 269, 282; "The Technicolor
    Adventures of Catalina Neon,"
    180–81, 269, 292; Wordstreet
    Champions, 180–81, 269, 294
high cultural pluralism, 122, 195,
    252–53; and multiculturalism, 122–23
Higher Education Act, 8, 61, 100, 118,
    251

Hillyer, Robert, 38, 59, 201, 224, 229,
    236, 282, 290
Hine, Daryl, 12
Hodsoll, Francis S. M., 158, 262–63, 282
Hoffman, Daniel, 128–29, 157, 210, 254
Hoffman, Tyler, 82, 84, 220, 235, 238–39
Holland, Spessard, 51
Hollywood Ten, 50–51
Holmes, Anne, 271, 282
Homeland Security Act of 2002, 164–65
Hopkins, Kenneth, 242, 282
Houghton Mifflin Harcourt, 218, 262
House Un-American Activities
    Committee (HUAC), 50–51
Howland, Harold E., 233
*Hudson Review, The*, 117, 149
Hughes, Langston, 168, 205
Hulme, T. E., 74, 238, 283
Huntington, Archer M., 215, 228
Huntington, Archibald, 230
Huntington Gift Fund, 130

IGM Models, 206
inaugural poem, vii, 3, 9, 22, 24–26, 54,
    68, 83–85, 89–92, 96–97, 99, 101, 107,
    118, 122, 140, 151, 153, 155–56, 166,
    168–69, 192–200, 202, 206, 213, 216,
    220, 236, 239, 241–42, 244–45, 247,
    271–72, 275–76, 278, 280, 289–90,
    293; "Dedication" (Frost), 89, 166,
    216, 220, 236, 239, 241, 280; "The
    Hill We Climb" (Gorman), 25, 206,
    213; "One Today" (Blanco), 25,
    192–99, 213, 271, 276, 278; "On the
    Pulse of Morning" (Angelou), 156,
    213
Internal Revenue Service (IRS), 35, 40
International Cooperation Year, 125–26
International Poetry Festival, 127
*In the American Tree*, 141, 256, 291
*Iowan, The*, 113

Iowa Writers' Workshop, 9, 22, 62, 69, 101–4, 108, 110, 113, 118, 126, 140, 175–76, 202, 245, 247–48, 279, 294; International Writing Program at, 9, 97, 114–15, 117, 126

*Jacket2*, 259, 287, 291
Jacobsen, Josephine, 210
Jameson, Fredric, 119, 252, 283
Jarrell, Randall, 36, 52–54, 65–66, 103, 210, 221, 228, 230, 276
Javadizadeh, Kamran, 15, 218, 283
Javits, Jacob K., 39
Jay, Paul, 219, 283
Jell-O, 164, 250
Johns Hopkins University, 35
Johns Hopkins Writing Seminars, 108, 246
Johnson, Lyndon B., 9, 51, 69, 102, 155
Jong, Erica, 134
Jordan, June, 145
Jung, Carl, 34, 38, 43, 222
Justice, Donald, 111, 249

Kealoha, 185
Kearns, Katherine, 84, 239, 284
Kempf, Christopher, 16, 218, 284
Kennedy, Jacqueline, 116
Kennedy, John F., 3, 15, 25, 68–70, 83–103, 114–118, 140, 151, 154, 156, 158, 166, 192, 202, 213, 215, 232, 235, 239, 241–45, 283, 287, 290, 293
Kennedy administration, 8, 22, 61, 88, 235
*Kenyon Review, The*, 117, 249
Kerr, Clark, 110, 248, 284
Khrushchev, Nikita, 3, 9, 22, 68, 84–85, 92–96, 241, 243, 293
Kindley, Evan, 15, 19, 137, 284
Kirby, Bruce, ix

Kitchen Table: Women of Color Press, 145
Knight, Etheridge, 137
Knopf, Alfred A., Inc., 262
Knowledge@Wharton, 266, 272, 288
Kooser, Ted, 23, 152, 157, 162, 164–67, 175–80, 189–90, 201, 209, 260, 267, 275, 284, 289; American Life in Poetry: A Project for Newspapers, 23, 161–62, 164, 166–67, 175–76, 260, 263–64, 267, 278, 289; *The Poetry Home Repair Manual*, 176, 267, 284
Krowl, Michelle, ix
Kumin, Maxine, 12–13, 117, 129, 131, 148, 210, 254, 293
Kunitz, Stanley, 157, 209–10

Language poets, 9, 18, 20, 23, 103–4, 141–42, 145–48, 153, 220, 257, 259, 287
Lathem, Edward Connery, 232, 235, 284, 292
Laugesen, Amanda, 219, 284
Lazard, Lloyd, 137, 256
Lea, Thomas C., 40, 224
Lederle, Cheryl, 270, 284
Lee, Don L., 255, 284
Lee, Elaine, 216, 253, 278; *Go Girl! The Black Woman's Book of Travel and Adventure*, 216, 253, 278
Lethbridge, Mary, 228, 284
Levine, Philip, 13, 179, 209, 268
Lewis, Anthony, 234, 284
Library of Congress, 13; Archive of Recorded Poetry and Literature, 28, 32–34, 53–55, 59, 90, 169; Coolidge Auditorium, 129, 136, 185, 188, 270; General Reference and Bibliography Division, 52, 58, 231–32, 234, 276; Humanities and Social Sciences Section, 13; Jefferson Building, 2–3,

31, 186, 189, 222, 270; *Library of Congress Gazette*, 150, 215, 260, 287; *Library of Congress Information Bulletin*, 216, 253, 255, 279, 280, 281, 290; Literary Initiatives Office (LIT), 202; Montpelier Room, 199; Poetry and Literature Center (PLC), ix, 6, 13–15, 23, 129, 131, 149, 155, 160, 178, 182, 189, 191, 202, 215–16, 228, 259–61, 267–70, 272, 275, 279, 281, 284, 286–90, 294; Poetry and Literature Program, 155; Poetry Office of the Library of Congress, vii, xi, 1–26, 31–34, 52, 57–58, 60, 62, 64, 67, 104–6, 115, 123–39, 149–51, 156–62, 179, 181, 189, 200, 204, 207, 209–11, 228, 230–34, 241, 252, 254, 256, 276, 289; Rebekah Johnson Bobbitt National Prize for Poetry, 155, 289

*Life*, 113

Lilly, Eli, 162

Lilly, Eli, III, 165, 201

Lilly, J. K., III, 12, 21, 32–33, 44, 46, 226

Lilly, Ruth, 7, 11–12, 23, 33, 46, 154, 162, 165, 179, 217, 244, 290

Lilly Endowment, 12, 21, 44–47, 164

Limón, Ada, 209

*Little Magazine and Contemporary Literature, a Symposium Held at the Library of Congress, The*, 252–53, 292

London Society, The, 71

Lorde, Audre, 129, 145

*Los Angeles Times*, 163

Lowell, Amy, 72, 80, 236

Lowell, Robert, 7, 9, 13, 17, 21, 27–31, 35–37, 49–61, 72, 96, 103–4, 126, 169, 211, 212, 216, 220–22, 225–226, 228, 230–32, 240, 244, 249, 276, 278, 281, 285, 292; distinction between raw and cooked, 17, 103–4

Luce, Henry, 113

Lyon, Janet, 258, 285

*Lyric*, 229

Lyric Foundation, 51, 229

Mabry, Thomas, 249

MacArthur, Marit, 242, 285

MacLeish, Archibald, 118, 120, 212, 216, 223, 225–26, 228, 234, 252, 255, 276, 285; "Ars Poetica," 120; "Voyage to the Moon," 118

Malraux, André, 232

Mao, David, 180

Mariani, Paul, 220–21, 285

Marsh Hawk Press, 262

Martin, Hansford, 249

Masters, Edgar Lee, 80

Matejka, Adrian, 185

Matsunaga, Senator Spark M., 130, 255

McCarthy, Richard, 251

McCarthy, Joseph, 21, 50

McGann, Jerome, 56

McGee, Micki, 221, 285

McGuire, William, 14–15, 105, 215–17, 221–24, 228–34, 241, 244–46, 251–56, 262, 285–86, 276–78, 285–89, 292, 294; *Bollingen: An Adventure in Collecting the Past*, 246, 285; *Poetry's Catbird Seat*, 14–15, 105, 216–17, 221–24, 228–32, 234, 244–45, 253–56, 262, 285

McGurl, Mark, 16, 106, 111, 121–22, 147, 195, 218, 246, 249, 252–53, 258–59, 271, 286

McKinlay, Alan, 245, 286

Mearns, David, 216

Medina, Juana, 181

Mellon, Mary Conover, 34, 222

Mellon, Paul, 6, 11, 21, 30, 32, 34–35, 38, 40, 54, 97, 222, 224

Meredith, William, 128–29, 210, 230

Merrill, James, 155, 261, 283

Merwin, W.S., 13, 179, 209, 268
MFA poet. *See* poet as creative writer
middle generation, 31, 103, 276
Milkweed Editions, 262
Miller, Shawn, ix, 183, 185–86, 189
Mish, Jeanetta Calhoun, 185
Mitchell, Larry, 188, 270
Modern Poetry Association, 6, 11, 23, 34, 38, 48, 98, 154, 162–63, 165, 167, 175, 224, 226–27, 279
Momaday, N. Scott, 128
Monro, Harold, 74, 77, 237–38
Monroe, Harriet, 75, 163, 165–66, 266, 278, 282, 286
Monteiro, George, 239, 286
Moore, Marianne, 13, 49, 221, 228
Moore, Merrill, 59
More, Paul Elmer, 248
Morison, Samuel Eliot, 212
Morrison, Kay, 223, 241
Morrissey, Marlene, 234
Mosher, Thomas, 76, 237
Muller, Robert, 188, 270
Mumford, L. Quincy., 8, 52–53, 65–66, 87, 96, 125–26, 216, 230, 233–35, 286
Murray, James F., Jr., 229
*Muse and the Librarian, The*, 230, 233, 240, 245, 272, 276
Muske-Dukes, Carol, 19
Mvskoke Nation, 24, 186, 188
Myers, D. G., 109–10, 218, 246–49, 286

*Nation, The*, 218, 237
national arts, 26, 67–68, 85, 88–89, 111, 115–18, 154, 166
National Council of Teachers of English, 157, 222, 289
National Cultural Center, 88, 115
National Defense Education Act of 1958, 251
National Endowment for the Arts (NEA), 6, 9–10, 22–23, 25, 61, 68, 88–89, 95, 102, 105, 116–18, 126, 130–31, 140, 153–54, 156–60, 160–66, 179, 187, 190–91, 203–4, 241, 250–51, 255, 261–62, 266, 276, 281–82; Operation Homecoming, 203
National Endowment for the Humanities (NEH), 25, 89, 130, 133; Jefferson Lecture, 133; Presidential Medal of Freedom, 133
National Humanities Metal, 179
national poetic voice, 7, 54, 96–99, 101, 119–21, 141–45, 148, 161, 169–70, 253
National Poetry Festival, 7, 9, 69, 96–101, 106, 111, 115, 125, 130, 147, 151, 157, 202
National Poetry Foundation (NPF), 141, 256–57, 275, 291
National Poetry Month, 153, 156–62, 167–68, 175, 179, 261–63, 277, 286
National Youth Administration, 248
NBC, 222, 250
Nemerov, Howard, 140, 149, 157, 210
New Criticism, 38, 47, 109, 111–12, 232, 249
New Frontier, 88
New Narrative, 145
*New Republic, The*, 51
New York City Department of Cultural Affairs, 157
*New Yorker, The*, 2, 56, 104, 218
*New York Review of Books, The*, 218
New York State Council on the Arts, 157
*New York Times, The*, 2, 30, 66, 71, 74, 78, 118, 163, 183, 185, 218, 221, 237, 241, 264, 266
Nims, John, 162, 217
Nixon, Richard M., 118

North, Joseph, 15–16
Norton, W. W., 262

Office of the President, 6, 156, 197, 199
official verse culture, 18, 104, 133, 141, 145, 148, 203–4; contrasted with state verse culture, 104, 106, 141, 148, 203–4
Ohnemus, Edward, 215–16, 260, 287
Osgood, Kenneth, 219, 287
Owen, Jane Blaffer, 227

Pack, Robert, 218, 282
Padgett, Ron, iv, 119, 287; "Voice," iv, 119
Panas, Jerold, 267, 287
Papyrus Greeting Cards, 157
Parini, Jay, 172, 242, 287
Parisi, Joseph, 163, 216–17, 264–65, 287, 293
*Parnassus*, 218
*Partisan Review*, 50, 223, 249, 276, 291
Patchen, Kenneth, 117
Patterson, James, 39
Paul Mellon Endowment, 30
Paz, Octavio, 168
PBS NewsHour Poetry Series, 179, 268
Penguin Books, 262
Perelman, Bob, x, 103, 141, 146, 257–59, 282, 287, 291; "Aesthetic Tendency and the Politics of Poetry: A Manifesto," 141, 146, 219–20, 257–58, 291; "A Counter-Response," 258–59, 287; *The Marginalization of Poetry: Language Writing and Literary History*, 259, 287, 291
Perloff, Marjorie, 141, 256, 287
Phi Beta Kappa, 241
phonocentrism, 9, 20, 22, 54, 68, 81, 83, 101, 142, 151–54, 168, 170, 172, 176–78, 180–84, 190

Piercy, Marge, 129
Pinsky, Robert, 7, 20, 23, 54, 151–54, 157, 159, 161, 164, 167–73, 176–78, 182–83, 188–90, 210, 220, 260–61, 263, 266–67, 276, 288; *Democracy, Culture, and the Voice of Poetry*, 167–70, 176, 263, 266, 288; *An Explanation of America*, 20, 172, 220, 266, 288; Favorite Poem Project, 20, 23, 55, 151, 154, 160–61, 164, 167–72, 176–77, 180, 182–83, 260–61, 263, 266, 275, 280, 288, 290; *Poetry and the World*, 170, 266, 288; *The Sounds of Poetry*, 170, 266, 288
poet as creative writer, vii, 22–23, 100–18, 122, 124, 146–47, 159, 199; as contrasted with poet-critic, 104, 107, 147, 159, 199
poet-critic, vii, 15–16, 22–23, 100–18, 123–24, 141–48, 153, 159, 199, 253, 258, 284; as contrasted with creative writer, 104, 107, 147, 159, 199
POETICS listserv, 17
poet laureateship in the United Kingdom, 91
*Poetry*, 6, 11, 21, 34, 41, 47, 49, 60, 69, 98, 159, 163, 165–66, 217, 229, 244; Ruth Lilly bequest to, 11–12, 23, 33, 154, 162, 165, 244
Poetry 180: A Poem a Day for American High Schools, 23, 152, 161, 167, 172–77, 180, 182, 184, 260, 263, 267–68, 280, 286, 288
*Poetry: A Magazine of Verse*. See *Poetry*
Poetry Coalition, 11, 189, 201, 217, 289
Poetry Foundation, xi, 6, 11–12, 15, 19, 23–24, 104, 131, 141, 154, 157, 160–67, 175–76, 179, 181–82, 190–91, 201, 203–6, 217, 220, 227, 256–57, 264–65, 267–69, 272, 275–76, 278, 282–83, 286, 288–89, 292–94;

Poetry Foundation (*continued*)
  Mark Twain Award for Humor, 163;
  "Poetry for the Mind's Joy," 179; Ruth
  Lilly Poetry Prize, 162, 179; "Young
  People's Poet Laureate," 205, 272, 294
Poetry for the People, 145
"Poetry-in-the-schools" (AAP), 157
*Poetry 180: A Turning Back to Poetry*, 161,
  174, 263, 267–68, 270, 278
*Poetry Review*, 74
*Poetry's Catbird Seat: The Consultantship
  in Poetry in the English Language at the
  Library of Congress, 1937–1987*, 14–15,
  105, 216–17, 221–24, 228–32, 234,
  244–45, 253–56, 262, 285
Poetry Society of America (PSA), 6, 11,
  38, 41, 51, 59–60, 69–74, 78, 97–98,
  104, 163–64, 176, 200–1, 236, 251,
  264, 289–90; College Poetry Society
  of America, 72, 237; Frost Medal, 72,
  88; Gold Medal for Distinguished
  Service, 72, 86; Round Table
  Workshop, 251
Poetry Society of England, London
  Poetry Society, 73
poetry wars, 17, 104, 107, 145
Poet's House (Indiana), 227
Poirier, Richard, 238–39, 280–81
Polanyi, Karl, 110
Porter, Katherine Anne, 35, 212, 225, 226
Pound, Ezra, 8, 11, 21, 29–32, 36–39, 43,
  47–48, 50–54, 56, 60, 65–67, 70, 72,
  74–81, 83, 155, 159, 173, 200, 221,
  223–26, 233–39, 247, 256, 276, 279,
  282, 284–85, 289, 291; *The Pisan
  Cantos*, 29, 30, 36–39, 47, 50, 65, 221,
  223, 249; review of *North of Boston*,
  70, 77–78
Presidential Task Force on the Arts and
  Humanities, 158, 263
Princeton University Press, 222

*The Program Era: Postwar Fiction and the
  Rise of Creative Writing*, 16, 105–7,
  121, 123, 137, 159, 176, 196, 218, 246,
  249, 252–53, 259, 268, 271, 286
Puerto Rico Oversight, Management,
  and Economic Stability Act
  (PROMESA), 205
Purser, John Thibaut, 132; *An Approach
  to Literature*, 132
Putnam, Herbert, 215, 228

Rago, Henry, 114
Randall, Dudley, 134
Random House, 157, 161, 173
Random House Children's Books, 157
Ransom, John Crowe, 35, 212
Rasula, Jed, 16, 35, 47, 222–23, 226, 234,
  289; *The American Poetry Wax
  Museum: Reality Effects, 1940–1990*, 16,
  222–23, 226, 289
Reagan, Ronald, 129
Reagan administration, 10, 131, 158
Reardon, T. J., Jr., 251
Rector, Liam, 159, 263, 289
Rees, Ted, 258
Reeve, Franklin D., 93–95, 243–44, 289
Rendell, Steven, 231, 279
Reynolds, Conger, 86
Rice, Isaac L., 72
Rich, Adrienne, 129, 131
Richardson, Mark, 239, 242, 276, 280–81
Rifkin, Libbie, 258, 290
Rittenhouse, Jessie, 71–74, 78–80,
  236–38, 290; *My House of Life*,
  236–38, 290; "The New Poetry and
  Democracy," 80, 238, 290; review of
  *North of Boston*, 71–72, 290
Robbins, Louise S., 220, 290
Robins, Natalie, 220, 290
Robinson, Edwin Arlington, 76, 168
Robinson, Vogue, 185

Rockefeller, David, 262
Rockefeller Foundation, 18, 61, 102, 110–12, 116–17, 120, 179, 249–50, 252
Roosevelt, Franklin D., Jr., 51
Rukeyser, Muriel, 36
Ryan, Kay, 178–79, 201, 209, 260, 268, 286; "Poetry for the Mind's Joy," 179

Salas Rivera, Raquel Salas, x–xi, 204–5, 272, 294; *lo terciario/the tertiary*, 205; as Philadelphia poet laureate, xi, 204–5; *We (Too) Are Philly*, 204–5, 272, 294
Salisbury, Harrison, 134
Sandburg, Carl, 89, 212
San Francisco Renaissance, 142, 218, 279
*Saturday Review of Literature, The*, 38, 41, 43, 45, 224, 226, 236, 279, 280, 282
Saunders, Frances Stonor, 235, 291
Sayre, Robert F., 218, 278
Schauffler, Robert Haven, 238
Schlesinger, Arthur, Jr., 116, 134
Schnitzer, Marcy, 264, 292
Scholastic, 157
Schramm, Wilbur, 248
Schwartz, Lisa K., 265
Sears, Donald, 246, 291
Seattle Pacific University Graduate Center, 262
Service, Robert, 129; "The Cremation of Sam McGee," 129
*Sewanee Review, The*, 249
Seymour, Charles, 42–43, 225
Shaffer, Richard, 256
Shapiro, Karl, 19, 21, 35–37, 47–49, 98, 104, 126, 163, 201, 211–12, 220, 223, 225–27, 249, 272, 276, 281, 283, 291; *Reports of My Death*, 36, 223, 227, 291; *Trial of a Poet*, 39, 291
Shelton, Richard, 129
Shivani, Anis, 104, 245, 291
Shockley, Evie, 184; "semiautomatic," 184

Silko, Leslie Marmon, 129
Silliman, Ron, 141–42, 145–47, 219–20, 256–59, 287, 291; "Aesthetic Tendency and the Politics of Poetry: A Manifesto," 141, 146, 219–20, 257–58, 291; *In the American Tree*, 141, 256, 291
Simic, Charles, 209, 268
Simpson, Louis, 218, 282
Sister Spit, 145
Smathers, George, 51
Smedley, Agnes, 30, 221
Smith, Chris, 245, 286
Smith, Harrison, 39, 224, 226, 228, 279
Smith, Thomas, 240, 291
Smith, Tracy K., xi, 7, 14, 23, 177–78, 182–85, 204, 209, 220, 268–70, 285, 288, 293; American Conversations: Celebrating Poems in Rural Communities, 23, 182, 275; *American Journal: Fifty Poems for Our Time*, 182, 269, 291, 293; "Political Poetry Is Hot Again," 183, 270, 291; "The United States Welcomes You," 184–85; *Wade in the Water: Poems*, 184–85, 270, 291
Smith, William Jay, 128, 210, 252, 254
*Social Text*, 141, 145, 219, 257, 272, 291, 294
Sontag, Susan, 134
Southern Agrarians, 132
*Southern Review*, 117–18
Soviet-American Writers Conference, 4, 134, 137
Spahr, Juliana, 15, 18–19, 67, 133–34, 164, 203, 219, 235, 255, 259, 264–65, 272, 281, 287, 291; *Du Bois's Telegram: Literary Resistance and State Containment*, 18–19, 67, 219, 235, 255, 291
Special Consultant on the Arts to the President, 68, 88, 95, 99

Spencer, Theodore, 35, 37, 212, 223, 225, 273
Spender, Stephen, 125–27, 210, 254; "Poem for a Public Occasion," 127
Stafford, William, 210
standard American English, 10, 20, 23, 104, 122, 152–53, 161, 189, 174, 177, 188, 196–97
State Department, 7, 9, 22, 25, 31, 50, 58, 61–62, 64, 68, 85, 87–88, 92, 97, 102, 110, 112, 115–17, 192, 197, 232, 234, 249, 281
state verse culture, 7, 9–11, 18, 21–24, 97, 99, 101–2, 104–6, 117, 123, 141, 146–48, 153–54, 156–57, 159, 166–67, 176, 192, 199, 203–5, 207; as distinct from official verse culture, 18, 104, 106, 141, 148, 203–4
Stanford University, 108, 128, 246
Stegner, Wallace, 108–10, 235, 248, 255, 277
Stein, Gertrude, 141, 257
Stephenson, Max, Jr., 264, 292
Stevens, David H., 112; *The Changing Humanities*, 112
Stevens, Hugh, 221, 292
Stevens, Roger L., 88, 115–17
Stevens, Wallace, 168, 173
St. John, David, 218, 292
Strand, Mark, 140, 210
Strobel, Marion, 48
Strongman, SaraEllen, x, 258
Summer Poetry Institutes, 168
Sun and Moon Press, 257, 282
Swallow, Alan, 108
Swenson, Cole, 218, 292

Taco Shop Collective, 145
Tate, Allen, 5, 34–35, 100, 110, 126, 211–12, 216, 223, 225, 226, 229, 248, 252, 276, 285, 287, 292
Taylor, Charles, 242, 292

Terkel, Studs, 134
Terrell, Carroll F., 256
Thomas, Edward, 237
Thomas, Mervyn, 79
Thompson, Lawrance, 232–33, 235, 240, 284, 292
Thorp, Willard, 35, 37, 212, 223, 225–26
*Time*, 113
Tompkins, Jane P., 218
Travisano, Thomas, 216, 220, 222, 228, 292
Trethewey, Natasha, 178–79, 194, 201, 209; Mississippi laureateship, 179; "Where Poetry Lives," 197, 268, 294
Truman administration, 27, 51, 85
Trump, Donald J., 25, 187
Tvardovsky, Alexander, 92

Udall, Stewart L., 63, 69, 89–90, 92–95, 215–16, 235–36, 240–44, 280, 291, 293
Udell, Geraldine, 49, 224
United States Congress Oversight Committee, 155
United States Information Agency, 64, 85–86, 97, 102
United States Information Service, 85, 102. *See also* United States Information Agency
University of Buffalo, 17
University of Denver, 108, 246
University of Iowa, 113–14, 116, 140, 246–47, 249; Writers' Workshop, 9, 22, 62, 69, 101–18, 126, 140, 175, 202, 245, 247, 248, 279, 294; School of Letters, 109, 248, 283
University of Maine at Orono, 141
University of Nebraska-Lincoln, 162
University of Notre Dame Press, 262
University of Pennsylvania, ix–x, 128, 205, 220, 268–70; Kelly Writers House, 205
University of Pittsburgh Press, 198

Untermeyer, Louis, 70, 72, 98, 210, 236, 238, 241, 244

Van Doren, Mark, 212
Van Duyn, Mona, 117, 139, 210
Vera, Dan, 254, 293
*Virginia Quarterly Review, The*, 118, 242
von Hallberg, Robert, 19–20, 150, 152–53, 174, 219–20, 260–61, 293; *American Poetry and Culture, 1945–1980*, 219, 293; on civil verse, 20, 23, 152–54, 160, 174, 178, 179, 184, 188, 190–91, 199, 204, 207, 260; *Lyric Powers*, 150, 220, 293

Wake Forest University Press, 262
Walcott, Derek, 90, 242, 293
Warren, Robert Penn, 10, 35, 37, 59, 105–6, 119, 131–33, 140–41, 149, 210–12, 225–26, 255, 290, 293; *An Approach to Literature*, 138; "The Briar Patch," 132; "Divided South Searches Its Soul," 132; *Segregation: The Inner Conflict in the South*, 133, 255, 293; *Understanding Poetry*, 132; *Who Speaks for the Negro?*, 133, 255, 293
Watten, Barrett, 141, 257, 291; "Aesthetic Tendency and the Politics of Poetry: A Manifesto," 141, 146, 219–20, 257–58, 291
Watkins, Evan, 247, 293
Wayne State University Press, 262
"Where Poetry Lives," 179, 268, 294
White House Arts Festival, 58, 103
Whitman, Walt, 71, 139, 168
Whittall, Gertrude Clarke, 65, 97–98, 139, 230, 234, 244
Whittall Fund, 65, 97–98, 139, 230, 234, 244

Whittemore, Reed, 123–26, 135, 139, 210, 228–29, 253, 294; "The Lines of an American Poet," 123; "Notes on a Certain Terribly Critical Piece," 124, 253
Wilbers, Stephen, 247–48, 294
Wilbur, Richard, 140, 149, 210, 230
Wilder, Thornton, 212
Williams, Flossie, 51, 229
Williams, Miller, 156, 213; "Of History and Hope," 213
Williams, William Carlos, 8, 13, 21, 33, 36, 50, 60, 65, 120, 210, 212, 219–20, 225–26, 228, 229, 252, 272, 285, 294; *Paterson*, 36, 252
Wilner, Eleanor, 203, 272, 294
Wiman, Christian, 163
Winnick, R. H., 232, 292
*Workshops of Empire: Stegner, Engle, and American Creative Writing During the Cold War*, 18, 67, 106, 235, 255, 277
Wright, Charles, 178, 209
Wright, James, 254
Writing Program at the University of Pennsylvania, x, 128

Yaddo Artists Colony, 28, 30, 31, 48, 50, 221, 264, 278, 285
Yale University, 8, 12, 32, 41, 43–44, 101, 217, 225
Yale University Library, 43
Yenser, Stephen, 19, 164–65
Young, Stephen, xi, 216–17, 220, 264–65, 271, 287
Yúdice, George, 272, 294

Zukofsky, Louis, 141, 252, 258, 290

GPSR Authorized Representative: Easy Access System Europe, Mustamäe tee 50, 10621 Tallinn, Estonia, gpsr.requests@easproject.com

www.ingramcontent.com/pod-product-compliance
Lightning Source LLC
Chambersburg PA
CBHW031233290426
44109CB00012B/281